Backgrounds to Blackamerican Literature

Chandler Publications in
BACKGROUNDS TO LITERATURE
RICHARD A. LEVINE, *Editor*

Backgrounds to Blackamerican Literature

EDITED BY

Ruth Miller, *State University of New York, Stony Brook*

CHANDLER PUBLISHING COMPANY

An Intext Publisher • Scranton / London / Toronto

INTERNATIONAL STANDARD BOOK NUMBER 0-8102-0413-4
LIBRARY OF CONGRESS CATALOG CARD NUMBER 76-140137
PRINTED IN THE UNITED STATES OF AMERICA

For

J. H. Franklin

and

H. J. Arnelle

CONTENTS

Backgrounds to Blackamerican Literature

INTRODUCTION

The proliferation of Black Studies programs across the country will renew interest in Blackamerican Literature. The collection of essays gathered here is designed to provide a guide to the background of this body of writing, whether the student approaches Blackamerican Literature as a single course of study or in conjunction with a more generalized inquiry.

Since there are very few contemporary Blackamerican works that do not reflect the writer's intense awareness of his past, and since one would wish to perceive as much as possible about the roots of the present-day turmoil — or to say it a different way, since one needs to know the grounds on which the present struggle is being waged — the first section of this book has been designed to indicate the salient issues, the major questions, and some of the more relevant documents of Blackamerican history.

Part I progresses from an account of the slave-ship experience (Equiano) to Woodson's discussion of the education of Blackamericans in colonial times, their participation in the Revolutionary War, and the origin of the "three-fifths of a man" concept devised in the Federalist Era; and then on to a consideration of the crucial antebellum era. After various slave insurrections are described (Williams), the actual life of the slave is narrated (Northup), the proslavery argument used by the Southern defenders of the institution appears (Franklin), and finally some specific information as to the conditions Blackamericans rebelled against is provided (Frazier).

The Civil War itself is too complex to be dealt with in a book of this type. Therefore, I have directed the student's attention to matters arising out of the upheaval: the problems of class and economy (Fortune), the problem of political reconstruction (Du Bois), and the conflict over the education of Blackamericans (Washington). In order to suggest what Blackamerican writers of the turn of the century and up to the first World War were striving against, Miller's account of lynching in the United States is included. The post-World War I period provides its moment of optimism (Locke), and one aspect of the post-World War II period may convey a sense of renewal to some and arouse dismay in others (Lincoln).

To be sure, the scope of this section is broad and sweeping — too generalized for the specialist, too special for the generalist — but the intent is to provide a *guide* to the background of Blackamerican literature, not the background itself.

The second section of the book is concerned with literary issues. First, the surpassingly important experience of jazz is put into perspective by a contemporary Black writer (Jones). Next, the problem of what constitutes appropriate subject matter for the Blackamerican writer is raised (Allen).

The selections that follow concern themselves with genre and tradition: first of drama (Turner and Cade), and then of fiction (Bontemps). And next, since most students are or wish to become well acquainted with the major contemporary Black writers, I have thought it useful to include examples of their literary criticism: Ralph Ellison and Richard Wright speak of their own work, James Baldwin discusses Richard Wright, and Eldridge Cleaver talks of Baldwin. Arthur P. Davis's essay on Gwendolyn Brooks exemplifies another dimension of criticism at the same time that it explores a different literary form. Finally, I have included two essays that illustrate the special relevance of the contemporary conflict in the field of Black Studies itself. The first is by Darwin T. Turner, who responds to the reappearance, in paperback, of a widely known study of the Negro novel written by a white scholar, Robert Bone; the second is by Ernest Kaiser, who analyzes the fictionalized account of Nat Turner's rebellion advanced by the white writer William Styron.

My selection of essays is not meant to be definitive. Rather, I intended these selections to be merely representative of what might be found in the field. Doubtless, alternative choices will come to mind; indeed, I believe that the more alternatives are suggested to the reader, the more successful my own enterprise will have been.

Stony Brook
1970

Ruth Miller

I

HISTORICAL BACKGROUNDS

The Slave Ship

Olaudah Equiano

The first object which saluted my eyes when I arrived on the coast was the sea, and a slave ship which was then riding at anchor and waiting for its cargo. These filled me with astonishment, which was soon converted into terror when I was carried on board. I was immediately handled and tossed up to see if I were sound by some of the crew, and I was now persuaded that I had gotten into a world of bad spirits and that they were going to kill me. Their complexions too differing so much from ours, their long hair and the language they spoke (which was very different from any I had ever heard) united to confirm me in this belief. Indeed such were the horrors of my views and fears at the moment that, if ten thousand worlds had been my own, I would have freely parted with them all to have exchanged my condition with that of the meanest slave in my own country. When I looked round the ship too and saw a large furnace or copper boiling and a multitude of black people of every description chained together, every one of their countenances expressing dejection and sorrow, I no longer doubted of my fate; and quite overpowered with horror and anguish, I fell motionless on the deck and fainted. When I recovered a little I found some black people about me, who I believed were some of those who had brought me on board and had been receiving their pay; they talked to me in order to cheer me, but all in vain. I asked them if we were not to be eaten by those white men with horrible looks, red faces, and loose hair. They told me I was not, and one of the crew brought me a small portion of spirituous liquor in a wine glass, but being afraid of him I would not take it out of his hand. One of the blacks therefore took it from him and gave it to me, and I took a little down my palate, which instead of reviving me, as they thought it would, threw me into the greatest consternation at the strange feeling it produced, having never tasted such any liquor before. Soon after this the blacks who brought me on board went off, and left me abandoned to despair.

I now saw myself deprived of all chance of returning to my native country or even the least glimpse of hope of gaining the shore, which I now considered as friendly; and I even wished for my former slavery in preference to my present situation, which was filled with horrors of every kind, still heightened by my ignorance of what I was to undergo. I was not long suffered

From *Equiano's Travels: His Autobiography, The Interesting Narrative of the Life of Olaudah Equiano or Gustavus Vassa, the African,* abridged and edited by Paul Edwards (New York: Frederick A. Praeger, 1967), pp. 25-32.

to indulge my grief; I was soon put down under the decks, and there I received such a salutation in my nostrils as I had never experienced in my life: so that with the loathsomeness of the stench and crying together, I became so sick and low that I was not able to eat, nor had I the least desire to taste anything. I now wished for the last friend, death, to relieve me; but soon, to my grief, two of the white men offered me eatables, and on my refusing to eat, one of them held me fast by the hands and laid me across I think the windlass, and tied my feet while the other flogged me severely. I had never experienced anything of this kind before, and although, not being used to the water, I naturally feared that element the first time I saw it, yet nevertheless could I have got over the nettings I would have jumped over the side, but I could not; and besides, the crew used to watch us very closely who were not chained down to the decks, lest we should leap into the water: and I have seen some of these poor African prisoners most severely cut for attempting to do so, and hourly whipped for not eating. This indeed was often the case with myself. In a little time after, amongst the poor chained men I found some of my own nation, which in a small degree gave ease to my mind. I inquired of these what was to be done with us; they gave me to understand we were to be carried to these white people's country to work for them. I then was a little revived, and thought if it were no worse than working, my situation was not so desperate: but still I feared I should be put to death, the white people looked and acted, as I thought, in so savage a manner; for I had never seen among my people such instances of brutal cruelty, and this not only shewn towards us blacks but also to some of the whites themselves. One white man in particular I saw, when we were permitted to be on deck, flogged so unmercifully with a large rope near the foremast that he died in consequence of it; and they tossed him over the side as they would have done a brute. This made me fear these people the more, and I expected nothing less than to be treated in the same manner. I could not help expressing my fears and apprehensions to some of my countrymen: I asked them if these people had no country but lived in this hollow place (the ship): they told me they did not, but came from a distant one. 'Then,' said I, 'how comes it in all our country we never heard of them?' They told me because they lived so very far off. I then asked where were their women? had they any like themselves? I was told they had: 'and why,' said I, 'do we not see them?' They answered, because they were left behind. I asked how the vessel could go? They told me they could not tell, but that there were cloths put upon the masts by the help of the ropes I saw, and then the vessel went on; and the white men had some spell or magic they put in the water when they liked in order to stop the vessel. I was exceedingly amazed at this account and really thought they were spirits. I therefore wished much to be from amongst them for I expected they would sacrifice me: but my wishes were vain, for we were so quartered that it was impossible for any of us to make our escape. While we stayed on the coast I was mostly on deck, and one day, to my great astonishment, I saw one of these vessels coming in with the sails up. As soon as the whites saw it they gave a great shout, at which we were amazed; and the more so as the vessel appeared larger by approaching nearer. At last she came to an anchor in my sight, and when the anchor was let go I and my countrymen who saw it were lost in astonishment to observe the vessel stop, and were now convinced it was done by magic. Soon after this the other ship got her boats out, and they came on board of us, and the people of both ships seemed very glad to see each other. Several of the strangers also shook hands with us black people, and made motions with their hands, signifying I suppose we were to go to their country; but we did not understand them. At last, when the ship we were in had got in all her cargo, they made ready with many fearful noises, and we were all put under deck so that we could not see how they managed the vessel. But this disappointment was the [least] of my sorrow. The stench of the hold while we were on the coast was so intolerably loathsome that it was dangerous to remain there for any time, and some of us had been permitted to stay on the deck for the fresh air; but now that the whole ship's cargo were confined together it became absolutely pestilential. The closeness of the place and the heat of the climate, added to the number in the ship, which was so crowded that each had scarcely room to turn himself, almost suffocated us. This produced copious perspirations, so that the air soon became unfit for respiration from a variety of loathsome smells, and brought on a sickness among the slaves, of which many died, thus falling victims to the improvident avarice, as I may call it, of their purchasers. This wretched situation was again aggravated by the galling of the chains, now become insupportable, and the filth of the necessary tubs, into which the children often fell and were almost suffocated. The shrieks of the women and the groans of the dying rendered the whole a scene of horror almost inconceivable. Happily perhaps for myself I was soon reduced so low here that it was thought necessary to keep me almost always on deck, and from my extreme youth I was not put in fetters. In this situation I expected every hour to share the fate of my companions, some of whom were almost daily brought upon deck at the point of death, which I began to hope would soon put an end to my miseries. Often did I think many of the inhabitants of the deep much more happy than myself. I envied them the freedom they enjoyed, and as often wished I could change my condition for theirs. Every circumstance I met with served only to render my state more painful, and heighten my apprehensions and my opinion of the cruelty of the whites. One day they had taken a number of fishes, and when they had killed and satisfied themselves with as many as they thought fit, to our astonishment who were on the deck, rather than give any of them to us to eat as we expected, they tossed the remaining fish into the sea again, although we begged and prayed for some as well as we could, but in vain; and some of my countrymen, being pressed by hunger, took an opportunity when they thought no one saw them of trying to get a little privately; but they were discovered, and the attempt procured them some very severe floggings. One day, when we had a smooth sea and moderate wind, two of my wearied countrymen who were chained together (I was near them at the time), preferring death to such a life of misery, somehow made through the nettings and jumped into the sea: immediately another quite dejected fellow, who on account of his illness was suffered to be out of irons, also followed their example; and I believe many more would very soon have done the same if they had not been prevented by the ship's crew, who were instantly alarmed. Those of us that were the most active were in a moment put down under the deck, and there was such a noise and confusion amongst the people of the ship as I never heard before, to stop her and get the boat out to go after the slaves. However two of the wretches were drowned, but they got the other and afterwards flogged him unmercifully for thus attempting to prefer death to slavery. In this manner we continued to undergo more hardships then I can now relate, hardships which are inseparable from this accursed trade. Many a time we were near suffocation from the want of fresh air, which we were often without for whole days together. This and the stench of the necessary tubs carried off many. During our passage I first saw flying fishes, which surprised me very much: they used frequently to fly across the ship and many of them fell on the deck. I also now first saw the use of the quadrant; I had often with astonishment seen the mariners make observations with it, and I could not think what it meant. They at last took notice of my surprise, and one of them, willing to increase it as well as to gratify my curiosity, made me one day look through it. The clouds appeared to me to be land, which disappeared as they passed along. This heightened my wonder, and I was now more persuaded than ever that I was in another world and that everything about me was magic. At last we came in sight of the island of Barbados, at which the whites on board gave a great shout and made many signs of joy to us. We did not know what to think of this, but as the vessel drew nearer we plainly saw the harbour and other ships of different kinds and sizes, and we soon anchored amongst them off Bridgetown. Many merchants and planters now came on board, though it was in the evening. They put us in separate parcels and examined us attentively. They also made us jump, and pointed to the land, signifying we were to go there. We thought by this we should be eaten by these ugly men, as they appeared to us; and when soon after we were all put down under the deck again, there was much dread and trembling among us, and nothing but bitter cries to be heard all the night from these apprehensions, insomuch that at last the white people got some old slaves from the land to pacify us. They told us we were not to be eaten but to work, and were soon to go on land where we should see many of our country people. This report eased us much; and sure enough soon after we were landed there came to us Africans of all languages. We were conducted immediately to the merchant's yard, where we were all pent up together like so many sheep in a fold without regard to sex or age. As every object was new to me everything I saw filled me with surprise. What struck me first was that the houses were built with storeys, and in every other respect different from those in Africa: but I was still more astonished on seeing people on horseback. I did not know what this could mean, and indeed I thought these people were full of nothing but magical arts. While I was in this astonishment one of my fellow prisoners spoke to a countryman of his about the horses, who said they were the same kind they had in their country. I understood them though they were from a distant part of Africa, and I thought it odd I had not seen any horses there; but afterwards when I came to converse with different Africans I found they had many horses amongst them, and much larger than those I then saw. We were not many days in the merchant's custody before we were sold after their usual manner, which is this: On a signal given, (as the beat of a drum) the buyers rush at once into the yard where the slaves are confined, and make choice of that parcel they like best. The noise and clamour with which this is attended and the eagerness visible in the countenances of the buyers serve not a little to increase the apprehensions of the terrified Africans, who may well be supposed to consider them as the ministers of that destruction to which they think themselves devoted. In this manner, without scruple, are relations and friends separated, most of them never to see each other again. I remember in the vessel in which I was brought over, in the men's apartment there were several brothers who, in the sale, were sold in different lots; and it was very moving on this occasion to see and hear their cries at parting. O, ye nominal Christians! might not an African ask you, Learned you this from your God who says unto you, Do unto all men as you would men should do unto you? Is it not enough that we are torn from our country and friends to toil for your luxury and lust of gain? Must every tender feeling be likewise sacrificed to your avarice? Are the dearest friends and relations, now rendered more dear by their separation from their kindred, still to be parted from each other and thus prevented from cheering the gloom of slavery with the small comfort of being together and mingling their sufferings and sorrows? Why are parents to lose their children, brother their sisters, or husbands their wives? Surely this is a new refinement in cruelty which, while it has no advantage to atone for it, thus aggravates distress and adds fresh horrors even to the wretchedness of slavery.

The Blackamerican in the Eighteenth Century

Carter G. Woodson

* * * *

There were [before the nineteenth century] in the American colonies many slaves whose condition constituted an exception to the rule. The slaves as a whole were much better treated at that time than they were during the nineteenth century. Most of them were then given some opportunity for enlightenment and religious instruction. Embracing these opportunities many of them early established themselves as freemen, constituting an essential factor in the economic life of their communities. Some became artisans of peculiar skill; others obtained the position of contractors; and not a few became planters themselves who owned extensive estates and numbers of slaves. Sir Thomas Gage found a number of such planters of color in Guatemala in the seventeenth century; the mixed breeds of Louisiana produced a number of this type. Even the English colonies along the coast were not always an exception to this rule, as is shown by the case of Anthony Johnson in Virginia, already mentioned as a Negro servant who attained the status of a slaveholder himself. Andrew Bryan, a Negro Baptist preacher, was widely known as a slaveholder in Savannah, Georgia, before 1790.

These exceptions resulted largely from the few white men who became interested in the welfare of the Negroes during the seventeenth and eighteenth centuries. Some of these liberal workers cooperated with the Society for the Propagation of the Gospel in Foreign Parts, to which the Negroes were indebted for most of their early enlightenment. These reformers contended that the gospel was sent also to the slaves and that they should be prepared by mental development to receive it. With the increasing interest in education it became more restricted to the clergy and such other well-chosen persons recommended by them and attached to the churches.

It was soon evident, however, that little could be effected in the enlightenment of these blacks without first teaching them the English language. In almost every case, therefore, during the eighteenth century, when the clergy undertook the teaching of the gospel among the blacks, it involved also instruction in the fundamentals of education, that their message might have the desired effect. In fact, in some of the colonies, the Negroes were about

From Carter G. Woodson, *The Negro In Our History* (Washington, D. C.: Associated Publishers, 1922), pp. 102-04, 120-29, 163-4. Published here under the editor's title.

as well provided with schools as the whites. The first school for the education of the whites in the Carolinas was established in 1716, and a school for the education of the Negroes was established in 1744. There were in a few colonies, schools not only for free Negroes but for slaves. They were sometimes taught in the classes with the children of their masters. In some cases, when the Negroes experienced sufficient mental development to qualify as teachers themselves, they were called upon to serve their masters' children in this capacity. In the eighteenth century there were schools for Negroes in almost all of the cities and towns where they were found.

It was fortunate for the Negroes that many schools of the middle colonies were conducted by the indentured servant class of low estate. It looks rather strange that our fathers should commit such an important task to the care of the convicts taken from the prisons in England and indentured in America. Yet this was the case. Jonathan Boucher said, in 1773, that two-thirds of the teachers in the colony of Maryland were such felons. As these were despised by the whites of the higher classes, they were forced to associate with the Negroes. The latter often learned from them how to read and write, and were thereby prepared to enlighten their own fellow men. Negro apprentices, moreover, as in the case of David James, a free Negro bound out in Virginia in 1727, had the right to instruction in the rudiments of learning and the handicrafts.

* * * *

Negroes were in the front rank of those openly protesting against the quartering and billeting of British soldiers in Boston to enforce the laws authorizing taxation in the colonies. In the clash itself Crispus Attucks, another Negro, was one of the first four to shed blood in behalf of American liberty. During the war numbers of Negroes, like Lemuel Haynes, served as minute men and later as regulars in the ranks, side by side with white men.

The organization of Negro soldiers on a larger scale as separate units soon followed after some opposition. The reasons for timidity in this respect were various. Having the idea that the Negroes were savages who should not be permitted to take part in a struggle between white men, Massachusetts protested against the enlistment of Negroes. The Committee of Safety, of which John Hancock and Joseph Ward were members, had this opinion. They contended that inasmuch as the contest then between Great Britain and her colonies respected the liberties and privileges of the latter, the admission of any persons but freemen as soldiers would be inconsistent with the principles supported and would reflect dishonor on the colony. Although this action did not apparently affect the enlistment of free persons of color, Washington, in taking command of the army at Cambridge, prohibited the enlistment of all Negroes. The matter was discussed in the Continental Congress and as a result Washington was instructed by that body to discharge all Negroes, whether slave or free. When the enlistment of Negroes came up again in the council of the army, it was unanimously agreed to reject slaves and by a large majority to refuse Negroes altogether. By these instructions, Washington, as commander of the army, was governed late in 1775.

Many of the colonists who desired to avail themselves of the support of the Negroes were afraid to set such an example. They were thinking that the British might outstrip them in playing the same game and might arm both the Indians and Negroes faster than the colonies could. A few were of the opinion that the Negroes, seizing the opportunity, might go over to Great Britain. On this account the delegates from Georgia to the Continental Congress had grave fears for the safety of the South. They believed that if one thousand regular troops should land in Georgia under a commander and with adequate supplies, and he should proclaim freedom to all Negroes, twenty thousand of them would join the British in a fortnight.

As a matter of fact, they had good reason for so thinking. When Lord Dunmore, governor of Virginia, was driven from the colony by the patriots, he summoned to his support several hundred Negroes to assist him in regaining his power. He promised such loyalists freedom from their masters. The British contemplated organizing a Negro regiment in Long Island. Sir Henry Clinton proclaimed in 1779 that all Negroes in arms should be purchased from their captors for the public service and that every Negro who might desert the "Rebel Standard" should have security to follow within the British lines any occupation which he might think proper . . . .

It was necessary, therefore, for the leaders of the country to recede from this position of refusing to enlist Negroes. Washington within a few weeks revoked his order prohibiting their enlistment. The committee in the Continental Congress considering the matter recommended the reënlistment of those Negroes who had served faithfully, and Congress, not wishing to infringe upon what they called States' rights, was disposed to leave the matter to the commonwealths. Most men of foresight, however, approved the recognition of the Negro as a soldier. James Madison suggested that the slaves be liberated and armed. Hamilton, like General Greene, urged that slaves be given their freedom with the sword, to secure their fidelity, animate their courage, and influence those remaining in bondage by an open door to their emancipation . . . . In his strait at Valley Forge, Washington was induced by General Varnum to enlist a battalion of Negroes in Rhode Island to fill his depleted ranks . . . .

The result of the increasing interest in the Negro was soon apparent. The Continental Congress prohibited the importation of slaves. With the exception of South Carolina and Georgia, a general effort in the extermination of slavery was made during the revolutionary epoch. The black codes were considerably moderated, and laws facilitating manumission were passed in most of the colonies. In 1772 Virginia repealed a measure forbidding emancipation except for military service. About the same time Maryland prohibited the importation of slaves and in like manner facilitated emancipation. New

York, New Jersey and Pennsylvania prohibited the slave traffic. Vermont, New Hampshire and Massachusetts exterminated slavery by constitutional provision; Rhode Island, Connecticut, New Jersey, New York and Pennsylvania washed their hands of the stain by gradual emancipation acts; and the Continental Congress excluded the evil from the Northwest Territory by the Ordinance of 1787. So sanguine did the friends of universal freedom become that they thought that later slavery of itself would gradually pass away in Maryland, Virginia and North Carolina.

* * * *

The Convention of 1787, called to frame the first constitution of the United States, desired to take very little interest in the antislavery movement in the organization of the new government. Oliver Ellsworth of Connecticut and Elbridge Gerry of Massachusetts thought the question of slavery should be settled by the States themselves. When this question came more prominently before this body, however, it had to be considered more seriously. It was necessary to consider a regulation for returning fugitive slaves, the prohibition of the slave trade, and the apportionment of representation. When the South wanted the Negroes to be counted to secure larger representation on the population basis, although it did not want thus to count the blacks in apportioning federal taxes, some sharp debate ensued. But the Northern antislavery delegates were not so much attached to the cause of universal freedom as to force their opinions on the proslavery group and thus lose their support in organizing a more stable form of government. They finally compromised by providing for representation of the States by two Senators from each, and for the representation of the people in the House by counting all whites and five Negroes as three whites. Another compromise was made in providing for the continuation of the slave trade until 1808, when it should be prohibited, and for a fugitive slave law to secure slaveholders in the possession of their peculiar property.

Immediately after the Federal Government was organized there seemed to be a tendency to ignore the claims of the Negro.

Negro Insurrections

George Washington Williams

The supposed docility of the American Negro was counted among the reasons why it was thought he could never gain his freedom on this continent. But this was a misinterpretation of his real character. Besides, it was next to impossible to learn the history of the Negro during the years of his enslavement at the South. The question was often asked: Why don't the Negroes rise at the South and exterminate their enslavers? Negatively, not because they lacked the courage, but because they lacked leaders [as has been stated already, they sought the North and their freedom through the Underground R. R.] to organize them. But notwithstanding this great disadvantage the Negroes *did* rise on several different occasions, and did effective work.

> "Three times, at intervals of thirty years, has a wave of unutterable terror swept across the Old Dominion, bringing thoughts of agony to every Virginian master, and of vague hope to every Virginian slave. Each time has one man's name become a spell of dismay and a symbol of deliverance. Each time has that name eclipsed its predecessor, while recalling it for a moment to fresher memory; John Brown revived the story of Nat. Turner, as in his day Nat. Turner recalled the vaster schemes of Gabriel."[1]

Mention has been made of the insurrection of slaves in South Carolina in the last century. Upon the very threshold of the nineteenth century, "General Gabriel," made the master-class of Virginia quail with mortal dread. He was a man of more than ordinary intelligence; and his plans were worthy of greater success. The following newspaper paragraph reveals the condition of the minds of Virginians respecting the Negroes:

> "For the week past, we have been under momentary expectation of a rising among the negroes, who have assembled to the number of nine hundred or a thousand, and threatened to massacre all the whites. They are armed with desperate weapons, and secrete themselves in the woods. God only knows our fate; we have strong guards every night under arms."

The above was communicated to the "United States Gazette," printed in Philadelphia, under date of September 8, 1800, by a Virginia correspondent. The people felt that they were sleeping over a magazine. The movement of Gabriel was to have taken place on Saturday, September 1st. The rendez-

[1] Atlantic Monthly, vol. x. p. 337.

From George Washington Williams, *History of the Negro Race in America* (New York: G. P. Putnam & Sons, 1883), Chapters VII and VIII. Footnotes renumbered.

vous of the Negro troops was a brook, about six miles from Richmond. The force was to comprise eleven hundred men, divided into three divisions. Richmond — then a town of eight thousand inhabitants — was the point of attack, which was to be effected under cover of night. The right wing was to fall suddenly upon the penitentiary, lately improvised into an arsenal; the left wing was to seize the powder-house; and, thus equipped and supplied with the munitions of war, the two columns were to assign the hard fighting to the third column. This column was to have possession of all the guns, swords, knives, and other weapons of modern warfare. It was to strike a sharp blow by entering the town from both ends, while the other two columns, armed with shovels, picks, clubs, etc., were to act as a reserve. The white troops were scarce, and the situation, plans, etc., of the Negroes were admirable.

"... the penitentiary held several thousand stand of arms; the powder-house was well-stocked; the capitol contained the State treasury; the mills would give them bread; the control of the bridge across James River would keep off enemies from beyond. Thus secured and provided, they planned to issue proclamations summoning to their standard 'their fellow-negroes and the friends of humanity throughout the continent.' In a week, it was estimated, they would have fifty thousand men on their side, with which force they could easily possess themselves of other towns; and, indeed, a slave named John Scott—possibly the dangerous possessor of ten dollars—was already appointed to head the attack on Petersburg. But in case of final failure, the project included a retreat to the mountains, with their new-found property. John Brown was therefore anticipated by Gabriel sixty years before, in believing the Virginia mountains to have been 'created, from the foundation of the world, as a place of refuge for fugitive slaves.'"[2]

The plot failed, but everybody, and the newspapers also, said the plan was well conceived.

In 1822 another Negro insurrection was planned in Charleston, S. C. The leader of this affair was Denmark Vesey.[3] This plot for an insurrection extended for forty-five or fifty miles around Charleston, and intrusted its secrets to thousands. Denmark Vesey, assisted by several other intelligent and trusty Negroes, had conceived the idea of slaughtering the whites in and about Charleston, and thus securing liberty for the blacks. A recruiting committee was formed, and every slave enlisted was sworn to secrecy. Household servants were rarely trusted. Talkative and intemperate slaves were not enlisted. Women were excluded from the affair that they might take care of the children. Peter Poyas, it was said, had enlisted six hundred without assistance. There were various opinions respecting the number enlisted. Some put it at hundreds, others thousands; one witness at the trial said there were nine thousand, another six thousand. But no white person ever succeeded in gaining the confidence of the black conspirators. Never was a plot so carefully guarded for so long a time.

[2] Atlantic Monthly, vol. x. p. 339.
[3] Atlantic Monthly, vol. vii. pp. 728, 744.

"During the excitement and the trial of the supposed conspirators, rumor proclaimed all, and doubtless more than all, the horrors of the plot. The city was to be fired in every quarter, the arsenal in the immediate vicinity was to be broken open, and the arms distributed to the insurgents, and an universal massacre of the white inhabitants to take place. Nor did there seem to be any doubt in the mind of the people that such would actually have been the result, had not the plot fortunately been detected before the time appointed for the outbreak. It was believed, as a matter of course, that every black in the city would join in the insurrection, and that, if the original design had been attempted, and the city taken by surprise, the negroes would have achieved a complete and easy victory. Nor does it seem at all impossible that such might have been or yet may be the case, if any well-arranged and resolute rising should take place."[4]

This bold plot failed because a Negro named William Paul began to make enlistments without authority. He revealed the secret to a household servant, just the very man he should have left to the skilful manipulations of Peter Poyas or Denmark Vesey. As an evidence of the perfection of the plot it should be stated that after a month of official investigation only fifteen out of the thousands had been apprehended!

"The leaders of this attempt at insurrection died as bravely as they had lived; and it is one of the marvels of the remarkable affair, that none of this class divulged any of their secrets to the court. The men who did the talking were those who knew but little."

The effect was to reveal the evils of slavery, to stir men to thought, and to hasten the day of freedom.

"Nat." Turner combined the lamb and lion. He was a Christian and a *man*. He was conscious that he was a man and not a "thing"; therefore, driven by religious fanaticism, he undertook a difficult and bloody task. Nathaniel Turner was born in Southampton County, Virginia, October 2, 1800. His master was one Benjamin Turner, a very wealthy and aristocratic man. He owned many slaves, and was a cruel and exacting master. Young "Nat." was born of slave parents, and carried to his grave many of the superstitions and traits of his father and mother. The former was a preacher; the latter a "mother in Israel." Both were unlettered, but, nevertheless, very pious people. The mother began when Nat. was quite young to teach him that he was born, like Moses, to be the deliverer of his race. She would sing to him snatches of wild, rapturous songs, and repeat portions of prophecy she had learned from the preachers of those times. Nat. listened with reverence and awe, and believed every thing his mother said. He imbibed the deep religious character of his parents, and soon manifested a desire to preach. He was solemnly set apart to "the Gospel Ministry" by his father, the Church, and visiting preachers. He was quite low in stature, dark, and had the genuine African features. His eyes were small, but sharp, and gleamed like fire when he was talking about his "mission," or preaching from some prophetic passage of Scripture. It is said that he never laughed. He was a dreamy sort

[4] Atlantic Monthly, vol. vii. p. 737.

of a man, and avoided the crowd. Like Moses, he lived in the solitudes of the mountains and brooded over the condition of his people. There was something grand to him in the rugged scenery that nature had surrounded him with. He believed that he was a prophet, a leader raised up by God to burst the bolts of the prison-house and set the oppressed free. The thunder, the hail, the storm-cloud, the air, the earth, the stars, at which he would sit and gaze half the night, all spake the language of the God of the oppressed. He was seldom seen in a large company, and never drank a drop of ardent spirits. Like John the Baptist, when he had delivered his message, he would retire to the fastness of the mountain, or seek the desert, where he could meditate upon his great work.

At length he declared that God spake to him. He began to dream dreams and to see visions. His grandmother, a very old and superstitious person, encouraged him in his dreaming. But, notwithstanding, he believed that he had communion with God, and saw the most remarkable visions, he denounced in the severest terms the familiar practices among slaves, known as "conjuring," "gufering," and fortune-telling. The people regarded him with mixed feelings of fear and reverence. He preached with great power and authority. He loved the prophecies, and drew his illustrations from nature. He presented God as the "*All-Powerful*"; he regarded him as a great "*Warrior.*" His master soon discovered that Nat. was the acknowledged leader among the slaves, and that his fame as "prophet" and "leader" was spreading throughout the State. The poor slaves on distant plantations regarded the name of Nat. Turner as very little removed from that of God. Though having never seen him, yet they believed in him as the man under whose lead they would some time march out of the land of bondage. His influence was equally great among the preachers, while many white people honored and feared him. His master thought it necessary to the safety of his property, to hire Nat. out to a most violent and cruel man. Perhaps he thought to have him "broke." If so, he was mistaken. Nat. Turner was the last slave to submit to an insult given by a white man. His new master could do nothing with him. He ran off, and spent thirty days in the swamps — but returned. He was upbraided by some of his fellow-slaves for not seeking, as he certainly could have done, "the land of the free." He answered by saying, that a voice said to him: "Return to your earthly master; for he who knoweth his Master's will and doeth it not, shall be beaten with many stripes." It was no direction to submit to an earthly master, but to return to him in order to carry out the will of his Heavenly Master. He related some of the visions he saw during his absence. "About that time I had a vision, and saw white spirits and black spirits engaged in battle; and the sun was darkened, the thunder rolled in the heavens, and blood flowed in streams; and I heard a voice saying: 'Such is your luck, such are you called on to see; and let it come, rough or smooth, you must surely bear it.' " It was not long after this when he saw another vision. He says a spirit appeared unto him and spake as follows: "The serpent is loosened, and Christ has laid down the yoke he has borne for the sins of men; and you must take it up and fight against the serpent, for the time is fast approaching when the first shall be last, and the last shall be first." These visions and many others enthused Nat., and led him to believe that the time was near when the Blacks would be "first" and the whites "last."

The plot for a general uprising was laid in the month of February, 1831. He had seen the last vision. He says: "I was told I should arise and prepare myself, and slay my enemies with their own weapons." He was now prepared to arrange the details of his plot. He appointed a meeting, to which he invited four trusted friends, Sam. Edwards, Hark Travis, Henry Porter, and Nelson Williams. A wild and desolate glen was chosen as the place of meeting, and night the time when they could perfect their plans without being molested by the whites. They brought with them provisions, and ate while they debated among themselves the methods by which to carry out their plan of blood and death. The main difficulty that confronted them was how to get arms. Nat. remembered that a spirit had instructed him to "slay my enemies with their own weapons," so they decided to follow these instructions. After they had decided upon a plan, "the prophet Nat." arose, and, like a great general, made a speech to his small but brave force. "Friends and brothers," said he, "we are to commence a great work to-night! Our race is to be delivered from slavery, and God has appointed us as the men to do his bidding; and let us be worthy of our calling. I am told to slay all the whites we encounter, without regard to age or sex. We have no arms or ammunition, but we will find these in the houses of our oppressors; and, as we go on, others can join us. Remember, we do not go forth for the sake of blood and carnage; but it is necessary that, in the commencement of this revolution, all the whites we meet should die, until we have an army strong enough to carry on the war upon a Christian basis. Remember that ours is not a war for robbery, nor to satisfy our passions; it is a *struggle for freedom*. Ours must be deeds, not words. Then let's away to the scene of action!"

The blow was struck on the night of the 21st of August, 1831, in Southampton County, near Jerusalem Court House. The latter place is about seventy miles from Richmond. Not only Southampton County but old Virginia reeled under the blow administered by the heavy hand of Nat. Turner. On their way to the first house they were to attack, that of a planter by the name of Joseph Travis, they were joined by a slave belonging to a neighboring plantation. We can find only one name for him, "Will." He was the slave of a cruel master, who had sold his wife to the "nigger traders." He was nearly six feet in height, well developed, and the most powerful and athletic man in the county. He was marked with an ugly scar, extending from his right eye to the extremity of the chin. He hated his master, hated slavery, and was glad of an opportunity to wreak his vengeance upon the whites. He armed himself with a sharp broadaxe, under whose cruel blade many a white man fell. Nat.'s speech gives us a very clear idea of the scope and spirit of his plan. We quote from his confession at the time of the trial, and will let him tell the story of this terrible insurrection.

"On returning to the house, Hark went to the door with an axe, for the purpose of breaking it open, as we knew we were strong enough to murder the family should they be awakened by the noise; but, reflecting that it might create an alarm in the neighborhood, we determined to enter the house secretly, and murder them whilst sleeping. Hark got a ladder and set it against the chimney, on which I ascended, and, hoisting a window, entered and came down stairs, unbarred the doors, and removed the guns from their places. It was then observed that I must spill the first blood, on which, armed with a hatchet and accompanied by Will., I entered my master's chamber. It being dark, I could not give a death-blow. The hatchet glanced from his head; he sprang from his bed and called his wife. It was his last word. Will. laid him dead with a blow of his axe."

After they had taken the lives of this family, they went from plantation to plantation, dealing death-blows to every white man, woman, or child they found. They visited vengeance upon every white household they came to. The excitement spread rapidly, and the whites arose and armed themselves in order to repel these insurrectionists.

"The first news concerning the affair was in the shape of a letter from Col. Trezvant, which reached Richmond Tuesday morning, too late for the columns of the (Richmond) "Enquirer," which was a tri-weekly. The letter was written on the 21st of August, and lacked definiteness, which gave rise to doubts in reference to the 'insurrection.' It was first sent to Petersburgh, and was then immediately dispatched to the Mayor of Richmond.

"Arms and ammunition were dispatched in wagons to the county of Southampton. The four volunteer companies of Petersburgh, the dragoons and Lafayette artillery company of Richmond, one volunteer company from Norfolk and one from Portsmouth, and the regiments of Southampton and Sussex, were at once ordered out. The cavalry and infantry took up their line of march on Tuesday evening, while the artillery embarked on the steamer 'Norfolk,' and landed at Smithfield. . . . A member of the Richmond dragoons, writing from Petersburgh, under date of the 23rd, after careful examination, thought that 'about two hundred and fifty negroes from a camp-meeting about the Dismal Swamp had murdered about sixty persons, none of them families much known.' "[5]

Will., the revengeful slave, proved himself the most destructive and cruel of Nat.'s followers. A hand to hand battle came. The whites were well armed, and by the force of their superior numbers overcame the army of the "Prophet,"—five men. Will. would not surrender. He laid three white men dead at his feet, when he fell mortally wounded. His last words were: "Bury my axe with me," believing that in the next world he would need it for a similar purpose. Nat. fought with great valor and skill with a short sword, and finding it useless to continue the struggle, escaped with some of his followers to the swamps, where he defied the vigilance of the military and the patient watching of the citizens for more than two months. He was finally compelled to surrender. When the Court asked: "Guilty or not guilty?" he

[5] Richmond Enquirer, August 26, 1831.

pleaded: "Not guilty." He was sustained during his trial by his unfaltering faith in God. Like Joan of Arc, he "heard the spirits," the "voices," and believed that God had "sent him to free His people."

In the impression of the "Enquirer" of the 30th of August, 1831, the first editorial, or leader, is under the caption of THE BANDITTE. The editor says:

> "They remind one of a parcel of blood-thirsty wolves rushing down from the Alps; or, rather like a former incursion of the Indians upon the white settlements. Nothing is spared: neither age nor sex respected—the helplessness of women and children pleads in vain for mercy . . . The case of Nat. Turner warns us. No black-man ought to be permitted to turn a Preacher through the country. The law must be enforced—or the tragedy of Southampton appeals to us in vain."[6]

A remarkable prophecy was made by Nat. The trial was hurried, and, like a handle on a pitcher, was on one side only. He was sentenced to die on the gallows. He received the announcement with stoic indifference, and was executed at Jerusalem, the county seat of Southampton, in April, 1831. He died like a man, bravely, calmly; looking into eternity, made radiant by a faith that had never faltered. He prophesied that on the day of his execution the sun would be darkened, and other evidences of divine disapprobation would be seen. The sheriff was much impressed by Nat.'s predictions, and consequently refused to have any thing to do with the hanging. No Colored man could be secured to cut the rope that held the trap. An old white man, degraded by drink and other vices, was engaged to act as executioner, and was brought forty miles. Whether it was a fulfilment of Nat.'s prophecy or not, the sun was hidden behind angry clouds, the thunder rolled, the lightning flashed, and the most terrific storm visited that county ever known. All this, in connection with Nat.'s predictions, made a wonderful impression upon the minds of the Colored people, and not a few white persons were frightened, and regretted the death of the "Prophet."

The results of this uprising, led by a lone man—he was alone, and yet he was not alone,—are apparent when we consider that fifty-seven whites and seventy-three Blacks were killed and many were wounded.

The first reliable list of the victims of the "tragedy" was written on the 24th of August, 1831.

> "List of the dead that have been buried:—At Mrs. Whiteheads', 7; Mrs. Waller's, 13; Mr. Williams', 3; Mr. Barrows', 2; Mr. Vaughn's, 5; Mrs. Turner's, 3; Mr. Travis's, 5; Mr. J. Williams', 5; Mr. Reice's, 4; Names unknown, 10; Total, 57."

Then there was a feeling of unrest among the slaves and a fear among the whites throughout the State. Even the proceedings of the trial of Nat. were suppressed for fear of evil consequences among the slaves. But now all are free, and the ex-planters will not gnash their teeth at this revelation. Nat. Turner's insurrection, like all other insurrections led by oppressed people,

[6] Richmond Enquirer, August 26 and 30, 1831.

lacked detail and method. History records but one successful uprising—San Domingo has the honor. Even France failed in 1789, and in 1848. There is always a zeal for freedom, but not according to knowledge. No stone marks the resting-place of this martyr to freedom, this great religious fanatic, this Black John Brown. And yet he has a prouder and more durable monument than was ever erected of stone or brass. The image of Nat. Turner is carved on the fleshy tablets of four million hearts. His history has been kept from the Colored people at the South, but the women have handed the tradition to their children, and the "Prophet Nat." is still marching on.

Of the character of this remarkable man, Mr. Gray, the gentleman to whom he made his confession, had the following to say:—

"It has been said that he was ignorant and cowardly, and that his object was to murder and rob, for the purpose of obtaining money to make his escape. It is notorious that he was never known to have a dollar in his life, to swear an oath, or drink a drop of spirits. As to his ignorance, he certainly never had the advantages of education; but he can read and write, and for natural intelligence and quickness of apprehension, is surpassed by few men I have ever seen. As to his being a coward, his reason, as given, for not resisting Mr. Phipps, shows the decision of his character. When he saw Mr. Phipps present his gun, he said he knew it was impossible for him to escape, as the woods were full of men; he therefore thought it was better for him to surrender, and trust to fortune for his escape.

"He is a complete fanatic, or plays his part most admirably. On other subjects he possesses an uncommon share of intelligence, with a mind capable of attaining any thing, but warped and perverted by the influence of early impressions. He is below the ordinary stature, though strong and active, having the true negro face, every feature of which is strongly marked. I shall not attempt to describe the effect of his narrative, as told and commented on by himself, in the condemned hole of the prison: the calm, deliberate composure with which he spoke of his late deeds and intentions; the expression of his fiend-like face, when excited by enthusiasm; still bearing the stains of the blood of helpless innocence about him, clothed with rags and covered with chains, yet daring to raise his manacled hands to Heaven, with a spirit soaring above the attributes of man. I looked on him, and the blood curdled in my veins."

In the "Richmond Enquirer," of September 2, 1831, appeared the following: "It is reported that a map was found, and said to have been drawn by Nat. Turner, with *polk-berry juice,* which was a description of the county of Southampton."

The influence of this bloody insurrection spread beyond the Old Dominion, and for years afterward, in nearly every Southern State the whites lived in a state of dread. To every dealer in flesh and blood the "Nat. Turner Insurrection" was a stroke of poetic justice.

The "Amistad" Captives

On the 28th of June, 1839, the "Amistad," a Spanish slaver (schooner), with Captain Ramon Ferrer in command, sailed from Havana, Cuba, for Porto Principe, a place in the island of Cuba, about 100 leagues distant. The passengers were Don Pedro Montes and Jose Ruiz, with fifty-four Africans just from their native country, Lemboko, as slaves. Among the slaves was one man, called in Spanish, Joseph Cinquez,[7] said to be the son of an African prince. He was possessed of wonderful natural abilities, and was endowed with all the elements of an intelligent and intrepid leader. The treatment these captives received was very cruel. They were chained down between the decks —space not more than four feet—by their wrists and ankles; forced to eat rice, sick or well, and whipped upon the slightest provocation. On the fifth night out, Cinquez chose a few trusty companions of his misfortunes, and made a successful attack upon the officers and crew. The captain and cook struck down, two sailors put ashore, the Negroes were in full possession of the vessel. Montes was compelled, under pain of death, to navigate the vessel to Africa. He steered eastwardly during the daytime, but at night put about hoping to touch the American shore. Thus the vessel wandered until it was cited off of the coast of the United States during the month of August. It was described as a "long, low, black schooner." Notice was sent to all the collectors of the ports along the Atlantic Coast, and a steamer and several revenue cutters were dispatched after her. Finally, on the 26th of August, 1839, Lieut. Gedney, U. S. Navy, captured the "Amistad," and took her into New London, Connecticut.

The two Spaniards and a Creole cabin boy were examined before Judge Andrew T. Judson, of the United States Court, who, without examining the Negroes, bound them over to be tried as pirates. The poor Africans were cast into the prison at New London. Public curiosity was at a high pitch; and for a long time the "*Amistad captives*" occupied a large place in public attention. The Africans proved to be natives of the Mendi country, and quite intelligent. The romantic story of their sufferings and meanderings was given to the country through a competent interpreter; and many Christian hearts turned toward them in their lonely captivity in a strange land. The trial was continued several months. During this time the anti-slavery friends provided instruction for the Africans. Their minds were active and receptive. They soon learned to read, write, and do sums in arithmetic. They cultivated a garden of some fifteen acres, and proved themselves an intelligent and industrious people.

The final decision of the court was that the "Amistad captives" were not slaves, but freemen, and, as such, were entitled to their liberty. The good and liberal Lewis Tappan had taken a lively interest in these people from the first, and now that they were released from prison, felt that they should be sent back to their native shores and a mission started amongst their countrymen. Accordingly he took charge of them and appeared before the public in a number of cities of New England. An admission fee of fifty cents was required at the door, and the proceeds were devoted to leasing a vessel to take them home. Large audiences greeted them everywhere, and the impression they made was of

7 Sometimes written Cinque.

the highest order. Mr. Tappan would state the desire of the people to return to their native land, appeal to the philanthropic to aid them, and then call upon the people to read the Scriptures, sing songs in their own language, and then in the English. Cinquez would then deliver an account of their capture, the horrors of the voyage, how he succeeded in getting his manacles off, how he aided his brethren to loose their fetters, how he invited them to follow him in an attempt to gain their liberty, the attack, and their rescue, etc., etc. He was a man of magnificent physique, commanding presence, graceful manners, and effective oratory. His speeches were delivered in Mendi, and translated into English by an interpreter.

"It is impossible," wrote Mr. Tappan from Boston, "to describe the novel and deeply interesting manner in which he acquitted himself. The subject of his speech was similar to that of his countrymen who had spoken in English; but he related more minutely and graphically the occurrences on board the "Amistad." The easy manner of Cinquez, his natural, graceful, and energetic action, the rapidity of his utterance, and the remarkable and various expressions of his countenance, excited admiration and applause. He was pronounced a powerful natural orator, and one born to sway the minds of his fellow-men. Should he be converted and become a preacher of the cross in Africa what delightful results may be anticipated!"

A little fellow called Kali, only eleven years of age, pleased the audience everywhere he went by his ability not only to spell any word in the Gospels, but sentences, without blundering. For example, he would spell out a sentence like the following sentence, naming each letter and syllable, and recapitulating as he went along, until he pronounced the whole sentence: "Blessed are the meek, for they shall inherit the earth."

Of their doings in Philadelphia, Mr. Joseph Sturge wrote:

"On this occasion, a very crowded and miscellaneous assembly collected to see and hear the Mendians, although the admission had been fixed as high as half a dollar, with the view of raising a fund to carry them to their native country. Fifteen of them were present, including one little boy and three girls. Cinque, their chief, spoke with great fluency in his native language; and his action and manner were very animated and graceful. Not much of his speech was translated, yet he greatly interested his audience. The little boy could speak our language with facility; and each of them read, without hesitation, one or two verses in the New Testament. It was impossible for any one to go away with the impression, that in native intellect these people were inferior to the whites. The information which I privately received from their tutor, and others who had full opportunities of appreciating their capacities and attainments, fully confirmed my own very favorable impressions."

But all the while their sad hearts were turning toward their home and the dear ones so far away. One of them eloquently declared: "If Merica men offer me as much gold as fill this cap full up, and give me houses, land, and every ting, so dat I stay in this country, I say: 'No! no! I want to see my father, my mother, my brother, my sister.' " Nothing could have been more tender and expressive. They were willing to endure any hardships short of life that they might once more see their own, their native land. The religious instruction they had enjoyed made a wonderful impression on their minds. One of them said: "We owe every thing to God; he keeps us alive, and makes us free. When we go to home to Mendi we tell our brethren about God, Jesus Christ, and heaven." Another one was asked: "What is faith?" and replied: "Believing in Jesus Christ, and trusting in him." Reverting to the murder of the captain and cook of the "Amistad," one of the Africans said that if it were to be done over again he would pray for rather than kill them. Cinquez, hearing this, smiled and shook his head. When asked if he would not pray for them, said: "Yes, I would pray for 'em, an' kill 'em too."

These captives were returned to their native country in the fall of 1841, accompanied by five missionaries. Their objective point was Sierra Leone, from which place the British Government assisted them to their homes. Their stay in the United States did the anti-slavery cause great good. Here were poor, naked, savage pagans, unable to speak English, in less than three years able to speak the English language and appreciate the blessings of a Christian civilization.

The Cotton Plantation

Solomon Northup

* * * *

[I]nasmuch as some may read this book who have never seen a cotton field, a description of the manner of its culture may not be out of place.

The ground is prepared by throwing up beds or ridges, with the plough—back-furrowing, it is called. Oxen and mules, the latter almost exclusively, are used in ploughing. The women as frequently as the men perform this labor, feeding, currying, and taking care of their teams, and in all respects doing the field and stable work, precisely as do the ploughboys of the North.

The beds, or ridges, are six feet wide, that is, from water furrow to water furrow. A plough drawn by one mule is then run along the top of the ridge or center of the bed, making the drill, into which a girl usually drops the seed, which she carries in a bag hung round her neck. Behind her comes a mule and harrow, covering up the seed, so that two mules, three slaves, a plough and harrow, are employed in planting a row of cotton. This is done in the months of March and April. Corn is planted in February. When there are no cold rains, the cotton usually makes its appearance in a week. In the course of eight or ten days afterwards the first hoeing is commenced. This is performed in part, also, by the aid of the plough and mule. The plough passes as near as possible to the cotton on both sides, throwing the furrow from it. Slaves follow with their hoes, cutting up the grass and cotton, leaving hills two feet and a half apart. This is called scraping cotton. In two weeks more commences the second hoeing. This time the furrow is thrown towards the cotton. Only one stalk, the largest, is now left standing in each hill. In another fortnight it is hoed the third time, throwing the furrow towards the cotton in the same manner as before, and killing all the grass between the rows. About the first of July, when it is a foot high or thereabouts, it is hoed the fourth and last time. Now the whole space between the rows is ploughed, leaving a deep water furrow in the center. During all these hoeings the overseer or driver follows the slaves on horseback with a whip . . . The fastest hoer takes the lead row. He is usually about a rod in advance of his companions. If one of them passes him, he is whipped. If one falls behind or is a moment idle, he is whipped. In fact, the lash is flying from morning until night, the whole day long. The hoeing season thus continues from April until July, a field having no sooner been finished once, than it is commenced again.

From *Twelve Years a Slave, Narrative of Solomon Northup* (Buffalo: Derby, Orton, and Mulligan, 1853), pp. 163-171.

In the latter part of August begins the cotton picking season. At this time each slave is presented with a sack. A strap is fastened to it, which goes over the neck, holding the mouth of the sack breast high, while the bottom reaches nearly to the ground. Each one is also presented with a large basket that will hold about two barrels. This is to put the cotton in when the sack is filled. The baskets are carried to the field and placed at the beginning of the rows.

When a new hand, one unaccustomed to the business, is sent for the first time into the field, he is whipped up smartly, and made for that day to pick as fast as he can possibly. At night it is weighed, so that his capability in cotton picking is known. He must bring in the same weight each night following. If it falls short, it is considered evidence that he has been laggard, and a greater or less number of lashes is the penalty.

An ordinary day's work is two hundred pounds. A slave who is accustomed to picking, is punished, if he or she brings in a less quantity than that. There is a great difference among them as regards this kind of labor. Some of them seem to have a natural knack, or quickness, which enables them to pick with great celerity, and with both hands, while others, with whatever practice or industry, are utterly unable to come up to the ordinary standard. Such hands are taken from the cotton field and employed in other business. Patsey . . . was known as the most remarkable cotton picker on Bayou Bœuf. She picked with both hands and with such surprising rapidity, that five hundred pounds a day was not unusual for her.

Each one is tasked, therefore, according to his picking abilities, none, however, to come short of two hundred weight. I, being unskillful always in that business, would have satisfied my master by bringing in the latter quantity, while on the other hand, Patsey would surely have been beaten if she failed to produce twice as much.

The cotton grows from five to seven feet high, each stalk having a great many branches, shooting out in all directions, and lapping each other above the water furrow.

There are few sights more pleasant to the eye, than a wide cotton field when it is in the bloom. It presents an appearance of purity, like an immaculate expanse of light, new-fallen snow.

Sometimes the slave picks down one side of a row, and back upon the other, but more usually, there is one on either side, gathering all that has blossomed, leaving the unopened bolls for a succeeding picking. When the sack is filled, it is emptied into the basket and trodden down. It is necessary to be extremely careful the first time going through the field, in order not to break the branches off the stalks. The cotton will not bloom upon a broken branch. [Master] Epps never failed to inflict the severest chastisement on the unlucky servant who, either carelessly or unavoidably, was guilty in the least degree in this respect.

The hands are required to be in the cotton field as soon as it is light in the morning, and, with the exception of ten or fifteen minutes, which is given them at noon to swallow their allowance of cold bacon, they are not permitted to be a moment idle until it is too dark to see, and when the moon is full, they often times labor till the middle of the night. They do not dare to stop even at dinner time, nor return to the quarters, however late it be, until the order to halt is given by the driver.

The day's work over in the field, the baskets are "toted," or in other words, carried to the gin-house, where the cotton is weighed. No matter how fatigued and weary he may be—no matter how much he longs for sleep and rest—a slave never approaches the gin-house with his basket of cotton but with fear. If it falls short in weight—if he has not performed the full task appointed him, he knows that he must suffer. And if he has exceeded it by ten or twenty pounds, in all probability his master will measure the next day's task accordingly. So, whether he has too little or too much, his approach to the gin-house is always with fear and trembling. Most frequently they have too little, and therefore it is they are not anxious to leave the field. After weighing, follow the whippings; and then the baskets are carried to the cotton house, and their contents stored away like hay, all hands being sent in to tramp it down. If the cotton is not dry, instead of taking it to the gin-house at once, it is laid upon platforms, two feet high, and some three times as wide, covered with boards or plank, with narrow walks running between them.

This done, the labor of the day is not yet ended, by any means. Each one must then attend to his respective chores. One feeds the mules, another the swine—another cuts the wood, and so forth; besides, the packing is all done by candle light. Finally, at a late hour, they reach the quarters, sleepy and overcome with the long day's toil. Then a fire must be kindled in the cabin, the corn ground in the small hand-mill, and supper, and dinner for the next day in the field, prepared. All that is allowed them is corn and bacon, which is given out at the corncrib and smoke-house every Sunday morning. Each one receives, as his weekly allowance, three and a half pounds of bacon, and corn enough to make a peck of meal. That is all—no tea, coffee, sugar, and with the exception of a very scanty sprinkling now and then, no salt. I can say, from a ten years' residence with Master Epps, that no slave of his is ever likely to suffer from the gout, superinduced by excessive high living. Master Epps' hogs were fed on *shelled* corn—it was thrown out to his "niggers" in the ear. The former, he thought, would fatten faster by shelling, and soaking it in the water—the latter, perhaps, if treated in the same manner, might grow too fat to labor. Master Epps was a shrewd calculator, and knew how to manage his own animals, drunk or sober.

The corn mill stands in the yard beneath a shelter. It is like a common coffee mill, the hopper holding about six quarts. There was one privilege which Master Epps granted freely to every slave he had. They might grind their corn nightly, in such small quantities as their daily wants required, or they might grind the whole week's allowance at one time, on Sundays, just as they preferred. A very generous man was Master Epps!

I kept my corn in a small wooden box, the meal in a gourd; and, by the way, the gourd is one of the most convenient and necessary utensils on a plantation. Besides supplying the place of all kinds of crockery in a slave cabin, it is used for carrying water to the fields. Another, also, contains the dinner. It dispenses with the necessity of pails, dippers, basins, and such tin and wooden superfluities altogether.

When the corn is ground, and fire is made, the bacon is taken down from the nail on which it hangs, a slice cut off and thrown upon the coals to broil. The majority of slaves have no knife, much less a fork. They cut their bacon with the axe at the woodpile. The corn meal is mixed with a little water, placed in the fire, and baked. When it is "done brown," the ashes are scraped off, and being placed upon a chip, which answers for a table, the tenant of the slave hut is ready to sit down upon the ground to supper. By this time it is usually midnight. The same fear of punishment with which they approach the gin-house, possesses them again on lying down to get a snatch of rest. It is the fear of oversleeping in the morning. Such an offence would certainly be attended with not less than twenty lashes. With a prayer that he may be on his feet and wide awake at the first sound of the horn, he sinks to his slumbers nightly.

The softest couches in the world are not to be found in the log mansion of the slave. The one whereon I reclined year after year, was a plank twelve inches wide and ten feet long. My pillow was a stick of wood. The bedding was a coarse blanket, and not a rag or shred beside. Moss might be used, were it not that it directly breeds a swarm of fleas.

The cabin is constructed of logs, without floor or window. The latter is altogether unnecessary, the crevices between the logs admitting sufficient light. In stormy weather the rain drives through them, rendering it comfortless and extremely disagreeable. The rude door hangs on great wooden hinges. In one end is constructed an awkward fire-place.

An hour before day light the horn is blown. Then the slaves arouse, prepare their breakfast, fill a gourd with water, in another deposit their dinner of cold bacon and corn cake, and hurry to the field again. It is an offence invariably followed by a flogging, to be found at the quarters after daybreak. Then the fears and labors of another day begin; and until its close there is no such thing as rest. He fears he will be caught lagging through the day; he fears to approach the gin-house with his basket-load of cotton at night; he fears, when he lies down, that he will oversleep himself in the morning. Such is a true, faithful, unexaggerated picture and description of the slave's daily life, during the time of cotton-picking, on the shores of Bayou Bœuf.

Defending the Cornerstone

John Hope Franklin

Slavery strengthened the military tradition in the South because owners found it desirable, even necessary, to build up a fighting force to keep the slaves under control. They also felt compelled to oppose outside attacks with a militant defense. They regarded the abolitionist attack as a war on their institutions. Calhoun called it "a war of religious and political fanaticism, mingled, on the part of the leaders, with ambition and the love of notoriety." The object being "to humble and debase us in our own estimation, and that of the world in general; to blast our reputation, while they overthrow our domestic institutions."[1] As they read antislavery literature, observed the establishment of organizations dedicated to the destruction of slavery, and felt the sting of "subversive" activities like the Underground Railroad, Southerners reasoned that they were the targets of an all-out offensive war.

In the early thirties the scope of the abolitionist offensive was felt. These years saw the establishment of numerous militant antislavery societies. This decade saw the appearance of Garrison's uncompromising *Liberator* and the revolt of the Negro Nat Turner in Virgina. Petitions against slavery began to pour into Congress, and abolitionist literature flowed in an ever-swelling stream. Calhoun admonished, "if we do not defend ourselves none will defend us; if we yield we will be more and more pressed as we recede; and if we submit we will be trampled underfoot . . . "[2] The editor of the *Southern Quarterly Review* took up the North's challenge in the first issue of that journal, saying, "all the south wants . . . is a fair field, fair weapons on both sides, and an opportunity to defend herself."[3] The people of the South would strike back with all the resources at their command. The assailants should be met, editor John Underwood cried, "and never suffered to enter the citadel until they walk over our prostrate bodies."[4]

These were more than rhetorical flourishes. As Garrison and his fellows forced the North to consider the danger of an ever increasing slave power, the Southern leaders asserted themselves. From dozens of pens came ardent

[1] John C. Calhoun, *The Works of John C. Calhoun* (New York, 1854), I, 483–484.

[2] *Ibid.*, II, 632–633. These remarks were made in the U. S. Senate on February 6, 1837, in the debate on the reception of abolition petitions.

[3] *Southern Quarterly Review*, I (January 1842), 51.

[4] John W. H. Underwood to Howell Cobb, February 2, 1844, in Phillips, "Correspondence of Toombs, Stephen, and Cobb," II, 54–55.

From John Hope Franklin, *The Militant South* (Cambridge, Mass.: The Belknap Press of Harvard University Press, 1956), Chapter 5.

defenses of a social structure by which they would live or die. In these "bloodless conquests of the pen" they hoped to surpass "in grandeur and extent the triumphs of war."[5] They evolved a defense of slavery that was as full of fight as a state militia called out to quell a slave uprising. Chancellor Harper, Professor Dew, Governor Hammond, Fitzhugh, and others seemed aware of the fact that, however sound or logical their proslavery arguments might be, they must infuse in them a fighting spirit. The successful defense of slavery, whether by argument or by force, depended on the development of a powerful justification based on race superiority that would bring to its support all — or almost all — white elements in the South. Thus they redefined the "facts" of history, the "teachings" of the Bible, the "principles" of economics.[6] Convinced that thought could not be free, they believed that there should be some positive modifications of the democratic principles enunciated by the founding fathers. They rejected the equalitarian teachings of Jefferson and asserted that the inequality of man was fundamental to all social organization. There were not rights that were natural or inalienable, they insisted. In his *Disquisition on Government*, Calhoun asserted that liberty was not the right of every man equally. Instead of being born free and equal, men "are born subject not only to parental authority, but to laws and institutions of the country where born, and under whose protection they draw their first breath."[7] Fiery Thomas Cooper stopped working on the South Carolina statutes long enough to observe wryly, "we talk a great deal of nonsense about the rights of man. We say that man is born free, and equal to every other man. Nothing can be more untrue: no human being ever was, now is, or ever will be born free."[8]

In the rejection of the principles of liberty and equality, political democracy was also rejected. "An unmixed democracy," said one Mississippian, "is capricious and unstable, and unless arrested by the hand of despotism, leads to anarchy . . ." There was too much talk about democracy and too little about the aristocratic tradition. "Too much liberty and equality beget a dissolute licentiousness and a contempt for law and order." Virginians and South Carolinians led the demand for a recognition of Southern honor because they were true to their ancient sentiments and "with constant pride they guard their unstained escutcheons."[9] Life, liberty, and the pursuit of happiness were not inalienable rights. Every government, South Carolina's Chancellor William Harper explained, deprives men of life and liberty for offenses against society, while "all the laws of society are intended for nothing else but to restrain men from the pursuit of happiness . . ." It followed, accordingly, that if the possession of a dark skin was dangerous to society,

[5] See William S. Jenkins, *Pro-slavery Thought in the Old South* (Chapel Hill, 1935); and E. N. Elliott, *Cotton is King and Pro-Slavery Arguments* (Charleston, 1852).

[6] *Southern Literary Messenger*, XXIII (October 1856), 247.

[7] Calhoun, *Works*, II, 58–59.

[8] Jenkins, *Pro-slavery Thought*, p. 125.

[9] Quoted in Edward Ingle, *Southern Sidelights* (New York, 1896), p. 31.

then that society had the right to "protect itself by disfranchising the possessor of civil privileges and to continue the disability to his posterity . . ."[10]

It was left to George Fitzhugh, that shrewd professional Southerner, to crystallize and summarize Southern thinking on social organization. Free society was an abject failure, he said; and its frantic, but serious consideration of radical movements like socialism, communism, and anarchism was a clear admission of its failure. If slavery was more widely accepted, man would not need to resort to the "unnatural remedies of woman's rights, limited marriages, voluntary divorces, and free love, as proposed by the abolitionists."[11] Only in a slave society were there proper safeguards against unemployment and all the evils that follow as a country becomes densely settled and the supply of labor exceeds its demand. Fitzhugh, with a sneer at the North, observed that the "invention and use of the word Sociology in a free society and the science of which it treats, and the absence of such word and science in slave society shows that the former is afflicted with disease, the latter healthy." It was bad enough that free communities were failures, but it was intolerable that they should try to impose their impossible practices on the South. "For thirty years," he argued, "the South has been a field on which abolitionists, foreign and domestic, have carried on offensive warfare. Let us now, in turn, act on the offensive, transfer the seat of war, and invade the enemy's territory."[12]

The South's society was to rest on the inequality of men in law and economics. Social efficiency and economic success demanded organization; and organization inevitably meant the enslavement of the ignorant and unfortunate. *Slavery was a positive good.* It was regarded by James H. Hammond as "the greatest of all the great blessings which a kind providence has bestowed." It made possible the transformation of the South from a wilderness into a garden, and gave the owners the leisure in which to cultivate their minds and create a civilization rich in culture and gentility. More than that, it gave to the white man the only basis on which he could do something for a group of "hopelessly and permanently inferior" human being.[13]

The idea of the inferiority of the Negro enjoyed wide acceptance among Southerners of all classes and was an important ingredient in the theory of society promulgated by Southern leaders. It was organized into a body of systematic thought by the scientists and social scientists of the South, out of which emerged a doctrine of racial superiority to justify any kind of control maintained over the slave. In 1826, Dr. Thomas Cooper had said that he had not the slightest doubt that Negroes were of an "inferior variety of the human species; and not capable of the same improvement as

[10] William Harper, *The Pro-slavery Argument* (Philadelphia, 1853), p. 11.

[11] George Fitzhugh, *Cannibals All! or Slaves Without Masters* (Richmond, 1857), pp. 97–98.

[12] George Fitzhugh, *Sociology for the South; or The Failure of Free Society* (Richmond, 1854), p. 222.

[13] *Selections From the Letters and Speeches of the Hon. James H. Hammond of South Carolina* (New York, 1866), p. 34.

the whites";[14] but, while a mere chemist was apparently unable to elaborate the theory, the leading physicians of the South were. Dr. S. C. Cartwright of the University of Louisiana was only one of a number of physicians who set themselves up as authorities on the ethnological inferiority of the Negro. In his view, the capacities of the Negro adult for learning were equal to those of a white infant; and the Negro could properly perform certain physiological functions only when under the control of white men. For example, Negroes "under the compulsive power of the white man . . . are made to labor or exercise, which makes the lungs perform the duty of vitalizing the blood more perfectly than is done when they are left free to indulge in idleness. It is the red, vital blood sent to the brain that liberates their mind when under the white man's control; and it is the want of a sufficiency of red, vital blood that chains their mind to ignorance and barbarism when in freedom." Because of his inferiority, liberty and republican institutions were not only unsuited to the Negro, but actually poisonous to his happiness.[15] Variations on this theme were still being played by many Southern "men of science" when Sumter was bombarded. Like racists in other parts of the world, Southerners sought support for their militant racist ideology by developing a common bond with the less privileged. The obvious basis was race, and outside the white race there was to be found no favor from God, no honor or respect from man. Indeed, those beyond the pale were the objects of scorn from the multitudes of the elect.[16] By the time that Europeans were reading Gobineau's *Inequality of Races*, Southerners were reading Cartwright's *Slavery in the Light of Ethnology*. In both cases the authors conceded "good race" to some, and withheld it from others. In admitting all whites into the pseudo-nobility of race, Cartwright won their enthusiastic support in the struggle to preserve the integrity and honor of *the* race.

While uniting the various economically divergent groups of whites, the concept of race also strengthened the ardor of most Southerners to fight for the preservation of slavery. All slaves belonged to a degraded, "inferior" race; and, by the same token, all whites, however wretched some of them might be, were superior. In a race-conscious society whites at the lowest rung could identify themselves with the most privileged and affluent of the community. Thomas R. Dew, Professor of Political Law at the College of William and Mary, made this point clear when he said that in the South "no white man feels such inferiority of rank as to be unworthy of association with those around him. Color alone is here the badge of distinction, the true mark of aristocracy, and all who are white are equal in spite of the

14 Thomas Cooper to Mahlon Dickerson, March 16, 1826, in "Letters of Dr. Thomas Cooper, 1825–1832." *American Historical Review,* VI (July, 1901), 729. The idea of Negro inferiority was believed by some Northerners, but it neither was as widespread in that section nor did it constitute a whole body of thought as it did in the South.

15 S. C. Cartwright, "Diseases and Peculiarities of the Negro," *The Industrial Resources, etc., of the Southern and Western States* (New Orleans, 1853), II, 316.

16 See Alfred Vagts, *A History of Militarism* (New York, 1937), pp. 165, 479.

variety of occupation."[17] De Bow asserted this even more vigorously in a widely circulated pamphlet published in 1860. At one point, he said that the non-slaveholding class was more deeply interested than any other in the maintenance of Southern institutions. He said that non-slaveholders were made up of two groups: those who desired slaves but were unable to purchase them; and those who were able but preferred to hire cheap white labor. He insisted that there was no group of whites in the South opposed to slavery. One of his principal arguments was that the non-slaveholder preserves the status of the white man "and is not regarded as an inferior or a dependent . . . No white man at the South serves another as a body servant, to clean his boots, wait on his table, and perform the menial services of his household. His blood revolts against this, and his necessities never drive him to it. He is a companion and an equal."[18]

Southern planters paid considerable attention to the non-slaveholding element whenever its support was needed in the intersectional struggle. Their common origins, at times involving actual kinship of planters and yeomen, gave them a basis for working together in a common cause. The opportunities for social mobility, however rare, provided the dreams of yeomen. These dreams strengthened their attachment to the planter class; while the fear of competition with a large group of freedmen was a nightmare. But *race*—the common membership in a superior order of beings of both planters and poorer whites — was apparenty the strongest point in the argument that the enslavement of the Negro was as good for small farmers as it was for large planters. The passion of the Southern planter and politician for oratory found ample release in the program to persuade Southern whites that theirs was a glorious civilization to be defended at all costs. In the absence of active and bitter class antagonisms, it was possible for the various white groups to cooperate especially against outside attacks and in behalf of slavery.[19]

Most Southerners were not satisfied merely to have their leaders restate the theory of Southern society and argue with abolitionists in Congress and other respectable places; they wanted to give effective and tangible support to their cause. Chancellor Harper had told them that, in the South as in Athens, "every citizen should be a soldier, and qualified to discharge efficiently the duties of a soldier."[20] In *De Bow's Review* "A Virginian" advised his fellows that *"without ceasing to be free citizens, they must cultivate the*

[17] Thomas R. Dew, *Review of the Debate in the Virginia Legislature of 1831 and 1832* (Richmond, 1832), pp. 112–113.

[18] J. D. B. De Bow, *The Interest in Slavery of the Southern Non-Slaveholder* (Charleston, 1860), pp. 3, 5, 8–10.

[19] For discussions of inter-class harmony in the South see Frank L. Owsley, *Plain Folk of the Old South* (Baton Rouge, 1949), pp. 133–134; and Paul H. Buck, "Poor Whites of the Ante-Bellum South," *American Historical Review*, XXXI (October 1925), 41, 51–52.

[20] Harper, *Pro-slavery Argument*, p. 80.

virtues, the sentiments, nay, the habits and manners of soldiers."[21] They should be ready for vigorous, militant action to protect and defend the South's institutions. James Buckingham believed that they were determined to do exactly that. In 1839, he remarked, "Here in Georgia . . . as everywhere throughout the South, slavery is a topic upon which no man, and, above all, a foreigner, can open his lips without imminent personal danger, unless it is to defend and uphold the system." He stated further that the violence of the measures taken against the few who ventured to speak in favor of abolition was such as to strike terror in others.[22]

There was no strong antislavery in the Southern states after 1830. Moreover, Northern antislavery organizations were doing little to incite the slaves to revolt or, except for sporadic underground railroad activities, to engage in other subversive activities. It was enough, however, for Southerners to believe either that abolitionists were active or that there was a possibility of their becoming active. This belief, running very strong at times, placed under suspicion everything Northern, including persons and ideas. "Upon a mere vague report, or bare suspicion," Harriet Martineau observed, "persons travelling through the South have been arrested, imprisoned, and, in some cases, flogged or otherwise tortured, on pretence that such persons desired to cause insurrection among the slaves. More than one innocent person has been hanged . . ." She reported with horror that, after William Ellery Channing published his attack on slavery, several South Carolinians vowed that, should he visit their state with a bodyguard of 20,000 men, he would not come out alive.[23]

After 1830, the South increased its vigilance over outside subversion, and pursued the elusive, at times wholly imaginary, abolitionist with an ardor born of desperation. When they could not lay hands on him they seized the incendiary publications that were the products of his "fiendish" mind. In the summer of 1835, overpowering the city guard, they stormed the post office in Charleston and burned a bag of abolitionist literature. According to the postmaster, this act was not perpetrated by any "ignorant or infuriated rabble."[24] In the same year, citizens of Fairfax County, Virginia, found local vigilance committees in each militia district "to detect and bring to speedy punishment all persons circulating abolitionst literature." A correspondence committee of twenty was to keep in touch with developments in other parts of the South.[25]

It was in 1835 that Sergeant S. Prentiss, rising to prominence in Missis-

21 "The Black Race in North America," *De Bow's Review,* XX (February 1856, 209. (Italics in original.)

22 Buckingham, *Slave States,* I, 183.

23 Martineau, *Society in America,* II, 349.

24 Alfred Huger to Amos Kendall, July 30, 1855, in Theodore D. Jervey, *Robert Y. Hayne,* pp. 379–380.

25 Eaton, "Mob Violence," p. 358.

sippi, wrote his mother who had remained at their Maine home, that fifteen Negroes and six whites had been hanged in connection with an insurrection plot that never materialized.[26] He added, "It certainly ought to serve as a warning to the abolitionists, not only of their own danger but of the great injury they are doing the slaves themselves by meddling with them."[27] The hunt was on. In the last decade before the Civil War, mobs and vigilance committees arrested Northern "peddlers, book agents, traveling salesmen, and . . . school teachers."[28] William Lloyd Garrison, indeed no impartial reporter of events, gathered enough information on the violent treatment of Northerners in the South to publish two tracts on the subject.[29] He reported that in one Alabama town the militia was called out to eject an agent who was selling Fleetwood's *Life of Christ*.[30] In Virginia "a company of brave and chivalrous militia was assembled, with muskets and bayonets in hand," to escort out of the community a Shaker who was peddling garden seeds.[31] He also reported that twenty-five vigilance committees had been set up in four Virginia counties to keep a strict eye on all suspicious persons "whose business is not known to be harmless or . . . who may express sentiments of sympathy . . . with abolitionists."[32]

These incidents were, of course, excellent grist for Garrison's mill; and allowance should be made for any exaggeration that might have come from his zeal in reporting such incidents. They bear a striking resemblance, however, to those reported by more disinterested sources. When John C. Underwood of Clark County, Virginia, went to the Republican National Convention in 1856, his neighbors were outraged. In a mass meeting they passed resolutions condemning him of moral treason and threatening him with violence if he ever returned to Virginia. He moved out of the state and remained away until 1864.

In the middle fifties a Texas legislator who had lived in the North expressed views on slavery that some of his fellows regarded as heretical. When it was announced that he was to speak in Galveston, a group of prominent citizens composed a letter to him which contained the following instructions:

> That your views . . . on slavery are unsound and dangerous is the fixed belief of this community . . . You are, therefore, explicity and premptorily notified that, in your speech you will not be permitted to touch in any manner on the subject of slavery . . . Your introduction of it in any manner will be the prompt signal for consequences to which we need not allude . . . This communication will be read to the assembled public before you proceed with your speech.[33]

[26] Sydnor, *Slavery in Mississippi*, p. 246.
[27] *Ibid.*, p. 246.
[28] Eaton, "Mob Violence," p. 366.
[29] *The New Reign of Terror in the Slaveholding States for 1859–60* (New York, 1860; and *A Fresh Catalogue of Southern Outrages upon Northern Citizens* (New York, 1860).
[30] Garrison, *New Reign of Terror*, p. 64.
[31] *Ibid*, p. 69.
[32] Clement Eaton, *Freedom of Thought in The Old South* (Durham, 1940), p. 245; and *Dictionary of American Biography*, XIX, 114.
[33] *De Bow's Review*, XXI (September 1856), 276–277.

All over the South mob action began to replace orderly judicial procedure, as the feeling against abolitionists mounted and as Southern views on race became crystallized. Even in North Carolina, where one citizen felt that there should be some distinction between that "civilized state and Mississippi and some other Western states," the fear of abolitionists caused many of its citizens to resort to drastic measures.[34] In 1850, two missionaries, Adam Crooks and Jesse McBride, came into the state from Ohio, ostensibly to preach to those North Carolina Methodists who had not joined the newly organized Methodist Episcopal Church, South.[35] Soon they were suspected of abolitionist activities, and McBride was convicted of distributing incendiary publications. According to one source they were "mobed and drove out of Gulford." Ten years later a vigilance committee threatened to deal violently with one John Stafford whose crime had been to give food and shelter to Crooks and McBride during their sojourn in the state.[36] This was the kind of activity that Professor Benjamin S. Hedrick, dismissed from the University of North Carolina for his free-soil views, deprecated. Safe in New York City he asked Thomas Ruffin, Chief Justice of the North Carolina Supreme Court, to use his influence "to arrest the terrorism and fanaticism" that was rampant in the South. "If the same spirit of terror, mobs, arrests and violence continue," he declared, "it will not be long before civil war will rage at the South."[37]

As the people of the South went about the grim task of exterminating persons and ideas hostile to their way of life, they began to give serious consideration to the relationship of slavery to their military strength. Since Revolutionary days critics had argued that slaves were a burden during periods of armed conflict. Despite Madison's warm attachment to the South he was convinced that slavery was a military liability. In the 1797 debates on the question of increasing the duty on imported slaves, he insisted that it was as much in the interest of Georgia and South Carolina as of the free states to end the slave trade altogether. "Every addition they receive to their number of slaves," he said, "tends to weaken and render them less capable of self-defense. In case of hostilities with foreign nations, they will be the means of inviting attack instead of repelling invasion."[38]

John Randolph of Roanoke, with his characteristic flair for the dramatic, made it clear that he regarded slaves as a liability in peace or in war. During the debates in Congress preceding the outbreak of the war of 1812 he declared that during the preceding ten years slaves had become more dan-

34 David W. Stone to Thomas Ruffin, May 3, 1842, in J. G. de Roulhac Hamilton, editor, *The Papers of Thomas Ruffin* (Raleigh, 1918), II, 206.

35 For a detailed account of the experiences of Crooks and McBride, see Eaton, *Freedom of Thought*, pp. 138–139.

36 John Stafford to Thomas Ruffin, January 24, 1860, in Hamilton, *Papers of Thomas Ruffin*, II, 65–67.

37 Benjamin S. Hedrick to Thomas Ruffin, January 16, 1860, in *Papers of Thomas Ruffin*, III, 64–65.

38 Olmsted, *Back Country*, p. 478.

gerous and that the equalitarian doctrines of the French Revolution had trickled down even to them. "God forbid," he said to his colleagues, "that the Southern states should ever see an enemy on their shores, with these infernal principles of French fraternity in the van . . . the night-bell never tolled for fires in Richmond, that the mother does not hug the infant more closely to her bosom."[39] Randolph, who was in Richmond at the time of the aborted Gabriel uprising in 1800, looked at slavery with an objectivity which few of his contemporaries possessed. He was convinced that slaves would strike for freedom whenever any crisis gave them the opportunity.

Few Southerners after Madison and Randolph entertained similar views regarding the military liability of slaves. But as these views lost favor in the South they found articulate supporters in the North. In 1840, Hildreth asserted that, in the hour of danger, slaves would "be regarded with more dread and terror even than the invaders themselves." In case of a threatened invasion they would "far from aiding in the defense of the country . . . create a powerful diversion in favor of the enemy." Slavery was clearly a military liability, for:

> Should the slaveholding states become involved in a war, which it would be necessary for them to prosecute from their own resources, they would be obliged to depend upon a standing army levied from among the dregs of the population. Such an army would be likely to become quite as much an object of terror to those for whose defence it would be levied, as to those against whom it would be raised.[40]

To Olmsted there was no question of the deleterious effect of slavery on the South's military strength. How could it be otherwise when so large a portion of the working force in the South "is the offspring of a subjected foreign people, itself held to labor without stipulated wages, not connected by marriage with the citizens, owning nothing of the property, having no voice in the state, in the lowest degree ignorant, and yet half barbarous in disposition and habits . . ." In a war the slave would, at the very first opportunity, strike for his freedom. Any other view was ridiculous.

> To suppose that in case of a war, either foreign or civil, the slave would be an element of strength to the South . . . seems to me, to be, on the face of it, a foundation upon which only the maddest theorist or the most impracticable of abstractionists could found a policy. Whether . . . in case of a civil war . . . northern men are likely to be more influenced by the cost of extra hazardous insurance policies on their manufactures and stores than southern gentlemen by the dread of losing the services of their slaves, we can best judge by the past.[41]

From the slaveholder's point of view it became necessary to nail such claims as lies. Regardless of how much the abolitionists wished it, slaves were not a military liability. Why should they be when the vast majority

[39] *Annals of Congress,* 12th Congress, 1st Session, p. 451. See also Hugh A. Garland, *The Life of John Randolph of Roanoke* (New York, 1854), I, 294–295.

[40] Hildreth, *Despotism in America,* pp. 108–110.

[41] Olmsted, *Back Country,* p. 477.

were happy and the whites had no fear of them? Indeed, Southerners protested almost too much that they had no fear of slaves. Hammond said that Randolph's description of the white mother clinging to her infant while fearing insurrection was "all a flourish." Of course, he admitted, "there may be nervous men and timid women, whose imaginations are haunted with unwonted fears . . . as there are in all communities on earth, but in no part of the world have men of ordinary firmness less fear of danger from their own operative than we have." In his celebrated letter to the English humanitarian Thomas Clarkson in 1845, Hammond made another concession to possible apprehension. He explained that "the habitual vigilance" of the South, "with its small guards in . . . cities and occasional patrols in the country" was responsible for the repose and security which the South enjoyed.[42] Two years later, a writer refused to make even these slight concessions regarding the possible danger of slaves. He said that the slaves had no disposition to violence. The security of the Southern states from a general revolt did not depend on a police force or military organization "or upon any measures of severity, but upon the general feeling that prevails between the two classes."[43] Edward Bryan added that as to any danger arising out of slavery, the South was "as safe as man can be."[44]

If slaves were not to be feared, the argument ran, there was no reason to look upon them as a military liability. A. P. Upshur, the Virginia publicist and jurist, put the proposition firmly but modestly when he said that if slavery added nothing to the owners' strength in war, it certainly took nothing from their power of resistance. Upshur went on to claim that in time of war slaves could, under the proper guidance, be turned into a distinct asset, for their diligent labor at home could release the entire white population for use in the struggle against the enemy. After surveying the whole sweep of history he was able to conclude that "those republics which have been most distinguished for their power, both in defensive and aggressive war, were, without exception, holders of slaves."[45]

History was frequently quoted by Southerners who wanted to prove that slavery did not undermine military strength. Hammond reminded Clarkson that slavery was not a source of weakness to Sparta, Athens, or Rome. What was more, their slaves were comparatively far more numerous than those of the South, "of the same color for the most part with themselves, and large numbers of them familiar with the use of arms."[46] Ruffin reminded critics that slavery had actually increased the military efficiency of the Greeks and Romans. He concluded that "History has nowhere shown that the holding of slaves was deemed a national weakness in war."[47] Another Southerner

42 Hammond, *Letters and Speeches,* pp. 477, 128.

43 *Southern Quarterly Review,* XII (July 1847), 122–123.

44 Bryan, *Rightful Remedy,* p. 47.

45 A. P. Upshur, "Domestic Slavery," *Southern Literary Messenger,* V (October 1839), 681.

46 Hammond, *Letters and Speeches,* p. 128.

47 Edmund Ruffin, "Consequences of Abolition Agitation," *De Bow's Review,* XXIII (December 1857), 597.

insisted that the slave system as a source of military weakness for the South existed only in the imagination of the abolitionist. "As we read history," he continued, "the slave institution has never been a source of weakness, and is in reality, one of strength. It has never enfeebled us in any foreign contest."[48]

Southern leaders argued so vehemently against the very idea of the slave as a military liability that they tended to hold him up as a distinct military asset. As wartime laborers their value was undeniable.

> Judging from what we all know ourselves of the character of the African in America . . . the idea that our slaves would embarrass and weaken us in time of war—even in a contest conducted for the express purpose of giving them liberty, appears to us to be wholly groundless. . . On the contrary, the proofs are conclusive that they would add vastly to our strength—that under the superintendence of a few they would cultivate the soil as diligently as they do now and maintain our agricultural resources undiminished, while the great body of our adult males would be fighting in the field . . .[49]

The suggestion was even made that slaves might be enlisted in military organizations to do battle for the cause of the South. Chancellor Harper seriously entertained that idea. He noted that some in the North and in Europe believed that, in the event that the South was engaged in a war, insurrection could be organized among the slaves and they could be used as a fighting force against their masters; this he stoutly denied. Because of their attachment to their masters, slaves were a "hundred fold" more available to the South than to any invading foe.

> They are already in our possession, and we might at will arm and organize them in any number that we might think proper. . . Thoroughly acquainted with their characters, and accustomed to command them, we might use any strictness of discipline which would be necessary to render them effective. . . Though morally most timid, they are by no means wanting in physical strength or nerve. . . With white officers and accompanied by a strong white cavalry, there are no troops in the world from whom there would be so little reason to apprehend insubordination or mutiny.[50]

Even the entertainment of such an idea reflects the extremes to which Southern thinking could go and the measures which desperation might force. While Harper recognized the dangers inherent in such a suggestion, he seems not to have realized that such action repudiated much which the South stood for. The South was more closely attached to the concepts of military service in feudal Europe than to those in ancient Sparta. Military service, like planting, was the pursuit of the gentleman. The term "gentleman" had been so loosely construed, at least for certain purposes, as to include most white men. To move to the point of including Negro slaves

[48] *Southern Quarterly Review,* XIV (July 1848), 61.
[49] *Southern Quarterly Review,* XV (July 1849), 306–307.
[50] Harper, *Pro-Slavery Argument,* p. 81.

was to move dangerously close to nullifying the entire Southern social order.

In the eyes of Southerners, Negro slavery had become not only a positive economic and social good, but also a positive military good. Slaves would work in the fields while their masters went to do battle against the enemy. If the masters needed help, the slaves might shoulder arms and save the day. In still another somewhat negative way, the institution of slavery was a positive military good: it could have a salutary effect on the nature of wars to come; it could eliminate aggressive warfare. One Southerner pointed out that, since it was unwise and inexpedient for masters to go away on expeditions of foreign conquest leaving their slaves undisciplined for long periods, aggressive warfare would be virtually eliminated as slavery spread over the world.[51]

Slavery might help to prevent war or, at least, to mitigate its horrors, President Dew claimed. By fixing the wanderer to the soil and establishing an interest in private property, slavery would moderate the savage temper of man and direct his attention toward establishing a society governed by law and dominated by civil institutions. Then the horrors and lawlessness of war would disappear.[52] Slavery could, therefore, be made to serve the interests of the pacifists or warmongers, depending on the point of view of the advocate. On the whole, however, there seems to be no doubt that it strengthened the military tradition, if not the hand, of the South.

51 *Southern Literary Messenger,* V (October 1839), 632.
52 Dew, *Review of the Debates,* p. 13.

Motherhood in Bondage

E. Franklin Frazier

Strange to say, the idealized picture of the Negro mother has not grown out of the stories of her sacrifices and devotion to her own children but has emerged from the tradition of the Negro mammy — a romantic figure in whom maternal love as a vicarious sentiment has become embodied. There is plenty of evidence to give a solid background to the familiar picture — stories of cold, and often inhuman, indifference toward her own offspring and undying devotion to the children of the master race. "The devotion of the nurses of these foster-children was greater than their love for their own" is the comment of one observer, Susan Smedes, who supports her generalizations with the following instance which she has recorded in *A Southern Planter*:

> One of them, with a baby at home very sick, left it to stay with the white child. This one she insisted on walking the night through, because he was roaring with the colic, though the mistress entirely disapproved and urged her to go home to her own child, whose illness was more serious, if less noisy, than the white nursling with its colic.[1]

This seems all the more strange when we recall the universal testimony of travelers and missionaries that the love of the African mother for her children is unsurpassed in any part of the world. "Maternal affection (neither suppressed by the restraints, nor diverted by the solicitudes of civilized life) is everywhere conspicuous among them," wrote Mungo Park, "and creates a correspondent return of tenderness in the child." He reports the following incident:

> In the course of the day, several women, hearing that I was going to Sego, came and begged me to inquire of Mansong, the King, what was become of their children. One woman in particular, told me that her son's name was Mamadee; that he was no heathen, but prayed to God morning and evening, and had been taken from her about three years ago, by Mansong's army; since which she had never heard of him. She said she often dreamed about him; and begged me, if I should see him, either in Bambarra, or in my own country, to tell him that his mother and sister were still alive.

Likewise, we learn that in East Africa mothers offered themselves to the

[1] Susan Smedes, *A Southern Planter,* Baltimore, 1887, p. 50.

From E. Franklin Frazier, *The Negro Family in the United States* (Chicago: University of Chicago Press, 1966), pp. 33-45.

slave-raiders in order to save their sons, and Hottentot women refused food during famines until their children were fed.

How are we to explain this contrast between the native Negro mother and her descendants in America? Surely transportation to the New World could not have eradicated fundamental impulses and instinctive feelings. Elizabeth Donnan, in the *Documents Illustrative of the History of Slave Trade to America*, of which she is editor, gives evidence that the dehumanizing of the Negro began before he left the shores of Africa. An official of the Dutch West India Company on the African coast wrote as follows concerning the Negro's reputed indifference to family ties where the slave trade was carried on: "Not a few in our country fondly imagine that parents here sell their children, men their wives, and one brother the other: but those who think so deceive themselves; for this never happens on any other account but that of necessity, or some great crime. But most of the slaves that are offered to us are prisoners of war, which are sold by the victors as their booty."[2]

To pregnant women who formed a part of the slave caravans motherhood meant only a burden and an accentuation of their miseries. Maternal feeling was choked and dried up in mothers who had to bear children, in addition to loads of corn or rice, on their backs during marches of eight to fourteen hours. Nor did life in the slave pens on the coast, where they were chained and branded and sometimes starved, mitigate the sufferings of motherhood.

In the selection of Negroes for the cargoes of the slave ships, their physical condition and their suitability for the specific requirements of the trade were the only factors of moment to the traders. When William Ellery, the father of one of the signers of the Declaration of Independence, instructed the captain of his slaver: "If you have a good Trade for Negroes may purchase forty or Fifty Negroes. get most of them mere Boys and Girl, some Men, let them be Young, No very small Children," it is unlikely that the faithful captain in obeying his orders cared much about the feelings of the Negro mothers who had to surrender their children. During the Middle Passage that followed the gathering of slaves on the coast, the last spark of maternal feeling was probably smothered in the breast of many mothers who were packed spoon fashion between decks and often gave birth to children in the scalding perspiration from the human cargo. Then whatever was left of maternal sentiment had to undergo another ordeal in the slave markets of the New World.

Scarcely more regard was shown for the humanity of the slaves in the American markets than in those of Africa. To be sure, humanitarian sentiment was more likely to make itself felt in the American communities than among the adventurers and criminals who frequented the slave markets

2 Elizabeth Donnan (ed.), *Documents Illustrative of the History of the Slave Trade to America,* Washington, D. C., 1930, I, 441.

of Africa. Moreover, in the slave markets of Charleston and Richmond it was to the economic advantage of those who bought and sold slaves to see that infants did not die because of the lack of maternal care. But since, as a South Carolina court held in 1809, "the young of slaves . . . . stand on the same footing as other animals," the relation of mothers to their children was recognized not because of its human or social significance but because of the property interests involved in the relationship.

In some cases the affectional ties between mother and children survived the ordeals of the slave markets and the Middle Passage and were perhaps strengthened by common suffering. But the characteristic attitudes and sentiments which the slave mother developed in America grew out of her experiences with pregnancy and childbirth and her relations with her offspring in the new environment. Where slave women were maintained as breeders and enjoyed certain indulgences and privileges because of their position, the experience of pregnancy and childbirth was likely to cause them to look upon their children as the source of these favors.

The following instructions were sent to an agent for the management of a plantation in Virginia in 1759: "The breeding wenches particularly, you must instruct the overseers to be kind and indulgent to, and not to force them when with child upon any service or hardship that will be injurious to them and that they have every necessary when in that condition that is needful for them, and the children to be well looked after and to give them every spring and fall the jerusalem oak seed for a week together and that none of them suffer in time of sickness for want of proper care."[3]

On the other hand, where slave women were forced into cohabitation and pregnancy, and childbirth brought no release from labor, they might develop a distinct antipathy toward their offspring. A former slave, Moses Grandy, wrote the following concerning the treatment of women by the overseer:

> On the estate I am speaking of, those women who had sucking children suffered much from their breasts becoming full of milk, the infants being left at home; they therefore could not keep up with the other hands: I have seen the overseer beat them with raw hide, so that the blood and milk flew mingled from their breasts. A woman who gives offence in the field, and is large in the family way, is compelled to lie down over a hole made to receive her corpulency, and is flogged with the whip, or beat with a paddle, which had holes in it; at every stroke comes a blister. One of my sisters was so severely punished in this way, that labor was brought on, and the child was born in the field. This very overseer, Mr. Brooks, killed in this manner a girl named Mary: her father and mother were in the field at the time.[4]

Even under the more normal conditions of slavery, childbirth could

[3] Arthur W. Calhoun, *A Social History of the American Family from Colonial Times to the Present,* Cleveland, 1917-18, I, 327.

[4] Moses Grandy, *Narrative of the Life of Moses Grandy; Late a Slave in the United States of America,* Boston, 1844, p. 18.

not have had the same significance for the slave mother as for the African mother. In Africa tribal customs and taboos tended to fix the mother's attitude toward her child before it was born. In America this traditional element in the shaping of maternal feeling was absent. Consequently, the development of maternal feeling was dependent largely upon the physiological and emotional responses of the mother to her child.

Concerning the biologically inherited elements in the so-called "maternal instinct," L. L. Bernard writes:

> It is difficult to separate early acquirements through the imitation process from biological inheritance without considerable intensive investigation. But it is doubtful if more than the response to touch, temperature and odor stimuli from the child by fondling, holding and licking or kissing, a more or less vague unorganized emotional response to its cries, which chiefly manifests itself in movement toward the child, vague answering cries and the discharge of milk upon certain definite stimuli of pressure upon the breast, can be said to be inherited by the human mother.[5]

Generally, during the period of pregnancy, the slave woman's labor was reduced, and on the birth of a child she received additional clothes and rations. But the following letter of an overseer indicates that the needs of the mothers and their newborn children were not always promptly met:

> Charlotte & Venus & Mary & Little Sary have all had children and have not received their baby clothes also Hetty & Sary & Coteler will want baby clothes. I see a Blanket for the old fellow Sampson he is dead. I thought I wrote to you that he was dead. Little Peggy Sarys daughter has not ever drawn any Blanket at all, and when they come I think it would be right to give her the Blanket that was sent to Sampson.[6]

As soon as possible after childbirth, the mother was required to return to the fields, often taking her unweaned child along. A former slave describes the situation as follows:

> The bell rings, at four o'clock in the morning, and they have half an hour to get ready. Men and women start together, and the women must work as steadily as the men, and perform the same tasks as the men. If the plantation is far from the house, the sucking children are taken out and kept in the field all day. If the cabins are near, the women are permitted to go in two or three times a day to their infant children. The mother is driven out when the child is three to four weeks old.[7]

In some cases the mothers were permitted to return to the cabin in order to nurse the infant who was left alone or in the charge of a child. "At this period," writes a former slave, John Brown, "my principal occupation was to nurse my little brother whilst my mother worked in the field. Almost

[5] L. L. Bernard, *Instinct: A Study in Social Psychology*, New York, 1924, p. 326.

[6] Letter of Elisha Cain, overseer, on Retreat Plantation, Jefferson County, Georgia, to his employer, Miss Mary Telfair, Savannah, November 20, 1836, in Phillips, *Documentary History of American Industrial Society: Plantation and Frontier*, Cleveland, I, 333-34.

[7] Lewis Clarke, *Narrative of the Sufferings of Lewis and Milton Clarke, Sons of a Soldier of the Revolution*, Boston, 1846, p. 127.

all the slave children have to do the nursing; the big taking care of the small, who often come poorly off in consequence. I know this was my little brother's case. I used to lay him in the shade, under a tree, sometimes, and go to play, or curl myself up under a hedge, and take a sleep."

The following situation described by Frances A. Kemble in her *Journal* was typical of many plantations:

> It is true that every able-bodied woman is made the most of in being driven afield as long as, under all and any circumstances, she is able to wield a hoe; but, on the other hand, stout, hale, hearty girls and boys, of from eight to twelve and older, are allowed to lounge about, filthy and idle, with no pretense of an occupation but what they call "tend baby," i.e., see to the life and limbs of the little slave infants, to whose mothers, working in distant fields, they carry them during the day to be suckled, and for the rest of the time leave them to crawl and kick in the filthy cabins or on the broiling sand which surrounds them.[8]

Consequently, where such limitations were placed upon the mother's spontaneous emotional responses to the needs of her children and where even her suckling and fondling of them were restricted, it was not unnatural that she often showed little attachment to her offspring.

A slaveholder, who loved "to recall the patriarchal responsibility and tenderness" which her father "felt for his poor, ignorant, dependent slaves," tells the following story to "show that the master's feelings are sometimes even deeper than the mother's":

> One of my slaves had an infant child two months old who was attacked with an affection of the windpipe. I never saw such extreme suffering; it was one continual spasm and struggle for breath. The physician visited it several times every day, but could give no relief. The poor little sufferer seemed as if it would neither live nor die. These extreme tortures lasted a whole week before it breathed its last; and my own mind was so excited by its sharp and constant convulsive shrieks, that I never left it night or day, and could not sleep, even a moment, sitting by its side; and yet its own mother slept soundly at the foot of the bed, not because she was fatigued, for she was required to do nothing but nurse the dying child.[9]

While the pathos expressed here is understandable, one would require a knowledge of the mother's experiences during pregnancy and childbirth and her subsequent relations with her infant in order to decide whether her behavior was unnatural or extraordinary. However, one might ask: Why were these slave women, in the words of the same informant, "the most enthusiastically fond foster-mothers, when they [were] called upon to nurse the infant child of their owners"?

Often the relations of the foster-mother or "mammy" to her "white chil-

[8] Frances A. Kemble, *Journal of a Residence on a Georgian Plantation,* New York, 1863, pp. 121-22.

[9] H. B. Schoolcraft, *By A Southern Lady: Letters on the Condition of the African Race in the United States,* Philadelphia, 1852, pp. 13-14.

dren" offered greater scope for the expression of the emotions and impulses characteristic of maternal love than the contacts which she had with her own offspring. The attachment and devotion which the "mammy" showed for the white children began before the children were born. The "mammy," who was always an important member of the household, attended her mistress during pregnancy and took under her care the infant as soon as it was born. Often she, instead of the mother, suckled the child and if the child was a girl, was never separated from her until she was grown. Miss Bremer has left a picture of one of these foster-mothers sitting "like a horrid specter, black and silent by the alter," during the wedding of her foster-child from whom she "could not bear the thought of parting." If these black foster-mothers showed more maternal affection and devotion for their charges than they or their black sisters showed for their own offspring, it was due to the emotional and biological dependence that developed between them as a result of this intimate association. Moreover, where this intimate association extended over several generations and the "mammy" became assimilated into the master's household, tradition tended to define her role and to inculcate in her sentiments proper to her status.

It should not be inferred from what has been said concerning the Negro woman's devotion to the children of the master race that she never developed a deep and lasting sentiment for her own children. In the slave cabin, where she was generally mistress, she often gathered about her a numerous progeny, in spite of miscarriages and a high infant mortality. Miss Kemble enters in her *Journal*, pp.190–91, the following information relative to the size of slave families, miscarriages, and infant mortality:

> "*Fanny* has had six children; all dead but one. She came to beg to have her work in the field lightened.
>
> "*Nanny* has had three children; two of them dead. She came to implore that the rule of sending them into the field three weeks after their confinement might be altered.
>
> "*Leah,* Caesar's wife, has had six children; three are dead.
>
> "*Sophy,* Lewis's wife, came to beg for some old linen. She is suffering fearfully; has had ten children; five of them are dead. The principal favor she asked was a piece of meat, which I gave her.
>
> "*Sally,* Scipio's wife, has had two miscarriages and three children born, one of whom is dead. She came complaining of incessant pain and weakness in her back. This woman was a mulatto daughter of a slave called Sophy, by a white man of the name of Walker, who visited the plantation.
>
> "*Charlotte,* Renty's wife, had had two miscarriages, and was with child again. She was almost crippled with rheumatism, and showed me a pair of poor swollen knees that made my heart ache. I have promised her a pair of flannel trowsers, which I must forthwith set about making.
>
> "*Sarah,* Stephen's wife—this woman's case and history were alike deplorable. She had had four miscarriages, had brought seven children into the world, five of whom were dead, and was again with child. She complained of dreadful pains in the back, and an internal tumor which swells with the exertion of working in the fields; probably, I think, she is ruptured."

The following entries concerning births and deaths of children were made by an overseer on a plantation in Florida, 1851.

BIRTHS ON THE PLANTATION IN 1851

Florer was confined this morning with a male Child, Jany. 27, 1851.
May 28th, Cate was delivered of a Female Child this morning.
June 4th, Martha was delivered of a male child at 12 o'clock today.
June 13th, Long Mariah was delivered of a male Child today at twelve o'clock.
August 17th, B. Mariah was delivered of a male child this morning.

DEATHS ON THE PLANTATION IN 1851

August 4th, Catherine, a child departed this life today at 2 o'clock.
September 18th, one Child Departed this life today at ten o'clock; by the name of Amy.
December 31. B. Mariers Child Billy died this morning.

After the day's labor in the field under an unsympathetic overseer, she could find warmth and sympathy and appreciation among her children and kinsmen. There the mother could give full rein to her tender feelings and kindly impulses. "One of my earliest recollections," writes Booker T. Washington, "is that of my mother cooking a chicken late at night, and awakening her children for the purpose of feeding them." The devotion of the mothers to their own children was often demonstrated in their sacrifices to see them when they were separated from them. Douglass' childhood recollections of his mother, who lived twelve miles from him, were of "a few hasty visits made in the night on foot, after the daily tasks were over, and when she was under the necessity of returning in time to respond to the driver's call to the field in the early morning."

It is not surprising, then, to find that slave mothers, instead of viewing with indifference the sale, or loss otherwise, of their children, often put up a stubborn resistance and suffered cruel punishments to prevent separation from them. The fact that slave families were often divided when it was to the economic advantage of the owners is too well established to take seriously the denials of those who have idealized slavery. Washington Irving, who regarded the separation of children from their parents as a peculiar evil of slavery, rationalized thus: "But are not white people so, by schooling, marriage, business, etc."[10]

When Loguen's brothers and sisters were taken from his mother, she was "taken into the room which was used for weaving coarse cloth for the negroes and fastened securely to the loom, where she remained, raving and moaning until morning." Another slave recounts his mother's efforts to prevent her children from being sold:

The master, Billy Grandy, whose slave I was born, was a hard drinking man; he sold away many slaves. I remember four sisters and four brothers; my mother had more

[10] *The Journals of Washington Irving,* ed. William P. Trent and George S. Hellman, Boston, 1919, III, 115.

children, but they were dead or sold away before I can remember. I was the youngest. I remember well my mother often hid us all in the woods, to prevent master selling us. When we wanted water, she sought for it in any hole or puddle, formed by falling trees or other wise: it was often full of tadpoles and insects: she strained it, and gave it round to each of us in the hollow of her hand. For food, she gathered berries in the woods, got potatoes, raw corn, &c. After a time the master would send word to her to come in, promising he would not sell us. But, at length, persons came, who agreed to give the price he set on us. His wife, with much to be done, prevailed on him not to sell me; but he sold my brother, who was a little boy. My mother, frantic with grief, resisted their taking her child away; she was beaten and held down: she fainted, and when she came to herself, her boy was gone. She made much outcry, for which the master tied her up to a peach tree in the yard, and flogged her.[11]

When Josiah Henson's master died, and it was necessary to sell the slaves in order to divide the estate among the heirs, he says:

We were all put up at auction and sold to the highest bidder, and scattered over various parts of the country. My brothers and sisters were bid off one by one, while my mother, holding my hand, looked on in an agony of grief, the cause of which I but ill understood at first, but which dawned on my mind with dreadful clearness, as the sale proceeded. My mother was then separated from me, and put up in her turn. She was bought by a man named Isaac R., residing in Montgomery county, and then I was offered to the assembled purchasers. My mother, half distracted with the parting forever from all her children, pushed through the crowd, while the bidding for me was going on, to the spot where R. was standing. She fell at his feet, and clung to his knees, entreating him in tones that a mother only could command, to buy her BABY as well as herself, and spare to her one of her little ones at least. Will it, can it be believed that this man, thus appealed to, was capable not merely of turning a deaf ear to her supplication, but of disengaging himself from her with such violent blows and kicks, as to reduce to the necessity of creeping out of his reach.[12]

We need not rely solely on the slave's word concerning the strength of the mother's affection for her children; indirect evidence, as well as contemporary observations, gives the same testimony. Concerning the slave mother's attachment for her children, the remark of an overseer in reply to another who spoke of the danger of losing slaves when they were taken North, is significant:

Oh, stuff and nonsense, I take care when my wife goes North with the children, to send Lucy with her; *her children are down here, and I defy all the Abolitionists in creation to get her to stay North.*

In the following accounts of a sale we learn that the mother's distress at the separation from her child was sufficient to cause it to be purchased with her:

Gambling v. *Read,* Meigs 281, December 1838. 1837, Gambling sold Read, Hannah, a female slave for $1200,.... Hannah had a young child, (a boy, three months old,)

[11] Grandy, *op. cit.*, pp. 5-6.

[12] *The Life of Josiah Henson, Formerly a Slave, Now an Inhabitant of Canada, as Narrated by Himself,* Boston, 1844, pp. 3-4.

and her distress at the separation from it induced Read to propose to purchase it;.... agreed that he should have it for 150 dollars.[13]

The *Alexandria Gazette's* comment on the slave trade in the national capital gives a vivid picture of the effect of selling children of the bereft mothers:

Here you may behold fathers and mothers leaving behind them the dearest objects of affection, and moving slowly along in the mute agony of despair; there, the young mother, sobbing over the infant whose innocent smile seems but to increase her misery. From some you will hear the burst of bitter lamentation, while from others the loud hysteric laugh breaks forth, denoting still deeper agony. Such is but a faint picture of the American slave-trade.

Let us return to the cabins at the quarters where the slave mothers lived with their children. A slave described the quarters where he lived as follows:

About a quarter of a mile from the dwelling house, were the huts, or cabins, of the plantation slaves, or field hands, standing in rows; much like the Indian villages which I have seen in the country of the Cherokees. These cabins were thirty-eight in number; generally about fifteen or sixteen feet square; built of hewn logs; covered with shingles, and provided with floors of pine boards. These houses were all dry and comfortable and were provided with chimnies; so that the people when in them, were all sheltered from the inclemencies of the weather. In this practice of keeping their slaves, well sheltered at night, the southern planters are pretty uniform; for they know that upon this circumstance, more than any other in that climate, depends the health of the slave, and consequently his value. In these thirty-eight cabins, were lodged two hundred and fifty people, of all ages, sexes, and sizes. Ten or twelve were generally employed in the garden about the house[14]

In spite of the numerous separations, the slave mother and her children, especially those under ten, were treated as a group. The following advertisement from the *Charleston* (S.C.) *City Gazette,* February 21, 1825, is typical of a sale of a group of slaves:

VALUABLE NEGROES FOR SALE

A Wench, complete cook, washer and ironer, and her 4 children—a Boy 12, another 9, a Girl 5, that sews; and a Girl about 4 years old.

Another Family—a Wench, complete washer and ironer, and her Daughter, 14 years old, accustomed to the house.

A Wench, a houseservant, and two male Children; one three years old, and the other 4 months.

A complete Seamstress and House Servant, with her male Child 7 years old.

Three Young Wenches, 18, 19, 21, all accustomed to house work.

A Mulatto Girl, about 17, a complete Seamstress and Waiting Maid, with her Grandmother.

Two Men, one a complete Coachman, and the other a Waiter. Apply at this Office, or at No. 19 Hasell-street, Feb. 19.

[13] Helen Tunnicliff Catterall (ed), *Judicial Cases concerning American Slavery and the Negro,* Washington, D. C., 1929, II, p. 507.

[14] Charles Ball, *Slavery in the United States,* Lewistown, Pa., 1836, p 107.

Sometimes more than one family occupied a cabin. "We all lived together with our mother," writes a former slave, "in a long cabin, containing two rooms, one of which we occupied; the other being inhabited by my mother's niece, Annike, and her children." Since the slaves were rationed according to families and under some circumstances were permitted to cultivate gardens for their own use, a sort of family economy gave a material foundation to their sentimental relationships.

A typical food ration list for 1856 is recorded in the *Florida Plantation Records,* pp. 513-14, as follows:

	Meal (Pecks)	Meat (Lb.)
Chesley and family	3	6½
Simon, Phillis, B. Peggy and 4 children	5	7½
England and family	4	5
Nathan and Coatney	2	5
Isaac	1	2½
Jacob and family	4	7
Esaw and Binah	2	5
O. Betty, O. Billy and family	6	9
Caesar and family	4¾	7½
Prophet, Joe and Cinder	3	7
Cupid	1	2½
B. Dick and family	4	5
Flora	1½	2½
Minda	1	2½
Kate and family	6½	9½
Nurse and Peggy	2	4½
Maria and Pollidor	4¼	5
L. Renty, Leah and two children	4	7
L. Dick	1	2½
Brave Boy	1	2½
Wallace	1	2
Jim and family	2½	5
Sucky	1	2½
L. Sarah	1	2
O. Sucky	1	2½
Frank	1	
pecks	68	119½

equal to 17 Bushels.

Pounds of Meat

Take off ½ lb. when you give a Pint of Syrup.

Although the families were recognized as more or less distinct units, the fact that life among the slaves was informal and familiar tended to bring them all into intimate relations. The orphans had little difficulty in finding mothers among the women at the quarters. Concerning a former slave, the biographer writes:

> Aunt Phyllis showed him tender sympathy and remarked to aunt Betty that it was a pity "ter-tek' dat po' child fum his sick mamma, and brung him on dis place whah he won't meet anybody but a pas'le o' low-down, good-for-nuthin strangers." This remark attached the boy to aunt Phyllis and he loved her ever afterward. He loved her, too, because she had the same name as his mother. Aunt Phyllis was a big-hearted old soul, and she looked with commiseration on all who suffered affliction or distress.[15]

But, in spite of this seemingly indiscriminate feeling toward children, mothers were likely to show special regard for their own offspring. Douglass, who was among the children placed under care of a cook, says:

[15] Charles Alexander, *Battles and Victories of Allen Allensworth,* Boston, 1914, p. 27.

She had a strong hold upon old master, for she was a first-rate cook, and very industrious. She was therefore greatly favored by him—as one mark of his favor she was the only mother who was permitted to retain her children around her, and even to these, her own children, she was often fiendishly in her brutality. Cruel, however, as she sometimes was to her own children, she was not destitute of maternal feeling, and in her instinct to satisfy their demands for food, she was often guilty of starving me and the other children.

When the mother was sold away or died, the oldest sister often assumed the role of mother to her brothers and sisters. A former slave wrote recently:

When my mother was sold I had one brother, William, and three sisters, Silva, Agga, and Emma. My father and mother were both pure blooded African Negros and there is not a drop of white blood in my veins, nor in those of my brother and sisters. When mother was taken away from us, Emma was a baby three years old. Silva, the oldest of the children, was fourteen, and she was a mother to the rest of us children. She took my mother's place in the kitchen as cook for my boss.[16]

We have spoken of the mother as the mistress of the cabin and as the head of the family. There is good reason for this. Not only did she have a more fundamental interest in her children than the father but, as a worker and free agent, except where the master's will was concerned, she developed a spirit of independence and a keen sense of her personal rights. An entry in a plantation journal represents her in one case requesting a divorce because of the burden of having so many children:

Lafayette Renty asked for Leaf to Marry Lear I also gave them Leaf. Rose, Rentys other wife, ses that she dont want to Libe with Renty on the account of his having so Many Children and they weare always quarling so I let them sepparate.

Usually the prospective son-in-law had to get the consent of the girl's mother. A slave complained that the mother of the girl whom he sought to marry opposed him because

she wanted her daughter to marry a slave who belonged to a very rich man living near by, and who was well known to be the son of his master. She thought no doubt that his master or father might chance to set him free before he died, which would enable him to do a better part to her daughter than I could.[17]

The dominating position of the mother is seen in the comment of a former slave on the character of her father and mother. Her father, she said, was "made after the timid kind" and "would never fuss back" at her mother who was constantly warning him: "Bob, I don't want no sorry nigger around me. I can't tolerate you if you ain't got no backbone."

[16] Robert Anderson, *From Slavery to Affluence; Memories of Robert Anderson, Ex-Slave,* Hemingsford, Neb., 1927, p. 5.

[17] Henry Bibb, *The Narrative of the Life and Adventures of Henry Bibb, an American Slave, Written by Himself, with an Introduction by Lucius Matlock,* New York, 1848, pp. 39-40.

Sometimes it happened that the husband and father played a more agressive role in the slave family.

In some lists of groups of slaves bought, the father appears:

NEGROES BOUGHT FEBY, 1839

Brave Boy, Carpenter, 40 years old
Phillis, his wife, 35
Pompey, Phillis's son, 16
Jack B. Boy & Phillis's son, 16
Chloe child do do
Primus B. Boy's son, 21
Cato Child, B. Boy's son
Jenny (Blind) B. Boy's mother
Nelly's husband in town, 30
Betty, her sister's child who died—child
Affey Nelly's child,—child, 11
Louisa her sister's child who is dead—child, 10
Sarah, Nelly's child, 8
Jack, Nelly's carpenter boy, 18
Ismel, Nelly's, 16
Lappo Phillis & Brave Boy's, 19

I paid cash for these 16 Negroes, $640. each—$10,240.00

Henson tells the following story of his father's defense of his mother:

The only incident I can remember, which occurred while my mother continued on N.'s farm, was the appearance of my father one day, with his head bloody and his back lacerated. He was in a state of great excitement, and though it was all a mystery to me at the age of three or four years, it was explained at a later period, and I understood that he had been suffering the cruel penalty of the Maryland law for beating a white man. His right ear had been cut off close to his head, and he had received a hundred lashes on his back. He had beaten the overseer for a brutal assault on my mother, and this was his punishment. Furious at such treatment, my father became a different man, and was so morose, disobedient, and intractable, that Mr. N. determined to sell him. He accordingly parted with him, not long after, to his son, who lived in Alabama; and neither mother nor I ever heard of him again.[18]

In some accounts of their families, former slaves included their father. For example, Steward wrote: "Our family consisted of my father and mother—whose names were Robert and Susan Steward—a sister, Mary, and myself." But generally the husband made regular visits to his wife and children. According to Bishop Heard, his father, who lived three miles away, "would come in on Wednesday nights after things had closed up at his home, and be back at his home by daylight, Thursday mornings; come again Saturday night, and return by daylight Monday morning."

The strength of the bond that sometimes existed between the father and his family is shown in such advertisements as the following:

$50 REWARD

Ran away from the subscriber his Negro man Pauladore, commonly called Paul. I understand Gen. R. Y. Hayne* *has purchased his wife and children from* H. L. Pinckney, Esq.,** and has them now on his plantation at Goose-creek, where, no doubt, the fellow is frequently lurking. T. Davis.

[18] Austin Steward, *Twenty-two Years a Slave, and Forty Years a Freeman,* Rochester, 1857, p. 13.

When Ball escaped from slavery in Georgia, he made his way back to his wife and children in Maryland. The apparently insignificant detail in the journal of an overseer: "To Eldesteno, old ben, to see his Grand son Samuel die," is an eloquent testimony to what some men felt in regard to their progeny. On the other hand, many slaves had the same relation with their fathers as Anderson, who says that, after his mother was sold away, "I frequently saw my father after that, but not sufficient to become familiar with him as a father and son should be. A few years later he married another woman from another plantation."

Generally speaking, the mother remained throughout slavery the dominant and important figure in the slave family. Although tradition has represented her as a devoted foster-parent to her master's children and indifferent to her own, it appears that, where this existed, the relations between the slave woman and the white child were similar to the relations which normally exist between mother and child. On the other hand, pregnancy and childbirth often meant only suffering for the slave mother who, because of her limited contacts with her young, never developed that attachment which grows out of physiological and emotional responses to its needs. Nevertheless, there is abundant evidence that slave mothers developed a deep and permanent love for their children, which often caused them to defy their masters and to undergo suffering to prevent separation from their young. This is only a part of the story of the slave mother, for there was another mother who bore children for the men of the master race . . . .

Classes in the South

T. Thomas Fortune

Since the war the people of the South are, from a Northern standpoint, very poor. There are very few millionaires among them. A man who has a bank account of fifty thousand dollars is regarded as very rich. I am reminded of an incident which shows that the Southern people fall down and worship a golden calf the same as their deluded brothers of the North and West.

A few years ago I was a resident of Jacksonville, the metropolis of Florida. Florida is a great Winter resort. The wealthy people of the country go there for a few months or weeks in the Winter. It is fashionable to do so. A great many wealthy northern men have acquired valuable landed interests in Jacksonville, among them the Astors of New York, who have a knack for pinning their interests in the soil. The people of Jacksonville were very proud to have as a resident and property holder, Mr. Wm. B. Astor. And Mr. Astor appeared to enjoy immensely the worship bestowed upon his money. He built one or two very fine buildings there, which must net him a handsome return for his investment by this time. Mr. Astor had with him a very shrewd "Man Friday," and this Man Friday got it into his head that he would like to be Mayor of Jacksonville, and he sought and obtained the support of his very powerful patron. It leaked out that Mr. Astor favored his Man Friday for Mayor. The "business interests" of the city took the matter "under advisement." After much "consultation" and preliminary skirmishing, it was decided that it would be unwise to antagonize Mr. Astor's Man Friday: and so he was placed in nomination as the "Citizens' Candidate." He was elected by a handsome majority. I believe it is a disputed question to-day, whether Mr. Astor's Man Friday was, or was not, a citizen of the place at the time he was elected Mayor. Be that as it may, it showed beyond question that the people knew how to go down upon their knees to the golden calf.

A condition of slavery or of serfdom produces two grievous evils, around which cluster many others of less importance, viz: the creation of vast landed estates, and the pauperization and debasement of labor. . . .

The operations of the vast landed estates of the South produced all the industrial disjointments which have afflicted the South since the war. The white man was taught to look upon labor as the natural portion of the black slave; and nothing could induce a white man to put his hand to the plow, but the gaunt visage of starvation at his door. He even preferred ignominious

---

From T. Thomas Fortune, *Black and White: Land, Labor, and Politics* (New York: Fords, Howard & Hulbert, 1884), pp. 196-210.

starvation to honest work; and, in desperate struggle to avoid the horror of the one and the disgrace of the other, he would sink himself lower in the scale of moral infamy than the black slave he despised. He would make of himself a monster of cruelty or of abject servility to avoid starvation or honest work. It was from this class of vermin that the planters secured their "Nigger drivers" or overseers, and a more pliable, servile, cruel heartless set of men never existed. They were commonly known as*"poor white trash,"* or "crackers." They were most heartily and righteously detested by the slave population. As the poor whites of the South were fifty years ago, so they are to-day—a careless, ignorant, lazy, but withal, arrogant set, who add nothing to the productive wealth of the community because they are too lazy to work, and who take nothing from that wealth because they are too poor to purchase. They have graded human wants to a point below which man could not go without starving. They live upon the poorest land in the South, the "piney woods," and raise a few potatoes and corn, and a few pigs, which never grow to be hogs, so sterile is the land upon which they are turned to "root, or die." These characteristic pigs are derisively called "shotes" by those who have seen their lean, lank and hungry development. They are awful counterparts of their pauper owners. It may be taken as an index of the quality of the soil and the condition of the people, to observe the condition of their live stock. Strange as it may appear, the faithful dog is the only animal which appears to thrive on "piney woods" land. The "piney woods" gopher, which may be not inappropriately termed a "highland turtle," is a great desideratum in the food supply of the pauper denizens of these portions of the South. There is nothing enticing about the appearance of the gopher. But his flesh, properly cooked, is passably palatable.

The poor white population of the South who live in the piney woods are sunk in the lowest ignorance, and practice vices too heinous to be breathed. They have no schools, and their mental condition hardly warrants the charitable inference that they would profit much if they were supplied with them. Still, I would like to see the experiment tried. Their horrible poverty, their appalling illiteracy, their deplorable moral enervation, deserve the pity of mankind and the assistance of philanthropic men and a thoughtful government. Though sunk to the lowest moral scale, *they are men,* and nothing should be omitted to improve their condition and make them more useful members of the communities in which they are now, more than an incubus.

It may not be out of place here to state that the Kuklux Klan, the White Liners League, the Knights of the White Camelia, and other lawless gangs which have in the past fifteen years made Southern chivalry a by-word and reproach among the nations of the earth, were largely recruited from this idle, vicious, ignorant class of Southerners. They needed no preparation for the bloody work perpetrated by those lawless organizations, those more cruel than Italian brigands. They instinctively hate the black man; because the condition of the black, his superior capacity for labor and receptivity of useful knowledge, place him a few pegs higher than themselves in the social scale. So these degraded white men, the very substratum of Southern population, were ready tools in the hands of the organized chivalrous brigands (as they had been of the slave oligarch), whose superior intelligence made them blush at the lawlessness they inspired, and who, therefore, gladly transferred to other hands the execution of those deeds of blood and death which make men shudder even now to think of them. It was long a common saying among the black population of the South that "I'd rudder be a niggah den a po' w'ite man!" and they were wise in their preference.

It is safe to say, that the peasantry of no country claiming to be civilized stands more in need of the labors of the schoolmaster and the preacher, than do the so-called "poor white trash" of the South. On their account, if no other, I am an advocate of a compulsory system of education, a National Board of Education, and a very large National appropriation for common school and industrial education.

I name this class first because it is the very lowest.

Next to this class is the great labor force of the South, the class upon whose ample shoulders have fallen the weight of Southern labor and inhumanity for lo! two hundred years—*the black man*. Time was, yesterday, it appears to me when this great class were all of *one* condition, driven from the rising to the setting of the sun to enrich men who were created out of the same sod, and in the construction of whose mysterious mechanism, mental and physical, the great God expended no more time or ingenuity. Up to the close of the Rebellion, of that gigantic conflict which shook the pillars of republican government to their center, the great black population were truly the "mudsills" of Southern society, upon which rested all the industrial burdens of that section; truly, "the hewers of wood and the drawers of water;" a people who, in the mysterious providence of God, were torn root and branch from their savage homes in that land which has now become to them a dream "more insubstantial than a pageant faded," to "dwell in a strange land, among strangers," to endure, like the children of Israel, a season of cruel probation, and then to begin life in earnest; to put their shoulders to the wheel and assist in making this vast continent, this asylum of the oppressed of the world, the grandest abode of mingled happiness and woe, and wealth and pauperization ever reared by the genius and governed by the selfishness and cupidity of man. And to-day, as in the dark days of the past, this people are the bone and sinew of the South, the great producers and partial consumers of her wealth; the despised, yet indispensable, "mudsills" of her industrial interests.

A Senator of the United States from the South, whose hands have been dyed in the blood of his fellow citizens, and who holds his high office by fraud and usurpation, not long since declared that his State could very well dispense with her black population. That population outnumbers the white three to one; and by the toil by which the State has been enriched, by the blood and the sweat of two hundred years which the soil of that State has absorbed, by the present production and consumption of wealth by that black population, we are amazed at the ignorance of the great man who has been placed in a "little brief authority." That black population cannot and will not be dispensed with; because it is so deeply rooted in the soil that it is a part of it—the most valuable part. And the time will come when it will hold its title to the land, by right of purchase, for a laborer is worthy of his hire, and is now free to invest that hire as it pleases him best. Already some of the very best soil of that State is held by the people this great magus in the Nation's councils would supersede in their divine rights.

When the war closed, as I said, the great black population of the South was distinctively a laboring class. It owned no lands, houses, banks, stores, or live stock, or other wealth. Not only was it the distinctively laboring class but the distinctively pauper class. It had neither money, intelligence nor morals with which to begin the hard struggle of life. It was absolutely at the bottom of the social ladder. It possessed nothing but health and muscle.

I have frequently contemplated with profound amazement the momentous mass of subjected human force, a force which had been educated by the lash and the bloodhound to despise labor, which was thrown upon itself by the wording of the Emancipation Proclamation and the surrender of Robert E. Lee. Nothing in the history of mankind is at all comparable, an exact counterpart, in all particulars, to that great event. A slavery of two hundred years had dwarfed the intelligence and morality of this people, and made them to look upon labor as the most baneful of all the curses a just God can inflict upon humankind; and they were turned loose upon the land, without a dollar in their hands, and, like the great Christ and the fowls of the air, without a place to lay their head.

And yet to-day, this people, who, only a few years ago, were bankrupts in morality, in intelligence, and in wealth, have leaped forward in the battle of progress like *veterans;* have built magnificent churches, with a membership of over two million souls; have preachers, learned and eloquent; have professors in colleges by the hundreds and schoolmasters by the thousands; have accumulated large landed interests in country, town and city; have established banking houses and railroads; manage large coal, grocery and merchant tailoring businesses; conduct with ability and success large and influential newspaper enterprises; in short, have come, and that very rapidly, into sharp competition with white men (who have the prestige of a thousand years of civilization and opportunity) in all the industrial interests which make a people great, respected and feared. The metamorphosis has been rapid, marvelous, astounding. Their home life has been largely transformed into the quality of purity and refinement which should characterize the home; they have now successful farmers, merchants, ministers, lawyers, editors, educators, physicians legislators—in short, they have entered every avenue of industry and thought. Their efforts are yet crude and their grasp uncertain, but they are in the field of competition, and will remain there and acquit themselves manfully.

Of course I speak in general terms of the progress the colored people have made. Individual effort and success, are the indicators of the vitality and genius of a people. When individuals rise out of the indistinguishable mass and make their mark, we may rest assured that the mass, is rich and capable of individual production. The great mass of every government, of every people, while adding to and creating greatness, go down in history unmentioned. But their glory, their genius, success and happiness, are expended and survive in the few great spirits their fortunate condition produced. The governments of antiquity were great and glorious, because their proletarians fade into vagueness, and are great only in the few great names which have been handed down to us. It has been said that a nation expends a hundred years of its vitality in the production of a great man of genius like Socrates, or Bacon, or Toussaint l'Overture, or Fulton. And this may be true. There can now be no question that the African race in the United States possess every element of vitality and genius possessed by their fellow citizens of other races, and any calculation of race possibilities in this country which assumes that they remain indefinitely the "mudsills" only of society will prove more brittle than ropes of sand.

At this time the colored people of the South are largely the industrial class; that is, they are the producing class. They are principally the agriculturists of the South; consequently, being wedded to the soil by life-long association and interest, and being principally the laboring class, they will naturally invest their surplus earnings in the purchase of the soil. Herein lies the great hope of the future. For the man who owns the soil largely owns and dictates to the men who are compelled to live upon it and derive their subsistence from it. The colored people of the South recognize this fact. And if there is any one idiosyncrasy more marked than another among them, it is their mania for buying land. They all live and labor in the cheerful anticipation of some day owning a home, a farm of their own. As the race grows in intelligence this mania for land owning becomes more and more pronounced. At first their impecuniosity will compel them to purchase poor hill-lands, but they will eventually get their grip upon the rich alluvial lands.

The class next to the great black class is the *small white farmers*. This class is composed of some of the "best families" of the South who were thrown upon their resources of brain and muscle by the results of the war, and some of the worst families drawn from the more thrifty poor white class. Southern political economists labor hard to make it appear that the vastly increased production of wealth in the South since the war is to be traced largely to the phenomenally increased percentum of small white farmers, but the assumption is too transparent to impose upon any save those most ignorant of the industrial conditions of the South, and the marvelous adaptability to the new conditions shown by colored men. I grant that these small white farmers, who were almost too inconsiderable in numbers to be taken into account before the war, have added largely to the development of the country and the production of wealth; but that the tremendous gains of free labor as against slave labor are to be placed principally to their intelligence and industry is too absurd to be seriously debated. The Charleston (S. C.) *News and Courier*, a pronounced anti-negro newspaper, recently made such a charge in all seriousness. The struggle for supremacy will largely come between the small white and black farmer; because each recurring year will augment the number of each class of small holders. A condition of freedom and open competition makes the fight equal, in many respects. Which will prove the more successful small holder, the black or the white?

The fourth class is composed of the *hereditary land-lords* of the South; the gentlemen with flowing locks, gentle blood and irascible tempers, who appeal to the code of honor (in times past) to settle small differences with their equals and shoot down their inferiors without premeditation or compunction, and who drown their sorrows, as well as their joviality in rye or Bourbon whiskey; the gentlemen who claim consanguinity with Europe's titled sharks, and vaunt their chivalry in contrast to the peasant or yeoman blood of all other Americans; the gentlemen who got their broad acres (however they came by their peculiar blood) by robbing black men, women and children of the produce of their toil under the system of slavery, and who maintain themselves in their reduced condition by driving hard bargains with white and black labor either as planters or shop-keepers, often as both, the dual occupations more effectually enabling them to make unreasonable contracts and exactions of those they live to victimize. They are the gentlemen who constantly declare that "this is a white man's government," and that "the Negro must be made to keep his place." They are the gentlemen who have their grip upon the throat of Southern labor; who hold vast areas of land, the product of robbery, for a rise in values; who run the stores and torture the small farmers to death by usurious charges for necessaries; these are the gentlemen who are opposed to the new conditions resultant from the war which their Hotspur impetuosity and Shylock greed made possible. In short, these gentlemen comprise the moneyed class. They are the gentlemen who are hastening the conflict of labor and capital in the South. And, when the black laborer and the white laborer come to their senses, join issues with the common enemy and pitch the tent of battle, then will come the tug of war.

The Ku Klux Klan

Organization and Principles 1868

Appellation

This Organization shall be styled and denominated, the Order of the * * *

Creed

We, the Order of the * * * , reverentially acknowledge the majesty and supremacy of the Divine Being, and recognize the goodness and providence of the same. And we recognize our relation to the United States Government, the supremacy of the Constitution, the Constitutional Laws thereof, and the Union of States thereunder.

Character and Objects of the Order

This is an institution of Chivalry, Humanity, Mercy, and Patriotism; embodying in its genius and its principles all that is chivalric in conduct, noble in sentiment, generous in manhood, and patriotic in purpose; its peculiar objects being

First: To protect the weak, the innocent, and the defenseless, from the indignities, wrongs, and outrages of the lawless, the violent, and the brutal; to relieve the injured and oppressed; to succor the suffering and unfortunate, and especially the widows and orphans of Confederate soldiers.

Second: To protect and defend the Constitution of the United States, and all laws passed in conformity thereto, and to protect the States and the people thereof from all invasion from any source whatever.

Third: To aid and assist in the execution of all constitutional laws, and to protect the people from unlawful seizure, and from trial except by their peers in conformity to the laws of the land.

Titles

Sec. 1. The officers of this Order shall consist of a Grand Wizard of the Empire, and his ten Genii; a Grand Dragon of the Realm, and his eight Hydras; a Grand Titan of the Dominion, and his six Furies; a Grand Giant of the Province, and his four Goblins; a Grand Cyclops of the Den, and his two Night Hawks; a Grand Magi, a Grand Monk, a Grand Scribe, a Grand Exchequer, a Grand Turk, and a Grand Sentinel.

Sec. 2. The body politic of this Order shall be known and designated as "Ghouls."

Territory and Its Divisions

Sec. 1. The territory embraced within the jurisdiction of this Order shall be coterminous with the States of Maryland, Virginia, North Carolina, South Carolina, Georgia, Florida, Alabama, Mississippi, Louisiana, Texas, Arkansas, Missouri, Kentucky, and Tennessee; all combined constituting the Empire.

Sec. 2. The Empire shall be divided into four departments, the first to be styled the Realm, and coterminous with the boundaries of the several States; the second to be styled the Dominion and to be coterminous with such counties as the Grand Dragons of the several Realms may assign to the charge of the Grand Titan. The third to be styled the Province, and to be coterminous with the several counties; *provided* the Grand Titan may, when he deems it necessary, assign two Grand Giants to one Province, prescribing, at the same time, the jurisdiction of each. The fourth department to be styled the Den, and shall embrace such part of a Province as the Grand Giant shall assign to the charge of a Grand Cyclops. . . .

Interrogations to Be Asked

1st. Have you ever been rejected, upon application for membership in the * * *, or have you ever been expelled from the same?

2d. Are you now, or have you ever been, a member of the Radical Republican party, or either of the organizations known as the "Loyal League" and the "Grand Army of the Republic?"

3d. Are you opposed to the principles and policy of the Radical party, and to the Loyal League, and the Grand Army of the Republic, so far as you are informed of the character and purposes of those organizations?

4th. Did you belong to the Federal army during the late war, and fight against the South during the existence of the same?

5th. Are you opposed to negro equality, both social and political?

6th. Are you in favor of a white man's government in this country?

7th. Are you in favor of Constitutional liberty, and a Government of equitable laws instead of a Government of violence and oppression?

8th. Are you in favor of maintaining the constitutional rights of the South?

9th. Are you in favor of the re-enfranchisement and emancipation of the white men of the South, and the restitution of the Southern people to all their rights, alike proprietary, civil, and political?

10th. Do you believe in the inalienable right of self-preservation of the people against the exercise of arbitrary and unlicensed power? . . .

. . . 9. The most profound and rigid secrecy concerning any and everything that relates to the Order, shall at all times be maintained.

10. Any member who shall reveal or betray the secrets of this Order, shall suffer the extreme penalty of the law.

Reconstruction and Its Benefits[1]

W. E. Burghardt Du Bois

There is danger to-day that between the intense feeling of the South and the conciliatory spirit of the North grave injustice will be done the negro American in the history of Reconstruction. Those who see in negro suffrage the cause of the main evils of Reconstruction must remember that if there had not been a single freedman left in the South after the war the problems of Reconstruction would still have been grave. Property in slaves to the extent of perhaps two thousand million dollars had suddenly disappeared. One thousand five hundred more millions, representing the Confederate war debt, had largely disappeared. Large amounts of real estate and other property had been destroyed, industry had been disorganized, 250,000 men had been killed and many more maimed. With this went the moral effect of an unsuccessful war with all its letting down of social standards and quickening of hatred and discouragement — a situation which would make it difficult under any circumstances to reconstruct a new government and a new civilization. Add to all this the presence of four million freedmen and the situation is further complicated. But this complication is very largely a matter of well-known historical causes. Any human being "doomed in his own person, and his posterity, to live without knowledge, and without the capacity to make anything his own, and to toil that another may reap the fruits",[2] is bound, on sudden emancipation, to loom like a great dread on the horizon.

How to train and treat these ex-slaves easily became a central problem of Reconstruction, although by no means the only problem. Three agencies undertook the solution of this problem at first and their influence is apt to be forgotten. Without them the problems of Reconstruction would have been far graver than they were. These agencies were: (a) the negro church, (b) the negro school, and (c) the Freedmen's Bureau. After the war the white churches of the South got rid of their negro members and the negro church organizations of the North invaded the South. The 20,000 members of the African Methodist Episcopal Church in 1856 leaped to 75,000 in 1866 and 200,000 in 1876, while their property increased sevenfold. The negro Baptists with 150,000 members in 1850 had fully a half million in

1 Paper read at the annual meeting of the American Historical Association in New York, December, 1909.

2 State *v.* Mann, *North Carolina Reports,* 2 Devereux 263.

From the *American Historical Review,* XV (July, 1910), pp. 781-799.

1870. There were, before the end of Reconstruction, perhaps 10,000 local bodies touching the majority of the freed population, centering almost the whole of their social life, and teaching them organization and autonomy. They were primitive, ill-governed, at times fantastic groups of human beings, and yet it is difficult to exaggerate the influence of this new responsibility — the first social institution fully controlled by black men in America, with traditions that rooted back to Africa and with possibilities which make the 35,000 negro American churches to-day, with their three and one-half million members, the most powerful negro institutions in the world.

With the Negro church, but separate from it, arose the school as the first expression of the missionary activity of Northern religious bodies. Seldom in the history of the world has an almost totally illiterate population been given the means of self-education in so short a time. The movement started with the negroes themselves and they continued to form the dynamic force behind it. "This great multitude rose up simultaneously and asked for intelligence."[3] The education of this mass had to begin at the top with the training of teachers, and within a few years a dozen colleges and normal schools started; by 1877, 571,506 negro children were in school. There can be no doubt that these schools were a great conservative steadying force to which the South owes much. It must not be forgotten that among the agents of the Freedmen's Bureau were not only soldiers and politicians but school-teachers and educational leaders like Ware and Cravath.

Granted that the situation was in any case bad and that negro churches and schools stood as conservative educative forces, how far did negro suffrage hinder progress, and was it expedient? The difficulties that stared Reconstruction politicians in the face were these: (a) They must act quickly. (b) Emancipation had increased the political power of the South by one-sixth: could this increased political power be put in the hands of those who, in defense of slavery, had disrupted the Union? (c) How was the abolition of slavery to be made effective? (d) What was to be the political position of the freedmen?

Andrew Johnson said in 1864, in regard to calling a convention to restore the state of Tennessee,

> who shall restore and re-establish it? Shall the man who gave his influence and his means to destroy the Government? Is he to participate in the great work of re-organization? Shall he who brought this misery upon the State be permitted to control its destinies? If this be so, then all this precious blood of our brave soldiers and officers so freely poured out will have been wantonly spilled.[4]

To settle these and other difficulties, three ways were suggested: (1) the Freedmen's Bureau, (2) partial negro suffrage, and (3) full manhood suffrage for negroes.

[3] First General Report of the Inspector of Schools, Freedmen's Bureau.
[4] McPherson, *Reconstruction*, p. 46.

The Freedmen's Bureau was an attempt to establish a government guardianship over the negroes and insure their economic and civil rights. Its establishment was a herculean task both physically and socially, and it not only met the solid opposition of the white South, but even the North looked at the new thing as socialistic and over-paternal. It accomplished a great task but it was repudiated. Carl Schurz in 1865 felt warranted in saying

> that not half of the labor that has been done in the south this year, or will be done there next year, would have been or would be done but for the exertions of the Freedmen's Bureau.... No other agency, except one placed there by the national government, could have wielded that moral power whose interposition was so necessary to prevent the southern society from falling at once into the chaos of a general collision between its different elements.[5]

Notwithstanding this the Bureau was temporary, was regarded as a makeshift and soon abandoned.

Meantime, partial negro suffrage seemed not only just but almost inevitable. Lincoln in 1864 "cautiously suggested" to Louisiana's private consideration, "whether some of the colored people may not be let in, as, for instance, the very intelligent, and especially those who have fought gallantly in our ranks. They would probably help, in some trying time to come, to keep the jewel of liberty in the family of freedom."[6] Indeed, the "family of freedom" in Louisiana being somewhat small just then, who else was to be intrusted with the "jewel"? Later and for different reasons, Johnson in 1865 wrote to Mississippi:

> If you could extend the elective franchise to all persons of color who can read the Constitution of the United States in English and write their names, and to all persons of color who own real estate valued at not less than two hundred and fifty dollars, and pay taxes thereon, you would completely disarm the adversary and set an example the other States will follow. This you can do with perfect safety, and you thus place the southern States, in reference to free persons of color, upon the same basis with the free States. I hope and trust your convention will do this.[7]

Meantime the negroes themselves began to ask for the suffrage — the Georgia Convention in August, 1866, advocating "a proposition to give those who could write and read well, and possessed a certain property qualification, the right of suffrage". The reply of the South to these suggestions was decisive. In Tennessee alone was any action attempted that even suggested possible negro suffrage in the future, and that failed. In all other states the "Black Codes" adopted were certainly not reassuring to friends of freedom. To be sure it was not a time for calm, cool, thoughtful action on the part of the white South. Their economic condition was pitiable, their fear of negro freedom genuine; yet it was reasonable to expect from them something

[5] Schurz. Report to the President, 1865. *Senate Ex. Doc. No. 2,* 39 Cong., I sess., p. 40.

[6] Letter to Hahn, March 13. McPherson, p. 20.

[7] Johnson to Sharkey, August 15. *Ibid.*, p. 19.

less than repression and utter reaction toward slavery. To some extent this expectation was fulfilled: the abolition of slavery was recognized and the civil rights of owning property and appearing as a witness in cases in which he was a party was generally granted the negro; yet with these went in many cases harsh and unbearable regulations which largely neutralized the concessions and certainly gave ground for the assumption that once free the South would virtually re-enslave the negro. The colored people themselves naturally feared this and protested as in Mississippi "against the reactionary policy prevailing, and expressing the fear that the Legislature will pass such proscriptive laws as will drive the freedmen from the State, or practically re-enslave them".[8]

The Codes spoke for themselves. They have often been reprinted and quoted. No open-minded student can read them without being convinced that they meant nothing more nor less than slavery in daily toil. Not only this but as Professor Burgess (whom no one accuses of being negrophile) says:

> Almost every act, word or gesture of the Negro, not consonant with good taste and good manners as well as good morals, was made a crime or misdemeanor, for which he could first be fined by the magistrates and then be consigned to a condition of almost slavery for an indefinite time, if he could not pay the bill.

These laws might have been interpreted and applied liberally, but the picture painted by Carl Schurz does not lead one to anticipate this:

> Some planters held back their former slaves on their plantations by brute force. Armed bands of white men patrolled the country roads to drive back the negroes wandering about. Dead bodies of murdered negroes were found on and near the highways and by-paths. Gruesome reports came from the hospitals—reports of colored men and women whose ears had been cut off, whose skulls had been broken by blows, whose bodies had been slashed by knives or lacerated with scourges. A number of such cases I had occasion to examine myself. A veritable reign of terror prevailed in many parts of the South. The negro found scant justice in the local courts against the white man. He could look for protection only to the military forces of the United States still garrisoning the "States lately in rebellion" and to the Freedmen's Bureau.

All things considered, it seems probably that if the South had been permitted to have its way in 1865 the harshness of negro slavery would have been mitigated so as to make slave-trading difficult, and to make it possible for a negro to hold property and appear in some cases in court; but that in most other respects the blacks would have remained in slavery.

What could prevent this? A Freedmen's Bureau, established for ten, twenty or forty years with a careful distribution of land and capital and a system of education for the children, might have prevented such an extension of slavery. But the country would not listen to such a comprehensive plan. A restricted grant of the suffrage voluntarily made by the states would have been

[8] October 7, 1865.

a reassuring proof of a desire to treat the freedmen fairly, and would have balanced, in part at least, the increased political power of the South. There was no such disposition evident. On the other hand, there was ground for the conclusion in the Reconstruction report of June 18, 1866, that so far as slavery was concerned "the language of all the provisions and ordinances of these States on the subject amounts to nothing more than an unwilling admission of an unwelcome truth." This was of course natural, but was it unnatural that the North should feel that better guarantees were needed to abolish slavery? Carl Schurz wrote:

> I deem it proper, however, to offer a few remarks on the assertion frequently put forth, that the franchise is likely to be extended to the colored man by the voluntary action of the Southern whites themselves. My observation leads me to a contrary opinion. Aside from a very few enlightened men, I found but one class of people in favor of the enfranchisement of the blacks: it was the class of Unionists who found themselves politically ostracised and looked upon the enfranchisement of the loyal negroes as the salvation of the whole loyal element.... The masses are strongly opposed to colored suffrage; anybody that dares to advocate it is stigmatized as a dangerous fanatic.
>
> The only manner in which, in my opinion, the southern people can be induced to grant to the freedman some measure of self-protecting power in the form of suffrage, is to make it a condition precedent to "readmission".[9]

Even in Louisiana, under the proposed reconstruction

> not one negro was allowed to vote, though at that very time the wealthy intelligent free colored people of the state paid taxes on property assessed at $15,000,000 and many of them were well known for their patriotic zeal and love for the Union. Thousands of colored men whose homes were in Louisiana, served bravely in the national army and navy, and many of the so-called negroes in New Orleans could not be distinguished by the most intelligent strangers from the best class of white gentlemen, either by color or manner, dress or language, still, as it was known by tradition and common fame that they were not of pure Caucasian descent, they could not vote.[10]

The United States government might now have taken any one of three courses:

> 1. Allowed the whites to reorganize the states and take no measures to enfranchise the freedmen.
>
> 2. Allowed the whites to reorganize the states but provided that after the lapse of a reasonable length of time there should be no discrimination in the right of suffrage on account of "race, color or previous condition of servitude".
>
> 3. Admitted all men, black and white, to take part in reorganizing the states and then provided that future restrictions on the suffrage should be made on any basis except "race, color and previous condition of servitude".

The first course was clearly inadmissible since it meant virtually giving up the great principle on which the war was largely fought and won, *i. e.*, human

9 Report to the President, 1865. *Senate Ex. Doc. 2,* 39 Cong., 1 sess., p. 44.

10 Brewster, ***Sketches of Southern Mystery, Treason, and Murder,*** p. 116.

freedom; a giving of freedom which contented itself with an edict, and then turned the "freed" slaves over to the tender mercies of their impoverished and angry ex-masters was no gift at all. The second course was theoretically attractive but practically impossible. It meant at least a prolongation of slavery and instead of attempts to raise the freedmen, it gave the white community strong incentives for keeping the blacks down so that as few as possible would ever qualify for the suffrage. Negro schools would have been discouraged and economic fetters would have held the black man as a serf for an indefinite time. On the other hand, the arguments for universal negro suffrage from the start were strong and are still strong, and no one would question their strength were it not for the assumption that the experiment failed. Frederick Douglass said to President Johnson: "Your noble and human predecessor placed in our hands the sword to assist in saving the nation, and we do hope that you, his able successor, will favorably regard the placing in our hands the ballot with which to save ourselves."[11] And when Johnson demurred on account of the hostility between blacks and poor whites, a committee of prominent colored men replied:

> Even if it were true, as you allege, that the hostility of the blacks toward the poor whites must necessarily project itself into a state of freedom, and that this enmity between the two races is even more intense in a state of freedom than in a state of slavery, in the name of Heaven, we reverently ask, how can you, in view of your professed desire to promote the welfare of the black man, deprive him of all means of defense, and clothe him whom you regard as his enemy in the panoply of political power?[12]

Carl Schurz expressed this argument most emphatically:

> The emancipation of the slaves is submitted to only in so far as chattel slavery in the old form could not be kept up. But although the freedman is no longer considered the property of the individual master, he is considered the slave of society, and all independent State legislation will share the tendency to make him such.
>
> The solution of the problem would be very much facilitated by enabling all the loyal and free-labor elements in the south to exercise a healthy influence upon legislation. It will hardly be possible to secure the freedom against oppressive class legislation and private persecution, unless he be endowed with a certain measure of political power.[13]

To the argument of ignorance Schurz replied:

> The effect of the extension of the franchise to the colored people upon the development of free labor and upon the security of human rights in the south being the principal object in view, the objections raised on the ground of the ignorance of the freedmen become unimportant. Practical liberty is a good school. . . . It is idle to say that it will be time to speak of negro suffrage when the whole colored race will be educated, for the ballot may be necessary to him to secure his education.[14]

[11] Frederick Douglass to Johnson, February 7, 1866. McPherson, p. 52.
[12] McPherson, p. 56.
[13] Report to the President, 1865. *Senate Ex. Doc. No. 2,* 39 Cong., 1 sess., p. 45.
[14] *Ibid.,* p. 43.

The granting of full negro suffrage meant one of two alternatives to the South: (a) the uplift of the negro for sheer self-preservation; this is what Schurz and the saner North expected; as one Southern superintendent said: "the elevation of this class is a matter of prime importance since a ballot in the hands of a black citizen is quite as potent as in the hands of a white one." Or (b) a determined concentration of Southern effort by actual force to deprive the negro of the ballot or nullify its use. This is what happened, but even in this case so much energy was taken in keeping the negro from voting that the plan for keeping him in virtual slavery and denying him education failed. It took ten years to nullify negro suffrage in part and twenty years to escape the fear of federal intervention. In these twenty years a vast number of negroes had risen so far as to escape slavery forever. Debt peonage could be fastened on part of the rural South, and was, but even here the new negro landholder appeared. Thus despite everything the Fifteenth Amendment and that alone struck the death knell of slavery.

The steps that ended in the Fifteenth Amendment were not, however, taken suddenly. The negroes were given the right by universal suffrage to join in reconstructing the state governments and the reasons for it were cogently set forth in the report of the Joint Committee on Reconstruction in 1866, which began as follows:

> A large proportion of the population had become, instead of mere chattels, free men and citizens. Through all the past struggle these had remained true and loyal, and had, in large numbers, fought on the side of the Union. It was impossible to abandon them without securing them their rights as free men and citizens. The whole civilized world would have cried out against such base ingratitude, and the bare idea is offensive to all right-thinking men. Hence it became important to inquire what could be done to secure their rights, civil and political.[15]

The report then proceeded to emphasize the increased political power of the South and recommended the Fourteenth Amendment, since

> It appeared to your committee that the rights of these persons by whom the basis of representation had been thus increased should be recognized by the General Government. While slaves, they were not considered as having any rights, civil or political. It did not seem just or proper that all the political advantages derived from their becoming free should be confined to their former masters, who had fought against the Union, and withheld from themselves, who had always been loyal.[16]

It was soon seen that this expedient of the Fourteenth Amendment was going to prove abortive and that determined and organized effort would be used to deprive the freedmen of the ballot. Thereupon the United States said the final word of simple justice, namely: the states may still regulate the suffrage as they please but they may not deprive a man of the right to vote simply because he is a negro.

[15] *House Reports No. 30,* 39 Cong., 1 sess., p. xiii.
[16] *Ibid.*

For such reasons the negro was enfranchised. What was the result? No language has been spared to describe these results as the worst imaginable. Nor is it necessary to dispute for a moment that there were bad results, and bad results arising from negro suffrage; but it may be questioned if the results were as bad as painted or if negro suffrage was the prime cause.

Let us not forget that the white South believed it to be of vital interest to its welfare that the experiment of negro suffrage should fail ignominiously, and that almost to a man the whites were willing to insure this failure either by active force or passive acquiescence; that beside this there were, as might be expected, men black and white, Northern and Southern, only too eager to take advantage of such a situation for feathering their own nests. The results in such case had to be evil but to charge the evil to negro suffrage is unfair. It may be charged to anger, poverty, venality, and ignorance; but the anger and poverty were the almost inevitable aftermath of war; the venality was much greater among whites than negroes, and while ignorance was the curse of the negroes, the fault was not theirs, and they took the initiative to correct it.

The chief charges against the negro governments are extravagance, theft, and incompetency of officials. There is no serious charge that these governments threatened civilization or the foundations of social order. The charge is that they threatened property, and that they were inefficient. These charges are in part undoubtedly true, but they are often exaggerated. When a man has, in his opinion, been robbed and maltreated he is sensitive about money matters. The South had been terribly impoverished and saddled with new social burdens. In other words, a state with smaller resources was asked not only to do a work of restoration but a larger social work. The property-holders were aghast. They not only demurred, but, predicting ruin and revolution, they appealed to secret societies, to intimidation, force, and murder. They refused to believe that these novices in government and their friends were aught but scamps and fools. Under the circumstances occurring directly after the war, the wisest statesman would have been compelled to resort to increased taxation and would in turn have been execrated as extravagant and even dishonest. When now, in addition to this, the new legislators, white and black, were undoubtedly in a large number of cases extravagant, dishonest, and incompetent, it is easy to see what flaming and incredible stories of Reconstruction governments could gain wide currency and belief. In fact, the extravagance, although great, was not universal, and much of it was due to the extravagant spirit pervading the whole country in a day of inflated currency and speculation. The ignorance was deplorable but a deliberate legacy from the past, and some of the extravagance and much of the effort was to remedy this ignorance. The incompetency was in part real and in part emphasized by the attitude of the whites of the better class.

When incompetency gains political power in an extravagant age the result is widespread dishonesty. The dishonesty in the reconstruction of the South was helped on by three circumstances:

1. The former dishonesty in the political South.
2. The presence of many dishonest Northern politicians.
3. The temptation to Southern politicians at once to profit by dishonesty and to discredit negro government.
4. The poverty of the negro.

(1) Dishonesty in public life has no monopoly of time or place in America. To take one state: In 1839 it was reported in Mississippi that ninety per cent. of the fines collected by sheriffs and clerks were unaccounted for. In 1841 the state treasurer acknowledges himself "at a loss to determine the precise liabilities of the state and her means of paying the same". And in 1839 the auditor's books had not been posted for eighteen months, no entries made for a year, and no vouchers examined for three years. Congress gave Jefferson College, Natchez, more than 46,000 acres of land; before the war this whole property had "disappeared" and the college was closed. Congress gave to Mississippi among other states the "16th section" of the public lands for schools. In thirty years the proceeds of this land in Mississippi were embezzled to the amount of at least one and a half millions of dollars. In Columbus, Mississippi, a receiver of public moneys stole $100,000 and resigned. His successor stole $55,000, and a treasury agent wrote: "Another receiver would probably follow in the footsteps of the two. You will not be surprised if I recommend his being retained in preference to another appointment." From 1830 to 1860 Southern men in federal offices alone embezzled more than a million dollars—a far larger sum then than now. There might have been less stealing in the South during Reconstruction without negro suffrage but it is certainly highly instructive to remember that the mark of the thief which dragged its slime across nearly every great Northern state and almost up to the presidential chair could not certainly in those cases be charged against the vote of black men. This was the day when a national secretary of war was caught stealing, a vice-president presumably took bribes, a private secretary of the president, a chief clerk of the Treasury, and eighty-six government officials stole millions in the whiskey frauds, while the Credit Mobilier filched fifty millions and bribed the government to an extent never fully revealed; not to mention less distinguished thieves like Tweed.

Is it surprising that in such an atmosphere a new race learning the a-b-c of government should have become the tools of thieves? And when they did was the stealing their fault or was it justly chargeable to their enfranchisement?

Undoubtedly there were many ridiculous things connected with Reconstruction governments: the placing of ignorant field-hands who could neither read nor write in the legislature, the gold spittoons of South Carolina, the enormous public printing bill of Mississippi—all these were extravagant and funny, and yet somehow, to one who sees beneath all that is bizarre, the real human tragedy of the upward striving of down-trodden men, the groping for light among people born in darkness, there is less tendency to laugh and gibe than among shallower minds and easier consciences. All that is funny is not bad.

Then too a careful examination of the alleged stealing in the South reveals much. First, there is repeated exaggeration. For instance it is said that the taxation in Mississippi was fourteen times as great in 1874 as in 1869. This sounds staggering until we learn that the state taxation in 1869 was only ten cents on one hundred dollars, and that the expenses of government in 1874 were only twice as great as in 1860, and that too with a depreciated currency. It could certainly be argued that the state government in Mississippi was doing enough additional work in 1874 to warrant greatly increased cost. A Southern white historian acknowledges that

> the work of restoration which the government was obliged to undertake, made increased expenses necessary. During the period of the war, and for several years thereafter, public buildings and state institutions were permitted to fall into decay. The state house and grounds, the executive mansion, the penitentiary, the insane asylum, and the buildings for the blind, deaf, and dumb were in a dilapidated condition, and had to be extended and repaired. A new building for the blind was purchased and fitted up. The reconstructionists established a public school system and spent money to maintain and support it, perhaps too freely, in view of the impoverishment of the people. When they took hold, warrants were worth but sixty or seventy cents on the dollar, a fact which made the price of building materials used in the work of construction correspondingly higher. So far as the conduct of state officials who were intrusted with the custody of public funds is concerned, it may be said that there were no great embezzlements or other cases of misappropriation during the period of Republican rule.[17]

The state debt of Mississippi was said to have been increased from a half million to twenty million when in fact it had not been increased at all.

The character of the real thieving shows that white men must have been the chief beneficiaries and that as a former South Carolina slaveholder said:

> The legislature, ignorant as it is, could not have been bribed without money, that must have been furnished from some source that it is our duty to discover. A legislature composed chiefly of our former slaves has been bribed. One prominent feature of this transaction is the part which native Carolinians have played in it, some of our own household men whom the state, in the past, has delighted to honor, appealing to their cupidity and avarice make them the instruments to effect the robbery of their impoverished white brethren. Our former slaves have been bribed by these men to give them the privilege by law of plundering the property-holders of the state.[18]

The character of much of the stealing shows who were the thieves. The frauds through the manipulation of state and railway bonds and of bank-notes must have inured chiefly to the benefit of experienced white men, and this must have been largely the case in the furnishing and printing frauds. It was chiefly in the extravagance for "sundries and incidentals" and direct money payments for votes that the negroes received their share.

[17] Garner, *Reconstruction in Mississippi,* p. 322.
[18] Hon. F. F. Warley in Brewster's *Sketches,* p. 150.

That the negroes led by astute thieves became tools and received a small share of the spoils is true. But two considerations must be added: much of the legislation which resulted in fraud was represented to the negroes as good legislation, and thus their votes were secured by deliberate misrepresentation. Take for instance the land frauds of South Carolina. A wise negro leader of that state, advocating the state purchase of lands, said:

> One of the greatest of slavery bulwarks was the infernal plantation system, one man owning his thousand, another his twenty, another fifty thousand acres of land. This is the only way by which we will break up that system, and I maintain that our freedom will be of no effect if we allow it to continue. What is the main cause of the prosperity of the North? It is because every man has his own farm and is free and independent. Let the lands of the South be similarly divided.

From such arguments the negroes were induced to aid a scheme to buy land and distribute it; yet a large part of $800,000 appropriated was wasted and went to the white landholder's pockets. The railroad schemes were in most cases feasible and eventually carried out; it was not the object but the method that was wrong.

Granted then that the negroes were to some extent venal but to a much larger extent ignorant and deceived, the question is: did they show any signs of a disposition to learn better things? The theory of democratic government is not that the will of the people is always right, but rather that normal human beings of average intelligence will, if given a chance, learn the right and best course by bitter experience. This is precisely what the negro voters showed indubitable signs of doing. First, they strove for schools to abolish ignorance, and, second, a large and growing number of them revolted against the carnival of extravagance and stealing that marred the beginning of Reconstruction, and joined with the best elements to institute reform; and the greatest stigma on the white South is not that it opposed negro suffrage and resented theft and incompetence, but that when it saw the reform movement growing and even in some cases triumphing, and a larger and larger number of black voters learning to vote for honesty and ability, it still preferred a Reign of Terror to a campaign of education, and disfranchised negroes instead of punishing rascals.

No one has expressed this more convincingly than a negro who was himself a member of the Reconstruction legislature of South Carolina and who spoke at the convention which disfranchised him, against one of the onslaughts of Tillman:

> The gentleman from Edgefield [Mr. Tillman] speaks of the piling up of the State debt; of jobbery and peculation during the period between 1869 and 1873 in South Carolina, but he has not found voice eloquent enough, nor pen exact enough to mention those imperishable gifts bestowed upon South Carolina between 1873 and 1876 by Negro legislators—the law relative to finance, the building of penal and charitable institutions, and, greatest of all, the establishment of the public school system. Starting as infants in legislation in 1869, many wise measures were not thought of, many injudicious acts were

passed. But in the administration of affairs for the next four years, having learned by experience the result of bad acts, we immediately passed reformatory laws touching every department of state, county, municipal and town governments. These enactments are today upon the statute books of South Carolina. They stand as living witnesses of the Negro's fitness to vote and legislate upon the rights of mankind.

When we came into power town governments could lend the credit of their respective towns to secure funds at any rate of interest that the council saw fit to pay. Some of the towns paid as high as twenty per cent. We passed an act prohibiting town governments from pledging the credit of their hamlets for money bearing a greater rate of interest than five per cent.

Up to 1874, inclusive, the State Treasurer had the power to pay out State funds as he pleased. He could elect whether he would pay out the funds on appropriations that would place the money in the hands of the speculators, or would apply them to appropriations that were honest and necessary. We saw the evil of this and passed an act making specific levies and collections of taxes for specific appropriations.

Another source of profligacy in the expenditure of funds was the law that provided for and empowered the levying and collecting of special taxes by school districts, in the name of the schools. We saw its evil and by a constitutional amendment provided that there should only be levied and collected annually a tax of two mills for school purposes, and took away from the school districts the power to levy and to collect taxes of any kind. By this act we cured the evils that had been inflicted upon us in the name of the schools, settled the public school question for all time to come, and established the system upon an honest, financial basis.

Next, we learned during the period from 1869 to 1874, inclusive, that what was denominated the floating indebtedness, covering the printing schemes and other indefinite expenditures, amounted to nearly $2,000,000. A conference was called of the leading Negro representatives in the two houses together with the State Treasurer, also a Negro. After this conference we passed an act for the purpose of ascertaining the bona fide floating debt and found that it did not amount to more than $250,000 for the four years; we created a commission to sift that indebtedness and to scale it. Hence when the Democratic party came into power they found the floating debt covering the legislative and all other expenditures, fixed at the certain sum of $250,000. This same class of Negro legislators led by the State Treasurer, Mr. F. L. Cardoza, knowing that there were millions of fraudulent bonds charged against the credit of the State, passed another act to ascertain the true bonded indebtedness, and to provide for its settlement. Under this law, at one sweep, those entrusted with the power to do so, through Negro legislators, stamped six millions of bonds, denominated as conversion bonds, "fraudulent". The commission did not finish its work before 1876. In that year, when the Hampton government came into power, there were still to be examined into and settled under the terms of the act passed by us providing for the legitimate bonded indebtedness of the state, a little over two and a half million dollars worth of bonds and coupons which had not been passed upon.

Governor Hampton, General Hagood, Judge Simonton, Judge Wallace and in fact, all of the conservative thinking Democrats aligned themselves under the provision enacted by us for the certain and final settlement of the bonded indebtedness and appealed to their Democratic legislatures to stand by the Republican legislation on the subject and to confirm it. A faction in the Democratic party obtained a majority of the Democrats in the legislature against settling the question and they endeavored to open up anew the whole subject of the state debt. We had a little over thirty members in the house and enough Republican senators to sustain the Hampton conservative faction and to stand up for honest finance, or by our votes place the debt question of the old state into the hands of the plunderers and peculators. We were appealed to by General Hagood, through me, and my answer to him was in these words: "General, our people have learned the difference between profligate and honest legislation. We have passed acts of financial reform, and with the assistance of God when the vote shall have been taken, you will be able to record for the thirty odd Negroes, slandered though they have been through the press, that they voted solidly with you all for honest legislation and the preservation of the credit of the State." The thirty odd Negroes in the legislature and their senators, by their votes did settle the debt question and saved the state $13,000,000. We were eight years in power. We had built school houses, established charitable institutions, built and maintained the penitentiary system, provided for the education of the deaf and dumb, rebuilt the jails and court houses, rebuilt the bridges and re-established the ferries. In short, we had reconstructed the State and placed it upon the road to prosperity and, at the same time, by our acts of financial reform transmitted to the Hampton Government an indebtedness not greater by more than $2,500,000 than was the bonded debt of the State in 1868, before the Republican Negroes and their white allies came into power.[19]

So, too, in Louisiana in 1872 and in Mississippi later the better element of the Republicans triumphed at the polls and joining with the Democrats instituted reforms, repudiated the worst extravagance, and started toward better things. But unfortunately there was one thing that the white South feared more than negro dishonesty, ignorance, and incompetency, and that was negro honesty, knowledge, and efficiency.

In the midst of all these difficulties the negro governments in the South accomplished much of positive good. We may recognize three things which negro rule gave to the South:

1. Democratic government.
2. Free public schools.
3. New social legislation.

Two states will illustrate conditions of government in the South before and after negro rule. In South Carolina there was before the war a property qualification for office-holders, and, in part, for voters. The Constitution of 1868, on the other hand, was a modern democratic document starting (in marked contrast to the old constitutions) with a declaration that "We, the People", framed it, and preceded by a broad Declaration of Rights which did away with property qualifications and based representation directly on population instead of property. It especially took up new subjects of social legislation, declaring navigable rivers free public highways, instituting homestead exemptions, establishing boards of county commissioners, providing for a new penal code of laws, establishing universal manhood suffrage "without distinction of race or color", devoting six sections to charitable and penal institutions and six to corporations, providing separate property for married women, etc. Above all, eleven sections of the Tenth Article were devoted to the establishment of a complete public-school system.

So satisfactory was the constitution thus adopted by negro suffrage and by a convention composed of a majority of blacks that the state lived twenty-seven

[19] Speech of Thomas E. Miller, one of the six negro members of the South Carolina Constitutional Convention of 1895. The speech was not published in the *Journal* but may be found in the *Occasional Papers* of the American Negro Academy, no. 6, pp. 11–13.

years under it without essential change and when the constitution was revised in 1895, the revision was practically nothing more than an amplification of the Constitution of 1868. No essential advance step of the former document was changed except the suffrage article.

In Mississippi the Constitution of 1868 was, as compared with that before the war, more democratic. It not only forbade distinctions on account of color but abolished all property qualifications for jury service, and property and educational qualifications for suffrage; it required less rigorous qualifications for office; it prohibited the lending of the credit of the state for private corporations—an abuse dating back as far as 1830. It increased the powers of the governor, raised the low state salaries, and increased the number of state officials. New ideas like the public-school system and the immigration bureau were introduced and in general the activity of the state greatly and necessarily enlarged. Finally, that was the only constitution ever submitted to popular approval at the polls. This constitution remained in force twenty-two years.

In general the words of Judge Albion W. Tourgee, a "carpetbagger", are true when he says of the negro governments:

> They obeyed the Constitution of the United States, and annulled the bonds of states, counties, and cities which had been issued to carry on the war of rebellion and maintain armies in the field against the Union. They instituted a public school system in a realm where public schools had been unknown. They opened the ballot box and jury box to thousands of white men who had been debarred from them by a lack of earthly possessions. They introduced home rule into the South. They abolished the whipping post, the branding iron, the stocks and other barbarous forms of punishment which had up to that time prevailed. They reduced capital felonies from about twenty to two or three. In an age of extravagance they were extravagant in the sums appropriated for public works. In all of that time no man's rights of person were invaded under the forms of law. Every Democrat's life, home, fireside and business were safe. No man obstructed any white man's way to the ballot box, interfered with his freedom of speech, or boycotted him on account of his political faith. [20]

A thorough study of the legislation accompanying these constitutions and its changes since would of course be necessary before a full picture of the situation could be given. This has not been done, but so far as my studies have gone I have been surprised at the comparatively small amount of change in law and government which the overthrow of negro rule brought about. There were sharp and often hurtful economies introduced marking the return of property to power, there was a sweeping change of officials, but the main body of Reconstruction legislation stood.

This democracy brought forward new leaders and men and definitely overthrew the old Southern aristocracy. Among these new men were negroes of worth and ability. John R. Lynch when speaker of the Mississippi house of

[20] *Occasional Papers* of the American Negro Academy, no. 6, p. 10; Chicago *Weekly Inter Ocean,* December 26, 1890.

representatives was given a public testimonial by Republicans and Democrats and the leading Democratic paper said:

> His bearing in office had been so proper, and his rulings in such marked contrast to the partisan conduct of the ignoble whites of his party who have aspired to be leaders of the blacks, that the conservatives cheerfully joined in the testimonial.[21]

Of the colored treasurer of South Carolina, Governor Chamberlain said:

> I have never heard one word or seen one act of Mr. Cardozo's which did not confirm my confidence in his personal integrity and his political honor and zeal for the honest administration of the State Government. On every occasion, and under all circumstances, he has been against fraud and jobbery, and in favor of good measures and good men.[22]

Jonathan C. Gibbs, a colored man and the first state superintendent of instruction in Florida, was a graduate of Dartmouth. He established the system and brought it to success, dying in harness in 1874. Such men—and there were others—ought not to be forgotten or confounded with other types of colored and white Reconstruction leaders.

There is no doubt but that the thirst of the black man for knowledge—a thirst which has been too persistent and durable to be mere curiosity or whim—gave birth to the public free-school system of the South. It was the question upon which black voters and legislators insisted more than anything else and while it is possible to find some vestiges of free schools in some of the Southern States before the war yet a universal, well-established system dates from the day that the black man got political power. Common-school instruction in the South, in the modern sense of the term, was begun for negroes by the Freedmen's Bureau and missionary societies, and the state public-school systems for all children were formed mainly by negro Reconstruction governments. The earlier state constitutions of Mississippi "from 1817 to 1865 contained a declaration that 'Religion, morality and knowledge being necessary to good government, the preservation of liberty and the happiness of mankind, schools and the means of education shall forever be encouraged.' It was not, however, until 1868 that encouragement was given to any general system of public schools meant to embrace the whole youthful population." The Constitution of 1868 makes it the duty of the legislature to establish 'a uniform system of free public schools, by taxation or otherwise, for all children between the ages of five and twenty-one years". In Alabama the Reconstruction Constitution of 1868 provided that "It shall be the duty of the Board of Education to establish throughout the State, in each township or other school district which it may have created, one or more schools at which all the children of the State between the ages of five and twenty-one years

[21] Jackson (Mississippi) *Clarion,* April 24, 1873.
[22] Allen, *Governor Chamberlain's Administration in South Carolina,* p. 82.

may attend free of charge." Arkansas in 1868, Florida in 1869, Louisiana in 1868, North Carolina in 1869, South Carolina in 1868, and Virginia in 1870, established school systems. The Constitution of 1868 in Louisiana required the general assembly to establish "at least one free public school in every parish", and that these schools should make no "distinction of race, color or previous condition". Georgia's system was not fully established until 1873.

We are apt to forget that in all human probability the granting of negro manhood suffrage and the passage of the Fifteenth Amendment were decisive in rendering permanent the foundation of the negro common school. Even after the overthrow of the negro governments, if the negroes had been left a servile caste, personally free, but politically powerless, it is not reasonable to think that a system of common schools would have been provided for them by the Southern States. Serfdom and education have ever proven contradictory terms. But when Congress, backed by the nation, determined to make the negroes full-fledged voting citizens, the South had a hard dilemma before her: either to keep the negroes under as an ignorant proletariat and stand the chance of being ruled eventually from the slums and jails, or to join in helping to raise these wards of the nation to a position of intelligence and thrift by means of a public-school system. The "carpet-bag" governments hastened the decision of the South, and although there was a period of hesitation and retrogression after the overthrow of negro rule in the early seventies, yet the South saw that to abolish negro schools in addition to nullifying the negro vote would invite Northern interference; and thus eventually every Southern state confirmed the work of the negro legislators and maintained the negro public schools along with the white.

Finally, in legislation covering property, the wider functions of the state, the punishment of crime and the like, it is sufficient to say that the laws on these points established by Reconstruction legislatures were not only different from and even revolutionary to the laws in the older South, but they were so wise and so well suited to the needs of the new South that in spite of a retrogressive movement following the overthrow of the negro governments the mass of this legislation, with elaboration and development, still stands on the statute books of the South.

Reconstruction constitutions, practically unaltered, were kept in

Florida, 1868–1885 .... 17 years.
Virginia, 1870–1902 .... 32 years.
South Carolina, 1868–1895 .... 27 years.
Mississippi, 1868–1890 .... 22 years.

Even in the case of states like Alabama, Georgia, North Carolina, and Louisiana, which adopted new constitutions to signify the overthrow of negro rule, the new constitutions are nearer the model of the Reconstruction document than they are to the previous constitutions. They differ from the negro constitutions in minor details but very little in general conception.

Besides this there stands on the statute books of the South to-day law after law passed between 1868 and 1876, and which has been found wise, effective, and worthy of preservation.

Paint the "carpet-bag" governments and negro rule as black as may be, the fact remains that the essence of the revolution which the overturning of the negro governments made was to put these black men and their friends out of power. Outside the curtailing of expenses and stopping of extravagance, not only did their successors make few changes in the work which these legislatures and conventions had done, but they largely carried out their plans, followed their suggestions, and strengthened their institutions. Practically the whole new growth of the South has been accomplished under laws which black men helped to frame thirty years ago. I know of no greater compliment to negro suffrage.

The Future of the American Negro

Booker T. Washington

In order that the reader may understand me and why I lay so much stress upon the importance of pushing the doctrine of industrial education for the Negro, it is necessary, first of all, to review the condition of affairs at the present time in the Southern States. For years I have had something of an opportunity to study the Negro at first-hand; and I feel that I know him pretty well, —him and his needs, his failures and his successes, his desires and the likelihood of their fulfilment. I have studied him and his relations with his white neighbours, and striven to find how these relations may be made more conducive to the general peace and welfare both of the South and of the country at large.

In the Southern part of the United States there are twenty-two millions of people who are bound to the fifty millions of the North by ties which neither can tear asunder if they would. The most intelligent in a New York community has his intelligence darkened by the ignorance of a fellow-citizen in the Mississippi bottoms. The most wealthy in New York City would be more wealthy but for the poverty of a fellow-being in the Carolina rice swamps. The most moral and religious men in Massachusetts have their religion and morality modified by the degradation of the man in the South whose religion is a mere matter of form or of emotionalism. The vote of the man in Maine that is cast for the highest and purest form of government is largely neutralised by the vote of the man in Louisiana whose ballot is stolen or cast in ignorance. Therefore, when the South is ignorant, the North is ignorant; when the South is poor, the North is poor; when the South commits crime, the nation commits crime. For the citizens of the North there is no escape; they must help raise the character of the civilisation in the South, or theirs will be lowered. No member of the white race in any part of the country can harm the weakest or meanest member of the black race without the proudest and bluest blood of the nation being degraded.

It seems to me that there never was a time in the history of the country when those interested in education should the more earnestly consider to what extent the mere acquiring of the ability to read and write, the mere acquisition of a knowledge of literature and science, makes men producers, lovers of labour, independent, honest, unselfish, and, above all, good. Call education by what name you please, if it fails to bring about these results

From Booker T. Washington, *The Future of the American Negro* (New York, 1899), Chapter II.

among the masses, it falls short of its highest end. The science, the art, the literature, that fails to reach down and bring the humblest up to the enjoyment of the fullest blessings of our government, is weak, no matter how costly the buildings or apparatus used or how modern the methods of instruction employed. The study of arithmetic that does not result in making men conscientious in receiving and counting the ballots of their fellow-men is faulty. The study of art that does not result in making the strong less willing to oppress the weak means little. How I wish that from the most cultured and highly endowed university in the great North to the humblest log cabin school-house in Alabama, we could burn, as it were, into the hearts and heads of all that usefulness, that service to our brother, is the supreme end of education. Putting the thought more directly as it applies to conditions in the South, can you make the intelligence of the North affect the South in the same ratio that the ignorance of the South affects the North? Let us take a not improbable case: A great national case is to be decided, one that involves peace or war, the honour or dishonour of our nation,—yea, the very existence of the government. The North and West are divided. There are five million votes to be cast in the South; and, of this number, one-half are ignorant. Not only are one-half the voters ignorant; but, because of the ignorant votes they cast, corruption and dishonesty in a dozen forms have crept into the exercise of the political franchise to such an extent that the conscience of the intelligent class is seared in its attempts to defeat the will of the ignorant voters. Here, then, you have on the one hand an ignorant vote, on the other an intelligent vote minus a conscience. The time may not be far off when to this kind of jury we shall have to look for the votes which shall decide in a large measure the destiny of our democratic institutions.

When a great national calamity stares us in the face, we are, I fear, too much given to depending on a short "campaign of education" to do on the hustings what should have been accomplished in the school.

With this idea in view, let us examine with more care the condition of civilisation in the South, and the work to be done there before all classes will be fit for the high duties of citizenship. In reference to the Negro race, I am confronted with some embarrassment at the outset, because of the various and conflicting opinions as to what is to be its final place in our economic and political life.

Within the last thirty years—and, I might add, within the last three months,—it has been proven by eminent authority that the Negro is increasing in numbers so fast that it is only a question of a few years before he will far outnumber the white race in the South, and it has also been proven that the Negro is fast dying out, and it is only a question of a few years before he will have completely disappeared. It has also been proven that education helps the Negro and that education hurts him, that he is fast leaving the South and taking up his residence in the North and West, and that his tendency is to drift toward the low lands of the Mississippi bottoms. It has been proven that education unfits the Negro for work and that education makes him more valuable as a labourer, that he is our greatest criminal and that he is our most law-abiding citizen. In the midst of these conflicting opinions, it is hard to hit upon the truth.

But, also, in the midst of this confusion, there are a few things of which I am certain,—things which furnish a basis for thought and action. I know that whether the Negroes are increasing or decreasing, whether they are growing better or worse, whether they are valuable or valueless, that a few years ago some fourteen of them were brought into this country, and that now those fourteen are nearly ten millions. I know that, whether in slavery or freedom, they have always been loyal to the Stars and Stripes, that no school-house has been opened for them that has not been filled, that the 2,000,000 ballots that they have the right to cast are as potent for weal or woe as an equal number cast by the wisest and most influential men in America. I know that wherever Negro life touches the life of the nation it helps or it hinders, that wherever the life of the white race touches the black it makes it stronger or weaker. Further, I know that almost every other race that has tried to look the white man in the face has disappeared. I know, despite all the conflicting opinions, and with a full knowledge of all the Negroes' weaknesses, that only a few centuries ago they went into slavery in this country pagans, that they came out Christians; they went into slavery as so much property, they came out American citizens; they went into slavery without a language, they came out speaking the proud Anglo-Saxon tongue; they went into slavery with the chains clanking about their wrists, they came out with the American ballot in their hands.

I submit it to the candid and sober judgment of all men, if a race that is capable of such a test, such a transformation, is not worth saving and making a part, in reality as well as in name, of our democratic government. That the Negro may be fitted for the fullest enjoyment of the privileges and responsibilities of our citizenship, it is important that the nation be honest and candid with him, whether honesty and candour for the time being pleases or displeases him. It is with an ignorant race as it is with a child: it craves at first the superficial, the ornamental signs of progress rather than the reality. The ignorant race is tempted to jump, at one bound, to the position that it has required years of hard struggle for others to reach.

It seems to me that, as a general thing, the temptation in the past in educational and missionary work has been to do for the new people that which was done a thousand years ago, or that which is being done for a people a thousand miles away, without making a careful study of the needs and conditions of the people whom it is designed to help. The temptation is to run all people through a certain educational mould, regardless of the condition of the subject or the end to be accomplished. This has been the case too often in the South in the past, I am sure. Men have tried to use, with these simple people just freed from slavery and with no past, no inherited traditions of learning, the same methods of education which they have used in New England, with all its inherited traditions and desires. The Negro is behind the white man because he has not had the same chance, and not from any inherent difference in his nature and desires. What the race accomplishes in these first fifty years of freedom will at the end of these years, in a large measure, constitute its past. It is, indeed, a responsibility that rests upon this nation,—the foundation laying for a people of its past, present, and future at one and the same time.

One of the weakest points in connection with the present development of the race is that so many get the idea that the mere filling of the head with a knowledge of mathematics, the sciences, and literature, means success in life. Let it be understood, in every corner of the South, among the Negro youth at least, that knowledge will benefit little except as it is harnessed, except as its power is pointed in a direction that will bear upon the present needs and condition of the race. There is in the heads of the Negro youth of the South enough general and floating knowledge of chemistry, of botany, of zoölogy, of geology, of mechanics, of electricity, of mathematics, to reconstruct and develop a large part of the agricultural, mechanical, and domestic life of the race. But how much of it is brought to a focus along lines of practical work? In cities of the South like Atlanta, how many coloured mechanical engineers are there? or how many machinists? how many civil engineers? how many architects? how many house decorators? In the whole State of Georgia, where eighty per cent. of the coloured people depend upon agriculture, how many men are there who are well grounded in the principles and practices of scientific farming? or dairy work? or fruit culture? or floriculture?

For example, not very long ago I had a conversation with a young coloured man who is a graduate of one of the prominent universities of this country. The father of this man is comparatively ignorant, but by hard work and the exercise of common sense he has become the owner of two thousand acres of land. He owns more than a score of horses, cows, and mules and swine in large numbers, and is considered a prosperous farmer. In college the son of this farmer has studied chemistry, botany, zoölogy, surveying, and political economy. In my conversation I asked this young man how many acres his father cultivated in cotton and how many in corn. With a far-off gaze up into the heavens he answered that he did not know. When I asked him the classification of the soils on his father's farm, he did not know. He did not know how many horses or cows his father owned nor of what breeds they were, and seemed surprised that he should be asked such questions. It never seemed to have entered his mind that on his father's farm was the place to make his chemistry, his mathematics, and his literature penetrate and reflect itself in every acre of land, every bushel of corn, every cow, and every pig.

Let me give other examples of this mistaken sort of education. When a mere boy, I saw a young coloured man, who had spent several years in school, sitting in a common cabin in the South, studying a French grammar. I noted the poverty, the untidiness, the want of system and thrift, that existed about the cabin, notwithstanding his knowledge of French and other academic studies.

Again, not long ago I saw a coloured minister preparing his Sunday sermon just as the New England minister prepares his sermon. But this coloured minister was in a broken-down, leaky, rented log cabin, with weeds in the yard, surrounded by evidences of poverty, filth, and want of thrift. This minister had spent some time in school studying theology. How much better it would have been to have had this minister taught the dignity of labour, taught theoretical and practical farming in connection with his theology, so that he could have added to his meagre salary, and set an example for his people in the matter of living in a decent house, and having a knowledge of correct farming! In a word, this minister should have been taught that his condition, and that of his people, was not that of a New England community; and he should have been so trained as to meet the actual needs and conditions of the coloured people in this community, so that a foundation might be laid that would, in the future, make a community like New England communities.

Since the Civil War, no one object has been more misunderstood than that of the object and value of industrial education for the Negro. To begin with, it must be borne in mind that the condition that existed in the South immediately after the war, and that now exists, is a peculiar one, without a parallel in history. This being true, it seems to me that the wise and honest thing to do is to make a study of the actual condition and environment of the Negro, and do that which is best for him, regardless of whether the same thing has been done for another race in exactly the same way. There are those among the white race and those among the black race who assert, with a good deal of earnestness, that there is no difference between the white man and the black man in this country. This sounds very pleasant and tickles the fancy; but, when the test of hard, cold logic is applied to it, it must be acknowledged that there is a difference,—not an inherent one, not a racial one, but a difference growing out of unequal opportunities in the past.

If I may be permitted to criticise the educational work that has been done in the South, I would say that the weak point has been in the failure to recognise this difference.

Negro education, immediately after the war in most cases, was begun too nearly at the point where New England education had ended. Let me illustrate. One of the saddest sights I ever saw was the placing of a three hundred dollar rosewood piano in a country school in the South that was located in the midst of the "Black Belt." Am I arguing against the teaching of instrumental music to the Negroes in that community? Not at all: only I should have deferred those music lessons about twenty-five years. There are numbers of such pianos in thousands of New England homes. But behind the piano in the New England home there are one hundred years of toil, sacrifice, and economy; there is the small manufacturing industry, started several years ago by hand power, now grown into a great business; there is ownership in land, a comfortable home, free from debt, and a bank account. In this "Black Belt" community where this piano went, four-fifths of the people owned no land, many lived in rented one-room cabins, many were in debt for food supplies, many mortgaged their crops for the food on which to live, and not one had a bank account. In this case, how much wiser it would have been to have taught the girls in this community sewing, intelligent and economical cooking, housekeeping, something of dairying and horticulture? The boys should have been taught something of farming in connection with their common-school education, instead of awakening in them a desire for a musical instrument which resulted in their parents going into debt for a third-rate piano or organ before a home was purchased. Industrial lessons would have awakened, in this community, a desire for homes, and would have given the people the ability to free themselves from industrial slavery to the extent that most of them would have soon purchased homes. After the home and the necessaries of life were supplied could come the piano. One piano lesson in a home of one's own is worth twenty in a rented log cabin.

All that I have just written, and the various examples illustrating it, show the present helpless condition of my people in the South,—how fearfully they lack the primary training for good living and good citizenship, how much they stand in need of a solid foundation on which to build their future success. I believe, as I have many times said in my various addresses in the North and in the South, that the main reason for the existence of this curious state of affairs is the lack of practical training in the ways of life.

There is, too, a great lack of money with which to carry on the educational work in the South. I was in a county in a Southern State not long ago where there are some thirty thousand coloured people and about seven thousand whites. In this county not a single public school for Negroes had been open that year longer than three months, not a single coloured teacher had been paid more than $15 per month for his teaching. Not one of these schools was taught in a building that was worthy of the name of school-house. In this county the State or public authorities do not own a single dollar's worth of school property,—not a school-house, a blackboard, or a piece of Crayon. Each coloured child had had spent on him that year for his education about fifty cents, while each child in New York or Massachusetts had had spent on him that year for education not far from $20. And yet each citizen of this county is expected to share the burdens and privileges of our democratic form of government just as intelligently and conscientiously as the citizens of New York or Boston. A vote in this county means as much to the nation as a vote in the city of Boston. Crime in this county is as truly an arrow aimed at the heart of the government as a crime committed in the streets of Boston.

A single school-house built this year in a town near Boston to shelter about three hundred pupils cost more for building alone than is spent yearly for the education, including buildings, apparatus, teachers, for the whole coloured school population of Alabama. The Commissioner of Education for the State of Georgia not long ago reported to the State legislature that in that

State there were two hundred thousand children that had entered no school the year past and one hundred thousand more who were at school but a few days, making practically three hundred thousand children between six and eighteen years of age that are growing up in ignorance in one Southern State alone. The same report stated that outside of the cities and towns, while the average number of school-houses in a county was sixty, all of these sixty school-houses were worth in lump less than $2,000, and the report further added that many of the school-houses in Georgia were not fit for horse stables. I am glad to say, however, that vast improvement over this condition is being made in Georgia under the inspired leadership of State Commissioner Glenn, and in Alabama under the no less zealous leadership of Commissioner Abercrombie.

These illustrations, so far as they concern the Gulf States, are not exceptional cases; nor are they overdrawn.

Until there is industrial independence, it is hardly possible to have good living and a pure ballot in the county districts. In these States it is safe to say that not more than one black man in twenty owns the land he cultivates. Where so large a proportion of a people are dependent, live in other people's houses, eat other people's food, and wear clothes they have not paid for, it is pretty hard to expect them to live fairly and vote honestly.

I have thus far referred mainly to the Negro race. But there is another side. The longer I live and the more I study the question, the more I am convinced that it is not so much a problem as to what the white man will do with the Negro as what the Negro will do with the white man and his civilisation. In considering this side of the subject, I thank God that I have grown to the point where I can sympathise with a white man as much as I can sympathise with a black man. I have grown to the point where I can sympathise with a Southern white man as much as I can sympathise with a Northern white man.

As bearing upon the future of our civilisation, I ask of the North what of their white brethren in the South,—those who have suffered and are still suffering the consequences of American slavery, for which both North and South were responsible? These of the great and prosperous North still owe to their less fortunate brethren of the Caucasian race in the South, not less than to themselves, a serious and uncompleted duty. What was the task the North asked the South to perform? Returning to their destitute homes after years of war to face blasted hopes, devastation, a shattered industrial system, they asked them to add to their own burdens that of preparing in education, politics, and economics, in a few short years, for citizenship, four millions of former slaves. That the South, staggering under the burden, made blunders, and that in a measure there has been disappointment, no one need be surprised. The educators, the statesmen, the philanthropists, have imperfectly comprehended their duty toward the millions of poor whites in the South who were buffeted for two hundred years between slavery and freedom, between civilisation and degradation, who were disregarded by both master and slave. It needs no prophet to tell the character of our future civilisation when the poor white boy in the country districts of the South receives one dollar's worth of education and the boy of the same class in the North twenty dollar's worth, when one never enters a reading-room or library and the other has reading-rooms and libraries in every ward and town, when one hears lectures and sermons once in two months and the other can hear a lecture or a sermon every day in the year.

The time has come, it seems to me, when in this matter we should rise above party or race or sectionalism into the region of duty of man to man, of citizen to citizen, of Christian to Christian; and if the Negro, who has been oppressed and denied his rights in a Chrstian land, can help the whites of the North and South to rise, can be the inspiration of their rising, into this atmosphere of generous Christian brotherhood and self-forgetfulness, he will see in it a recompense for all that he has suffered in the past.

The Sport of the Ghouls

Kelly Miller

*　　*　　*　　*

The democratic ideal of America is tainted with a disregard for law, the only foundation upon which a democracy can endure. She is impelled by a wild and reckless intrepidity of spirit.

> "That bids her make the laws she flouts—
> That bids her flout the laws she makes."

The United States has the largest percentage of murders and homicides and the lowest average of legal executions of any civilized institution on the face of the earth. Ex-President, now Chief-Justice Taft, in a notable address some years ago, stated that there had been 131,951 murders and homicides in the United States between 1885 and 1908, and only 2,286 legal executions. In 1912, there were 9,152 homicides and only 145 executions.

Lawlessness is universally deplored as America's overshadowing national sin. In partial explanation of this deplorable state of things, it might be said that in a new country where the self-assertive Saxon was confronted by two primitive races, his personal authority was subject to little or no legal restraint. His word was law, and his judgment the final source of appeal. It was the imperialism of race that destroyed the Indian and enslaved the Negro. The spirit of self-sufficiency of judgment in dealing with primitive races survives long after evoking conditions have passed away.

Lynching is a peculiar American institution. This country has contributed a new word to the English language. The term, itself, is said to be derived from a Virginia slaveholder named Lynch who was in the habit of taking the law into his own hands in dealing with runaway slaves and white outlaws who sought shelter in the Dismal Swamp. Mr. Lynch is said to have contributed the name to Lynchburg, Va. The word has come to mean the infliction of summary punishment without due process of law. But the process is so generally applied to the Negro offender that it has grown to connote a mode of racial punishment.

*　　*　　*　　*

The practice of lynching is apt to be manifested on the frontiers of civilization where a lower culture is brought into contact with a higher. The sons of God are prone to wreak summary vengeance upon the children of men who dare dispute their higher prerogative. The flaming sword of wrath still

---

From Kelly Miller, *The Everlasting Stain* (Washington, D. C.: Associated Publishers, 1924), pp. 314-332.

guards the forbidden fruit from the excluded aspirant of lower degree. Race hatred is the cause of most human outrages. The massacre of Armenian by Turk, pogroms of the Poles against the Jews, and lynching of Negroes in America grow out of the same basal instinct.

In most cases the outbreak between races takes on the form of mass assault and is inspired by political, religious or economic motive. Race riots, a somewhat new phase of race conflict in America, partakes largely of this nature. In case of lynching, the mob forms around an individual who is alleged to have committed some flagrant offense, and proceeds to execute the offender without waiting for the formal sanction of the court of law.

Violence is usually limited to the individual offender and does not involve wholesale slaughter. While the Negro is the usual victim of lynching, he is by no means the only one. During the thirty years, 1889-1918, there were 702 white men lynched in the United States. A larger number of white men were lynched in America than in all the rest of the civilized world. When the evil passion has once been aroused, it is impossible to limit its viciousness to any one race or class. The iniquities visited upon the Negro today will be meted out to the white man tomorrow. The evil inherent in race contact consists in a double standard of dealing. The methods devised for special application to the inferior race will inevitably tend to the demoralization of all. Water seeks its lowest level. So evil practice always tends to gravitate to the lowest ethical standard.

It is interesting to inquire why lynching is almost wholly limited to the United States of America. The self-reliant spirit of democracy, especially in pioneer communities, makes the individual feel that, in the final analysis, he is a law unto himself. The individual and not the social conscience becomes the immediate guide. The self-responsible individual or group that feels that its sensibilities have been ruthlessly outraged, justifies itself in wreaking summary vengeance upon the offender, especially when he falls outside the pale of its own race and class. In the anti-slavery controversy, those who went on the side of liberty often appealed to what they called the higher law, which took precedence over the law of the land. This is a dangerous doctrine, to be indulged only in case of extreme moral emergencies. If it is allowed to become the practice of individuals or groups not accustomed to exercise rigid-self-restraint, it is sure to lead to gross abuse. In a democracy such ultra procedure is apt to be indulged either for good or ill.

Each Southern plantation constituted a jurisdiction within itself where the owner was juror, judge and executioner. He possessed the power of life and death over his slaves. His influence over public sentiment was so powerful that his will and judgment became the law of the community. The slaveholders were to the manor born, and felt that they rightfully exercised the power of life and death over their slaves for the good of society. When the master murdered his slave, he was considered the chief loser. The community felt little concern. The constraint of conscience and the restraint of self-interest tended to reduce the practice to a minimum under the old régime of master and slave. But the slaveholders constituted a relatively small proportion of the white population of the South. Not one in ten of the white population of the Southern states belonged in this class. The poor whites who were unable to own slaves were held in a degree of contempt and disesteem scarcely above the level of the blacks. They were subject to the direction and control of the aristocratic class, and were as amenable to their personal and public authority as slaves themselves. Their color, which preëmpted them from forced servitude, was the principal advantage which they enjoyed. They naturally developed a hatred for the Negroes who were their indirect industrial rivals, and felt that, as white men, they were required to live on a higher level than the blacks, and as freemen they could not enter into competition with the slave labor.

After the emancipation of the Negro and the overthrow of the reconstruction régime in the South, the non-slaveholding whites, for the first time, gained consciousness of their political power. Animosity against the old aristocratic white element was scarcely less vehement than their venom against the Negro. The voice of the new man became dominant in the state. They drove the slaveholding oligarchy from power and took the reins of government into their own hands. Public feeling was lashed into fury against the Negro. Lynching was urged as a suitable mode of punishment whenever the black man threatened or jeopardized the prerogative of the white race. The late Senator Benjamin R. Tillman was the mouthpiece and oracle of this ruthless program. It is noticeable that under slavery lynchings were rare and almost unheard of. Under the reconstruction government they were infrequent. The practice rose simultaneously with the rise of the non-slaveholding whites to power in the states.

A people who begin their existence with violent protest against authority to which they were once subject are apt to carry the protestant spirit beyond the limit of its original intendment. The Protestant religion will reach its logical goal when all ecclesiastical authority is abolished over the individual conscience and judgment. The Boston Tea Party embodied the spirit of disregard for law as much as a mob of lynchers. If it is rejoined that the Puritan lawbreakers were impelled by patriotic motives which rose above the law, so the mob might retort that its hasty passion is also promoting immediate or ultimate social aims. The lawless habit acquired for some worthy purpose seeks exercise on unworthy objects when that purpose has been subserved. It is to be hoped that the democracies which are achieved by more orderly and regular procedure will escape this evil concomitant.

The term "social equality" has come to signify the deadline of relationship between the races. Any semblance of attempt on part of the Negro to cross this deadline in the South is vested with summary punishment. Every white man feels that he bears a racial commission to act in the emergency. His acts, however outrageous, will be sure to meet with public favor, if he can show that they were committed in the name and at the behest of social equality. The phrase has taken on frenzied meaning. It has become the tocsin and rallying cry of the white supremacy propaganda. Men worship and bow down at its shrine as a heathen before his graven god. No crime is too heinous to be committed at its dictation. That the races must be kept apart is the gospel of the South, more sacred than Holy Writ. There is no provision of the sacred Scripture that may not be violated to attain this great objective. Any act on the part of an individual or group of individuals which tends to this end is justified in public opinion.

Lynching is sought to be justified on the ground of assault on white women by colored men. But it is not the crime so much as the color of the criminal that provokes the punishment. The assault of a Negro on a white woman arouses all of the passion and animosity of the white race. It is easier to inflame public opinion over the color of the criminal than over the nature of the crime. Social intimacy and physical mixture of the races must be prevented at all hazards, is the philosophy of those who justify lynching.

Race hatred and lynching do not heed the obvious facts and formulas of logic. The mixture of the races has already taken place on a gigantic scale. The presence of three million mulattoes indicates clearly that the danger of intermixture does not come through assault of the black male upon the white female. The result will be just as effective through the lust of the white male after the black female. The fact of mixed progeny is stubborn and persistent. The laws of biology care nothing for the social creeds of the day. It makes little or no difference how mixed progeny is produced. The essential thing is the product, not the process.

Lynching of Negroes does not involve risk of danger, nor does it evoke the many qualities of courage or daring. It is a safe pastime which appeals to the coward and the bully. There is a total lack of the zest of sportsmanship. A mob of five hundred men armed to the teeth wreaking vengeance on a defenseless Negro already in custody of the law does not present an heroic spectacle. The complacent sheriff is easily "overpowered" and renders the keys for the asking. The culprit is spirited away to be strung up to the limb of a tree. His body is riddled with bullets and ticketed with a placard to remind all Negroes of the superiority of the white race. In the South a white man is rarely ever punished for killing a Negro. Of the thousands of homicides and murders of black men during the past fifty years, instances of legal execution may be counted on the fingers of one's hand. The white man in the South, either as an individual, or as part of the mob, may kill a Negro with all but absolute impunity. Lynching is apt to continue until the participant is made to pay the penalty for his part in the murderous pact. Men will override the law at their convenience when they can do so with impunity. Salutary fear of the law is persuasive to obedience of law.

Although lynchings occur most frequently in the South, they are by no means confined to that section. They have occurred in all but six states of the United States. They are not limited by geographical boundaries or lines of latitude.

The following table indicates the number of white and colored persons lynched in the United States from 1889 to 1920:

Year	Total	White	Colored
1889	175	80	95
1890	91	3	88
1891	194	67	127
1892	226	71	155
1893	153	39	114
1894	182	54	128
1895	178	68	110
1896	125	46	79
1897	162	38	124
1898	127	24	103
1899	109	22	87
1900	101	12	89
1901	135	27	108
1902	94	10	84
1903	104	17	87
1904	86	7	79
1905	65	5	60
1906	68	4	64
1907	62	3	59
1908	100	8	92
1909	89	14	75
1910	90	10	80
1911	71	8	63
1912	64	3	61
1913	48	1	47
1914	54	5	49
1915	96	43	53
1916	58	7	51
1917	50	2	48
1918	67	4	63
1919	83	6	77
1920	65	8	57
	3372	716	2656

The one hopeful indication of the table is the gradual diminution with the years.

NUMBER OF PERSONS LYNCHED—BY STATES OF THE UNITED STATES, 1889–1920

State	Number	State	Number
Main	1	West Virginia	32
New Hampshire	0	North Carolina	59
Vermont	0	South Carolina	124
Massachusetts	0	Georgia	415

Rhode Island	0	Florida	196
Connecticut	0	Kentucky	170
New York	3	Tennessee	198
New Jersey	1	Alabama	290
Pennsylvania	4	Mississippi	392
Ohio	13	Arkansas	225
Indiana	19	Louisiana	321
Illinois	24	Oklahoma	99
Michigan	4	Texas	348
Wisconsin	4	Montana	23
Minnesota	7	Idaho	11
Iowa	8	Wyoming	34
Missouri	84	Colorado	20
North Dakota	2	New Mexico	13
South Dakota	13	Arizona	8
Nebraska	17	Utah	0
Kansas	24	Nevada	4
Delaware	1	Washington	16
Maryland	17	Oregon	4
Virginia	79	California	26
Alaska	4	Places Unknown	11

This table shows how widespread the evil practice is distributed throughout the whole area. There are 2,953 counties in the states of the United States, with an approximate average area of 1,000 square miles. If these lynchings were equally distributed over the whole territory, there would be something like 1 lynching in each county during the past thirty years.

Women and girls have not escaped the bloodthirsty vengeance of the American mob. The following table shows the number of lynchings of the female sex distributed by state and color from 1889 to 1918:

WOMEN AND GIRLS LYNCHED—BY STATES—1889–1918

	Total	White	Colored
United States	61	11	50
Alabama		..	7
Arkansas		..	5
Florida		..	2
Georgia		..	5
Kentucky		1	3
Louisiana		1	..
Mississippi		1	11
Nebraska		1	..
North Carolina		1	..
Oklahoma		..	2
South Carolina		..	4
Tennessee		2	1
Texas		3	6
Virginia		1	..

It will be seen that white women as well as colored women have not escaped mob fury.

Of 3,224 of these cases of lynchings the causes or alleged causes are as follows:

NUMBER OF PERSONS LYNCHED, BY OFFENSES CHARGED AND BY COLOR, 1889–1918

	Murder	Rape	Attacks upon Women	Other Crimes against the Person	Crimes against Property	Miscellaneous Crimes	Absence of Crimes
White	319	46	13	62	121	135	6
Negro	900	477	237	253	210	303	142
Total	1219	523	250	315	331	438	148

Only 19 per cent of the lynchings of Negroes were on account of allegement of rape, and 9.4 per cent for attack upon women. It must always be borne in mind that the offenses were only alleged. In few cases have they been proved by a court of competent jurisdiction. In numerous instances mistaken identity has been established after the victim has been dispatched to his doom. Hundreds have met their fate with the protestation of innocence on their dying lips.

Effort has been made to besmirch the Negro race by branding it with evil reputation. Lynching has sought justification because of the alleged lecherous propensity of the Negro race. And yet not one case of lynching in five can even plead allegement of rape in justification. The Negro in Africa, South America and the West Indies is not afflicted with such evil propensity. During the days of the Civil War, when the master left his family in charge of the slaves, not one case of violated honor is on record.

White men commit assault on women all over the world. The criminal statistics of every European state show its due quota of cases of rape and assault upon women. In 1910 there were committed to prison in the United States 1,082 white men and 380 Negroes on the charge of rape. All of which goes to prove that lynching is not due to any "usual crime" or to any peculiar evil racial characteristic, but to the prevalent disposition to disregard law and orderly procedure where the Negro commits an offense against the white race.

The cruelty and barbarity of lynchings are indescribable for horror and atrocity. When we contemplate the deep damnation of the taking off of helpless victims, we question the efficacy of civilization to assuage the innate savagery of human nature. Victims have been drowned, hanged, shot, burned alive, beaten to death, dismembered while thousands gloated over their groanings with ghoulish glee. Women with child have been disemboweled in the public gaze. The United States enjoys the evil distinction of being the only civilized nation of the earth whose people take delight in the burning and torturing of human beings. Nowhere else in the civilized world do men, women and children dance with glee and fight for ghastly souvenirs of quivering human flesh, and mock with laughter the dying groans of the helpless victim which sicken the air while the flickering flames of the funeral pyre light up the midnight sky with their dismal glare.

But the United States is seriously conscious of the evil reputation which lynching imposes upon the nation. And yet it cannot plead exculpation on the ground that only the evil-minded few perpetrate and participate in this evil. Any nation is held justly accountable for the characteristic conduct of its citizens. The practice is too widespread in time and space to plead national irresponsibility. The nation commits what it permits. The American people, when clothed in their right mind and speaking with their true voice denounce the evil practice in every mood and tense of condemnation. They hope and pray that the reproach might be rolled away. When the nation would assume the asserted place as moral monitor among the nations of the earth, and condemn other people for their sins, it must face the age-old retort: "Thou hypocrite, first cast out the beam out of thine own eye."

President Wilson, in his deep chagrin, found that the practice of lynching in America belied or belittled his high-minded assumption of moral responsibility and leadership among the nations of mankind. In the midst of a war for democracy his people were discrediting at home the ideals which he was proclaiming abroad. In July 1918 he issued a proclamation to the American people on the evils of mob action, which was both an indictment and an appeal:

MY FELLOW COUNTRYMEN:

I take the liberty of addressing you upon a subject which so vitally affects the honor of the nation and the very character and integrity of our institutions that I trust you will think me justified in speaking very plainly about it.

There have been many lynchings, and every one of them has been a blow at the heart of ordered law and humane justice. No man who loves America, no man who really cares for her fame and honor and character, or who is truly loyal to her institutions can justify mob action while the courts of justice are open and the governments of the States and the nation are ready and able to do their duty.

We are at this very moment fighting lawless passion. We proudly claim to be the champions of democracy. If we really are, in deed and truth, let us see to it that we do not discredit our own. I say plainly that every American who takes part in the action of a mob or gives it any sort of countenance is no true son of this great democracy, but its betrayer, and does more to discredit her by that single disloyalty to her standards of law and right than the words of her statesmen or the sacrifices of her heroic boys in the trenches can do to make suffering people believe her to be their saviour. How shall we commend democracy to the acceptance of other peoples if we disgrace our own by proving that it is after all, no protection to the weak. Every mob contributes to German lies about the United States what her most gifted liars cannot improve upon by way of calumny. They can at least say that such things cannot happen in Germany except in time of revolution, when law is swept away.

WOODROW WILSON.

July 25, 1918.

But in spite of the President's proclamation there were 83 lynchings in 1919, 65 in 1920, and over 60 in 1921. The conscience of the nation is pricked to the core. All of America's resourcefulness must be asserted to exterminate this national disgrace lest the home of freedom in the Western World lose its boasted reputation as the land of liberty, and become known among nations as the land of lynchers.

The New Negro

Alain Locke

In the last decade something beyond the watch and guard of statistics has happened in the life of the American Negro and the three norns who have traditionally presided over the Negro problem have a changeling in their laps. The Sociologist, the Philanthropist, the Race-leader are not unaware of the New Negro, but they are at a loss to account for him. He simply cannot be swathed in their formulæ. For the younger generation is vibrant with a new psychology; the new spirit is awake in the masses, and under the very eyes of the professional observers is transforming what has been a perennial problem into the progressive phases of contemporary Negro life.

Could such a metamorphosis have taken place as suddenly as it has appeared to? The answer is no; not because the New Negro is not here, but because the Old Negro had long become more of a myth than a man. The Old Negro, we must remember, was a creature of moral debate and historical controversy. His has been a stock figure perpetuated as an historical fiction partly in innocent sentimentalism, partly in deliberate reactionism. The Negro himself has contributed his share to this through a sort of protective social mimicry forced upon him by the adverse circumstances of dependence. So for generations in the mind of America, the Negro has been more of a formula than a human being — a something to be argued about, condemned or defended, to be "kept down," or "in his place," or "helped up," to be worried with or worried over, harassed or patronized, a social bogey or a social burden. The thinking Negro even has been induced to share this general attitude, to focus his attention on controversial issues, to see himself in the distorted perspective of a social problem. His shadow, so to speak, has been more real to him than his personality. Through having had to appeal from the unjust stereotypes of his oppressors and traducers to those of his liberators, friends and benefactors he has had to subscribe to the traditional positions from which his case has been viewed. Little true social or self-understanding has or could come from such a situation.

But while the minds of most of us, black and white, have thus burrowed in the trenches of the Civil War and Reconstruction, the actual march of development has simply flanked these positions, necessitating a sudden reorientation of view. We have not been watching in the right direction; set

---

From Alain Locke, *The New Negro* (New York: Albert & Charles Boni, Inc., 1925), pp. 3-16.

North and South on a sectional axis, we have not noticed the East till the sun has us blinking.

Recall how suddenly the Negro spirituals revealed themselves; suppressed for generations under the stereotypes of Wesleyan hymn harmony, secretive, half-ashamed, until the courage of being natural brought them out — and behold, there was folk-music. Similarly the mind of the Negro seems suddenly to have slipped from under the tyranny of social intimidation and to be shaking off the psychology of imitation and implied inferiority. By shedding the old chrysalis of the Negro problem we are achieving something like a spiritual emancipation. Until recently, lacking self-understanding, we have been almost as much of a problem to ourselves as we still are to others. But the decade that found us with a problem has left us with only a task. The multitude perhaps feels as yet only a strange relief and new vague urge, but the thinking few know that in the reaction the vital inner grip of prejudice has been broken.

With this renewed self-respect and self-dependence, the life of the Negro community is bound to enter a new dynamic phase, the buoyancy from within compensating for whatever pressure there may be of conditions from without. The migrant masses, shifting from countryside to city, hurdle several generations of experience at a leap, but more important, the same thing happens spiritually in the life-attitudes and self-expression of the Young Negro, in his poetry, his art, his education and his new outlook, with the additional advantage, of course, of the poise and greater certainty of knowing what it is all about. From this comes the promise and warrant of a new leadership. As one of them has discerningly put it:

> We have tomorrow
> Bright before us
> Like a flame.
>
> Yesterday, a night-gone thing
> A sun-down name.
>
> And dawn today
> Broad arch above the road we came.
> We march!

This is what, even more than any "most creditable record of fifty years of freedom," requires that the Negro of to-day be seen through other than the dusty spectacles of past controversy. The day of "aunties," "uncles" and "mammies" is equally gone. Uncle Tom and Sambo have passed on, and even the "Colonel" and "George" play barnstorm rôles from which they escape with relief when the public spotlight is off. The popular melodrama has about played itself out, and it is time to scrap the fictions, garret the bogeys and settle down to a realistic facing of facts.

First we must observe some of the changes which since the traditional lines of opinion were drawn have rendered these quite obsolete. A main change has been, of course, that shifting of the Negro population which has made the Negro problem no longer exclusively or even predominantly Southern. Why should our minds remain sectionalized, when the problem itself no longer is? Then the trend of migration has not only been toward the North and the Central Midwest, but city-ward and to the great centers of industry — the problems of adjustment are new, practical, local and not peculiarly racial. Rather they are an integral part of the large industrial and social problems of our present-day democracy. And finally, with the Negro rapidly in process of class differentiation, if it ever was warrantable to regard and treat the Negro *en masse* it is becoming with every day less possible, more unjust and more ridiculous.

In the very process of being transplanted, the Negro is becoming transformed.

The tide of Negro migration, northward and city-ward, is not to be fully explained as a blind flood started by the demands of war industry coupled with the shutting off of foreign migration, or by the pressure of poor crops coupled with increased social terrorism in certain sections of the South and Southwest. Neither labor demand, the boll-weevil nor the Ku Klux Klan is a basic factor, however contributory any or all of them may have been. The wash and rush of this human tide on the beach line of the northern city centers is to be explained primarily in terms of a new vision of opportunity, of social and economic freedom, of a spirit to seize, even in the face of an extortionate and heavy toll, a chance for the improvement of conditions. With each successive wave of it, the movement of the Negro becomes more and more a mass movement toward the larger and the more democratic chance — in the Negro's case a deliberate flight not only from countryside to city, but from medieval America to modern.

Take Harlem as an instance of this. Here in Manhattan is not merely the largest Negro community in the world, but the first concentration in history of so many diverse elements of Negro life. It has attracted the African, the West Indian, the Negro American; has brought together the Negro of the North and the Negro of the South; the man from the city and the man from the town and village; the peasant, the student, the business man, the professional man, artist, poet, musician, adventurer and worker, preacher and criminal, exploiter and social outcast. Each group has come with its own separate motives and for its own special ends, but their greatest experience has been the finding of one another. Proscription and prejudice have thrown these dissimilar elements into a common area of contact and interaction. Within this area, race sympathy and unity have determined a further fusing of sentiment and experience. So what began in terms of segregation becomes more and more, as its elements mix and react, the laboratory of a great race-welding. Hitherto, it must be admitted that American Negroes have been a race more in name than in fact, or to be exact, more in sentiment than in experience. The chief bond between them has been that of a common condition rather than a common consciousness; a problem in common rather than a life in common. In Harlem, Negro life is seizing upon its first chances for group expression and self-determination. It is — or promises at least to be — a race capital. That is why our comparison is taken with those nascent centers of folk-expression and self-determination which are playing a creative part in the world to-day. Without pretense to their political significance, Harlem has the same rôle to play for the New Negro as Dublin has had for the New Ireland or Prague for the New Czechslovakia.

Harlem, I grant you, isn't typical — but it is significant, it is prophetic. No sane observer, however sympathetic to the new trend, would contend that the great masses are articulate as yet, but they stir, they move, they are more than physically restless. The challenge of the new intellectuals among them is clear enough — the "race radicals" and realists who have broken with the old epoch of philanthropic guidance, sentimental appeal and protest. But are we after all only reading into the stirring of a sleeping giant the dreams of an agitator? The answer is in the migrating peasant. It is the "man farthest down" who is most active in getting up. One of the most characteristic symptoms of this is the professional man, himself migrating to recapture his constituency after a vain effort to maintain in some Southern corner what for years back seemed an established living and clientele. The clergyman following his errant flock, the physician or lawyer trailing his clients, supply the true clues. In a real sense it is the rank and file who are leading, and the leaders who are following. A transformed and transforming psychology permeates the masses.

When the racial leaders of twenty years ago spoke of developing race-pride and stimulating race-consciousness, and of the desirability of race solidarity, they could not in any accurate degree have anticipated the abrupt feeling that has surged up and now pervades the awakened centers. Some of the recognized Negro leaders and a powerful section of white opinion identified with "race work" of the older order have indeed attempted to discount this feeling as a "passing phase," an attack of "race nerves" so to speak, an "aftermath of the war," and the like. It has not abated, however, if we are to gauge by the present tone and temper of the Negro press, or by the shift in popular support from the officially recognized and orthodox spokesmen to those of the independent, popular, and often radical type who are unmistakable symptoms of a new order. It is a social disservice to blunt the fact that the Negro of the Northern centers has reached a stage where tutelage, even of the most interested and well-intentioned sort, must give place to new relationships, where positive self-direction must be reckoned with in ever increasing measure. The American mind must reckon with a fundamentally changed Negro.

The Negro too, for his part, has idols of the tribe to smash. If on the one hand the white man has erred in making the Negro appear to be that which would excuse or extenuate his treatment of him, the Negro, in turn, has too often unnecessarily excused himself because of the way he has been treated. The intelligent Negro of to-day is resolved not to make discrimination an extenuation for his shortcomings in performance, individual or collective; he is trying to hold himself at par, neither inflated by sentimental allowances nor depreciated by current social discounts. For this he must know himself and be known for precisely what he is, and for that reason he welcomes the new scientific rather than the old sentimental interest. Sentimental interest in the Negro has ebbed. We used to lament this as the falling off of our friends; now we rejoice and pray to be delivered both from self-pity and condescension. The mind of each racial group has had a bitter weaning, apathy or hatred on one side matching disillusionment or resentement on the other; but they face each other to-day with the possibility at least of entirely new mutual attitudes.

It does not follow that if the Negro were better known, he would be better liked or better treated. But mutual understanding is basic for any subsequent coöperation and adjustment. The effort toward this will at least have the effect of remedying in large part what has been the most unsatisfactory feature of our present stage of race relationships in America, namely the fact that the more intelligent and representative elements of the two race groups have at so many points got quite out of vital touch with one another.

The fiction is that the life of the races is separate, and increasingly so. The fact is that they have touched too closely at the unfavorable and too lightly at the favorable levels.

While inter-racial councils have sprung up in the South, drawing on forward elements of both races, in the Northern cities manual laborers may brush elbows in their everyday work, but the community and business leaders have experienced no such interplay or far too little of it. These segments must achieve contact or the race situation in America becomes desperate. Fortunately this is happening. There is a growing realization that in social effort the co-operative basis must supplant long-distance philanthropy, and that the only safeguard for mass relations in the future must be provided in the carefully maintained contacts of the enlightened minorities of both race groups. In the intellectual realm a renewed and keen curiosity is replacing the recent apathy; the Negro is being carefully studied, not just talked about and discussed. In art and letters, instead of being wholly caricatured, he is being seriously portrayed and painted.

To all of this the New Negro is keenly responsive as an augury of a new democracy in American culture. He is contributing his share to the new social understanding. But the desire to be understood would never in itself have been sufficient to have opened so completely the protectively closed portals of the thinking Negro's mind. There is still too much possibility of being snubbed or patronized for that. It was rather the necessity for fuller, truer self-expression, the realization of the unwisdom of allowing social discrimination to segregate him mentally, and a counter-attitude to cramp and fetter his own living — and so the "spite-wall" that the intellectuals built over the "color-line" has happily been taken down. Much of this reopening of intellectual contact has centered in New York and has been richly fruitful not merely in the enlarging of personal experience, but in the definite enrichment of American art and letters and in the clarifying of our common vision of the social tasks ahead.

The particular significance in the re-establishment of contact between the more advanced and representative classes is that it promises to offset some of the unfavorable reactions of the past, or at least to re-surface race contacts somewhat for the future. Subtly the conditions that are molding a New Negro are molding a new American attitude.

However, this new phrase of things is delicate; it will call for less charity but more justice; less help, but infinitely closer understanding. This is indeed a critical stage of race relationships because of the likelihood, if the new temper is not understood, of engendering sharp group antagonism and a second crop of more calculated prejudice. In some quarters, it has already done so. Having weaned the Negro, public opinion cannot continue to paternalize. The Negro to-day is inevitably moving forward under the control largely of his own objectives. What are these objectives? Those of his outer life are happily already well and finally formulated, for they are none other than the ideals of American institutions and democracy. Those of his inner life are yet in process of formation, for the new psychology at present is more of a consensus of feeling than of opinion, of attitude rather than of program. Still some points seem to have crystallized.

Up to the present one may adequately describe the Negro's "inner objectives" as an attempt to repair a damaged group psychology and reshape a warped social perspective. Their realization has required a new mentality for the American Negro. And as it matures we begin to see its effects; at first, negative, iconoclastic, and then positive and constructive. In this new group psychology we note the lapse of sentimental appeal, then the development of a more positive self-respect and self-reliance; the repudiation of social dependence, and then the gradual recovery from hyper-sensitiveness and "touchy" nerves, the repudiation of the double standard of judgment with its special philanthropic allowances and then the sturdier desire for objective and scientific appraisal; and finally the rise from social disillusionment to race pride, from the sense of social debt to the responsibilities of social contribution, and offsetting the necessary working and commonsense acceptance of restricted conditions, the belief in ultimate esteem and recognition. Therefore the Negro to-day wishes to be known for what he is, even in his faults and shortcomings, and scorns a craven and precarious survival at the price of seeming to be what he is not. He resents being spoken of as a social ward or minor, even by his own, and to being regarded a chronic patient for the sociological clinic, the sick man of American Democracy. For the same reasons, he himself is through with those social nostrums and panaceas, the so-called "solutions" of his "problem," with which he and the country have been so liberally dosed in the past. Religion, freedom, education, money—in turn, he has ardently hoped for and peculiarly trusted these things; he still believes in them, but not in blind trust that they alone will solve his life-problems.

Each generation, however, will have its creed, and that of the present is the belief in the efficacy of collective effort, in race co-operation. This deep feeling of race is at present the mainspring of Negro life. It seems to be the outcome of the reaction to proscription and prejudice; an attempt, fairly successful on the whole, to convert a defensive into an offensive position, a handicap into an incentive. It is radical in tone, but not in purpose and only the most stupid forms of opposition, misunderstanding or persecution could make it otherwise. Of course, the thinking Negro has shifted a little toward the left with the world-trend, and there is an increasing group who affiliate with radical and liberal movements. But fundamentally for the present the Negro is radical on race matters, conservative on others, in other words, a "forced radical," a social protestant rather than a genuine radical. Yet under further pressure and injustice iconoclastic thought and motives will inevitably increase. Harlem's quixotic radicalisms call for their ounce of democracy to-day lest to-morrow they be beyond cure.

The Negro mind reaches out as yet to nothing but American wants, American ideas. But this forced attempt to build his Americanism on race values is a unique social experiment, and its ultimate success is impossible except through the fullest sharing of American culture and institutions. There should be no delusion about this. American nerves in sections unstrung with race hysteria are often fed the opiate that the trend of Negro advance is wholly separatist, and that the effect of its operation will be to encyst the Negro as a benign foreign body in the body politic. This cannot be—even if it were desirable. The racialism of the Negro is no limitation or reservation with respect to American life; it is only a constructive effort to build the obstructions in the stream of his progress into an efficient dam of social energy and power. Democracy itself is obstructed and stagnated to the extent that any of its channels are closed. Indeed they cannot be selectively closed. So the choice is not between one way for the Negro and another way for the rest, but between American institutions frustrated on the one hand and American ideals progressively fulfilled and realized on the other.

There is, of course, a warrantably comfortable feeling in being on the right side of the country's professed ideals. We realize that we cannot be undone without America's undoing. It is within the gamut of this attitude that the thinking Negro faces America, but with variations of mood that are if anything more significant than the attitude itself. Sometimes we have it taken with the defiant ironic challenge of McKay:

Mine is the future grinding down to-day
Like a great landslip moving to the sea,
Bearing its freight of débris far away
Where the green hungry waters restlessly
Heave mammoth pyramids, and break and roar
Their eerie challenge to the crumbling shore.

Sometimes, perhaps more frequently as yet, it is taken in the fervent and almost filial appeal and counsel of Weldon Johnson's:

O Southland, dear Southland!
Then why do you still cling
To an idle age and a musty page,
To a dead and useless thing?

But between defiance and appeal, midway almost between cynicism and hope, the prevailing mind stands in the mood of the same author's *To America,* an attitude of sober query and stoical challenge:

How would you have us, as we are?
Or sinking 'neath the load we bear,
Our eyes fixed forward on a star,
Or gazing empty at despair?
Rising or falling? Men or things?
With dragging pace or footsteps fleet?
Strong, willing sinews in your wings,
Or tightening chains about your feet?

More and more, however, an intelligent realization of the great discrepancy between the American social creed and the American social practice forces upon the Negro the taking of the moral advantage that is his. Only the steadying and sobering effect of a truly characteristic gentleness of spirit prevents the rapid rise of a definite cynicism and counter-hate and a defiant superiority feeling. Human as this reaction would be, the majority still deprecate its advent, and would gladly see it forestalled by the speedy amelioration of its causes. We wish our race pride to be a healthier, more positive achievement than a feeling based upon a realization of the shortcomings of others. But all paths toward the attainment of a sound social attitude have been difficult; only a relatively few enlightened minds have been able as the phrase puts it "to rise above" prejudice. The ordinary man has had until recently only a hard choice between the alternatives of supine and humiliating submission and stimulating but hurtful counter-prejudice. Fortunately from some inner, desperate resourcefulness has recently sprung up the simple expedient of fighting prejudice by mental passive resistance, in other words by trying to ignore it. For the few, this manna may perhaps be effective, but the masses cannot thrive upon it.

Fortunately there are constructive channels opening out into which the balked social feelings of the American Negro can flow freely.

Without them there would be much more pressure and danger than there is. These compensating interests are racial but in a new and enlarged way. One is the consciousness of acting as the advance-guard of the African peoples in their contact with Twentieth Century civilization; the other, the sense of a mission of rehabilitating the race in world esteem from that loss of prestige for which the fate and conditions of slavery have so largely been responsible. Harlem, as we shall see, is the center of both these movements; she is the home of the Negro's "Zionism." The pulse of the Negro world has begun to beat in Harlem. A Negro newspaper carrying news material in English, French and Spanish, gathered from all quarters of America, the West Indies and Africa has maintained itself in Harlem for over five years. Two important magazines, both edited from New York, maintain their news and circulation consistently on a cosmopolitan scale. Under American auspices and backing, three pan-African congresses have been held abroad for the discussion of common interests, colonial questions and the future co-operative development of Africa. In terms of the race question as a world problem, the Negro mind has leapt, so to speak, upon the parapets of prejudice and extended its cramped horizons. In so doing it has linked up with the growing group consciousness of the dark-peoples and gradually learning their common interests. As one of our writers has recently put it: "It is imperative that we understand the white world in its relations to the non-white world." As with the Jew, persecution is making the Negro international.

As a world phenomenon this wider race consciousness is a different thing from the much asserted rising tide of color. Its inevitable causes are not of our making. The consequences are not necessarily damaging to the best interests of civilization. Whether it actually brings into being new Armadas of conflict or argosies of cultural exchange and enlightenment can only be decided by the attitude of the dominant races in an era of critical change. With the American Negro, his new internationalism is primarily an effort to recapture contact with the scattered peoples of African derivation. Garveyism[1] may be a transient, if spectacular, phenomenon, but the possible rôle of the

[1] WHAT WE BELIEVE

The Universal Negro Improvement Association advocates the uniting and blending of all Negroes into one strong, healthy race. It is against miscegenation and race suicide.

It believes that the Negro race is as good as any other, and therefore should be as proud of itself as others are.

It believes in the purity of the Negro race and the purity of the white race.

It is against rich blacks marrying poor whites.

It is against rich or poor whites taking advantages of Negro women.

It believes in the spiritual Fatherhood of God and the Brotherhood of Man.

It believes in the social and political physical separation of all peoples to the extent that they promote their own ideals and civilization, with the privilege of trading and doing business with each other. It believes in the promotion of a strong and powerful Negro nation in Africa.

It believes in the rights of all men.

UNIVERSAL NEGRO IMPROVEMENT ASSOCIATION.

MARCUS GARVEY, President-General.

January 1, 1924.

American Negro in the future development of Africa is one of the most constructive and universally helpful missions that any modern people can lay claim to.

Constructive participation in such causes cannot help giving the Negro valuable group incentives, as well as increased prestige at home and abroad. Our greatest rehabilitation may possibly come through such channels, but for the present, more immediate hope rests in the revaluation by white and black alike of the Negro in terms of his artistic endowments and cultural contributions, past and prospective. It must be increasingly recognized that the Negro has already made very substantial contributions, not only in his folk-art, music especially, which has always found appreciation, but in larger, though humbler and less acknowledged ways. For generations the Negro has been the peasant matrix of the section of America which has most undervalued him, and here he has contributed not only materially in labor and in social patience, but spiritually as well. The South has unconsciously absorbed the gift of his folk-temperament. In less than half a generation it will be easier to recognize this, but the fact remains that a leaven of humor, sentiment, imagination and tropic nonchalance has gone into the making of the South from a humble, unacknowledged source. A second crop of the Negro's gifts promises still more largely. He now becomes a conscious contributor and lays aside the status of a beneficiary and ward for that of a collaborator and participant in American civilization. The great social gain in this is the releasing of our talented group from the arid fields of controversy and debate to the productive fields of creative expression. The especially cultural recognition they win should in turn prove the key to that revaluation of the Negro which must precede or accompany any considerable further betterment of race relationships. But whatever the general effect, the present generation will have added the motives of self-expression and spiritual development to the old and still unfinished task of making material headway and progress. No one who understandingly faces the situation with its substantial accomplishment or views the new scene with its still more abundant promise can be entirely without hope. And certainly, if in our lifetime the Negro should not be able to celebrate his full initiation into American democracy, he can at least, on the warrant of these things, celebrate the attainment of a significant and satisfying new phase of group development, and with a spiritual Coming of Age.

The Black Muslims as a Protest Movement

C. Eric Lincoln

The social movement called the "Black Muslims" is symptomatic of the anxiety and unrest which characterizes the contemporary world situation. It is not an isolated phenomenon; for it has its counterparts in Asia, in Africa, in South America, in Europe, and wherever the peoples of the world are striving for a realignment of power and position. Such conditions of social anxiety generally follow in the wake of major disturbances in the power equilibrium, or in anticipation of such disturbances. Wars ("hot" or "cold"), major political changes, in short, whatever is perceived as a threat to the continued existence of the group, or the values without which existence would be interpreted (by the group) as meaningless, contributes to a condition of anxiety which may well be reflected in various forms of conflict—of which the protest movement is one.

We may restate our thesis in another way: Whenever there is an actual or a felt discrepancy in the power relations of discrete systems or subsystems, a condition of social anxiety will emerge.

A protest movement is an expression of the pervasive anxiety and discontent of a group in negative reaction to what is perceived as a discrepancy of power. Power is the control over decisions. The protest movement is a reaction protesting that control, or the character of its expression.

Conflict may also derive from a persistent inequity in the distribution of scarce values within a society. By scarce values I mean such tangibles as jobs, food, houses, and recreational facilities (*resource scarcity*); and such intangibles as status, recognition, respect, and acceptance (*position scarcity*).[1]

Such conflict may exist at one of several possible levels: It may be (1) *latent,* with the subordinated group unorganized in the recognized presence of a vastly superior power. The conflict may be (2) *nascent,* a situation in which an organization for conflict is in existence or under development, but the conflict has not yet become overt. Again, conflict may be (3) *ritualized*

[1] " 'Resource scarcity' is a condition in which the supply of desired objects (or states of affairs) is limited so that parties may not have *all* they want of anything." " 'Position scarity' is a condition in which . . . a role cannot be simultaneously occupied or performed by two or more actors, and different prescribed behavior cannot be carried out simultaneously." Raymond W. Mack and Richard C. Snyder, "The Analysis of Social Conflict–Toward an Overview and Synthesis," *Conflict Resolution,* I, No. 2 (1957), 218.

From Arnold M. Rose, ed., *Assuring Freedom to the Free* (Detroit: Wayne State University Press, 1964), pp. 220-240.

by the contending parties, thereby assuming a nonviolent expression. Very often conflict is (4) *suppressed,* by proscription of the organizations of the subordinated group, or by force or the threat of force. In extreme circumstances conflict becomes (5) *violent,* resulting in the destruction of life and property.[2]

The Black Muslims are a symbol and a product of social conflict. They represent a point at the extreme edge of a spectrum of protest organizations and movements which involves, directly or indirectly, probably every Negro in America. The spectrum of protest begins on the near side with the conservative churches, then shades progressively into the relatively more militant congregations, the Urban League, the NAACP, the SCLC, the SNCC, CORE, and finally the unknown number of black nationalist organizations of which the Black Muslim movement is the largest and the best known. The organizations mentioned do not exhaust the roster of protest by any means. Some of the protest movements have sizeable memberships in spite of their amorphous character. Some have no more than ten or twelve members. Some do not even have names.

But almost every church, every social club, sorority, or fraternity, every business or civic association doubles as a protest organization. The effort is total, or very nearly total. In some cities the protest membership is quite fluid, with individuals moving freely from group to group within a defined range as they become more activist-oriented, or perhaps less certain of the final efficacy of the action groups. The wide range of affiliative possibilities is both functional and dyfunctional to the protest interests. Because there are many organizations, there is greater opportunity for a wider variety of personal expression than was possible when the Urban League and the NAACP had the field to themselves. However, the supply of leadership material has not kept pace with the proliferation of movements and organizations. The most effective leadership remains concentrated in a few organizations, while the energies and enthusiasms of a good number of the lesser-known protest groups are dissipated for want of planning and direction. Theirs is an inarticulate protest—unknown and ineffective.

The Black Muslims are among the best organized and most articulate of the protest movements. In terms of their immediate internal objectives, they have a highly effective leadership, some of which has been recruited from the Christian churches and retrained by Elijah Muhammad to serve the cause of Black Islam. Their newspapers and magazines are superior in layout and technical quality to much of the Negro press; and their financial support of the movement is probably higher in proportion to income than that of any similar group. Yet, the Black Muslims are not generally acceptable to the spirit of protest which has won universal respect and frequent admiration for some other members of the Negro's spectrum of protest. To understand why this is

[2] See St. Clair Drake, "Some Observations on Interethnic Conflict as One Type of Intergroup Conflict," *op. cit.*, p. 162.

so, it will be fruitful to offer some analysis of the circumstances out of which the movement was born, the character of its membership, and the nature of its goal.

The psychological heritage of the Black Muslim movement, in common with that of all other Negro protest organizations, is at least as old as the institution of slavery in America. Protest has been a distinctive although frequently a subdued thread widely distributed across the whole fabric of white-black relations throughout the history of white and Negro contact in America. The successive roles of masters and bondsmen, masters and slaves, white men and freedmen, majority and minority groups, have been successive arrangements of hegemony and subordination in which the Negro's role *vis à vis* that of the white man has not changed. From time to time, especially since the Second World War, there have been varying degrees of adjustment *within the system of arrangements,* but the power relationship has remained constant. Hence, the capacity of Negroes to affect decisions relating to themselves and the system of values they hold to be important is not appreciable.

Even the Negro's limited capacity to affect decisions and produce change depends primarily upon the conscience and the convenience of the white man, rather than upon any existing corpus of power possessed by Negroes. Indeed, it is unlikely that the Negro will ever have a dependable share in the control of the decision-making apparatus of his country until he either controls a significant segment of the economy, or a much larger percentage of the vote than he does at present. His inordinate dependence upon "protest" derives precisely from his failure to achieve the more dependable protection for his interests that comes from sharing the white man's power rather than appealing to the white man's conscience.

A protest movement is an aggressive expression of a subordinated group. It is the organization of the resources of the subordinated group to resist the coercive power of the dominant group, or to challenge the morality or the justice of the expression of that power. The Negro did not wait until he was delivered in America to begin his protestation of the white man's concept of the black man's "place" in the caste system to be established here. Available records show that no fewer than fifty-five slave revolts occurred at sea between 1700 and 1845. During the height of the slave period—the two hundred years from 1664 to 1864, there are recorded accounts of at least 109 slave insurrections which occurred within the continental United States. Since it was customary to suppress all news and information concerning revolts lest they become infectious, it is reasonable to assume that the reported cases were of some magnitude, that very many cases were not reported, and that some cases which were reported have not yet been made available to research.

Protest was not limited to armed insurrection. The rate of infanticide was high. Suicide became a problem of such magnitude as to require the slave owners to devise "the strongest argument possible," (supported by religious and social taboos) to reduce the rate of self-destruction. Sabotage of livestock, machinery, and agricultural produce was not unknown. "Taking" (from the white man, as distinct from "stealing" from each other) was routine. Running away was a form of protest so common as to have been considered a disease. Southern physicians described its symptoms in the journals of the period and gave it the name monomania—"a disease [it was said] to which the Negro is peculiarly subject."[3]

As slavery became increasingly profitable, the slavocracy became concerned to offer a moral justification for its peculiar institution. At the same time, it sought to inculcate the illiterate slaves (as it sought later to indoctrinate the freedmen and their abolitionist friends), with an image of the Negro shrewdly designed to discourage protest and to encourage resignation and accommodation. This was the "Myth of the Magnolias," so called because it was usually accompanied by a fantasy of banjo-strumming darkies lounging peacefully under the sweet-scented magnolias behind the big house—happy and contented in their station, and forever loyal to the kindhearted master and his arrangements for their mutual felicities. The Magnolia myth explained the Negro's condition in terms of "his *natural docility,* his *instinctive servility,* and his *inherent imbecility."* It alleged that the Negro's "docile nature" led to his willing acceptance of his condition of bondage, and that his "instinctive servility" made him an ideal slave—a being equipped psychologically to submit his will completely to that of another; who sensed his own inferiority, and who willed that his body be at the complete disposal of the more sophisticated will of his master. His alleged "imbecility" derived, it was argued, from an inherent incapacity to be creative, or to learn at a level beyond the simple abilities of a child. This was a principal intent of the Magnolia myth—to perpetuate an image of the Negro as being inherently intellectually inferior, and therefore incapable of mastering the complex requirements of adult citizenship and self-determination. The Negro was a child who could never grow up. He would never be "ready." This was the image he was required to accept for himself. This was the image the world was asked to accept.

The historians, the novelists, the politicians, and a varied assortment of other myth-makers have done America a great disservice. Each repetition of the myth makes it more difficult for those segments of the white majority who believe it, to understand the behavior of Negroes; and each repetition of the myth increases the determination of the Negro minority to belie it. Both science and history have discredited the Magnolia Myth, but the protest movements provide the most dramatic refutation. There are, for example, no docile Muslims. There are no servile students participating in the sit-ins. And considering its success before our highest tribunal, it is hard to believe that the legal staff of the NAACP is a council of imbeciles.

[3] See Melville J. Herskovits, *The Myth of the Negro Past* (Boston: Beacon Press, 1941), pp. 86-109.

The Magnolia Myth with local modifications remains a pervasive influence in our society. Our information media have done little to refute it. The editors of the texts we use to educate our children have done even less. It has remained then to the Negro to destroy the myth himself. The Black Muslims have gone a step further and have created for themselves a counter-myth, *the myth of black supremacy.*

The Black Muslims movement had its beginning in the black ghetto of Detroit. The time was 1930. It was the first year of the Great Depression—a time of hunger, confusion, disillusionment, despair, and discontent. It was a period of wide spread fear and anxiety. Between 1900 and 1930 two-and-a-quarter-million Negroes left the farms and plantations of the South. Most of them emigrated to selected urban areas of the North—New York, Philadelphia, Chicago, and Detroit being among the most popular destinations. The Negro population of Detroit, for example, increased 611 per cent during the ten years of 1910 to 1920. During the same period, the total Negro population in the North increased from a mere 75,000 to 300,000, an increase of 400 per cent.

Floods, crop failures, boll weevils, and the revival of the Ku Klux Klan all served to hasten the Negro's departure from the South. One hundred Negroes were lynched during the first year of the twentieth century. By the outbreak of the First World War in 1914, the number stood at 1,100. When the war was over, the practice was resumed—28 Negroes being burned alive between 1918 and 1921. Scores of other were hanged, dragged behind automobiles, shot, drowned, or hacked to death.

The Negroes who left the South were temporarily welcomed in the North, although the congenialities of the North have always been of a most impersonal sort. Many industries sent agents into the South to lure the Negroes north with promises of good jobs. But the Negro was soon to find that it was his labor, not his presence, that was wanted. It was a common practice for the agents to purchase tickets for whole families and to move them *en masse* for resettlement in the great industrial cities. The war had drained away the white manpower needed to build the ships, work the steel, pack the meat, and man the machines; and it had also cut off the normal supply of immigrant labor from Europe.

After the war was over, the Negro's welcome wore thin. It became increasingly hard for Negroes to get jobs except as strike-breakers. Soon there were not enough jobs to go around, and thousands of Negroes were fired and replaced with white men. There was not enough housing, and most Negroes were crowded into the black ghettos in the most deteriorated part of the inner city. Landlords and law-enforcement agencies alike were unsympathetic. But still the Negroes came out of the South. Few had skills; many were illiterate. All were filled with hope for something better than what they had left. Soon there was hunger and crime and delinquency—and trouble with the police.

The bright promise of the North had failed. Hope turned to desperation. In desperation is the onset of anxiety.

It is an interesting historical phenomenon that when a people reach the precipice of despair, there is so often waiting in the wings a savior—a messiah to snatch them back from the edge of the abyss. So it was that in Detroit there appeared in the black ghetto a mysterious Mullah who called himself W. D. Farad Muhammad. He had come, he told the handful of Negroes who gathered to hear him, from the holy city of Mecca. His mission, as he described it, was "to wake the 'Dead Nation in the West',[4] to teach [them] the truth about the white man, and to prepare [them] for the Armageddon." The Armageddon? What did this apocalyptic concept have to do with the problems of the Negro in America? Farad was explicit on the point: In the Book of Revelation it is promised that there will be a final battle between good and evil, and that this decisive battle will take place at Har-Magedon, "the Mountain of Megiddo," in the Great Plain of Esdraelon in Asia Minor.[5] But the Bible has a cryptic message for the initiated of Black Islam (even as it has for more familiar sects). The forces of "good and evil" are the forces of "black and white." "The Valley of Esdraelon" symbolizes "the Wilderness of North America." The Battle of Armageddon is to be the Black Man's final confrontation of the race which has so long oppressed him.

At first Farad (who was at the time thought to be a prophet, but who was after his departure recognized as Allah himself) met from house to house with small groups of Negroes. He went about his mission as unobtrusively as possible, listening to the problems of the destitute Negroes, sharing whatever they had to offer him. A contemporary convert recalls his *modus operandi*:

> He came first to our house selling raincoats, and afterwards silks. In this way he could get into the people's houses. . . . If we asked him to eat with us, he would eat whatever we had on the table, but after the meal he began to talk. . . .[6]

What he had to say must have been electrifying. Another Muslim describes his first encounter with the Prophet as follows:

> Up to that time I always went to the Baptist church. After I heard that sermon from the Prophet, I was turned around completely. When I went home and heard that dinner was ready, I said: "I don't want any dinner, I just want to go back to the meetings." I wouldn't eat my meals but I [went] back that night and I [went] to every meeting after that. . . . That changed everything for me.[7]

The fame of the Prophet spread and he soon established in Detroit the first of the Temples of Islam. As his following increased he grew more bold in his

[4] I.e., American Negroes.

[5] "Armageddon" is Greek transliteration from the Hebrew "Har-Magedon."

[6] Eradmann Beynon, "The Voodoo Cult Among Negro Migrants in Detroit," *The American Journal of Sociology*, XLIII (July 1937-May 1938), 895.

[7] *Ibid*, p. 896.

attacks upon the habits and the culture symbols the Negroes had always taken for granted. In the first place, he taught his followers that they were not "Negroes," but "Black Men." The word "Negro" was alleged to be an invention of the white man designed to identify his victims better and to separate them from their Asian and African brothers. Further, the so-called Negro was not an American, but an "Asiatic," for his forefathers had been stolen from the Afro-Asian continent by the white slavemasters who came in the name of Jesus. Christianity, the Prophet taught, was a white man's religion, a contrivance designed for the enslavement of nonwhite peoples. Wherever Christianity has gone, he declared, men have lost their liberty and their freedom. Islam was declared to be "the natural religion of the Black Man." Only in Islam could the so-called Negroes find freedom, justice, and equality.

Little by little the Prophet began to enlighten these disillusioned migrants from the South about their true history and their place in the future. Black Man was the "Original Man," he taught. On the continent of Afro-Asia black civilizations flourished "long before the white man stood up on his hind legs and crept out of the caves of Europe." Further, the white man was pictured as "a devil by nature." He is, the Prophet taught, the physical embodiment of the principle of evil, and he is incapable of doing good. Further, said Farad, "the white man is the eternal adversary of the one true God whose right and proper name is Allah."

By "tricknology" the blue-eyed devils had enslaved the Black man, the chosen people of Allah. The devils had taken away the slaves' native language (which was Arabic), and forced them to speak a foreign tongue. The white devils had taken away their names (i.e. their identity), and given them European names (which are to be hated as badges of slavery). Above all, the cruel slavemasters took away their natural religion (which is Islam) and made them worship a blue-eyed Jesus with blond hair, telling them that this was their God.

The so-called Negroes, although unknown to themselves, comprised "The Nation of Islam in the West." They had been brainwashed and given a false image of themselves by their white teachers, especially the Christian preachers who lulled them into submission by promising them a home "over Jordan" when they would no longer hew the wood and draw the water for the white man's comfort.

"The wheel must turn," the Prophet insisted. The Nation of Islam had a manifest destiny. The Armageddon must come. It would come as soon as the Black Man in America learned who he himself was, and accepted the truth about the white man, which the Prophet had been sent to declare.

Not all of Farad's energies were spent in attacking the white man. He taught his followers cleanliness and thrift. He persuaded them to give up liquor and such "unclean" foods as pork, cornbread, peas, possums, and catfish, bidding them to separate themselves from the habits they acquired in slavery. He established a school where homemaking, Negro history, Arabic, and other subjects of interest to the Muslims were taught. He demanded that his followers be clean at all times, bathing at least once each day. He taught them to give an honest day's work for an honest day's pay. He taught them to be respectful of others, and above all, to respect themselves. They must obey "all constituted authority," but they must require an eye for an eye and a tooth for a tooth. The *lex talionis* was the law of survival.

The Prophet's first appearance in Detroit is dated as July 4, 1930, and no one remembers seeing him after June 30, 1934. There are many legends, but no authentic information on where he came from, or where he went. But four years of preaching left a legacy of good and evil for eight thousand Negroes who had come to call themselves Muslims.

In the troubled times of the early 1930's, men and women everywhere were looking for some panacea to save them from the desperate circumstances of the Depression. Large numbers of people found that they could not cope rationally with the excruciating anxiety—the uncertainties with which they were confronted from day to day. Some escapists leaped from the roof-tops of the very buildings which were symbols of more stable times. Some clairvoyants, who thought they could discern the wave of the future in Marxist philosophy, found their panacea in the Communist party. The Negro's escapism tended to be of a more practical nature. Instead of taking the long route to heaven, he built himself "heavens" here on earth in the cults of Father Divine and Daddy Grace.

The followers of Farad were both escapists and clairvoyants. Farad himself was the messiah who had come to lead the so-called Negroes into the millennium which was to follow the Battle of Armageddon. He was the Prophet who had foreseen and foretold the Golden Age that would be theirs when the Black Nation in the West had thrown off the yoke of the white slavemasters. But Farad had disappeared.

The Prophet had not left himself without a witness. Very early in his brief ministry in Detroit he had attracted the admiration and the loyalty of a young Negro from the town of Sanderville, Georgia. Elijah Poole, son of a Baptist minister, was already embittered by the harshness of race relations in the South when he left Georgia and migrated to Detroit with his family in the early 1920's. In Detroit, his disillusionment with the "promised land" was almost immediate, for he soon discovered that the limitations which prescribed his place in the North differed only in degree from the familiar pattern of circumscription in the South. For a time, better jobs were available in the North, but Poole was soon to discover that the job security operated on a racial basis. Housing was more strictly segregated than in the South, and living conditions in the black ghetto were often worse than they had been in the sharecropper's cabin. The lynchings in the South had their counterparts in the race riots of the North. There seemed to exist a universal conspiracy to make life in America as untenable as possible for Negroes.

The belittling paternalism of the South had been replaced by the cold indifference of the North, and Elijah Poole found himself and his family with no better chance of assimilation in the great "melting pot" of the North than he had left in the South. As a matter of fact, his daily contact with foreign-born elements speaking in strange "un-American" accents and wearing "foreign" clothes increased his feelings of isolation and resentment. He saw the jobs of Negroes taken from them and given to white men who had not fought for this country, and who in some cases had fought against it. Inevitably the Georgia-born Poole arrived at the conclusion that even in the North the color of a man's skin, not the fact of his citizenship nor the quality of his intrinsic worth, was the determining factor in all his social relationships.

Elijah was now ready for the racist doctrines of Wali Farad. From their first meeting he became the Prophet's most dedicated apostle and his chief amanuensis. Farad had identified the Black Man's oppressor in terms never before heard in the Negro community. He had exposed the white man as a devil—a *literal* devil, created on the Isle of Patmos by a mad scientist whose name was Yakub. This was the secret of the white man's power, his cruelty, *and* his vulnerability. Allah had given the devil a certain time to rule, and the time of the devil was up. *The Black Man must prepare himself for the Armageddon!* Poole was impressed. Farad had the explanation of the white man's cruelty as well as the key to his power. Eventually, Farad entrusted his mantle and his mission to Elijah. He made Poole First Minister of Islam and put the Muslim school, the training of ministers, and the highly secret FOI (the Fruit of Islam, the leadership training corps "for the coming Armageddon") under his direction. Later, Poole was sent to Chicago to found Temple No. 2, the present headquarters of the movement.

In recognition of Poole's dedicated leadership, Farad relieved him of his "slave-name" (i.e. "Poole") and honored him with the Muslim name "Muhammad." Thereafter, Farad's public appearances were progressively less frequent until the day of his final disappearance.

Under Elijah Muhammad, the new "Messenger of Islam," the movement spread from the initial temple in Detroit to almost every major city in the country where there is a sizable Negro population. In most of these cities there is a temple; in others, where the movement is less strong, there are missions. Where there are no missions there are likely to be representatives of the movement who are in contact with the Muslim leadership in nearby cities.

The black ghetto is the principal source of Muslim recruitment. There, in the dirty streets and crowded tenements where life is cheap and hope is minimal, where isolation from the common values of society and from the common privileges of citizenship is most acute, the voice of the Messenger does not fall upon deaf ears. So often, his is the only message directed to the pimps, the prostitutes, the con-men, the prisoners, the ex-cons, the alcoholics, the addicts, the unemployed whom the responsible society has forgotten. It is a voice challenging them to recover their self-respect, urging them to repudiate the white man's religion and the white man's culture, daring them to believe in black supremacy, offering them a Black God and a Black Nation, promising them that the day will come when "we will be masters . . . and we are going to treat the white man the way he should be treated,"[8] demanding of them that "if anyone comes to take advantage of you, *lay down your life!* and the Black Man will be respected all over the Planet Earth."[9]

"Never be the aggressor," the voice proclaims, "never look for trouble. But if any man molests you, may Allah bless you."[10]

"We must take things into our own hands," the Messenger insists. "We must return to the Mosaic law of an eye for an eye and a tooth for a tooth. What does it matter if 10 million of us die? There will be 7 million of us left and they will enjoy justice and freedom."[11]

Such is the challenge of Elijah Muhammad who is hailed by his ministers as "the most fearless black man in America." His followers are, with few exceptions, from America's most underprivileged class. They are denizens of the black ghetto. To them, the voice of Elijah Muhammad is a voice raised against injustice— real or imagined. Muhammad is a paladin who has taken up the cudgel against the "devil" responsible for all of their miseries and their failures. The resentments and the hostilities that breed in the ghetto are finally brought to focus upon a single object—*the white man.* Outside the black ghetto there are Muslim units in many of the state and federal prisons across the country. Here the movement finds its prison audiences to be ready made and highly receptive, for the racial character of the law-enforcement agencies, the courts and the custodial personnel, is a key factor in sharpening the Negro prisoner's resentments and his sense of persecution.

I have tried to present a developmental background for the Black Muslim movement against which we may now more profitably examine their demands as a protest group. Generally speaking, the movement has been a protest directed at the whole value-construct of the white Christian society of which the Black Muslims feel themselves (as Negroes) to be an isolated and unappreciated appendage. Hence, the burden of their protest is against their "retention" in a society where they are not wanted. This is the soft side of the "Armageddon complex" which looks to the removal of the source of their discomfiture rather than to going anywhere themselves. Mr. Muhammad teaches that "the white man's home is in Europe," and that "there will be no peace until every man is in his own country."

In a recent issue of the official Muslim newspaper, *Mr. Muhammad Speaks,* the Muslims stated their protest in the form of the following ten propositions:

[8] *Chicago's American,* February 22, 1960.

[9] See "Tensions Outside the Movement," C. Eric Lincoln, *The Black Muslims in America* (Boston: Beacon Press, 1961), pp. 135-78.

[10] *Op. cit.,* p. 5.

[11] *Chicago's American,* February 23, 1960.

1. We want freedom. We want a full and complete freedom.
2. We want justice. Equal justice under the law. We want justice applied equally to all, regardless of creed or class or color.
3. We want equality of opportunity. We want equal membership in society with the best in civilized society.
4. We want our people in America whose parents or grandparents were descendants from slaves, to be allowed to establish a separate state or territory of their own. . . .
5. We want freedom for all Believers of Islam now held in federal prisons. We want freedom for all black men and women now under death sentence in innumerable prisons in the North as well as the South.
   We want every black man and woman to have the freedom to accept or reject being separated from the slave master's children and establish a land of their own. . . .
6. We want an immediate end to the police brutality and mob attacks against the so-called Negro throughout the United States.
7. As long as we are not allowed to establish a state or territory of our own, we demand not only equal justice under the laws of the United States, but equal employment opportunities—NOW! . . . .
8. We want the government of the United States to exempt our people from ALL taxation as long as we are deprived of equal justice under the laws of the land.
9. We want equal education—but separate schools up to 16 for boys and 18 for girls on the condition that the girls be sent to women's colleges and universities. We want all black children educated, taught without hindrance or suppression.
10. We believe that intermarriage or race mixing should be prohibited. We want the religion of Islam taught without hindrance or suppression.
    These are some of the things that we, the Muslims, want for our people in North America.[12]

Some of the proposals of the Muslims are obviously unrealistic, and we need not discuss them here. Other tests and demands of the Black Muslims as stated in the foregoing propositions do not seem unreasonable. I do not know any Americans who do not "want freedom," for example. Justice under the law, equality of opportunity, and freedom of worship are all "approved values" in our society, and they find their sanctions in the American creed. Further, they are all objectives which are implicit in the programs of all other movements within the Negro spectrum of protest. What, then, are the factors which qualify the Muslim protest movement and make it unacceptable to the general American public?

The fundamental differences between the attitudes, the behavior, and the goals of the Black Muslims as compared to other Negro protest organizations may be explained in terms of their differing degrees of dissociation deriving from the unusual anxiety and frustration incident to their status in the American social arrangement. Negroes, as a caste, are *all* outside the assimilative process, and they exhibit from time to time the frustrations which are the corollaries of their marginality. However, the dissociation of the Muslim membership from the larger society, and even from the general Negro subgroup (which ordinarily seeks to identify itself with the American

[12] July 31, 1962.

mainstream), may be considered extreme. In reacting to the unique pressures of their day-to-day experiences as low-caste Negroes in a white-oriented society, the Muslims have abandoned the fundamental principles of the American creed and have substituted in its place a new system of values perceived as more consistent with the realities of their circumstances.

It is meaningless to label the Muslims as "unAmerican," for the American creed is not a legal or constitutional document against which the political loyalty of a group may be measured.[13] The American creed is a common set of beliefs and values in which all Americans have normally found consensus. It is a body of ideals, a social philosophy which affirms the basic dignity of every individual and the existence of certain inalienable rights without reference to race, creed, or color. The roots of the American creed are deep in the equalitarian doctrines of the eighteenth-century Enlightenment, Protestant Christianity and English law. For most of us, it has been the cultural matrix within which all discordant socio-political attitudes converge, and from which derives the great diversity of social and political interpretations which makes democracy possible in a society of widely variant populations.

The Black Muslims, by the nature of certain of their goals and institutions, have excepted themselves from the aegis of the American creed. The Black Muslims repudiate American citizenship in favor of a somewhat dubious membership in a mystical "Asiatic" confraternity, and they are violently opposed to Christianity, the principles of which are fundamental to our understanding of the democratic ideal. Not only do they resist assimilation and avoid interracial participation in the life of the community, but the Muslim creed assigns all nonblacks to the subhuman status of "devils" (and promises to treat them as such); the sustaining philosophy is one of black supremacy nurtured by a careful inculcation of hatred for the white man and his characteristic institutions. By their own choice the Black Muslims exclude themselves from the body of principles and the system of values within the framework of which Americans have customarily sought to negotiate their grievances.

Other groups advocate white supremacy, resist the assimilation of Negroes and others, practice hatred rather than love, yet they retain an idealistic loyalty to the principles of the American creed. The point is that although the creed is violated constantly in practice, it remains an *ideal* to which all give their asservation — in which all believe, and from which we continue to derive our laws and our moral values in spite of our failures to honor them completely.

The Black Muslim movement does not conceive itself to be in violation of the principles and values of the American creed. Rather, the movement

[13] For an excellent interpretation of the American creed see Arnold Rose, *The Negro in America* (Boston: Beacon Press, 1957), pp. 1ff.

views itself as having substituted new principles, new values, and a new creed based on a radically different interpretation of history from that expressed in the American creed. Muhammad promises a new order based on the primacy of a nation of Black Men with a manifest destiny under a Black God. His is a nation radically different from those now shaping the existing American society. In spite of the fact that the Black Muslim movement shares at some points the immediate goals of the lesser Negro protest movements, its oppugnance to traditional values limits its general acceptability as a protest organization. The action impact of the movement on the general Negro community has been negligible considering the fact that most of America's twenty million black citizens live under conditions considerably more iniquitous than those which at other times and places have been productive of the gravest social consequences. This is not to suggest that Negroes are not aware of the movement. They are. And there are important pockets of sympathy among Negroes for the Muslims as a class more oppressed than other Negro classes, and a certain covert admiration for their militant, nonaccommodative stance against the traditional aggressions of the white man.

Nevertheless, the depth of the Negro's commitment *as a class* to the democratic procedures implicit in the American creed has operated successfully to contain the Muslim movement — eliminating it as a serious threat to racial peace or national security. But the Black Muslims remain a somber symbol of the social callousness that is possible even in an equalitarian democracy. Such movements do not "just happen." The Muslims are the most insistent symptoms of the failure of this society to meet effectively the minimum needs of one-tenth of its population to find a meaningful level of participation in the significant social values most Americans take for granted.

The Muslims represent that segment of the Negro subgroup who, being deprived of traditional incentives, have finally turned to search for alternatives outside the commonly accepted value structure. They are the products of social anxiety — people who are repeatedly frustrated in their attempts to make satisfactory adjustments in a society unaware of their existence except as the faceless subjects of statistical data. As Negroes, their future was unpromising. As Muslims, theirs is a creed of futility. As Americans, the responsibility for what they are, or what they will become, is our own.

Rules of the Black Panther Party

Central Headquarters, Oakland, California

Every member of the BLACK PANTHER PARTY throughout this country of racist America must abide by these rules as functional members of this party. CENTRAL COMMITTEE members, CENTRAL STAFFS, and LOCAL STAFFS, including all captains subordinate to either national, state, and local leadership of the BLACK PANTHER PARTY will enforce these rules. Length of suspension or other disciplinary actions necessary for violation of these rules will depend on national decisions by national, state or state area, and local committees and staffs where said rule or rules of the BLACK PANTHER PARTY WERE VIOLATED.

Every member of the party must know these verbatum by heart. And apply them daily. Every member must report any violation of these rules to their leadership or they are counter-revolutionary and are also subjected to suspension by the BLACK PANTHER PARTY.

The Rules Are:

1. No party member can have narcotics or weed in his possession while doing party work.
2. Any party member found shooting narcotics will be expelled from this party.
3. No party member can be DRUNK while doing daily party work.
4. No party member will violate rules relating to office work, general meetings of the BLACK PANTHER PARTY, and meetings of the BLACK PANTHER PARTY ANYWHERE.
5. No party member will USE, POINT, or FIRE a weapon of any kind unnecessarily or accidentally at anyone.
6. No party member can join any other army force other than the BLACK LIBERATION ARMY.
7. No party member can have a weapon in his possession while DRUNK or loaded off narcotics or weed.
8. No party member will commit any crimes against other party members or BLACK people at all, and cannot steal or take from the people, not even a needle or a piece of thread.
9. When arrested BLACK PANTHER MEMBERS will give only name, address, and will sign nothing. Legal first aid must be understood by all Party members.

10. The Ten Point Program and platform of the BLACK PANTHER PARTY must be known and understood by each Party member.

11. Party Communications must be National and Local.

12. The 10-10-10-program should be known by all members and also understood by all members.

13. All Finance officers will operate under the jurisdiction of the Ministry of Finance.

14. Each person will submit a report of daily work.

15. Each Sub-Section Leader, Section Leader, Lieutenant, and Captain must submit Daily reports of work.

16. All Panthers must learn to operate and service weapons correctly.

17. All Leadership personnel who expel a member must submit this information to the Editor of the Newspaper, so that it will be published in the paper and will be known by all chapters and branches.

18. Political Education Classes are mandatory for the general membership.

19. Only office personnel assigned to respective offices each day should be there. All others are to sell papers and do Political work out in the community, including Captains, Section Leaders, etc.

20. COMMUNICATIONS — all chapters must submit weekly reports in writing to the National Headquarters.

21. All Branches must implement First Aid and/or Medical Cadres.

22. All Chapters, Branches, and components of the BLACK PANTHER PARTY must submit a monthly Financial Report to the Ministry of Finance, and also the Central Committee.

23. Everyone in a leadership position must read no less than two hours per day to keep abreast of the changing political situation.

24. No chapter or branch shall accept grants, poverty funds, money or any other aid from any government agency without contacting the National Headquarters.

25. All chapters must adhere to the policy and the ideology laid down by the CENTRAL COMMITTEE of the BLACK PANTHER PARTY.

26. All Branches must submit weekly reports in writing to their respective Chapters.

8 Points of Attention

1) Speak politely.
2) Pay fairly for what you buy.
3) Return everything you borrow.
4) Pay for anything you damage.
5) Do not hit or swear at people.
6) Do not damage property or crops of the poor, oppressed masses.
7) Do not take liberties with women.
8) If we ever have to take captives do not ill-treat them.

3 Main Rules of Discipline

1) Obey orders in all your actions.
2) Do not take a single needle or a piece of thread from the poor and oppressed masses.
3) Turn in everything captured from the attacking enemy.

II

LITERARY BACKGROUNDS

Primitive Blues and Primitive Jazz

LeRoi Jones

A slave cannot be a man. A man does not, or is not supposed to, work all of his life without recourse to the other areas of human existence. The emotional limitations that slavery must enforce are monstrous: the weight of his bondage makes impossible for the slave a great many alternatives into which the shabbiest of free men can project himself. There is not even a separate identity the ego can claim. "What are you going to be when you grow up?" "A slave."

The work song is a limited social possibility. The shouts and hollers were strident laments, more than anything. They were also chronicles, but of such a mean kind of existence that they could not assume the universality any lasting musical form must have. The work songs and later blues forms differ very profoundly not only in their form but in their lyrics and *intent*.

Oh, Lawd, I'm tired, uuh
Oh, Lawd, I'm tired, uuh
Oh, Lawd, I'm tired, uuh
Oh, Lawd, I'm tired, a dis mess.

(*repeated*)

Primitive blues-singing actually came into being because of the Civil War, in one sense. The emancipation of the slaves proposed for them a normal human existence, a humanity impossible under slavery. Of course, even after slavery the average Negro's life in America was, using the more ebullient standards of the average American white man, a shabby, barren existence. But still this was the black man's first experience of time when he could be alone. The leisure that could be extracted from even the most desolate sharecropper's shack in Mississippi was a novelty, and it served as an important catalyst for the next form blues took.

Many Negroes who were sharecroppers, or who managed to purchase one of the tiny farms that dotted the less fertile lands of the South, worked in their fields alone or with their families. The old shouts and hollers were still their accompaniment for the arduous work of clearing land, planting, or harvesting crops. But there was a solitude to this work that had never been present in the old slave times. The huge plantation fields had many slaves,

From LeRoi Jones, *Blues People: Negro Music in White America* (New York: William Morrow and Company, 1963), pp. 60-81.

and they sang together. On the smaller farms with fewer slaves where the older African forms died out quicker, the eight- and sixteen-bar "ballits," imitations of the songs of the white masters, were heard along with the shouts. Of course, there must have been lyrics to some of the songs that the slave could not wisely sing in front of his master. But the small farms and sharecroppers' plots produced not only what I think must have been a less self-conscious work song but a form of song or shout that did not necessarily have to be concerned with, or inspired by, *labor*. Each man had his own voice and his own way of shouting — his own life to sing about. The tenders of those thousands of small farms became almost identified by their individual shouts. "That's George Jones, down in Hartsville, shoutin' like that."

Along with this leisure there was also that personal freedom to conduct or ruin one's life as one saw fit. In the 1870's there were thousands of black migrant workers moving all through the South. There were also men who just moved around from place to place, not really migratory laborers, just footloose wanderers. There could come now to these ex-slaves a much fuller idea of what exactly America was. A slave on a Georgia plantation, unless he was sold or escaped, usually was born, grew to manhood, and died right in Georgia. To him, the whole of America would be Georgia, and it would have to conform strictly to what he had experienced. St. Louis, Houston, Shreveport, New Orleans, simply did not exist (and certainly not New York). But now for many Negroes there was a life of movement from farm to farm, from town to town. The limited social and emotional alternatives of the work song could no longer contain the growing experience of this country that Negroes began to respond to. Also, the entrance of Negroes into the more complicated social situation of self-reliance proposed multitudes of social and cultural problems that they never had to deal with as slaves. The music of the Negro began to reflect these social and cultural complexities and change.

Very early blues did not have the "classic" twelve-bar, three-line, AAB structure. For a while, as I mentioned before, blues-type songs utilized the structure of the early English ballad, and sometimes these songs were eight, ten, or sixteen bars. The shout as much as the African call-and-response singing dictated the form blues took. Blues issued directly out of the shout and, of course, the spiritual. The three-line structure of blues was a feature of the shout. The first two lines of the song were repeated, it would seem, while the singer was waiting for the next line to come. Or, as was characteristic of the hollers and shouts, the single line could be repeated again and again, either because the singer especially liked it, or because he could not think of another line. The repeated phrase also carries into instrumental jazz as the *riff*.

Another reason for the changes in musical form was the change of speech patterns among a great many Negroes. By now the language of America was mastered for casual use by most Negroes. While the work song or shout had only a few English words, or was composed of Africanized English words or some patois-like language that seemed more a separate language than an attempt at mastering English, early blues had already moved toward pure American lyrics (with the intent that the song be understood by other Americans). The endlessly repeated line of the shout or holler might also have been due to the relative paucity of American words the average field Negro possessed, the rhyme line being much more difficult to supply because of the actual limitation singing in American imposed. The lines came more easily as the language was mastered more completely. Blues was a kind of singing that utilized a language that was almost strictly American. It was not until the ex-slaves had mastered this language in whatever appropriation of it they made that blues began to be more evident than shouts and hollers.

The end of the almost exclusive hold of the Christian Church on the black man's leisure also resulted in a great many changes of emphasis in his music. The blues is formed out of the same social and musical fabric that the spiritual issued from, but with blues the social emphasis becomes more personal, the "Jordan" of the song much more intensely a *human* accomplishment. The end of slavery could be regarded as a Jordan, and not a metaphysical one either, although the analogy of the deliverance of the Jews and the Emancipation must have been much too cogent a point for proselytizing to be lost on the local black minister. There was a definite change of *direction* in the primitive blues. The metaphysical Jordan of life after death was beginning to be replaced by the more pragmatic Jordan of the American master: the Jordan of what the ex-slave could see vaguely as self-determination. Not that that idea or emotion hadn't been with the very first Africans who had been brought here; the difference was that the American Negro wanted some degree of self-determination where he was living. The desperation to return to Africa had begun to be replaced by another even more hopeless one. The Negro began to feel a desire to be more in this country, America, than chattel. "The sun's gonna shine in my back door someday!"

The leisure and movement allowed to Negroes after the Civil War helped to standardize the new blues form as well as spread the best verses that were made up. Although there were regional differences in the way blues began to be sung, there were also certain recurring, soon "classical," blues verses and techniques that turned up in a great many places simply because a man had been there from Georgia or Louisiana or South Carolina and shown the locals what his town or region produced.

But the thousands of black blues shouters and ballit singers who wandered throughout the South around the turn of the century moved from place to place not only because Negroes were allowed to travel after the

Civil War, but because for a great many Negroes, emancipation meant a constant desperate search for employment (although there must also have been those people who, having been released from their bondage, set out at once to see what this country was really about). Not only the migratory workers who followed the crop harvests but the young men who wanted any kind of work had to tramp all over the South in search of it. It is also a strange note that once the Negroes were free, it was always the men who had the harder time finding work. Women could always find work as domestics wherever they were. But the black man who had done agricultural labor, as most Negroes had, found it difficult to find work because the impoverished whites of the South suddenly had to pay wages to their workers. The Negro had to have wages to live: for the first time he needed money and had to enter into the fierce struggle for economic security like any other poor man in this country. Again, even the economic status of the Negro after his freedom proposed new changes for his music. "I never had to have no money befo'/And now they want it everywhere I go." The content of blues verse had become much changed from the strictly extemporized lyrics of the shouts and hollers.

It seems possible to me that some kind of graph could be set up using samplings of Negro music proper to whatever moment of the Negro's social history was selected, and that in each grouping of songs a certain frequency of reference could pretty well determine his social, economic, and psychological states at that particular period. From the neo-African slave chants through the primitive and classical blues to the scat-singing of the beboppers: all would show definite insistences of reference that would isolate each group from the others as a social entity. No slave song need speak about the slave's lack of money; no early Afro-American slave song would make reference to the Christian Church; almost no classical blues song would, or could, make direct or *positive* mention of Africa. Each phase of the Negro's music issued directly from the dictates of his social and psychological environment. Hence the black man who began after slavery to eliminate as much of the Negro culture from his life as possible became by this very act a certain kind of *Negro*. And if this certain kind of Negro still endeavored to make music, albeit with the strict provision that this music not be a Negro music, he could still not escape the final "insult" of this music being evaluated socially, psychologically, and musically as a kind of *Negro* music. The movement of the Negro into a position where he would be able to escape even this separation from the white mainstream of America is a central theme of this book.

Even with the relative formalization of secular Negro music, blues was still an extremely personal music. There were the songs extolling the merits and adventures of heroes or heroic archetypes, John Henry, Stagger Lee,

Dupree, etc., but even as the blues began to expand its references it still remained a kind of singing that told about the exploits of the singer. Heroic archetypes or cowardly archetypes were used to point up some part of the singer's life.

In come a nigger named Billy Go-helf
Coon was so mean was skeered of hisself;
Loaded wid razors an' guns, so they say,
Cause he killed a coon most every day.

And this intensely personal nature of blues-singing is also the result of what can be called the Negro's "American experience." African songs dealt, as did the songs of a great many of the preliterate or classical civilizations, with the exploits of the social unit, usually the tribe. There were songs about the gods, their works and lives, about nature and the elements, about the nature of a man's life on the earth and what he could expect after he died, but the insistence of blues verse on the life of the individual and his individual trials and successes on earth is a manifestation of the whole Western concept of man's life, and it is a development that could only be found in an American black man's music. From the American black leader's acceptance of Adam Smith "laissez faire" social inferences to some less fortunate black man's relegation to a lonely patch of useless earth in South Carolina, the weight of Western tradition, or to make it more specific and local, the weight of just what social circumstance and accident came together to produce the America that the Negro was part of, had to make itself part of his life as well. The whole concept of the *solo*, of a man singing or playing by himself, was relatively unknown in West African music.

But if the blues was a music that developed because of the Negro's adaptation to, and adoption of, America, it was also a music that developed because of the Negro's peculiar position in this country. Early blues, as it came to differ from the shout and the Afro-Christian religious music, was also perhaps the most impressive expression of the Negro's individuality within the superstructure of American society. Even though its birth and growth seems connected finally to the general movement of the mass of black Americans into the central culture of the country, blues still went back for its impetus and emotional meaning to the individual, to his completely personal life and death. Because of this, blues could remain for a long time a very fresh and singular form of expression. Though certain techniques and verses came to be standardized among blues singers, the singing itself remained as arbitrary and personal as the shout. Each man sang a different blues: the Peatie Wheatstraw blues, the Blind Lemon blues, the Blind Willie Johnson blues, etc. The music remained that personal because it began with the performers themselves, and not with formalized notions of how it was to be performed. Early blues developed as a music to be sung for *pleasure*, a casual music, and that was its strength and its weakness.

I don't want you to be no slave,
I don't want you to work all day,
I don't want you to be true,
I just want to make love to you.

Since most Negroes before and after slavery were agricultural laborers, the corn songs and arwhoolies, the shouts and hollers, issued from one kind of work. Some of the work songs, for instance, use as their measure the grunt of a man pushing a heavy weight or the blow of a hammer against a stone to provide the metrical precision and rhythmical impetus behind the singer. ("Take this hammer, uh,/ Take it to the captain, uh,/Take it to the captain, uh,/Tell him I'm gone.") Contemporary work songs, for example, songs recorded by Negro convicts working in the South — laying railroad ties, felling trees, breaking rocks, take their impetus from the work being done, and the form of the singing itself is dictated by the work. These workers for the most part do not sing blues. The labor is central to the song: not only is the recurring grunt or moan of these work songs some kind of metrical and rhythmical insistence, it is the very catalyst for the song. On one recent record, the Louisiana Folklore Society's, *Prison Work-songs* recorded in Angola, Louisiana, at the Louisiana State Penitentiary there, one song listed as *Take This Hammer* begins as that song, but lasts as that for only about three "bars" (three strokes of the hammer) and then wanders irresolutely into *Alberta, Berta,* several blues verses, and a few lines from a spiritual. The point is that the primitive blues was at once a more formal music since the three-line, twelve-bar song became rapidly standardized, and was also a more liberated music since there was literally *more* to sing about. In one's leisure one can begin to formalize a method of singing as well as find new things to sing about. (It is an interesting thought that perhaps all the music that Negroes in America have made might have been quite different if the work that they were brought here to do had been different. Suppose Negroes had been brought to this country to make vases or play basketball. How might the blues have developed then from the impetus of work songs geared to those occupations?)

Work songs and shouts were, of course, almost always *a capella.* It would have been extremely difficult for a man to pick cotton or shuck corn and play an instrument at the same time. For this reason pre-blues secular singing did not have the discipline or strict formality that a kind of singing employing instruments must have. But it is obvious from the very earliest form of the blues that instrumental accompaniment was beginning to be taken into consideration. The twelve-bar blues — the more or less final form of blues — is constructed so that each verse is of three lines, each line about four bars long. The words of the song usually occupy about one-half of each line, leaving a space of two bars for either a sung answer or an instrumental response.

It may seem strange that the formal blues should evolve *after* slavery, after so many years of bondage and exposure by the slaves to the larger Western cultural unit, into a form that is patently non-Western; the three-line verse form of the blues springs from no readily apparent Western source. But the use of instruments on a large scale was also something that happened after the Emancipation; the very possession of instruments, except those few made from African models, was rare in the early days of slavery. The stereotyped pictures that many of the apologists for the Southern way of life used as flyleaves for their numerous novels after the Civil War, depicting a happy-go-lucky black existentialist strumming merrily on his banjo while sitting on a bale of cotton, were, I'm sure, more romantic fiction than fact. The slave would hardly have had the time to sit on his master's bale of cotton during the work day, and the only instruments that were in common usage among the slaves were drums, rattles, tambourines, scrapers (the jawbone of a horse over which a piece of wood was scraped), and the like; even such an African instrument as the banjo was very scarce. The guitar was not commonly played by Negroes until much after the Civil War. An instrument like the harmonica grew in popularity among a great many Negroes simply because it took up almost no space and was so easy to carry around. But even the harmonica did not come into common use until after slavery, and certainly the possession and mastery of European instruments did not occur until much later.

When primitive or country blues did begin to be influenced by instruments, it was the guitar that had the most effect on the singers. And when the great masses of Negroes were just beginning to learn the instrument, the relatively simple chords of the country blues were probably what they learned. Conceivably, this also brought about another change: blues, a vocal music, was made to conform to an instrument's range. But, of course, the blues widened the range of the instrument, too. Blues guitar was not the same as classical or "legitimate" guitar: the strings had to make vocal sounds, to imitate the human voice and its eerie cacophonies. Perhaps the reason why the guitar was at once so popular was not only because it was much like the African instrument, the banjo (or *banjor*), but because it was an instrument that still permitted the performer to *sing*.

When the Negro finally did take up the brass instruments for strictly instrumental blues or jazz, the players still persisted in singing in the "breaks." This could be done easily in the blues tradition with the call-and-response form of blues. Even much later in the jazz tradition, not only were instruments made to sound like the human voice but a great many of the predominantly instrumental songs were still partially sung. The first great soloist of jazz, Louis Armstrong, was a formidable blues singer, as was the great jazz pianist Jelly Roll Morton. Both men sang blues almost as beautifully as they played their instruments.

The primitive blues was still very much a vocal music; the singers relied on the unpredictability and mobility of the human voice for their imaginative catalysts. But the growing use of European instruments such as brass and reeds almost precluded song, except as accompaniment or as an interlude. When Negroes began to master more and more "European" instruments and began to think musically in terms of their timbres, as opposed to, or in conjunction with, the voice, blues began to change, and the era of jazz was at hand.

"Jazz began in New Orleans and worked its way up the river to Chicago," is the announcement most investigators of mainstream popular culture are apt to make when dealing with the vague subject of jazz and its origins. And while that is certainly a rational explanation, charmingly simple, etc., it is more than likely untrue. Jazz, or purely instrumental blues, could no more have begun in one area of the country than could blues. The mass migrations of Negroes throughout the South and the general liberating effect of the Emancipation make it extremely difficult to say just exactly where and when jazz, or purely instrumental blues (with European instruments), originated. It *is* easy to point out that jazz is a music that could not have existed without blues and its various antecedents. However, jazz should not be thought of as a *successor* to blues, but as a very original music that developed out of, and was concomitant with, blues and moved off into its own path of development. One interesting point is that although jazz developed out of a kind of blues, blues in its later popular connotation came to mean *a way of playing jazz,* and by the swing era the widespread popularity of the blues singer had already been replaced by the jazz player's. By then, blues was for a great many people no longer a separate music.

Even though New Orleans cannot be thought of with any historical veracity as "the birthplace of jazz," there has been so much investigation of the jazz and earlier music characteristic there in the first part of the twentieth century, that from New Orleans conclusions may be drawn concerning the social and cultural phenomena that led to the creation of jazz. Also, the various effects of the development of this music upon Negroes in the area can be considered and certain essential analogies made.

I have mentioned Congo Square in New Orleans as a place where African Negroes in the earlier years of slavery met to play what was certainly an African music. Marshall Stearns quotes an architect, Benjamin Latrobe, who visited Congo Square in 1819:

"The music consisted of two drums and a stringed instrument. An old man sat astride of a cylindrical drum about a foot in diameter, and beat it with incredible quickness with the edge of his hand and fingers. The other drum was an open staved thing held between the knees and beaten in the same manner. . . . The most curious instrument, however, was a stringed instrument which no doubt was imported from Africa. On the top of the finger board was the rude figure of a man in a sitting posture, and two pegs behind him to which the strings were fastened. The body was a calabash . . . One, which from the color of the wood seemed new, consisted of a block cut into something of the form of a cricket bat with a long and deep mortice down the center . . . being beaten lustily on the side by a short stick. In the same orchestra was a square drum, looking like a stool . . . also a calabash with a round hole in it, the hole studded with brass nails, which was beaten by a woman with two short sticks."[1]

This kind of gathering in Congo Square was usually the only chance Negroes had to sing and play at length. And, of course, even this was supervised by the local authorities: the slaves were brought to the square and brought back by their masters. Still, the Congo Square sessions were said to have included many African songs that were supposedly banned by the whites for being part of the vodun or voodoo rites. The slaves also danced French quadrilles and sang patois ditties in addition to the more African chants that they shouted above the "great drums."

Nowhere else in the United States is the French influence so apparent as in New Orleans; it was this predominantly French culture that set the tone for the Europeanization of African slaves in the area. The mulattoes, or light-skinned Negroes, in New Orleans, who were the result usually of some less than legal union between the French masters and black slave women, even adopted the name *Creole* to distinguish themselves from the other Negroes, although this term originally meant any white settler of French or Spanish blood. The Creoles, in much the same manner as the house Negroes on plantations in other areas, adopted as much of the French culture as they could and turned their backs on the "darker" culture of their half-brothers. It is safe to assume, for instance, that there were no black Creoles dancing in Congo Square.

The black man must have been impressed not only by the words and dances of the quadrilles and minuets he learned from the French settlers of New Orleans, but by the instruments the white Creoles employed to play them. So New Orleans Negroes became interested in the tubas, clarinets, trombones, and trumpets of the white marching bands, which were also popular in New Orleans as well as in many other Southern cities. (In the time of Napoleon, the popularity of the military band soon spread from France to all the settlements in the New World influenced by French culture.) The "exotic" rhythms of the quadrilles (2/4 and 6/8) and the military marching bands (4/4) also made a great impression on the slaves, and they tried to incorporate these meters into their own music. The black Creoles, however, tried to adopt these elements of French culture completely, learning the quadrilles by rote. Still slavery and the circumstance of the Negroes' bondage played a big role in this kind of assimilation as well. Many of the Creoles were freedmen by virtue of the accident of their birth, or at

[1] *The Story of Jazz* (New York, Oxford University Press, 1956), p. 43.

least were house servants long before the Emancipation. They had direct access to European music and instruments long before the rest of the Negroes in the area.

The marching bands that were started by Negroes in imitation of the Napoleonic military marching bands of the white Creoles also fell into two distinct categories. There were the comparatively finely trained bands of the Creoles and the untutored, raw bands of the Uptown, darker New Orleans Negroes (which did not begin until well after slavery was abolished). These bands were used for all kinds of affairs; in addition to the famous funeral processions, they played for picnics, dances, boating trips, and the like. One reason for the formation of these bands was the organization of a great number of clubs and secret societies and fraternities in the Negro communities (white and black) after the Emancipation. These societies and fraternities were an important part of the Negro's life, and drained a lot of the black community away from the Christian Church, which had been the sole place the slaves could spend their leisure time. But it was not unusual for a Negro to belong to the Christian Church (in New Orleans, after the Black Codes of 1724, Negroes were only allowed to become Catholics) and to also belong to a number of secret societies. These societies still thrive today all over the country in most Negro communities, though for the most part their actual "secrecy" is the secrecy of any fraternal organization. The Masons and the Elks have claimed most urban and Northern Negroes, and the old vodun-tinged secret orders, sometimes banned by whites, have for the most part (except in the rural areas) disappeared completely.

One example of the way Negroes used European rhythms in conjunction with their own West African rhythms was the funeral processions. The march to the cemetery was played in slow, dirgelike 4/4 cadence. It was usually a spiritual that was played, but made into a kind of raw and bluesy Napoleonic military march. The band was followed by the mourners — relatives, members of the deceased's fraternal order or secret society, and well-wishers. (All night before the burial, or on as many nights as there were that intervened between the death and the burial, the mourners came into the house of the deceased to weep and wail and kiss the body. But these "wakes" or "mourning times" usually turned into house parties.) After the burial, the band, once removed some good distance from the cemetery, usually broke into the uptempo part of the march at some approximation of the 2/4 quadrille time. *Didn't He Ramble* and *When the Saints Go Marchin' In* were two of the most frequently played tunes — both transmuted religious songs. Even in this kind of march music the influence of the blues was very heavy, at least for the Uptown or "darker" brass bands — the Downtown Creole bands would have nothing to do with the "raw and raucous playing of those dark folks." The form of the Creole funerals must have differed also if the Downtown mourners were emulating their white Creole models. Certainly a great many self-respecting Creoles must have frowned on the antics the darker Negroes performed when burying a member of their community. The long period of jovial mourning, complete with banquets and dancing, was certainly outside the pale of either Catholic or Protestant religious practice. Herskovits cites these burial customs as originating in West Africa, especially among the large Dahomey tribes. (An interesting note about the New Orleans funeral is that recently, in 1955, *Ebony*, the vehicle of American middle-class aspirations, announced that when PaPa Celestin, the great New Orleans trumpet player, died, no jazz was played — "out of respect for PaPa.")

By the time the marching and brass bands were in vogue in New Orleans and some other parts of the South, Negroes had already begun to master a great many other European instruments besides the guitar and the harmonica. The trumpets, trombones, and tubas of the brass bands were played with a varying amount of skill, though when a man has learned enough about an instrument to play the music he wants to play, "skill" becomes an arbitrary consideration.The black brass bands of New Orleans around the turn of the century had certainly mastered the European brass instruments as well as the Downtown Creole bands, but by now they were simply "doing it the way they felt it." By the time the first non-marching, instrumental, blues-oriented groups started to appear in numbers, *i.e.*, the "jass" or "dirty" bands, the instrumentation was a pastiche of the brass bands and the lighter quadrille groups. In 1897, Buddy Bolden's group consisted of cornet, trombone, clarinet (the first reed instrument Negroes began to play with any frequency), violin, guitar, string bass (already an innovation over the tuba, the first "time-keeping" instrument in these bands), and drums.

The repressive "white supremacy" measures that were put into effect after the Civil War had a great deal of effect on the music of New Orleans. By 1894, there was a legislative act enforcing segregation which hit the black Creoles hardest. It also, in the long run, helped redirect their social and musical energies. Up until the time of the infamous discriminative codes, the Creoles enjoyed an autonomy of social and economic status; to a certain extent they had the same economic and social advantages as the whites. Many of them had been educated in France and also sent their children to France to be educated, where many remained. Quite a few Creole families were among the richest families in New Orleans, and still others were well-known artisans and craftsmen. In a great many cases Creoles worked side by side with whites. They also enjoyed the cultural side of eighteenth and nineteenth-century New Orleans life: Creoles had their own boxes at the opera, and they participated in all the Downtown or white parades with their own highly trained military-style marching bands. But with the segregation acts of the late nineteenth century, Creoles began to lose the jobs where they had been working with whites, and they were no longer permitted to play Downtown, neither in the homes of the rich whites nor in the military parades.

It was about this time that the darker, blues-oriented musicians from Uptown New Orleans were beginning to play their "dirty" instrumental music in saloons and dance halls, at parties, picnics, and some of the places where the older brass marching bands used to hold forth. It was still a "marchy" kind of music, but the strict 4/4 march tempo had given way to the ragged 2/4 tempo, and the timbres and tones that people like Bolden began to use were radically removed from the pure sonorities of European-style marching bands. Theirs was a much more vocal kind of playing compared to the way brass horns had been used before. Again, this seems part of a definable cycle in the response of the Negro to the cultural and social stimuli of this country. The blues moved through much the same cycle, developing out of what seemed like imitations of European music into a form (and content) that was relatively autonomous. Primitive blues is much more a Negro music than a great deal of the music it grew out of.

Miss Kemble in her diary reports hearing Negroes singing a song "while they labored" on river boats that was very much like *Coming Through the Rye*. It is quite probable that it was *Coming Through the Rye*. Most slaves in the early part of the nineteenth century could not have sung the words to the song, but could change them into: "Jenny shake her toe at me,/ Jenny gone away;/Jenny shake her toe at me,/Jenny gone away./Hurrah! Miss Susy, oh/Jenny gone away;/Hurrah! Miss Susy, oh!/Jenny gone away." Also relevant are the best of Miss Kemble's observations about Negro music — presumably their work songs, since she would hardly have observed them at any other time:

"Except the extemporaneous chants in our honor . . . I have never heard the Negroes sing any words that could be said to have any sense. To one, an extremely pretty, plaintive, and original air, there was but one line, which was repeated with a sort of wailing chorus —

> Oh! my massa told me, there's no grass in Georgia.

Upon inquiring the meaning of which, I was told it was supposed to be the lamentation of a slave from one of the more northerly states, Virginia or Carolina, where the labor of hoeing the weeds, or grass as they call it, is not nearly so severe as here, in the rice and cotton lands of Georgia. Another very pretty and pathetic tune began with words that seemed to promise something sentimental —

> Fare you well, and good-by, oh, oh!
> I'm goin' away to leave you, oh! oh!

but immediately went into nonsense verses about gentlemen in the parlor drinking wine and cordial, and ladies in the drawing room drinking tea and coffee, etc. I have heard that many of the masters and overseers on these plantations prohibit melancholy tunes or words, and encourage nothing but cheerful music and senseless words, deprecating the effect of sadder strains upon the slaves, whose peculiar musical sensibility might be expected to make them especially excitable by any songs of a plaintive character, and having any reference to their peculiar hardships."[2]

And so we have perhaps another reason why the Negro's secular music matured only after the end of slavery. The blues, as it came into its own strict form, was the most plaintive and melancholy music imaginable. And the content, the meaning, Miss Kemble searched for in vain in the work songs, was certainly quite evident in the later music.

Although the instrumental music moved toward an autonomous form only after the Emancipation, in only a few years after the beginning of the twentieth century, there was such a thing as a jazz band. And in a few more years this kind of band was throwing off most of its musical ties with the brass marching bands or the string groups of the white Creoles.

When the Creoles "of color" began to lose their Downtown jobs or found that they were no longer permitted to play for white affairs, some of them began to make the trip Uptown to sit in with their darker half-brothers. By this time, near the turn of the century, there was a marked difference in the playing and music of the Uptown and Downtown Negroes. The Creoles had received formal musical training, sometimes under the aegis of white French teachers. They had mastered the European instrumental techniques, and the music they played was European. The Uptown Negroes, who had usually learned their instruments by ear and never received formal and technical training, developed an instrumental technique and music of their own, a music that relied heavily on the non-European vocal tradition of blues. Many Creoles who had turned their backs on this "darker" tradition now began to try to learn it again.

An important idea to consider here is that jazz as it developed was predominantly a blues-based music. The blues timbre and spirit had come to jazz virtually unchanged, even though the early Negro musicians using European instruments had to learn to play them with the strict European march music as a model. The "classical" timbre of the trumpet, the timbre that Creoles imitated, was not the timbre that came into jazz. The purity of tone that the European trumpet player desired was put aside by the Negro trumpeter for the more humanly expressive sound of the voice. The brass sound came to the blues, but it was a brass sound hardly related to its European models. The rough, raw sound the black man forced out of these European instruments was a sound he had cultivated in this country for two hundred years. It was an American sound, something indigenous to a certain kind of cultural existence in this country.

Creoles like violinist Paul Domingues, when he said, "See, us Downtown people, we didn't think so much of this rough Uptown jazz until we couldn't

[2] *Op. cit.*, pp. 163-64.

make a living otherwise. . . . I don't know how they do it. But goddam, they'll do it. Can't tell you what's there on the paper, but just play the hell out of it,"[3] were expressing perhaps the basic conflict to arise regarding the way the ex-slave was to make his way in America. Adaptation or assimilation? It was not much of a problem for most Negroes in the nineteenth century, although, to be sure, there must have been quite a few who had already disappeared (culturally) into the white world. The Creoles, for instance, had already made that move, but New Orleans was a special situation. Adaptation was the Negro's way earlier; he had little choice. He had not sufficient knowledge of, or experience in, the dominant culture to become completely assimilated within it. He went along the path of least resistance, which was to fashion something out of that culture for himself, girded by the strength of the still evident African culture. The Uptown musicians made jazz in this manner. The Creoles resisted "Negro" music because they thought they had found a place within white society which would preclude their being Negroes. But they were unsuccessful in their attempt to "disappear" because the whites themselves reminded them that they were still, for all their assimilation, "coons." And this seems to me an extremely important idea since it is just this bitter insistence that has kept what can be called Negro culture a brilliant amalgam of diverse influences.

There was always a border beyond which the Negro could not go, whether musically or socially. There was always a possible limitation to any dilution or excession of cultural or spiritual references. The Negro could not ever become white and that was his strength; at some point, always, he could not participate in the dominant tenor of the white man's culture. It was at this juncture that he had to make use of other resources, whether African, subcultural, or hermetic. And it was this boundary, this no man's land, that provided the logic and beauty of his music.

[3] Alan Lomax, *Mr. Jelly Roll* (New York, Duell, Sloan & Pearce, 1950), pp. 15-16.

Negritude and Its Relevance for the American Negro Writer

Samuel W. Allen

In discussing the future direction of creative endeavor, it is least possible to be doctrinaire.[1] The creative effort appears to be in large measure a refusal to be bound, a breaking forth, a reaction to prescription. And all critical preoccupation with the future of any area of creative activity is apt to be proven vain, in error, and subject to reversal by the superior court of hindsight.

Turning, then, to negritude, we see that it has developed principally among the poets of African descent writing in the French language, including not only the poets of the African continent itself but also those of the Caribbean area, of Martinique, etc., who are also writing in French. Among these are Aimé Césaire, the late Jacques Roumain, René Dépestre, Léon Damas, Laleau, Niger and others who, remote from what they feel to be a lost homeland that exists in the nostalgic, collective memory, are more intense in their reaction to the estrangement of the African in Western society than the poets of the continent are.

In passing, we may note that this term, negritude, is unsettling to many, perhaps because it puts into the realm of the explicit that which might more comfortably remain in the area of the implicit. The Negro is denied an acceptable identity in Western culture, and the term negritude focuses and carries with it the pejorative implications of that denial. The fact that it was possible for the term to emerge in the literature is undoubtedly symbolic of the necessity of the development it represents. It is the latter with which we are principally concerned; what to call it, while important, is secondary.

The work of these poets of the Caribbean and of those of the continent—Leopold Senghor, David Diop, Birago Diop, and, among those writing in English, Efua Morgue, Dei Anang, Carey Thomas, Adeboye Babalola, has served and is serving to cast off the cultural imprint of colonial Europe; it is a type of reconnaissance in the formation of a new imaginative world free

[1] This paper was written in 1959 and, although minor revisions have been made, both its terminology and its concern reflect to some degree that period when black affirmation was still much more suspect than it is today.

Originally published in slightly different form in *The American Negro Writer and His Roots* (New York: The American Society of African Culture, 1960), pp. 8-20.

from the proscriptions of a racist West. Their creative activity reveals an effort toward a renewal of their lost organic vision of the universe, which is inextricably involved in, and as crucial as, the political and economic enfranchisement presently occurring. The African finds himself bound fast in the culture prison of the Western World, which has held him for centuries in derision and contempt; his poetic concern has been with his liberation from this prison, with the creation of a truer sense of identity, and with the establishment of his dignity as a man. This preoccupation led to the birth in the French language of the central concept of negritude, principally in the work of Leopold Senghor and Aimé Césaire. The term is not amenable to easy definition. It appears to serve in somewhat varying roles for those who employ it. It represents in one sense the Negro African poet's endeavor to recover for his race a normal self-pride, a confidence in himself shattered for centuries when the enslaver suddenly loomed in the village pathway; to recover a world in which he once again could have a sense of unashamed identity and an *un*subordinate role. Jean Paul Sartre wrote an excellent preface to Senghor's 1947 anthology of African poetry in the French language, and in this, he likened negritude to an African Eurydice, recovered by the song of Orpheus from Pluto. It is the African's lost beloved, his complete and ultimate self, his vision of the world, not the spirit of a culture in which he dwells on sufferance or which holds him in veiled and unveiled disdain. It is not simply a goal to be accomplished, but rather, more functionally, an affective disposition. In Heidegger's existentialist term, it indicates the Negro's "being-in-the-world." Senghor points out that the negritude of a poem is less the theme than the style, its characteristic manner, the intensity of its passion, its rhythmic flow or the quality of its imagery, whether he writes of a ritual dance in Dahomey, of the Brittany seacoast, or of the nature of God and man. Negritude includes the characteristic impulses, traits and habits which may be considered more markedly Negro African than white or European. It is thus something which the poet possesses in the wells of his being and simultaneously something which he is seeking to recover, to make manifest; and again it is a subjective disposition which is affirmed and which objectivizes itself in the poem.

Aimé Césaire writes:

> My négritude is not a rock, its deafness hurled against the clamor
> of the day
> My négritude is not a film of dead water on the dead eye of the
> earth
> My négritude is neither a tower nor a cathedral
> It plunges into the red flesh of the earth
> It plunges into the burning flesh of the sky
> It pierces the opaque prostration by its upright patience.

In these lines, Césaire emphasizes the dynamic quality of this concept; negritude is an act, an active becoming, a vital force patiently and stubbornly active in the earth and the sky and the elements. Amid the insufferable tensions of his estrangement, negritude is that area the poet has carved out for himself in the poem where he may live and dwell and have his true and absolute being:

> The words surpass themselves. It is indeed toward a sky and a land whose height and depth can not be troubled. It is made of the old geography. Yet there now emerges at a certain level an area curiously breathable. At the gaseous level of the solid and liquid organism, white and black, night and day.

We should note that a common reaction among Americans—tutored in a society strongly egalitarian and integrationist in avowed direction and ideal, however derelict in deed—is one of surprise that the Negro African, who above all has been the victim of racial persecution, should affirm qualities. However, a consideration of the historical circumstances giving rise to its development tends to made clear its justification, and more, its necessity. The reaction to centuries of humiliation and contempt is not one of calm objectivity. The pendulum can only gradually achieve dead center. Each age, each people has its own historical necessity. In this connection, Sartre has used Hegelian concepts, which serve well here, to describe this movement. Negritude in African poetry is an antiracist racism; it is the moment of negativity in reaction to the thesis of white supremacy. It is the antithesis in a dialectical progression which leads to an ultimate synthesis of a common humanity without racism. This is undoubtedly too neat a formula for the actual operation of the influences involved; yet it does provide a ready and roughly accurate framework for the comprehension of the conflicting tendencies at play here. We see, too, that these poets are deeply aware that man, ultimately, is man and that his race is an attribute, only, of his more basic membership in the human community. Jacques Romain gives particularly poignant testimony:

> Africa I guard your memory Africa
> you are in me as the shaft is in the wound
> as the guardian fetish in the center of the village
> make of me the stone of your sling
> of my mouth the lips of your sores
> of my knees the broken columns of your humiliation
> and yet
> I wish to be only of your race
> fellow workers of every land.

We have considered this concept, this esthetic, this rebel to analysis—negritude—confining our remarks thus far to the work of African and French West Indian writers and the role negritude has played in their development. Let us consider briefly the possible relevance of this concept to the work of the American Negro writer or, to put it differently, its validity for a writer in our cultural situation.

I think it has a role. This is not necessarily so for all of us, the writer not being a soldier marching to command. He writes, when he writes most creatively, pursuant to his own individual and most deeply felt need. The racial accident of his birth may have little or only indirect influence on the thrust of his writing, although for a black writer in America this is difficult to imagine. It is probably true also that it was not by chance that this concept, negritude, originated among the poets rather than among those working in prose. Except for certain highly imaginative works, the novelist writes within a framework of what we term reality. He must in part concern himself with Plato's shadows—with plot and setting. His characters, unlike Orphan Annie, must grow up. He is constrained to a certain degree of reasonableness. The poet has probably a greater chance to penetrate, at once without apology and without a setting of the worldly stage, to the deepest levels of his creative concern. And so, perhaps what we are saying may have greater applicability to poetry than to prose.

I think there is little disagreement that our cultural situation is substantially different from that of Amos Tutuola, of Efua Morgue of Ghana, of the Senegalese, resident of Paris since his university day, or of the Haitian or Jamaican writer. Our contact with Africa has been remote for centuries, and both the natural and the consciously directed impacts of the enslavement were to shatter the African cultural heritage. Further, the American Negro, uprooted from his homeland, has been subjected in a manner unparalleled among other people of African descent to the cultural imprint of a powerful, dominant majority in a strange and unfriendly land. The Ashanti, the Senegalese, the Yoruba were overwhelmed militarily and politically and subjected to a foreign culture; but they were on their home ground, and they retained the morale afforded by the mystic attachment to the soil of their ancestors. The colonizing European, though controlling, was a minority, and the African remained in large part Senegalese, Ashanti, Yoruba. And even in South Africa, the Zulu, uprooted and driven into the mines, remained upon his own continent. The West Indian, though like the Negro of the United States, captive and transplanted across the ocean, at least retained the advantage of numbers and an infrequency of contact with a ruling and relatively restrained elite. In contrast, the American Negro has undergone a physical and spiritual alienation without parallel in modern history. Overwhelmed militarily, uprooted and transplanted 3,000 miles from his native soil, he has been subjected for centuries to the close, daily cultural impress not only of a dominant elite but also of the lowest elements of what Claude McKay has termed a "cultured hell," created by a powerful, materialistic and brutal, frontier society, uncertain of its own identity and seeking to assure itself of status in part by the denial of status to its victims. Rightfully resentful of the privilege of the old world, our American society itself fell victim to a psychological complex of denigration—a complex which, it is perfectly patent today, has redounded to its own disadvantage in the assault upon the intellectual, in the rock-throwing at the egghead, in the triumph in America of a cultural mediocrity.

The question, then, is posed whether this unparalleled alienation and our partial entrance into what is termed the mainstream of American life precludes our exploration and affirmation of our identity as a minority of African descent and our recourse to the African heritage as a fructifying source of our creative endeavor. (And this, basically, has been the function of negritude—to serve as a means toward the achievement of a sense of full cultural identity and a normal self-pride within the cultural context.) Lest there be some confusion, it should be pointed out that we are dealing here not with the question of social segregation on the basis of race, but with an analysis of our cultural situation and an exploration of the aspects of our identity, which, though thwarted by the prevailing racial mores, may nonetheless be a fertile source of creative inspiration. It is evident that such an exploration is a necessity not only for the African but for the Afro-American as well.

There may be differences, as there were in the debate in Paris between Aimé Césaire and some of the American delegation, as to whether the American Negro is, or has been, subjected to a species of colonialism. The fact is he has felt himself to be in an alien, not a native, land, to plagiarize Willard Savoy and Richard Wright. He too feels about him, as Countee Cullen says in "Heritage," a culture prison. This feeling is evident to the observer. The African visitor to America, we frequently hear, finds the American of African descent "diminué"—diminished. Henry Wallace, visiting the West Indies, noted what he felt to be a greater personal stature on the part of the West Indian. I have heard Mr. Killens say that Dorothy Dandridge was struck by the deep sense of assurance and quiet pride she found in the Senegalese. I understand that the psychologists Kardiner and Okesey have recently traced the psychological profile of the American Negro in their book *The Mark of Oppression.* Dubose Heyward portrays the effect of this culture prison in *Porgy,* in which the hero, the American Negro, is symbolically a cripple, and in which the only man of full stature is the character who never in the course of the play experiences a confrontation with the all-powerful white authorities, and who refuses reasonably to conform and to make the best of the social pattern. He is the outlaw, the gambler, the near rapist, the murderer, who is symbolically named Crown.

Thus do we see the effect of the dominant cultural pattern. I think it a significant commentary upon the direction of that pattern that it is necessary, with perhaps some exceptions, to return to the nineteenth century to find among America's outstanding writers—in the great-souled Melville, in the mystic Thoreau, in the cosmic vision of Whitman—the spiritual dimension to comprehend and to transcend the fact of race in America.

When we consider, then, the nature of the role the Negro has occupied in America's cultural design, when we consider the materialistic stamp of America's contemporary contributions to man's progress, it appears we should be wary of making too eager, too anxious, too precipitous a jump into what is termed the mainstream of that culture. That the Negro is an American is a fact of history. And though it may be true, as T. S. Eliot said, that the time-and-place social history of the artist is not necessarily his *significant* prior experience as far as his creative direction is concerned, yet it is probable that his creative effort will bear the strong imprint of his experience within his society. However, and this is the focal point of the discussion, it does the Negro writer a disservice to think of his work as a tributary to some major American stream, an attitude implicit in the frequent injunction to enter into the mainstream of American culture.

Hegel has somewhere said that the slave must not only break the chain; he must also shatter the image in both his and his former master's mind before he can truly become free. The mainstream of American arts and letters, it is obvious, falls woefully short of reflecting the Negro with dignity and with psychological integrity. To think merely of joining that stream or to think of our creative effort simply as part of that stream would mean to fall to a substantial degree under the influence of its direction and to perpetrate in part its cultural prototypes. (Here we should distinguish between a mastery of the content and techniques of a literature and the danger of a self-immolating submission to it.) It would be, and has proved in large measure in the Negro Rennaissance of the twenties to be, a more fruitful approach for the American Negro to write out of his own felt need, looking to the creative sources of his inclination, defining himself in terms of the deeper wells of his being as he may discover them in the direction of his particular interests, talents and emotional reactions. He should seek his inspiration in what life in this society has meant to *him* and, if he finds it seminal, in the history, mythology and folklore of Africa, in the battles of Chaka, in Benin bronze, in the Bantu philosophy of vital force, forgetting for the time being the necessity of an American mainstream. There is small chance that the body of creative effort of the American Negro will not reflect his American experience. But it is only in an emphasis upon the development of his own identity in that experience that he will be able to make ultimately his fullest contribution to the whole, within and without the nation.

Because this culture prison to which we have referred has imposed a wall between him and his origins, it is to those origins that the artist is drawn to recover that lost fullness of self. Thus, for example, Amos Tutuola, author of the celebrated *Palm Wine Drinkard,* was able, by pursuing his own ancestral experience and developing his own style of expression, to create something totally divergent from current British literary trends. Though to a sophisticated London ear, his syntax may leave something to be desired, he has gone far toward creating an African mythology and resurrecting the magic of his African heritage, which he undoubtedly would not have accomplished had he been more alert and responsive to English literary trends. Here in America, it was not in pursuit of a mainstream that Langston Hughes created something new under the literary sun when he contained on paper the haunting refrains of the blues. And, similarly, it was in a retreat to the sources of his own identity that James Weldon Johnson captured the beauty and the power of the Southern Negro preacher in *God's Trombones* without the caricature characteristic of the American white writers who have dealt with the theme.

I think it may, moreover, be worthwhile to ask what is this mainstream of the contribution of the United States to world culture? It is not chauvinism but an objective determination of fact to remark that in the area of both popular and religious music, the American Negro is not a tributary; he is substantially the stream. With the alchemy of his particular talent, he transformed and practically preëmpted the field of American popular music through jazz and the blues. Out of his American passion, he created the tragic glory of the spirituals and his own inimitable gospel music, and he remains decisive in their development. And this he did not do through a preoccupation with the "respectable" or accepted musical forms about him, but in response to the interior demands of his being.

Thus far the United States as a nation—young, frontier, and materialistic—has made but a modest contribution to the world's cultural riches. The American Negro, with his esthetic talent and with the deeper spiritual insight of his long and not yet ended ordeal, may well betray not only his future possibilities in the United States but, more importantly, his potential cultural and spiritual contribution to humanity by fixing in his mind a pattern of his role as a subordinate part of a greater whole, a whole which has traditionally denied him dignity and his full stature as a human being.

James Weldon Johnson wrote in *Along This Way* that the Negro may be ultimately merged in America, but that he had beforehand a distinct cultural contribution to make. Cedrec Dover, the Indian writer, at the Paris Congress three years ago, decried the fact that the drive toward integration in the United States seems to mean for many American Negroes a desire for obliteration and passive absorption by the majority. He remarked that a close and fruitful rapport between people can occur only where there is complete respect for the identity of the one by the other. It is this truth that Ralph Waldo Emerson, who keynoted a second independence from Britain, undoubtedly had in mind when he said in effect that a quality of the highest type of friendship was the ability to do without.

And to achieve this birth of freedom from the culture prison, let us finally consider more precisely whether the American Negro writer has an interest in looking to that phase of what the French African terms negritude, the African heritage. Is he cut off by 300 years of his American experience? Undoubtedly, he will never draw upon this experience in the manner or with the intensity of the writer on the African continent. But since the dominant American image of the Negro, which is held by Negro and white alike and which robs the Negro of his full stature, is due in large measure to the popular distorted impression of Africa and her peoples as a continent of barbarism, would it not be valuable, even imperative, to break through that culture prison and to deal with this poisonous current that feeds the American stream?

It is a necessary task, and in the historical light of the interaction of cultures, there is no reason why the African heritage may not be, for those who are so inclined, a fertile source of inspiration. For these it will be futile to admonish that our roots are American only, that our roots go back to the Virginia shore in 1619 and stop at the water's edge amid the branding and the cries and trance-like intonations such as those of Cassandra when carried by Agamemnon back to Greece: "What isle, what land is this?"

Perhaps, therefore, our concern with Africa should stop with 1619. But here in New York a German philosopher once said the connective most applicable to man is not "therefore," but "nonetheless." What was the direct line from Greece to Arabia? And yet through Arabian scholars such as Avicenna and Avarroes, a milennium removed, antiquity was recaptured and became the inspiration for the Rennaissance of Western Europe. When Derain chanced upon a piece of African statuary in a street in France, his remoteness from the former continent did not prevent him, or Picasso and others of the cubists and the "fauves," from finding in that work an inspiration for an entirely new direction—a new dimension in Western art. A more immediate example: last year at the Schomburg collection in Harlem, Randy Weston, a jazz pianist and composer, was doing research in African rhythms, which he has employed in the creations he has since played here at the Birdland and elsewhere. In literature, the poetry of Countee Cullen, Langston Hughes, Melvin Tolson and Claude McKay has already, in varying degrees, occupied itself with the African past.

It is impossible to know beforehand to what extent the African heritage may be utilized by the American Negro writer or by any American writer for that matter. Experience, not a predetermined chart, will provide the answer. I do not feel that the Negro writer's identity as an American precludes him from a substantial participation in that rich heritage.

On the South Atlantic coastline of this country there is an expression which has survived slavery—the expression "gone to Guinea." When the old African woman was weary from her labor in the fields or from her chores about the house, when she was overcome by the troubles of the world, she would say that soon she would be "gone to Guinea," that is, she would die and go to heaven. Guinea *was* heaven. Guinea was the West Coast of Africa which remained but faintly, nostalgically in the memory of her shattered past. As part of the continuing effort of the American Negro to find his roots, to achieve his full stature not only in his American society but as a contributor to a world culture, I think it may be fruitful to go back for a moment in our cultural reconnaissance—to go back to Guinea.

In conclusion, it should be pointed out again that there are two phases of this development among the African poets. We have just considered the preoccupation with the content of the African past. Here, the fact that the social, economical and political organization of the American Negro is part of the American society is evident. It could not be otherwise. And although Carter Woodson, W. E. B. Dubois and others mounted a continuing attack upon the Robert S. Park school of thought that the Negro was completely bereft of his cultural past when he was transplanted to these shores, yet it appears undisputed that there was no substantial African influence in the shaping of American institutions. This fact, however, as we have seen in the history of the interaction of cultures, is by no means decisive as to the value of the one in affording a source of inspiration and renewal for the other. The American Negro as a group will undoubtedly in the long run be preëminently concerned with the American scene. Yet Africa may well serve for many as a leaven, enriching in large measure the cultural loaf.

There is, finally, that aspect of negritude which, as we have pointed out, has not to do with an African content, but which is simply an affirmation of self, of that dwarfed self, denied realization because of the root of its identity. (And that is the meaning of the word "race." It comes from "raiz," meaning "root.") It is clear that the American Negro, like the African, has an imposing interest in the development of his image of the universe, in the correction of the distorted image of himself in this society, and in an exploration and a fuller expression of his particular talents, whatever the subject matter with which he deals. It is true, though historically oppressed and excluded from its privileges, we are part of the American whole and subject to its influences. The problem is one of emphasis within a continuing dialectic of forces. Both points of view have their reality. But we cannot resolve the argument by a kind of generous eclecticism. It is vital to assess the degree of emphasis and the particular emphasis appropriate to our cultural situation. That emphasis at present would most fruitfully be in the insistence upon our unique creative personality; and it should continue to be so until we have achieved our full identity, implicit in our culture without the necessity of affirmation, until we have purged the empoisoned mainstream, until the metamorphosis implicit in the lines of Césaire has taken place:

"bird of their scorn, bird reborn, brother in the sun."

This may be termed a kind of cultural treason. It is not. It may be termed, in a pejorative sense, romanticism. Again, it is not. But pleading in the alternative, if it be, it is our opportunity to make the most of it.

The Negro Dramatist's Image of the Universe, 1920-1960

Darwin T. Turner

In drama, as in his other media of self-expression, the Negro artist has retouched his image of the universe as the Negro's shifting position in American society has afforded new perspectives. For the Negro, the stage represented, first a pulpit from which to denounce the injustices meted out to him in America or a platform on which to parade idealized heroes to supplant the grinning, dancing Jim Crows of the white playwrights. His universe was a checkerboard of black and white: the white purity lauding both the Negro and the benevolent people who struggled to elevate the Negro; the black of corruption castigating both the treacherous Uncle Toms and the people who chained the race in ignorance and deprivation. As the Negro has been guaranteed additional rights, however, the playwrights have perceived a universe of shades of grey, a universe of non-noble, non-villainous human beings who wrestle with life.

Beginning as a crusader, a preacher, an instructor, the Negro dramatist has become a delineator, a psychologist cognizant of his artistic responsibility to represent life faithfully. The maturing of the Negro dramatist to a standard-conscious, accurate painter of his universe can be observed by comparing characteristic images in Negro dramas of the Twenties and Thirties with similar images in dramas of the Fifties. In order to restrict the topic, the examination will be limited to the dramatist's delineating of the hero; his treatment of education, religion, and superstition; his attitude towards life in the North, and his discernment of the relationship between Negroes and the larger American society.

The Image of the Hero

Since most individuals view the universe as a macrocosm and themselves as the microcosm, the first aspect of the Negro's image of the universe which warrants study is his image of himself. To efface the Negro stereotype paraded in plantation novels of the "Old South" tradition and exhibited in minstrel shows, the Negro protest dramatists of the Twenties and Thirties created a

From *CLA Journal,* V (December, 1961), 106-120.

counter stereotype: a dark-skinned, physically impressive adult—noble, courageous, rebellious, and proud.

Carving his characters to the "noble savage" Indian prototype of Aphra Behn and James Fenimore Cooper, Willis Richardson emphasized the physical strength, the nobility, and the courage of his heroes. In *The Flight of the Natives* (1927), Mose refuses to permit any man to flog him. When his master, cowed from the attempt, threatens to sell him "down the river," Mose reluctantly decides to escape without his wife, who is physically incapable of withstanding the rigors of flight. As he leaves, however, he swears to rescue her eventually. The heroes of *The Black Horseman* (1929) are tall, athletic Africans eulogized for their bravery. Massinissa, a tall, dark-skinned hero, contrasts with Syphax, his smaller, fairer antagonist. Massinissa unmasks a Roman spy by torturing him. An African, he argues, would never reveal secrets, no matter how severely he might be tortured. In both works, Richardson glorified qualities which he considered intrinsic virtues of the Negro: dignity, nobility, and courage.

Although John Matheus, in *Ti Yette* (1929), centered his story about a Creole quadroon, Matheus invested him with qualities typical of Richardson's heroes. Racine, the quadroon, idolizes Negroes who have died rather than submit to indignity. Determined to marry his sister to an African prince, Racine kills her when he learns that she plans to reject her African ancestor in order to marry a white man.

One of the most productive Negro dramatists of the Thirties, S. Randolph Edmonds, continued the pattern in such dramas as *Bad Man* and *Nat Turner,* both published in 1934. Thea Dugger, the Bad Man, leaps from the mold of Bret Harte's heroes. Although his animal savagery has wrenched fearful respect from Negro workers in a saw-mill camp, a girl's faith ennobles him. When the sister of one of the workers visits her lover in the camp, Thea, flattered by her admiration, protects her from the other workers. When a lynch mob attacks the camp to capture the murderer of a white man, Thea prefers to sacrifice himself rather than to risk endangering the girl's life in a fight.

Proud and courageous, he detests cowards. When the lynchers approach, he refuses to join the Negroes who seek escape. He will fight, or he will die; he will not run.

Edmonds' Nat Turner possesses Thea's courage although he lacks Thea's physical strength. Respected by some of his enslaved followers, feared as a witch-doctor by others, judged untrustworthy or even insane by still others, Nat desires to inspire the Virginia slaves with his pride and his fearlessness. "No real man," he tells them, "ain' willing tuh be wurked lak a mule in de field, whupped lak a dog, and tied tuh one farm and one master. . . . We mus' let dem know dat jes' because our skins is black we is not afraid tuh die."[1]

Thea and Nat project a twin image dominant in the protest dramas of the

[1] Randolph Edmonds, *Six Plays for a Negro Theatre* (Boston, 1934), pp. 71-72.

Twenties and the Thirties. Thea typifies the hero whose pride and physical strength provoke his defying tyranny. He sometimes wins followers when others seek the protection of his strength; he sometimes becomes a martyr when he refuses to bend even though he stands alone. In contrast, Nat Turner typifies the leader who, less strong physically, uses religion and inspiration to teach other Negroes the necessity of rebelling.

The submissive Negro, trusting God and the white man to resolve his problems, rarely is the protagonist of the protest dramas. Such a character can be observed in Frank Wilson's *Meek Mose* (1928). Scorned by his neighbors, who call him a white man's tool, Mose suffers eviction and an attempt upon his life. Continuing to advise faith in God, he triumphs when oil is discovered.

More often, however, the submissive Negro is the villain. In both *Nat Turner* and *Bad Man,* the despicable characters are the cowards who advise surrender.

Significantly, although they drew stereotypes, Negro dramatists revealed weaknesses in their heroes by the mid-Thirties. Thea bullies weaker Negroes. Nat is fanatic. Their virtues are magnified, but their vices distinguish them from the noble savages of Richardson's dramas.

The hero image in the more recent dramas has been that of an ordinary human being rather than an idealized stereotype. Three significant developments merit attention.

First, although the hero or protagonist elicits sympathy, he does not necessarily arouse admiration. Richard Wright's Bigger Thomas, in *Native Son* (1941),[2] embodies Thea Dugger's weaknesses with none of Thea's redeeming qualities. Uncouth and cowardly, he lies, rapes, and murders; yet he is the sympathetic protagonist of a protest drama.

Recognizing the unreality of both the "noble-savage" drawn by Negro polemicists and the "savage-beast" drawn by Dixon and other Negrophobes, Wright blended in Bigger the weaknesses for which the race has been criticized. Then he charged non-Negro America with the responsibility of breeding such individuals. Although he offered a stereotype as obvious as Massinissa had been, Wright evidenced the new confidence of the Negro writer in revealing the vices of race, not in comedy, but in work intended to evoke sympathy.

In the Forties and the Fifties, Negro dramatists have delineated credible protagonists both in dramas intended to be produced before Negroes and in those intended to be produced before predominantly non-Negro audiences. In A. Clifton Lamb's *Roughshod up the Mountain* (1956), the central figure, an uneducated minister desiring to retain his post, ignores his inability to guide his sophisticated, educated congregation.

The hero of Langston Hughes' *Simply Heavenly* (1957) is Jesse B. Semple. Ordinary—even weak in character, Semple carouses, squanders his money,

2 Dramatized by Richard Wright and Paul Green.

and philanders. A comic and a pathetic figure, he typifies the dramatist's realistic appraisal of some Negroes who comprise the group which Hughes has described as the lower class of Negro society. But *Simply Heavenly* does not dramatize the problems of all Negroes of that group: it tells the story of Jesse B. Semple. Hughes displayed Semple before the Broadway audience confident that the Negro had attained sufficient dignity in American life that the audience would not confuse Semple with all Negroes.

To point to Biggers and Semples is not to imply that the stereotyped noble Negro has disappeared from the stage. He lives in idealizations of school teachers who sacrifice life and love for their children and in idealizations of such leaders as Frederick Douglass. Nevertheless, the contemporary Negro dramatist exercises greater freedom in delineating the weaknesses of a character whom he wishes to have accepted as an individual rather than as a representative of a race.

A second development in the characterization of Negro protagonists has been that the educated Negro is no longer regarded as an individual significantly different from other Negroes. The development undoubtedly reflects the change in the Negro's position. Whereas in the Twenties and the Thirties, a college education was still considered an opportunity for only the "Talented Tenth" or those whose families possessed wealth, today a college education lies within the reach of many Negroes in urban communities.

Evidence of the earlier attitude toward the educated Negro appears in May Miller's *Riding the Goat* (1929). Jones, the antagonist of the play, dislikes Dr. Carter because he believes that Carter's education has enabled him to win the love of Ruth Chapman. Even Ann Hetty, Ruth's grandmother, suspects Carter's education. She says, "Course I thinks Doctor's all right in some ways, but them educated chaps always manages to think a little diff'rent."[3]

In contrast, in *Simply Heavenly* (1957), Boyd, a young, educated Negro, gains respect as a person who will succeed in life. Significantly, however, the protagonist is not Boyd but Jesse Semple, who survives by means of common sense rather than formal education. Hughes has not ridiculed the educated Negro; at the same time, however, he has not pedestaled Boyd as the individual carrying the hopes of the race.

Third, recent dramatists have studied the intelligent or even intellectual hero as an individual rather than as a representative of the race. In *Bad Man,* Ted James had cried, "We ain't s'posed tuh pay no 'tention tuh a burnin' man . . . but ef de people wid larnin' can't do nothin' 'bout hit, 'tain nothing we can do."[4] Implicit in the cry is a prayer for an educated Negro to solve the race's problems.

In *Simply Heavenly,* Boyd attracts not as a leader but as a respected individual.

[3] May Miller, "Riding the Goat," *Plays and Pageants of Negro Life,* Willis Richardson, ed. (Washington, 1930), p. 156.

[4] Randolph Edmonds, *op. cit.,* p. 35.

In Louis Peterson's *Take a Giant Step* (1953), the hero is a sensitive, intelligent young Negro who acquires education routinely. Although he discerns a difference between himself and the people whom he encounters when he seeks companionship in a tavern, he does not envision himself as a person with a mission. He desires merely to adjust to a society which accepts him intellectually but not socially.

Education, Superstition, and Religion

The new attitude toward the education of the hero reflects a changed attitude towards a second area of his universe: education, superstition, and religion.

As has been suggested, most dramatists of the Twenties and Thirties, writing during a time in which the average Negro could not secure a college education, viewed education as the curse of individuals or as the hope of the race, an attitude still evidenced occasionally in such a work as William Robinson's *The Passing Grade* (1958), which castigates the unjust administration of the rural Negro schools in the South. Those who hailed education as the need of the race assumed ignorance to be a major cause of the Negro's inferior position and echoed Dr. W. E. B. DuBois' pleas for educated men and women to serve as spokesmen and as leaders. Those distrusting education demonstrated an anti-intellectualism characteristic of American society as a whole rather than of the Negro race alone. From the first American comedy, Royall Tyler's *The Contrast* (1787), through the era of Will Rogers, to the present disparagement of "eggheads," American society has mocked the college-bred, cultured individual and has praised the shrewd, ingenious wit educated in the school of hard knocks. Consequently, the reflection of that attitude in dramas by Negroes should surprise no one.

Negro playwrights of the Twenties and Thirties who pictured superstition as a characteristic of the race used it for three purposes: local color, criticism, and comedy. Significantly, however, by associating superstition with the older characters in the plays, they identified it with the past rather than with the future of the race.

In John Matheus's *'Cruiter,* for example, the grandmother superstitiously anticipates bad fortune for business begun on Friday. Matheus has characterized her, however, as one of the older Negroes bound to tradition. Although she sends her son and her daughter North to find a freedom impossible in the South, she refuses to accompany them.

Similarly, in Edmonds' *The New Window* (1934), Lizzie, the middle-aged wife, superstitiously awaits fortuitous omens while Hester, her daughter, assists destiny. Offered an opportunity to free herself from sixteen years of marriage to a bully, Lizzie is impotent; but knowing his intentions to fight a duel, Hester dulls the firing pin of his gun so that he will be killed.

The danger of depending upon superstitions provided a theme for Georgia

D. Johnson's *Plumes*. Distrusting modern medical practice, Charity Brown, a middle-aged woman, debates the advisability of submitting her child to an operation. Before she decides whether to risk the operation, the child dies.

Often, a satirical treatment of superstition has distinguished the older generation from the younger generation. In James W. Butcher's *The Seer,* Bucephalus Wilson, a charlatan, has preyed upon the superstitions of older Negroes in order to further his selfish plans. When Wilson schemes to use Ivory Toles' fear of ghosts as an instrument to force Toles to consent to Wilson's marrying Toles' daughter, the girl's young suitor unmasks Wilson by posing as a ghost. All three of the comedy's older characters—Toles, Wilson, and Wilson's henchman—behave superstitiously. Even Wilson, who recognizes most of the ignorance of superstition, fears ghosts. In contrast, the intelligent, ingenious young hero and heroine fear nothing.

In *The Conjure Man Dies* (1936) Rudolph Fisher used voodoo and sorcery as a background for melodrama and horror. Although they have employed superstition for their dramatic purposes, most Negro dramatists have avoided picturing voodoo as a unique, important, or necessary part of the Negro's faith.

Perhaps because it has been considered characteristic of Negro thought, religion has been a popular element for dramatists, who have used it both as a theme and as background for the plot. Some dramatists have suggested the hope which Negroes have sought in religion. Mammy, in Edmonds' *Breeders* (1934), verbalizes the attitude: "Lawd, Ah don't want tuh question Yo' justice an' murcy, but Ah kain't help but axe how long Yuh will let Yo' chilluns be sold down de river lak horses an' cows, an' beat wussen de mules dey water down at de waterin' branch. . . . Stop it soon, Lawd! Stop it soon an' let Yo' chilluns drink of de water of freedom, an' put on de garments of righteousness."[5]

Other dramatists, however, have criticized the delusion of accepting religion as a panacea. In *Meek Mose* (1928), Wilson suggested that religion is offered to Negroes to make them forget the discriminatory practices of American society. In *Bleeding Hearts* (1934), Edmonds revealed the despair of a Negro who could not find solace in religion. In *Divine Comedy* (1938), Owen Dodson castigated the religious fanatics who delude Negroes just as charlatans have deceived them with superstition.

Other dramatists have not suggested attitudes toward religion but have used it merely as background for purposes of humor, history, local color, or social criticism In *Jedgement Day* Pawley contrasted Zeke's superstition with the sincere religious conviction of his wife and of the minister. George Norwood dramatized the Father Divine movement in *Joy Exceeding Glory*. A. Clifton Lamb, in *Roughshod up the Mountain* (1956), used religion as a vehicle for dramatizing the conflict in Negro society resulting from the transition of the race. Having ascended to the pulpit when "the call" has inspired him to leave

5 Randolph Edmonds, *op. cit.*, p. 101.

his trade as a brick-layer, a Negro minister attempts unsuccessfully to prevent his congregation from replacing him with a young minister trained in the Harvard School of Divinity. To the author, however, the theme is not religious but social: it states the demand of the Negro populace for educated and rational, rather than emotional, leadership.

Two interesting aspects of the Negro dramatist's treatment of education and religion appear in the plays. First, dramatists have ignored the Negro's interest in culture and in the fine arts. Perhaps part of the reason for the neglect of this phase of Negro life lies in the dramatists' tendency to focus upon Negroes of lower economic positions.

Second, as protest drama has diminished, dramatists have become less constrained in their treatment of immorality. Many protest dramatists created images to refute the allegation that sexual immorality characterizes Negro behavior. In *The Flight of the Natives* the Negroes remain faithful to their mates even though they have not been married legally. In *Breeders* the heroine kills herself rather than submit to a relationship with the plantation stud.

Recent playrights, however, have depicted immoral sexual relationships more objectively; sometimes they have even sanctioned such relationships. The young hero of *Take a Giant Step* attempts to prove his masculinity and to weld himself to Negro society by consummating a physical relationship with a prostitute after his desire for a more spiritual relationship has been rebuffed by a seemingly virtuous young woman who, weary of poverty, wishes to offer her body to any man who has enough money to escort her on a tour of night-clubs. In *Roughshod up the Mountain,* the young minister who represents the intelligence of the new Negro is romantically associated with a reformed prostitute, a twentieth century Mary Magdalene. Although the heroine of *Simply Heavenly* refuses to risk remaining alone with Semple before their marriage, the hero sometimes relapses into the arms of another woman, who wears morality more loosely.

Attitudes Towards the North

A third important facet of the Negro's image of his universe is his attitude towards life in the North, particularly Harlem. In much of the drama of the Twenties and the Thirties, the North represented a vaguely defined section of America in which the Negro might find freedom. Harlem, however, often symbolized a modern Babylon in which damnation awaited the unsuspecting Southern Negro.

The conflicting attitudes towards the North appear in Frank Wilson's *Sugar Cane* (1920). Paul Cain distrusts all Northern Negroes whereas his son envisions the North as a place where Negroes can acquire education. In Jean Toomer's *Balo* (1927), Balo's father desires to remain in Georgia to farm and preach. The mother, however, dreams of the happiness which she can find only in the North. Although Granny, in *'Cruiter,* sends her grandson North to find economic security in a munitions factory, she prefers to remain in the section which has been her home.

Historical, anti-slavery dramas, of course, pictured the North as a world of freedom for Negroes, to whom any place would have offered more happiness than the South offered. The same attitude persisted in early protest dramas. For instance, in *Bleeding Hearts,* embittered because his employer has refused to permit him to stop work to comfort his dying wife, Joggison Taylor leaves the South. He fears that he will kill his employer if he remains.

The contrasting attitude—suspicion of the North—is evident in *Harlem* (1922), by Wallace Thurman, a Negro, in collaboration with William J. Rapp. After their migration to Harlem from South Carolina, the Williams family experiences only misery. Cordelia, the daughter, prostitutes herself. Financial failure forces the family to give rent parties. Cordelia becomes involved in murder when her West Indian lover is accused of having murdered a gambler who had been a former suitor. Eulalie Spence, in *The Starter* (1927), has satirized Negro life which spawns such individuals as T. J., indolent, conceited, dependent upon the support of Georgia, his industrious sweetheart. The most violent condemnation of the North in drama of the Twenties and Thirties, however, is Edmonds' *Old Man Pete.* Having come North at their children's invitation, Pete Collier and his wife offend their sophisticated children by shouting in church and by dressing and conducting themselves in rural, Southern ways which the children wish to forget. When the parents realize the children's feelings, they decide to return to the South. Trying to walk from Harlem to Grand Central Station on the coldest night in the history of New York, they freeze to death while resting in Central Park.

Recent dramatists, such as Hughes and Peterson, however, have depicted life in the North more objectively, revealing the vices of life among the lower classes but viewing the North neither as a heaven nor a hell.

Negro Society

The final aspect of Negro life to be examined is the Negro's picture of his society and of the relationship between that society and America.

Perhaps because they dramatized protest themes, many Negro playwrights of the Twenties and Thirties saw Negro society only as it was affected by white society. In such works as *Sugar Cane* (1920, *'Cruiter, Ti Yette* (1929), *Bad Man* (1934), and *Bleeding Hearts* (1934)—as well as those works which condemn slavery, the basic conflict results from the inability of Negroes to protect themselves from unjust impingements by other Americans. In *Sugar Cane* and *Ti Yette,* white men exploit Negro women sexually. In *Bad Man,* friction between the races costs Negro life, and in *Bleeding Hearts,* the inhumanity of the white employer precipitates the conflict. The attitude of these dramatists is effectively expressed in *'Cruiter* when Sonny says, "Whatevah whi' folks wants o' we-all, we-all jes' nacherly got tuh do, Ah spose."[6]

Interference with the lives of Negroes is dramatized effectively in Ransom Rideout's *Going Home* (1928). Having settled abroad after World War I, Israel Du Bois marries a European girl who believes him to be a wealthy American. When American troops pass through the town where Du Bois lives, Major Powell, the son of the family which reared Du Bois as a servant, foments a race war but finally persuades Du Bois to leave his wife and to return to America.

In some of the drama of the Twenties and the Thirties, however, and in more recent plays, the Negro playwright has considered conflicts caused by internal rather than external forces. Richardson's The *Broken Banjo* (1925) describes the problems of a Negro betrayed by his wife's parasitic relatives. Langston Hughes's *Soul Gone Home* (1938) introduces the ghost of a son who charges his mother with misconduct because she was not able to provide him with the food, the clothing, and the example of moral purity which a child should have.

Other dramatists have drawn their characters so racelessly that one cannot identify them as Negroes. In *The House of Sham* (1929), Richardson dramatized the problem of a real estate broker who, by fraudulent practices, enables his wife and his daughter to live extravagantly. Thelma Duncan, in *Sacrifice* (1930), told the story of a youth who protects a friend by assuming the blame for stealing an examination. In *The Anger of One Young Man* (1959), William Robinson has described the frustration of a writer whose idealism is blighted by the mercenary materialism of the publishing trade.

Still other dramatists have emphasized the uniquely Negroid existence of their characters. In *Big White Fog* (1938), Theodore Ward dramatized problems of a Negro family affected by the depression, Communism, domestic quarrels, and anti-Semitism. As Americans they respond to issues which touch all Americans. As Negroes they react to such other matters as Garveyism and the attempt of a white man to buy the affection of one of his daughters.

The Harlemites of *Simply Heavenly* dwell in an isolated world. The central problem is Semple's effort to amass enough money to persuade Joyce to marry him. Conflicts within that society and the economic status of the characters remind the audience that the figures are lower class Negroes. Rather than being embarrassed about their lives, however, they defend their ways. When a Negro stranger condemns as stereotypes the other Negroes in a neighborhood tavern, Mamie justifies her enjoyment of watermelons, chitterlings, red dresses, gin and black-eyed peas and rice. "I didn't come here to Harlem to get away from my people," she says. "I come here because ther's more of 'em. I loves my race. I loves my people."[7]

[6] John Matheus, " 'Cruiter," *The Negro Caravan,* Sterling Brown and others, eds. (New York, 1941), p. 192.

[7] Langston Hughes, "Simply Heavenly," *The Langston Hughes Reader* (New York, 1958), p. 258.

In *Take a Giant Step,* Louis Peterson has dramatized the manner in which an educated Negro may become isolated from both Negro and white society. When he reaches the age at which he and his friends begin to seek the companionship of females, Spencer Scott, whose family is the only Negro one in the neighborhood, is rebuffed by his former playmates. Seeking association within his race, he perceives equally his inability to adjust to the Negroes who visit taverns.

A. Clifton Lamb, in *Roughshod up the Mountain,* has pictured the chasm dividing the traditional Negro society from the new Negro society. On one side are the uneducated Negro laborers; on the other side are Negroes who, by means of education, have attained professional positions.

Perhaps the most dominant and the most important idea in recent drama by Negroes is the impossibility of typifying the Negro race. Lorraine Hansberry's *A Raisin in the Sun* (1959) effectively dramatizes this idea.

Lorraine Hansberry has not idealized the Younger family. Descended from five generations of slaves and sharecroppers, the Youngers, domestic laborers, have little which other people would covet. Desiring to free his wife and his mother from the burden of helping to support the family and desiring to provide his son with an inheritance of which he can be proud, Walter Lee Younger experiences bitter frustration because no one else in his family agrees to his scheme to invest his mother's insurance money in a liquor store. Far from epitomizing nobility, he searches for pride and for maturity. As he says, "I'm thirty-five years old; I been married eleven years and I got a boy who sleeps in the living room—and all I got to give him is stories about how rich white people live."[8] He believes that the Negro who wishes to succeed must imitate white people.

In contrast, his sister, Beneatha (Bennie), inspired partly by racial pride and partly by the lectures of her African suitor, argues against the assimilation of the Negro race into the American culture. Whereas Walter materialistically concentrates upon acquiring money, Bennie wants to become a doctor because her desire since childhood has been to help other people.

Concerned neither with money nor with crusades, their mother desires merely to provide cleanliness and decency for her family. When she receives the insurance money left by her husband, she restrains herself from donating the ten thousand dollars to the church only because she wishes to help her children realize their dreams. She wants her children to respect themselves and to respect others. She refuses to consent to her son's purchasing a liquor store because she believes that it is morally wrong to sell liquor. She wants to maintain a household characterized by the simplicity of Christian ethics. She sees herself symbolized in a ragged plant which she has nursed and has treasured because, in the North, she has never had sufficient space for the garden which she desires.

Separated by personality and belief, the members of the family conflict

[8] Lorraine Hansberry, *A Raisin in the Sun* (New York, 1959), p. 17.

incessantly in their attitudes towards education and religion. Although Walter does not oppose education, he resents the fact that Bennie's desire to become a doctor rather than a nurse will necessitate expenses which he wishes to avoid. Bennie, an atheist, seeks education, not to help her race collectively, but to help individuals. Lena Younger, their mother, comforts herself with the belief that God helps the good.

The Youngers are basically moral. Walter would not commit adultery; in fact, he argues that wives are excessively suspicious in believing that their husbands are running to other women when the husbands merely want to be alone. Bennie refuses to become involved in a casual affair with a man to whom she is attracted. To save money, however, Walter's wife, Ruth deliberates abortion, and Walter fails to oppose her.

The North has not brought prosperity to the Youngers, emigrants from the South. On the other hand, it has not harmed them. Life in the crowed slums of Southside Chicago has not been pleasant. They have shared a bathroom with other tenants, and they have lacked sufficient space for separate bedrooms or for a garden. Miss Hansberry has reported the situation, however, rather than used it as a basis for protest. The only major conflict with American society stems from the Youngers' decision to move into an all-white neighborhood because they cannot afford to purchase a home at the inflationary prices charged in suburban developments for Negroes.

The Youngers disagree even in their attitudes toward their race. Although Walter blames the backwardness of the race for the inferior economic status of the Negro, he responds to the rhythms of recordings of African music. Bennie recognizes the barrier which separates her from the snobbish Negroes who possess wealth; yet she considers herself a crusader for and a defender of her race. Individual in their characters and their attitudes towards life, the Youngers find unity only in their common belief in the importance of self-respect, a philosophy not unique to the Negro race.

The Future Images of Negro Drama

The changes in the Negro dramatist's image of his hero, his attitude toward education, his attitude toward the North, and his image of his society and its problems parallel those which can be observed in other media utilized by Negro literary artists: from idealization of Negroes to efface the caricatures created by white authors, to strident, self-conscious defense of the vices of Negroes, to objective appraisal. Unlike the Negro novelist, the dramatist cannot escape easily into a world of racelessness. It he employs Negroes to enact his stories, he identifies the characters with Negroes. For that reason, perhaps, the Negro dramatists, more than the novelists, have continued to emphasize problems unique to the Negro race. As reasons for protest have faded, however, they have become more concerned with dilemmas of individuals rather than of the entire race. They have created individuals in the confidence that

America has become educated to a stage at which audiences will not assume these characters to typify the Negro race. The Negro dramatists of the present and of the future are no longer compelled to regard themselves as spokesmen for a race which needs educated and talented writers to plead its cause. Now they can regard themselves as artists, writing about the Negro race only because that is the group with which they are the most familiar.

Black Theater

Toni Cade

There still seem to be a great many bothersome questions—for those who care to be bothered—in the use of the term Negro drama. An all-inclusive term to cover the long history of our singing strength? including the recent search for the authentic black voice? Should a survey course include African writers, West Indian, the minstrel past? Should an anthology make a distinction between white and black playwrights? And what of all-Negro casts in white shows? Negro scenes in white plays? And so forth. But there are, it would seem, very few questions with the term Black Theater. It is simply—the theater of Black People. Our theater of Black People. Our theater of the sixties.

It began sometime between the Baldwin opening and the Black Arts School closing. It began sometime between the death gasps of the Civil Rights Movement and the birth of the Black Liberation Movement. It is a birthday tribute to Malcolm X, a memorial to Langston Hughes. A program of poetry by LeRoi Jones with music by Graves and Pullens, a dance by Tally Beatty. It is Alvin Ailey and Eleo Pomare. It is the musical performances of Sun Ra, Archie Shepp. It is a New Breed Fashion show. It is children reciting poetry on an improvised stage on Speakers' Corner. It is a fund raising for Huey Newton. It is improvisational exercises by students' workshops. It is a survey course by Voices Inc., the Afro-American Folkloric troupe, and Pauline Meyers. It is even argued that Blacks playing Shakespeare, Bach, Ibsen, Folkine, Shaw, CBS is black theater, for "They put their own thing on it so tough these days—like what Ray Charles did for that sad ass song 'Margie'—indelible style, ya dig. That's what it's all about in the sixties—Black Theater." Just as the labor movement established the agit-prop theater, and the New Negro Movement established protest theater, the Black Liberation Movement established Black Theater.

Every time a southern sheriff unleashed the dogs, we moved further away from the dark town folly-blackbird revue mentality. Every political push within the colonized zones all over the world made the super neuter nigger hero on film seem all the more absurd. Every electric prod helped cauterize those dead tissues that layered over the vehement blackness just beneath the skin. Every assassin bullet propelled us toward historical awareness, a new sense of ourselves. And in the grips of grief and pride, the masks crumbled,

From *Black Expression: Essays by and about Black Americans in the Creative Arts*, edited by Addison Gayle, Jr. (New York: Weybright and Talley, 1969), pp. 134-143.

the intricate network of etiquette between black and white began to crumble too. And finally, some have gotten free from the superficiality and the mimicry to speak plainly and to tap that dramatic storehouse of black-white, black-black, black-self encounters. And Black Theater takes shape.

What seems to provide the essential conflict for the playwright, a tension which is invariably invested in the work, is that never yet resolved vacillation between assimilation and separateness, between the social responsibility of the black artist and the autonomy of art, the rogue's gallery of personae from polemicist, machine-gunner, troubadour, liquidator, colloborationist, witness, recorder, Kamikaze. The movement, though, seems to be an impulse away from. As Jones raises in *Blues People* and others have discussed at length, this impulse stems from the old assumption that Afro-Americans are as earnest and devoted in the defense of the American system as are American whites. The sixties' playwright as well as other thinkers have stepped back to smile at that assumption as they decide what parts of that system, which values are worth saving, adopting; which of those so-called mainstream preoccupations are worth transforming by injecting which of the so-called minority values; which of those forked-tongued values that have formed the American reality of fine sentiment and broken treaties, broken spirits, broken bodies are real for black people.

When James Baldwin returned from his terrifying journey South in the fifties, he had the germ of a play in the Emmett Till case. The young black boy had been mauled and murdered in Mississippi in 1955, and the white man who had gone to trial and been acquitted sold his story of the crime, confessional details and all, to William Bradford Huie for a magazine article. When the boy appeared on stage several years later as Richard Henry in *Blues for Mister Charlie,* the predominantly black audience of that preview evening cheered the bitter, bold ass bad braggart nigger who had come home to scream on everybody, pass his photos of white-women-I-have-had around, and wear away the already eroding dialogue between Cap'n and Rastus. They stood up for Juanita, the spirited young woman who loves Richard and has been holding onto her rage at all the games all the jiveass-mothers have been running on her and her people for so long. They fell in love with Mother Henry the wry old grandmother whose uhhunhs helped her survive and survive with dignity. They embraced Meridian Henry, the mixed-up minister who should've known better. They checked out the white editor, Parnell, as he narrated, interpreted, and got involved in the tensions—they found him impotent and laughable. They booed Lyle Britten the ofaypeckerwoodredneck-crackerbastard murderer. They dug where his wife Jo was at, they'd met her often enough. Complete strangers slapped palms, gave five, stomped feet, punched shoulders at every four-letter invective that boomed across the dark and stormy stage. And when the white actor yelled "You dirty nigger," "You black bastard," his counterparts in the auditorium tensed up and shouted out. No one at that moment seemed to mind the turpid rhetoric, the sprawling staging, the very nearly clumsy flash-back flash-forth whodunit machinery, the embarrassingly inept acting of the playwright's brother, the flat white cardboard grotesques, the oversharped cliché of black virility—white impotency, the pitiful-po'-me underneath the black characters' tirades. It was a rally. It was fire. It was energetic, vital, relevant, cathartic, upsetting. It was beautiful. It was the beginning—the beginning of polarization on stage and in the house. It was a distinct voice—distinct from the fairly muted voice of Negro drama of the fifties.

Black theater, however, did not grow on Broadway. It took hold in the community—in the community theaters, the library and school auditoriums, the writers' workshop studios, acting school lofts, the Y's, the mobile units of Harlem primarily, and in the off-Broadway areas where blacks were growing in numbers, and in the various counties of the Black Belt, the various ghettoes where troupes began to form and to tour. Black theater became a workshop for playwrights like Douglas Turner Ward, LeRoi Jones, Ron Milner, Ed Bullins; a showcase for performers like Lou Gossett, James Earl Jones, Cynthia Belgrave, Helen Ellis, Eleo Pomare, Milford Grave, Don Pullens, Moses Gunn; a forum for the spectators, musicians, designers, poets, dancers of Harlem, Bedford-Stuyvesant, the Lower East Side, the Village, the South, the campuses, the communities. Black theater became a possibility.

At the time of the *Blues* opening, the St. Mark's production of Jean Genet's *The Blacks* was about to go on tour. This production and the Sheridan Square production of Duberman's *In White America* were a beginning too. In the past, the black actor playing roles written by whites and directed by whites was severely hampered and tended to reveal, in spite of talent and craftmanship, the handicap—the inability to tap himself, to make use of whatever truth he was aware of, of what it means to be black, to somehow not get caught up and frozen in that other "truth," the stage truth, the stuff of his life as seen by someone else. The Duberman script, a survey of historic ordeals, a series of testimony and narrative, was at least flexible enough in its historical "truth" to allow the performers to finally, as the actor James Earl Jones has often stated, say something about what's behind the black face, to force the Other to see me through my color. And no one, sitting down with one or two actors from the Genet cast, can fail to notice how racialized many of those actors became in their attempt to translate the Africans into Afro-Americans, to translate the Outsider view to a Black view. Some agonizing moments occurred, it would seem, in those actors' attempts to decipher the text, to animate the roles, to fashion the charades into meaningful drama. The play called for obviously African-looking actors. Afro hair was important for the masque. Knowledge of that double life, the envy and mimicry of the oppressor, the rage and self-hate, the need for revenge—all were necessary to prevent the essentially anti-people script from breaking into a series of gratuitously aggressive episodes. And while the play was sinisterly biased in its assumption that revenge is what it is all about, not liberation but simply substitution of evil, there was nothing about the text that cut deeply into the essential truth of black anger or compromised the black actor too dreadfully. That play—staged with definite hostility—was a beginning too.

The LeRoi Jones plays from 1962 to 1964 were more than a beginning of Black Theater. It was. *Dutchman,* the game between the man on the margin and the seductive assassin, said all there is to say about the whole continuous pattern of the lure and the murder of black people. Jennifer West portrayed the white, sexy, bizarre Lula who entraps. And Robert Hooks portrayed the Negro-Black victim Clay who has imprisoned his self in Ivy League acceptance and is smoked out of his corner by the paranoia and promise of the girl and stabbed to death. *The Toilet,* an anecdotal short piece set in a boys' high school bathroom, was about a gang who beat up the lonely white boy who's made homosexual overtures to one of the group. When the others leave the bloody mess behind, Ray, another marginal type even on the outskirts of his own group, remains behind to minister the boy's wounds—sympathetic, in touch, caught up in the need to touch and be touched. *The Slave*, by far the most ambitious piece of dramaturgy, is about Walker, a black intellectual jammed between his Western-valued education and his people's call to arms. In the midst of revolution in the streets, he invades the home of his former wife, a white woman who just couldn't find personal immunity in his anti-whitey campaign. He speaks of their marriage, their children, identifies with the new husband, white, who shares his taste in music, philosophy, literature —one minute identifying, the next hell bent on extricating himself from everything white including those parts of himself that have been tainted. A tormented character, another Jones victim—portraying again the crisis drama within the "native" too much immersed in the colonial culture.

During the '64 season, several off-off Broadway and off-Broadway houses featured playlets and improvisations that attempted to dramatize the anguish of the black-white relationship. One of the more notable pieces was the Crickett production of Fugard's *The Blood Knot* with James Earl Jones, later Lou Gossett, and J. D. Cannon. It was a domestic-racial drama of two half brothers, white and black, who are living in a shanty in Port Elizabeth, South Africa. They play out the tensions of brothers who have various degrees of mobility and opportunity, they play out the horrors of that country's racial policies.

What signalled the new trend in the black-white relationship was not only the tension but the acknowledgement that the whole conquistador mentality was as murderous to the white psyche as to the black. And the tension did not arise out of some melodramatic moment when a white slipped and told a darky joke. New too was the curtain scene—no clasp of hands, no reaching toward brotherhood as the black forgives all past atrocities and promises not to marry his new ally's sister. The curtain tended to fall on an announcement that the end was near—the end of the traditional dialogue, the end of control, the end of the world as we knew it.

Since World War II, numerous writers have sounded the doomsday note: The West was in its decline. The big powers were on their way out. American life was falling apart. At the heart of white culture was a void. No one could any longer be convinced that the future lay in the adoption of a Western style of life. That way was suicide. LeRoi Jones' Walker says this, as he attempts to exorcise those parts of himself that harbor the seeds of decay. Jones had often argued the point in many of the essays of *Home* and in numerous sections of *Blues People.* He states in "The Revolutionary Theatre" that theater must teach white people their death. In many ways, the theater of the sixties—Black theater, Radical theater, and even mainstream theater—has done just that. Before Jones numerous people had made the case. Norman Mailer argued in "The White Negro" that the only hope for survival, the only way the white could move away from the wall, was in the adoption of the Blacks' hip life style. Sartre in "Black Orpheus" parallels the Mailer theme, indicating that the only alive literature, the only valid impulse left in letters, is negritude—the Cesaire–Senghor–Diop movement that might be shorthanded in the vernacular as soul plus revolt. George Orwell tolled the bell years ago. And Susan Sontag, Bob Dylan, the young Guthries, and others have recently chimed in. Allen Ginsburg has told us what happened to the best minds of his time. And even a quick glance at the films, literature, and social science disciplines of the majority culture seems to reveal the yes—our men are Madison Ave automatons, our women hungry and shorted out, love perverted and distorted by money and power, social realities built on lies, our heroes are murderers, bandits, degenerates, we're all caught up in mechanical habits, in love with brokendown institutions, our leaders the very dregs of the bestial swamps, and all the greedy grabbing for the top hasn't evolved a race of taller men. So some white people scamper away from white culture. Others study Chinese while the Third World rises. Others organize to tear it down. And others are just waiting for the end.

Several plays give voice to this theme. In many ways, Archie Shepp's not enough seen "jazz allegory" *Junebug Graduates Tonight* investigates the dying off of America and the alternative routes of survival—at least as some see them. An uneven production, hampered more by cowardly direction (at least a reluctance or inability to push actors to the center of their characters to find the seat of tensions and to provide the various pulls in the play) than by the loudmouth symbolism, it is a serious though patchwork discussion of the Muslim route, the Marxist view, the integrationist's stand, the fascist order. The protagonist Junebug is to make the valedictorian address on graduation night and more than wanting to make good or to look right, he wants to be right. The play depicts the forces in his life that will determine the spirit and content of his address.

The prologue opens with a song in a bombed-out church with one of the oddest curtain raiser lines I've ever heard—"A nigger is like a tree—dispensable." It makes more sense after we have met Uncle Sam, the huckster-con artist who insists he is a dirty ole man but is actually impotent except where money and power and gain are concerned, and America, a fat-leg predator all too eager to take the confused Junebug under her wing and skirt. The first scene, a five-part fugue in a kitchen, presents the family. There is the hard, bitter, nastymouth dike Jessie (played by Minnie Gentry who can burn any stage down with a little help from a gutsy director) who if unleashed could put a little muscle in the radical movement; Sonja, a young trick who is too easy bait for the white man and his dusky-negress fantasies despite her street hipness; a silly bloated aunt with babies who probably meets every crisis, personal and racial, with a trip to Rose Meta; Billy the pimp, a sorry commentary on what happens to black manhood caught between the white supremacist and the black matriarch—"You could've been a big time pimp," Julia sings to him, which prompts him to erectionless soapsuds of lyrical love which provokes raucous laughter from Jessie. "I'm a virgin," he laments. In the next scenes we meet the Muslim father, a cottonwood cracker, some Nazis and minutemen, Y.A.F.ers, hecklers and uncommitted bystanders. Junebug, recently immersed in Marx, delivers his speech. America is betrayed, Uncle Sam is outraged. An interesting piece, "Junebug"–pity it wasn't a Negro Ensemble or New Lafayette property.

The Douglas Turner Ward plays, *Days of Absence* and *Happy Ending,* present the notion that blacks and whites are more tied up with each other than either cares to admit. In *Happy Ending* a young militant nephew is scandalized because his aunts, two domestics, are weeping over the fact that their employers are getting a divorce. Good, he argues, their world is crashing around them, crumbling apart, and so forth. The aunts interrupt their tears long enough to point out that all these years they've been living comfortably by taking food, "losing" clothes, padding the bills, etc. The nephew quiets down. The other play, extremely well done in white face and natural, is about the whites of a Southern town who gradually notice to their confusion and finally realize to their horror that all the blacks in the town and from neighboring counties have mysteriously disappeared. Pandemonium breaks loose. An interesting comment on the old colonial myth that if the settlers should withdraw, the natives would fall back into their brutish ways and be lost forever.

The recent productions of the Negro Ensemble Company, particularly *Kongi's Harvest,* New Lafayette, American Place, particularly Bullins' plays, and two evenings of theater—the Malcolm X birthday tribute of the Onyx Society at the Mary McLeod Bethune school and the Black Theater for Black Panthers at the Fillmore East—seem to point the direction to total theater—dance, poetry, music, drama, films, song; and to the creation of a nationalist myth—international Blackness as the cultural matrix, homage to revolutionary heroes, institutionalization of Negritude, foregone conclusion of white decadence, the turning of the back.

Opening first at the American Place and later at the Martinique were three pieces by Ed Bullins, Minister of Culture of the Black Panther Party and resident playwright of the New Lafayette. *A Son Come Home*, an ephemeral playlet staged with a somewhat flabby montage effect, the mood sustained by the music of Gordon Watkins, portrays a mother-son relationship. He, recently out of jail for some nationalist (?) activities and now earnest in his desire to be a musician, returns home after nearly ten years to find that she, having done with sacrificing and travail, having decided that the best way to end the struggle is to abandon it, has sought refuge in a very exacting and bloodless religious sect. As they go over the past, upstage actors depict those experiences they cannot put words to, those background ordeals that have let the family fall to pieces. And the son, bewildered to find that his mother can no longer help him or even love him, is dismayed, too, realizing he can no longer fit into any of those old relationships anyway.

The second play, the very lively *Electronic Nigger*, is a scary bit of hilarity. Carpentier, an electronic eavesdropper agent from the Department of Correction, enters a creative writing class and usurps the position of the teacher—first night nerves, first novel failures, anxious, earnest, cultivated, well-read, square, co-opted, Carpentier is at first obnoxious, absurd in his jargon, and his program is wire-tapping and socio-eco-politico-case-history-computerized drama. The teacher feels that he is a disgrace to the race. A white student even calls him "Uncle Tom." But his madness, his program, his power prove very seductive and he pied-pipers the students to his corner while the teacher disintegrates like some breakaway bannister . . . or better yet like a machine gone wild: "Plato, Faulkner, Shaw, Ellison, Emily Dick—."

The last play, *Clara's Ole Man*, starts out like any other local color documentary with some of the folks coming and going through the slice of life. Then it moves into nightmare territory. Clara has invited young Jack in for the day while her ole man is supposed to be at work. Jack, a gentle, mildly ambitious ex-marine currently going to college prep school, enters the kitchen, which rapidly becomes more and more claustrophobic, and meets the somewhat bizarre family—Big Girl, a none too pleasant butch who displaces the air around her with fat, power, and profanity; Baby Girl, the spastic in the corner who seems to be the embodiment of disease and corruption once Big Girl goes into her spiel; some strange neighbors on strange missions; some street corner hardheads fresh in from a mugging. Jack's out-of-itness amuses Big Girl and the thugs; eventually his innocence irritates them. Finally, it aggravates them to the point of violence as Jack, finally realizing that Big Girl is Clara's ole man, attempts to leave only to have his exit cut off by the wandering-in wino.

The Bullins play at the Black Panther program, *How Do You Do*, is a duet between a black poet on stage creating and two conjured-up sassy types who move in and out of the various postures black folks are known to adopt — ladeda, down home, blacker-than-thou, middle-class, whiter-than-bright, I've-got-a-brand-new-this and dig-my-shoes, Sapphire is a grim sister, Rastus shouts black but sleeps white. A delight. What characterizes Bullins work is a complete nonchalance about mainstream acceptance. Many of the reviewers were forced to mention that they found the spirit of the play somewhat "alien to the white liberal conscience."

The Jones plays on the Panther program portrayed a black revolutionary (or maybe he was only an armed second-story man) who invades the home of a white family, played in white masks with gibberish language and haphazard gestures, not to be thoroughly confused by their foreignness, their toylike, not even childlike, behavior. He's come with some sinister (or is it revolutionary?) purpose but stays on amused as he directs the poor fools. A friend joins him, they damn near die laughing, pulling the strings with alarming expertise.

The work at the Malcolm program was a musical drama based on various Jones' poems, taking some of his more catchy lines for virtuoso playing. What informs most of Jones' work, unlike Bullins', is a messianic zeal to teach whites how stupid, how hateful, how doomed they are. I wonder if Albert Murray, in his essay "Something Different, Something More," isn't absolutely right when he maintains that the fuck-you-charlie school of drama is just a safe game in which whites read undernearth that they are being envied and wooed. I think perhaps the ignore-'em school makes better drama and perhaps better propaganda too.

What characterizes Black Theater, then, is a newness in content, direction, attitude, and purpose. Miscegenation is no longer the great dramatic moment on stage. The black character is no longer just a good guy like the boy next door with smoked cork on his face. The playwright need not any longer accommodate his vision to what the white conscience believes is the truth about this country, its past, its people, and their relationships. There is an undercurrent of pedagogy, sometimes called radicalism, that feels obliged to bomb blacks out of their corners, smoke whites out of hiding, and flush the shit out of the system. There is a concern for the details that make up the black world, its kitchens, its flamboyantly angry men, its torn women, its ambivalences, its fluctuating moods, its spirit distilled in the walk, the music, the language. Revolution was talked to death on the stages of the thirties. The residue hung in the air till the sixties. But at least revolutionary upheaval is taking place in a realer sense in our time which will either sustain dramatic writing or bump it off completely, made irrelevant. And even if the angry hero becomes too fixed and the white-man-listen spring dries up, the theatrical adventures of the sixties will at least have provided the lessons for the more genuine, more separate, more black, more liberated revolutionary theater of the seventies.

The Negro Renaissance: Jean Toomer and the Harlem Writers of the 1920's

Arna Bontemps

That story from one of the old countries about the man with the marriageable daughter comes to mind when I think of a leading literary pundit in the second decade of this century. In a land where brides were bartered it was, of course, not uncommon for subtle salesmanship to flourish. Sometimes it could become high pressured. In this old yarn the eager parent of the bride had recited so many of his daughter's excellent qualities the prospective husband began to wonder whether she had any human faults at all. "Well, yes," the father finally acknowledged. "A tiny one. She is just a little bit pregnant."

Similarly, in the Twenties the man whose comments on writing by or about Negroes were most respected was just a little bit Negro. He was William Stanley Braithwaite, literary critic for the Boston *Transcript* and editor of an annual series, "Anthologies of Magazine Verse, 1913–1929." In "Braithwaite's Anthologies," as they were commonly known, Spoon River poems by Edgar Lee Masters, chants by Vachel Lindsay, free verse by Carl Sandburg and the early works of many other important American poets were recognized and published before the authors had received general acceptance or acclaim.

But Braithwaite did not completely disassociate himself from Negroes, as he might have. Indeed, he was awarded the Spingarn medal in 1917 as "the Negro who, according to a committee appointed by the board [of the NAACP], has reached the highest achievement in his field of activity." His occasional observations on Negro writing in the decade preceding Harlem's golden era are therefore useful as prologue. In 1913, for example, Braithwaite took note of James Weldon Johnson's "Fiftieth Anniversary Ode" on the Emancipation and suggested that it represented a move by the Negro poet to disengage himself. A decade of near silence had followed Paul Laurence Dunbar's last lyrics, and Braithwaite's language created an image of the Negro poet in chains, seeking to free himself.

The reappearance of this Johnson poem in a collection called *Fifty Years and Other Poems*, in 1917 — the same year that Braithwaite was awarded

From *Anger and Beyond: The Negro Writer in the United States*, edited by Herbert Hill (New York: Harper & Row, 1966) pp. 20-36.

the Spingarn medal, incidentally — prompted Braithwaite to remark, in effect, that this could be the beginning of something big, like a new awakening among Negro writers, perhaps. But actually, Johnson's most significant poetic achievement was still a decade in the future, when his collection of folk sermons in verse was to be published as *God's Trombones* in 1927. Nevertheless, Braithwaite appears to have picked the right year for the first sign of "disengagement" or "awakening" or whatever it was. The year 1917 now stands out, where Negro poetry in the United States is concerned, as the year in which Claude McKay's poem "The Harlem Dancer" appeared in *The Seven Arts* magazine under the pen name of Eli Edwards. You may know the poem. It was in sonnet form:

Applauding youths laughed with young prostitutes
And watched her perfect, half-clothed body sway;
Her voice was like the sound of blended flutes
Blown by black players upon a picnic day.
She sang and danced on gracefully and calm,
The light gauze hanging loose about her form;
To me she seemed a proudly-swaying palm
Grown lovelier for passing through a storm.
Upon her swarthy neck black shiny curls
Luxuriant fell, and tossing coins in praise,
The wine-flushed, bold-eyed boys, and even the girls,
Devoured her shape with eager, passionate gaze;
But looking at her falsely-smiling face,
I know her self was not in that strange place.

Now this I submit was the anticipation and the theme of an early outburst of creativity later described as the Negro or Harlem Renaissance. When McKay's "The Harlem Dancer" reappeared in his collection *Harlem Shadows* in 1922, along with other poems so fragrant and fresh they almost drugged the senses, things immediately began to happen. Here was poetry written from experience, differing from poetry written from books and other cultural media in somewhat the same way that real flowers differ from artificial ones. A chorus of other new voices led by Jean Toomer, Langston Hughes and Countee Cullen promptly began to make the Twenties a decade which *Time* magazine has described as Harlem's "golden age."

Interestingly, Braithwaite recognized McKay as the first voice in this new chorus, but he spoke of him as "a genius meshed in [a] dilemma." It bothered Braithwaite that McKay seemed to "waver between the racial and the universal notes." In some of his poems, Braithwaite felt, McKay was clearly "contemplating life and nature with a wistful sympathetic passion," but in others the poet became what Braithwaite called a "strident propagandist, using his poetic gifts to clothe arrogant and defiant thoughts." Braithwaite thought this was bad. He cited McKay's "The Harlem Dancer" and his "Spring in New Hampshire" as instances of the former, his "If We Must Die" as a shameless instance of the latter. But, ironically, a generation later it was "If We Must Die," a poem that would undoubtedly stir the blood of almost any Black Muslim, that Sir Winston Churchill quoted as climax and conclusion of his oration before the joint houses of the American Congress when he was seeking to draw this nation into the common effort of World War II. McKay had written it as the Negro American's defiant answer to lynching and mob violence in the Southern states, Churchill made it the voice of the embattled Allies as he read aloud McKay's poem "If We Must Die."

Obviously neither Churchill nor McKay had at that time considered the possibilities of nonviolence. The poem does show, however, how a short span of years and certain historical developments can alter the meaning of a literary work. It also demonstrates the risk of trying to separate too soon the local or special subject from the universal.

But if Braithwaite's attitude toward Claude McKay was ambivalent, it was certainly unequivocal with respect to the second, and in some ways the most inspiring, of the writers who made the Harlem Renaissance significant in the long-range development of the Negro writer in the United States.

"In Jean Toomer, the author of *Cane*," Braithwaite wrote in 1925, "we come upon the very first artist of the race, who with all an artist's passion and sympathy for life, its hurts, its sympathies, its desires, its joys, its defeats and strange yearnings, can write about the Negro without the surrender or compromise of the artist's vision. So objective is it, that we feel that it is a mere accident that birth or association has thrown him into contact with the life he has written about. He would write just as well, just as poignantly, just as transmutingly, about the peasants of Russia, or the peasants of Ireland, had experience brought him in touch with their existence. *Cane* is a book of gold and bronze, of dusk and flame, of ecstasy and pain, and Jean Toomer is a bright morning star of a new day of the race in literature."

Cane was published in 1923 after portions of it had first appeared in *Broom, The Crisis, Double Dealer, Liberator, Little Review, Modern Review, Nomad, Prairie and S 4 N*. But *Cane* and Jean Toomer, its gifted author, presented an enigma—an enigma which has, if anything, deepened in the forty-three years since its publication. Given such a problem, perhaps one may be excused for not wishing to separate the man from his work. Indeed, so separated, Toomer's writing could scarcely be understood at all, and its significance would escape us now as it has escaped so many others in the past.

In any case, *Who's Who in Colored America* listed Toomer in 1927 and gave the following vita:

b. Dec. 26, 1894, Washington, D. C.; s. Nathan and Nina (Pinchback) Toomer; educ. Public Scho., Washington, D. C.; Dunbar, High Scho.; Univ. of Wisconsin, 1914–15;

taught schools, Sparta, Ga., for four months, traveled, worked numerous occupations; auth. *Cane,* pub. Boni and Liveright, 1923; Short Stories and Literary Criticisms in various magazines; address, c/o Civic Club, 439 W. 23rd St., New York, N. Y.

Needless to say, no subsequent listing of Toomer is to be found in this or any other directory of conspicuous Negro Americans. Judging by the above, however, Toomer had always been elusive, and the interest that *Cane* awakened did nothing to change this. Several years later Toomer faded completely into white obscurity leaving behind a literary mystery almost as intriguing as the disappearance of Ambrose Bierce into Mexico in 1913.

Why did he do it? What did it mean?

Concerned with writing, as we are, we automatically turn to Toomer's book for clues. This could be difficult, because copies are scarce. *Cane*'s two printings were small, and the few people who went quietly mad about the strange book were evidently unable to do much toward enlarging its audience. But among these few was practically the whole generation of young Negro writers then just begining to appear, and their reaction to Toomer's *Cane* marked an awakening that soon thereafter began to be called a Negro renaissance.

Cane's influence was not limited to the happy band that included Langston Hughes, Countee Cullen, Eric Walrond, Zora Neale Hurston, Wallace Thurman, Rudolph Fisher and their contemporaries of the Twenties. Subsequent writing by Negroes in the United States as well as in the West Indies and Africa has continued to reflect its mood and often its method, and, one feels, it also has influenced the writing about Negroes by others. And certainly no earlier volume of poetry or fiction or both had come close to expressing the ethos of the Negro in the Southern setting as *Cane* did.

There are many odd and provocative things about *Cane,* and not the least is its form. Reviewers who read it in 1923 were generally stumped. Poetry and prose were whipped together in a kind of frappé. Realism was mixed with what they called mysticism, and the result seemed to many of them confusing. Still, one of them could conclude that "*Cane* is an interesting, occasionally beautiful and often queer book of exploration into old country and new ways of writings." Another noted, "Toomer has not interviewed the Negro, has not asked opinions about him, has not drawn conclusions about him from his reactions to outside stimuli, but has made the much more searching, and much more self-forgetting effort of seeing life with him, through him."

Such comment was cautious, however, compared to the trumpetings of Waldo Frank in the Foreword he contributed:

> A poet has arisen among our American youth who has known how to turn the essence and materials of his Southland into the essences and materials of literature. A poet has arisen in that land who writes, not as a Southerner, not as a rebel against Southerners, not as Negro, not as apologist or priest or critic: who writes as a *poet.* The fashioning of beauty is ever foremost in his inspiration: not forcedly but simply, and because these

> ultimate aspects of his world are to him more real than all its specific problems. He has made songs and lovely stories of his land. . . .
>
> The gifted Negro has been too often thwarted from becoming a poet because his world was forever forcing him to recollect that he was a Negro. The artist must lose such lesser identities in the great well of life. . . . The whole will and mind of the creator must go below the surfaces of race. And this has been an almost impossible condition for the American Negro to achieve, forced every moment of his life into a specific and superficial plane of consciousness. . . .
>
> It seems to me, therefore, that this is a first book in more ways than one. It is a harbinger of the South's literary maturity: of its emergence from the obsession put upon its minds by the unending racial crisis. . . . It marks the dawn of direct and unafraid creation. And, as the initial work of a man of twenty-seven, it is the harbinger of a literary force of whose incalculable future I believe no reader of this book will doubt.

It is well to keep in mind the time of these remarks. Of the novels by which T. S. Stribling is remembered, only *Birthright* had been published. Julia Peterkin had not yet published a book. DuBose Heyward's *Porgy* was still two years away. William Faulkner's first novel was three years away. His Mississippi novels were six or more years in the future. Robert Penn Warren, a student at Vanderbilt University, was just beginning his association with the Fugitive poets. His first novel was still more than a decade and a half ahead. Tennessee Williams was just nine years old.

A chronology of Negro writers is equally revealing. James Weldon Johnson had written lyrics for popular songs, some of them minstrel style, and a sort of documentary novel obscurely published under a pseudonym, but *God's Trombones* was a good four years in the offing. Countee Cullen's *Color* was two and Langston Hughes' *The Weary Blues* three years away, though both of these poets had become known to readers of the Negro magazine *Crisis* while still in their teens, and Hughes at twenty-one, the year of *Cane*'s publication, could already be called a favorite.

The first fiction of the Negro Renaissance required apologies. It was not first-rate. But it was an anticipation of what was to come later. Even so, it followed *Cane* by a year or two, and Eric Walrond's *Tropic Death* did not come for three. Zora Neale Hurston's first novel was published in 1931, eight years after *Cane*. Richard Wright made his bow with *Uncle Tom's Children* in 1938, fifteen years later. *Invisible Man* by Ralph Ellison followed Toomer's *Cane* by just thirty years. James Baldwin was not born when Toomer began to publish.

Waldo Frank's use of "harbinger" as the word for *Cane* becomes both significant and ironic when we recognize the debt most of these individuals owe Toomer. Consciously or unconsciously, one after another they picked up his cue and began making the "more searching" effort to see life *with* the Negro, "through him." *Cane* heralded an awakening of artistic expression by Negroes that brought to light in less than a decade a surprising array of talents, and these in turn made way for others. An equally significant change in the writing about Negroes paralleled this awakening. Strangely, however, *Cane* was not at all the harbinger Frank seemed to imagine. Despite his promise—a promise which must impress anyone who puts this first book besides the early writings of either Faulkner or Hemingway, Toomer's contemporaries—Jean Toomer rejected his prospects and turned his back on greatness.

The book by which we remember this writer is as hard to classify as its author. At first glance it appears to consist of assorted sketches, stories and a novelette interspersed with poems. Some of the prose is poetic, and often Toomer slips from one form into the other almost imperceptibly. The novelette is constructed like a play.

His characters, always evoked with effortless strength, are as recognizable as they are unexpected in the fiction of that period. Fern is a "creamy brown" beauty so complicated men take her "but get no joy from it." Becky is a white outcast beside a Georgia road who bears two Negro children. Laymon, a preacher-teacher in the same area, "knows more than would be good for anyone other than a silent man." The name character in the novelette *Kabnis* is a languishing idealist finally redeemed from cynicism and dissipation by the discovery of underlying strength in his people.

It doesn't take long to dscover that *Cane* is not without design, however. A world of black peasantry in Georgia appears in the first section. The scene changes to the Negro community of Washington, D.C., in the second. Rural Georgia comes up again in the third. Changes in the concerns of Toomer's folk are noted as the setting moves from the Georgia pike to the bustling Negro section in the nation's capital. The change in the level of awareness that the author discloses is more subtle, but it is clearly discernible when he returns to the Georgia background.

A young poet-observer moves through the book. Drugged by beauty "perfect as dusk when the sun goes down," lifted and swayed by folk song, arrested by eyes that "desired nothing that *you* could give," silenced by "corn leaves swaying, rusty with talk," he recognized that "the Dixie Pike had grown from the goat path in Africa." A native richness is here, he concluded, and the poet embraces it with the passion of love.

This was the sensual power most critics noticed and most readers remembered about *Cane*. It was the basis for Alfred Kreymborg's remark in *Our Singing Strength* that "Jean Toomer is *one* of the finest artists among the dark people, if not *the* finest." The reviewer for the New York *Herald Tribune* had the rich imagery of *Cane* in mind when he said, "Here are the high brown and black and half-caste colored folk of the cane fields, the gin hovel and the brothel realized with a sure touch of artistry." But there remained much in the book that he could not understand or appreciate. Speaking of Toomer's "sometimes rather strident reactions to the Negro," he added that "at moments his outbursts of emotion approach the inarticulately maudlin," though he had to admit that *Cane* represented "a distinct achievement wholly unlike anything of this sort done before."

Others found "obscurity" and "mysticism" in the novelette which comprises the last third of the book. This is not surprising, for in Toomer's expressed creed "A symbol is as useful to the spirit as a tool is to the hand," and his fiction is full of them. Add to puzzling symbols an itch to find "new ways of writing" that led him to bold experimentation and one may begin to see why Toomer baffled as he pleased readers interested in writing by or about Negroes in the early Twenties.

Kreymborg spoke of Toomer as "a philosopher and a psychologist by temperament" and went on to say that "the Washington writer is now fascinated by the larger, rather than the parochial interest of the human race, and should some day compose a book in the grand manner."

Of course, Toomer didn't, or at least he has not published one up to now, and to this extent Kreymborg has failed as a prophet, but his reference to Toomer as philosopher and psychologist was certainly on the mark, and his rather large estimate of this writer's capacities was significant, considering its date. The "new criticism," as we have come to recognize it, had scarcely been heard from then, and apparently it has still not discovered Toomer, but the chances are it may yet find him challenging. He would have comforted them, I am almost sorry to say, incarnating, as he does, some of their favorite attitudes. But at the same time, he could have served as a healthy corrective for others. Whether or not he would prove less complex or less rewarding than Gertrude Stein or James Joyce, for example, remains to be determined.

Saunders Redding gave *Cane* a close reading fifteen years after its publication and saw it as an unfinished experiment, "the conclusion to which we are fearful of never knowing, for since 1923 Toomer has published practically nothing." He meant, one assumes, that Toomer had published little poetry or fiction, or anything else that seemed closely related to *Cane* or to *Cane*'s author. Toomer had published provocative articles here and there as well as a small book of definitions and aphorisms during that time, and since then he has allowed two of his lectures to be publshed semi-privately. But Redding must be included in the small group who recognized a problem in *Cane* that has yet to be explained.

To him Toomer was a young writer "fresh from the South," who found a paramount importance in establishing "racial kinship" with Negroes in order to treat them artistically. He was impressed by Toomer's "unashamed and unrestrained" love for the race and for the soil and setting that nourished it. He saw a relationship between the writer's "hot, colorful, primitive" moods and the "naïve hysteria of the spirituals," which he held in contrast to "the sophistic savagery of jazz and the blues." *Cane*, he concluded, "was a lesson in emotional release and freedom."

Chapters about Toomer were included in Paul Rosenfeld's *Men Seen* in 1925 and in Gorham B. Munson's *Destinations* in 1928, and elsewhere there are indications that Toomer continued to write and to experiment for at least a decade after the publication of *Cane.* Long stories by him appeared in the second and third volumes of the *American Caravan.* A thoughtful essay on "Race Problems and Modern Society" became part of a volume devoted to *Problems of Civilization* in Baker Brownell's series on "Man and His World." Seven years later, in the *New Caravan* of 1936, Toomer presented similar ideas in the long poem "Blue Meridian." Meanwhile, contributing a chapter to the book *America & Alfred Stieglitz* in 1934, Toomer was explicit about his own writing as well as several other matters.

The rumor that Toomer had crossed the color line began circulating when his name stopped appearing in print. But a reasonable effort to find out what it was Toomer was trying to say to us subsequently makes it hard to accept "passing" as the skeleton key to the Jean Toomer mystery. He seemed too concerned with truth to masquerade. One wants to believe that Toomer's mind came at last to reject the myth of race as it is fostered in our culture. A man of fair complexion, indistinguishable from the majority of white Americans, he had always had a free choice as to where he would take his place in a color-caste scheme. Having wandered extensively and worked at odd jobs in a variety of cities before he began contributing to little magazines, as he has stated, he could scarcely have escaped being taken at face value by strangers who had no way of knowing that the youth, who looked like Hollywood's conception of an Ivy League basketball star, but who spoke so beautifully, whose very presence was such an influence upon them, was not only a product of the Negro community but a grandson of the man whom the *Dictionary of American Biography* describes as the "typical Negro politician of the Reconstruction."

Men of this kind, such as Walter White of the NAACP or Adam Clayton Powell of the U.S. Congress, sometimes called voluntary Negroes when they elect to remain in the fold, so to speak, have in other circumstances been discovered in strange places in our society—in neo-fascist organizations in the United States, among big city bosses, on movie screens, in the student body at "Ole Miss"—but seldom if ever before in an organization working "for understanding between people." Yet Jean Toomer's first publication, following the rumors and the silence, was "An Interpretation of Friends Worship," published by the Committee on Religious Education of Friends General Conference, 1515 Cherry Street, Philadelphia, 1947. It was followed two years later by a pamphlet, "The Flavor of Man." The writing is eloquent with commitment. It reflects unhurried reading and contemplation, as was also true of his piece on "Race Problems and Modern Society." Toomer did not fail to remind his readers that certain racial attitudes could not be condoned. He certainly did not speak as a Negro bent on escaping secretly into white society. Jean Toomer, who, like his high-spirited grandfather, had exuberantly published his pride in his Negro heritage, appears to have reached a point in his thinking at which categories of this kind tend to clutter rather than classify. The stand he appears to have taken at first involved nothing more clandestine than the closing of a book or the changing of a subject.

Yet he is on record as having denied later that he was a Negro. That is a story in itself. Nevertheless, at that point, it seems, Jean Toomer stepped out of American letters. Despite the richness of his thought, his gift of expression, he ceased to be a writer and, as I have suggested, turned his back on greatness. His choice, whatever else may be said about it, reflects the human sacrifices in the field of the arts exacted by the racial myth on which so much writing in the United States is based. While he may have escaped its strictures and inconveniences in his personal life, he did not get away from the racial problem in any real sense. His dilemmas and frustrations as a writer are equally the dilemmas and frustrations of the Negro writers who have since emerged. The fact that most of them have not been provided with his invisible cloak makes little difference. He is their representative man. He stands as their prototype.

What, then, ordinarily happened to the Negro writer of Toomer's time in America after his first phase, after he had been published and taken his first steps? Encouraged by reviewers, assured that his talent was genuine, that he was not *just* a Negro writer but an American writer who happened to be a Negro, that his first book had broken new ground and that his next would be awaited with keen interest unrelated to any exotic qualities he may have shown but simply as arresting art, he was readily convinced. The "American writer" tag was especially appealing. It stuck in his mind, and when he got the bad news from the sales department, he coupled it with remarks he had heard from his publishers about a certain "resistance" in bookstores to books about "the problem." Obviously the solution for him, as an American writer, was not to write narrowly about Negroes but broadly about people.

So sooner or later he did it: a novel not intended to depict Negro life. The results may be examined: Paul Laurence Dunbar's *The Love of Landry*, Richard Wright's *Savage Holiday*, Chester B. Himes' *Cast the First Stone*, Ann Petry's *Country Place*, Zora Neale Hurston's *Seraph on the Suwanee*, James Baldwin's *Giovanni's Room*, along with Jean Toomer's *York Beach*. While the implication that books about whites are about people while those about Negroes are *not* should have provoked laughter, the young Negro writer was too excited to catch it. The discovery which followed was that the bookstore "resistance" was not removed by this switch. Moreover, he found to his dismay that friendly reviewers had in most instances become cool. In any case, none of these writers seemed sufficiently encouraged by the results to continue in the same direction. Whatever it was that blocked the

Negro writer of fiction, that denied him the kind of acceptance accorded the Negro maker of music, for example, was clearly not just the color of his characters.

Southern white novelists from T. S. Stribling to Julia Peterkin to DuBose Heyward to William Faulkner to Robert Penn Warren had thronged their novels with Negroes of all descriptions without appearing to meet reader resistance or critical coolness. So now it could be seen that the crucial issue was not the choice of subject but the author's attitude toward it. With this knowledge the young Negro writers pondered and then made their decisions. Dunbar chose drink. Wright and Himes went to Paris to think it over, as did James Baldwin, at first. Toomer disappeared into Bucks County, Pennsylvania. Frank Yerby, on the basis of a short story in *Harper's Magazine* and a manuscript novel that went the rounds without finding a publisher, took the position that "an unpublished writer, or even one published but unread, is no writer at all." He chose "entertainment" over "literature," and worked his way out of the segregated area of letters in the costume of a riverboat gambler. His book *The Foxes of Harrow* about the Mississippi riverboat gambler became the first successful non-Negro novel by a Negro American writer.

A curious historical irony is suggested. The memoirs of George H. Devol, published in 1887 under the title *Forty Years a Gambler on the Mississippi,* relates the following about a cabin boy called Pinch:

> I raised him and trained him. I took him out of a steamboat barber shop. I instructed him in the mysteries of card-playing, and he was an apt pupil. . . .

Devol recalled with much amusement a night they left New Orleans on the steamer *Doubloon*:

> There was a strong team of us—Tom Brown, Holly Chappell, and the boy Pinch. We sent Pinch and staked him to open a game of chuck-aluck with the Negro passengers on deck, while we opened up monte in the cabin. The run of luck that evening was something grand to behold. I do not think there was a solitary man on the boat that did not drop around in the course of the evening and lose his bundle. When about thirty miles from New Orleans a heavy fog overtook us, and it was our purpose to get off and walk about six miles to Kennersville, where we could take the cars to the city.
>
> Pinchback got our valises together, and a start was made. A drizzling rain was falling, and the darkness was so great that one could not see his hand before his face. Each of us grabbed a valise except Pinch, who carried along the faro tools. The walking was so slippery that we were in the mud about every ten steps, and poor Pinch he groaned under the load that he carried. At last he broke out:
>
> "Tell you what it is, Master Devol, I'll be dumbed if this aint rough on Pinch. Ise going to do better than this toting along old faro tools."
>
> "What's that, Pinch? What you going to do?"
>
> "Ise going to get into that good old Legislature and I'll make Rome howl if I get there."
>
> Of course I thought at the time that this was all bravado and brag; but the boy was in earnest, and sure enough he got into the Legislature, became Lieutenant Governor,

and by the death of the Governor he slipped into the gubernatorial chair, and at last crawled into the United States Senate.

Without necessarily accepting the gambler Devol as an authority on Reconstruction history we may still take his account as substantially factual. P. B. S. Pinchback himself often referred to his career on the river. He was still a prominent public figure when these memoirs were published. He could have denied them had he wished. That Frank Yerby, who became a teacher in a Negro college in Louisiana after his graduation from Fisk University, should center the story of *The Foxes of Harrow* around a Mississippi riverboat gambler is not an odd coincidence. But that Jean Toomer should be the grandson of Pinchback and one of the two people to accompany his body back to New Orleans for burial in 1921 suggests another historical irony.

The behavior pattern known sociologically as "passing for white," then, has its literary equivalent, and the question it raises is whether or not this is proper in the arts. The writer's desire to widen his audience by overcoming what has been called resistance to racial material is certainly understandable, but sooner or later the Negro novelist realizes that what he has encountered, as often critical as popular, is more subtle than that. What annoys some readers of fiction, it seems, is not so much that characters in a book are Negro or white or both as the *attitude of the writer* toward these characters. Does he accept the status quo with respect to the races? If so, any character or racial situation can be taken in stride, not excluding miscegenation. But rejection of traditional status, however reflected, tends to alienate these readers.

On the other hand, the Negro reader has little taste for any art in which the racial attitudes of the past are condoned or taken for granted. Since this is what he has come to expect in the fiction in which he sees himself, he too has developed resistance. His is a wider resistance to the whole world of the contemporary novel. To him literature means poetry, by and large. He knows Phillis Wheatley and Paul Laurence Dunbar far better than he knows any prose writers of the past. James Weldon Johnson and Countee Cullen are familiar and honored names. There is seldom a sermon in a Negro church, a commencement, a banquet, a program in which one of these or a contemporary poet like Hughes or Margaret Walker or Gwendolyn Brooks is not quoted. But the Negro novelists, aside from Richard Wright, possibly, are lumped with the whole questionable lot in the mind of this reader. When he is not offended by the image of himself that modern fiction has projected, he is at least embarrassed.

The Negro writer, like the white writer of the South, is a product of the Southern condition. Whether he wills it or not, he reflects the tensions and cross-purposes of that environment. Just as the myth of the old South weakens under close examination, the myth of literature divorced from what have been called sociological considerations dissolves in a bright light.

The fictional world on which most of us first opened our eyes, where the Negro is concerned, is epitomized by a remark made by a character in William Faulkner's *Sartoris*. "What us niggers want ter be free fer, anyhow?" asks old Uncle Simon. "Aint we got es many white folk now es we kin suppo't?"

The elusiveness of Jean Toomer in the face of complexities like these can well stand for the elusiveness of Negro writers from Charles W. Chesnutt to Frank Yerby. What Toomer was trying to indicate to us by the course he took still intrigues, but I suspect he realizes by now that there is no further need to *signify*. The secrets are out. As the song says, "There's no hiding place down here."

Dilemma of the Negro Novelist in the U.S.

Chester Himes

Any discussion of the Negro novelists in the U.S.A. must first examine the reasons why all novelists, whatever their race and nationality, write. The obvious answer, the one that first comes to mind, is that we write to express and perpetuate our intellectual and emotional experiences, our observations and conclusions. We write to relate to others the process of our thoughts, the creations of our imaginings. That is the pat answer.

We have a greater motive, a nobler aim, we are impelled by a higher cause. We write not only to express our experiences, our intellectual processes, but to interpret the meaning contained in them. We search for the meaning of life in the realities of our experiences, in the realities of our dreams, our hopes, our memories. Beauty finds reality in the emotion it produces, but that emotion must be articulated before we can understand it. Anger and hatred require expression as do love and charity.

The essential necessity of humanity is to find justification for existence. Man cannot live without some knowledge of the purpose of life. If he can find no purpose in life he creates one in the inevitability of death. We are maintained at our level of nobility by our incessant search for ourselves.

The writer seeks an interpretation of the whole of life from the sum of his experiences. When his experiences have been so brutalized, restricted, degraded, when his very soul has been so pulverized by oppression, his summations can not avoid bitterness, fear, hatred, protest; he is inclined to reveal only dwarfed, beaten personalities and life that is bereft of all meaning. But his logic will tell him that humanity can not accept the fact of existence without meaning. He must find the meaning regardless of the quality of his experiences. Then begins his slow, tortured progress toward truth.

The Negro writer, more than any other, is faced with this necessity. He must discover from his experiences the truth of his oppressed existence in terms that will provide some meaning to his life. Why he is here; why he continues to live. In fact, this writer's subject matter is in reality a Negro's search for truth.

From the start the American Negro writer is beset by conflicts. He is in

From *Beyond the Angry Black,* edited by John A. Williams (New York: Cooper Square Publishers, 1966), pp. 52-58.

conflict with himself, with his environment, with his public. The personal conflict will be the hardest. He must decide at the outset the extent of his honesty. He will find it no easy thing to reveal the truth of his experience or even to discover it. He will derive no pleasure from the recounting of his hurts. He will encounter more agony by his explorations into his own personality than most non-Negroes realize. For him to delineate the degrading effects of oppression will be like inflicting a wound upon himself. He will have begun an intellectual crusade that will take him through the horrors of the damned. And this must be his reward for his integrity: he will be reviled by the Negroes and whites alike. Most of all, he will find no valid interpretation of his experiences in terms of human values until the truth be known.

If he does not discover this truth, his life will be forever veiled in mystery, not only to whites but to himself; and he will be heir to all the weird interpretations of his personality.

The urge to submit to the pattern prescribed by oppression will be powerful. The appeal to retrench, equivocate, compromise, will be issued by friends and foe alike. The temptations to accede will be tempting, the rewards coercive. The oppressor pays, and sometimes well, for the submission of the oppressed.

To the American Negro writer's mind will come readily a number of rationalizations. He may say to himself: "I must free myself of all race consciousness before I can understand the true nature of human experiences, for it is not the Negro problem at all, but the human problem." Or he may attempt to return to African culture, not as a source but as an escape, and say: "This is my culture; I have no other culture." But he will find that he can not accomplish this departure because he is an American. He will realize in the end that he possesses this heritage of slavery; he is a product of this American culture; his thoughts and emotions and reactions have been fashioned by his American environment. He will discover that he can not free himself of race consciousness because he can not free himself of race; that is his motive in attempting to run away. But, to paraphrase a statement of Joe Louis', "He may run, but he can't hide."

Once the writer's inner conflict has been resolved and he has elected the course of honesty, he will begin his search for truth. But the conflict will not cease. He immediately enters into conflict with his environment. Various factors of American life and American culture will be raised to stay his pen. The most immediate of these various conflicts is with the publisher. From a strictly commercial point of view, most publishers consider honest novels by Negro writers on Negro subjects bad ventures. If there is nothing to alleviate the bitter truth, no glossing over of the harsh facts, compromising on the vital issues, most publishers feel that the book will not sell. And the average publisher today will not publish a novel he thinks will not sell.

However, should the Negro find a publisher guided by neither profit nor prejudice (a very rare publisher indeed), he may run into the barrier of preconception. Many truly liberal white people are strongly opinionated on the racial theme, and consider as false or overdrawn any conception that does not agree with their own. Oft-times these people feel that their experiences *with* Negroes (unfortunately not *as* Negroes) establish them as authorities on the subject. But quite often their opinions are derived from other Negroes who have attained financial success or material security, in fact fame and great esteem, through a trenchant sort of dishonesty, an elaborate and highly convincing technique of modern uncle-tomism. It is unfortunate that so many white people who take an active and sympathetic interest in the solution of the American racial dilemma become indoctrinated first by such Negroes. Instead of receiving a true picture of Negroes' personalities, they are presented with comforting illusions. Should the publisher be of this group, he concludes that the honest Negro writer is psychotic, that his evaluations are based on personal experiences which are in no way typical of his race. This publisher does not realize that his own reasoning is self-contradictory; that any American Negro's racial experiences, be they psychotic or not, are typical of all Negroes' racial experiences for the simple reason that the source is not the Negro but oppression.

Then there is, of course, the publisher with such a high content of racial bias as to reject violently any work that does not present the Negro as a happy contented soul. But there will be no conflict between the Negro writer and this publisher; it will never begin.

Once the writer's work is past the printer, his inner conflict having been resolved and his publisher convinced, there begins a whole turbulent sea of conflict between the novelist and his public.

If this novelist, because he has prepared an honest and revealing work on Negro life anticipates the support and encouragement of middle-class Negro people, he is doomed to disappointment. He must be prepared for the hatred and antagonism of many of his own people, for attacks from his leaders, the clergy and the press; he must be ready to have his name reviled at every level, intellectual or otherwise. This is not hard to understand. The American Negro seeks to hide his beaten, battered soul, his dwarfed personality, his scars of oppression. He does not want it known that he has been so badly injured for fear he will be taken out of the game. The American Negro's highest ambition is to be included in the stream of American life, to be permitted to "play the game" as any other American, and he is opposed to anything he thinks will aid to his exclusion. The American Negro, we must remember, is an American; the face may be the face of Africa, but the heart has the beat of Wall Street.

But Negroes will themselves oppress other Negroes, given the opportunity, in as vile a manner as anyone else. The Negro writer must be able to foresee this reaction. The antagonism and opposition of the white American, he has already expected. These oppressors who have brutally ravaged the personality of a race, dare their victims to reveal the scars thus inflicted.

The scars of those assaulted personalities are not only reminders, but affronts.

It is in this guilt which now we all know of and understand, that keeps the oppressor outraged and unrelenting. It is his fear that he will have to resolve a condition which is as much his heritage as slavery is our own. The guilt, revolving in this fear is a condition the oppressor dare not aggravate. Yet, he can not permit or accept it, a fact which traps the white oppressor in his own greatest contradiction. The oppressor can not look upon the effects of his oppression without being aware of this contradiction; he doesn't want to be confronted with this evil, but neither can he escape or resolve it. He will go to any extent, from the bestial to the ridiculous, to avoid confrontation with this issue.

As Horace Clayton wrote in *Race Conflict in Modern Society,*

"To relieve himself of his guilt, to justify his hate, and to expel his fear, white men have erected an elaborate facade of justifications and rationalizations. The Negro is a primitive, dangerous person who must be kept in subordination. Negroes do not have the same high sensibilities as do whites and do not mind exploitation and rejection. Negroes are passive children of nature and are incapable of participating in and enjoying the higher aspects of the general American culture. Negroes would rather be by themselves. Negroes are eaten with tuberculosis and syphilis. But all these rationalizations do not quell the gnawing knowledge that they, Americans who believe in freedom, believe in the dignity of the human personality, are actively or passively perpetuating a society which defiles all that is human in other human beings."

We already know that attacks upon the honest American Negro novelist will emanate from the white race. However, the tragedy is that among white liberal groups are people who, themselves, are guiltless of any desire to oppress, but suffer the same guilt as do the active oppressors. Because of this they abhor with equal intensity the true revelations of Negroes' personalities. There are, of course, truly thoughtful, sincere, sympathetic white people who will shudder in protest at the statement that all American Negroes hate all American whites.

Of course, Negroes hate white people, far more actively than white people hate Negroes. What sort of idiocy is it that reasons American Negroes don't hate American whites? Can you abuse, enslave, persecute, segregate and generally oppress a people, and have them love you for it? Are white people expected not to hate *their* oppressors? Could any people be expected to escape the natural reaction to oppression? Let us be sensible. To hate white people is one of the first emotions an American Negro develops when he becomes old enough to learn what his status is in American society. He must, of necessity, hate white people. He would not be—and it would not be human if he did not—develop a hatred for his oppressors. At some time in the lives of every American Negro there has been this hatred for white people; there are no exceptions. It could not possibly be otherwise.

To the Negro writer who would plumb the depth of the Negro personality, there is no question of whether Negroes hate white people—but how does this hatred affect the Negro's personality? How much of himself is destroyed by this necessity to hate those who oppress him? Certainly hate is a destructive emotion. In the case of the Negro, hate is doubly destructive. The American Negro experiences two forms of hate. He hates first his oppressor, and then because he lives in constant fear of this hatred being discovered, he hates himself—because of this fear.

Yes, hate is an ugly word. It is an ugly emotion. It would be wonderful to say there is no hate; to say, we do not hate. But to merely speak the words would not make it so; it would not help us, who are Negroes, rid ourselves of hate. It would not help you, who are not Negroes, rid yourselves of hate. And it would not aid in the removal of the causes for which we hate. The question the Negro writer must answer is: how does the fear he feels as a Negro in white American society, affect his, the Negro personality?

There can be no understanding of Negro life, of Negroes' compulsions, reactions and actions; there can be no understanding of the sexual impulses, of Negro crime, of Negro marital relations, of our spiritual entreaties, our ambitions and our defeats, until this fear has been revealed at work behind the false fronted facades of our ghettoes; until others have experienced with us to the same extent the impact of fear upon our personalities. It is no longer enough to say the Negro is a victim of a stupid myth. We must know the truth and what it does to us.

If this plumbing for the truth reveals within the Negro personality, homicidal mania, lust for white women, a pathetic sense of inferiority, paradoxical anti-Semitism, arrogance, uncle tomism, hate and fear and self-hate, this then is the effect of oppression on the human personality. These are the daily horrors, the daily realities, the daily experiences of an oppressed minority.

And if it appears that the honest American Negro writer is trying to convince his audience that the whole Negro race in America, as a result of centuries of oppression, is sick at soul, the conclusion is unavoidable. It could not conceivably be otherwise.

The dilemma of the Negro writer lies not so much in what he must reveal, but in the reactions of his audience, in the intellectual limitations of the reader which so often confine men to habit and withhold from them the nobler instruments of reason and conscience. There should be no indictment of the writer who reveals this truth, but of the conditions that have produced it.

Himes logic has noted that American Negroes *have* written honest books and that they have been published and read. That is evidence that the dominant white group in America is not entirely given over to an irrevocable course of oppression.

There is an indomitable quality within the human spirit that can not be destroyed; a face deep within the human personality that is impregnable to all assaults. This quality, this force, exists deep within the Negro also; he is human. They rest so deeply that prejudice, oppression, lynchings, riots, time or weariness can never corrode or destroy them. During the three hundred years Negroes have lived in America as slaves and near subhumans, the whole moral fibre and personality of those Negroes now living would be a total waste; we would be drooling idiots, dangerous maniacs, raving beasts—if it were not for that quality and force within all humans that cries: "I will live!"

There is no other explanation of how so many Negroes have been able to break through the restrictions of oppression, retain their integrity, and attain eminence, and make valuable contributions to our whole culture. The Negro writer must not only reveal the truth, but also reveal and underline these higher qualities of humanity.

My definition of this quality within the human spirit that can not be destroyed is a single word: *Growth.* Growth is the surviving influence in all lives. The tree will send up its trunk in thick profusion from land burned black by atom bombs. Children will grow from poverty and filth and oppression and develop honor, develop integrity, contribute to all mankind.

It is a long way, a hard way from the hatred of the faces to the hatred of evil, a longer way still to the brotherhood of men. Once on the road, however, the Negro will discover that he is not alone. The white people whom he will encounter along the way may not appear to be accompanying him. But all, black and white, will be growing. When the American Negro writer has discovered that nothing ever becomes permanent but change, he will have rounded out his knowledge of the truth. And he will have performed his service as an artist.

Hidden Name and Complex Fate

Ralph Ellison

A Writer's Experience in the United States

In *Green Hills of Africa* Ernest Hemingway reminds us that both Tolstoy and Stendhal had seen war, that Flaubert had seen a revolution and the Commune, that Dostoievsky had been sent to Siberia and that such experiences were important in shaping the art of these great masters. And he goes on to observe that "writers are forged in injustice as a sword is forged." He declined to describe the many personal forms which injustice may take in this chaotic world—who would be so mad as to try?—nor does he go into the personal wounds which each of these writers sustained. Now, however, thanks to his brother and sister, we do know something of the injustice in which he himself was forged, and this knowledge has been added to what we have long known of Hemingway's artistic temper.

In the end, however, it is the quality of his art which is primary. It is the art which allows the wars and revolutions which he knew, and the personal and social injustices which he suffered, to lay claims upon our attention; for it was through his art that they achieved their most enduring meaning. It is a matter of outrageous irony, perhaps, but in literature the great social clashes of history no less than the painful experience of the individual are secondary to the meaning which they take on through the skill, the talent, the imagination and personal vision of the writer who transforms them into art. Here they are reduced to more manageable proportions; here they are imbued with humane values; here, injustice and catastrophe become less important in themselves than what the writer makes of them. This is *not* true, however, of the writer's struggle with that recalcitrant angel called Art; and it was through *this* specific struggle that Ernest Hemingway became *Hemingway* (now refined to a total body of transcendent work, after forty years of being endlessly dismembered and resurrected, as it continues to be, in the styles, the themes, the sense of life and literature of countless other writers). And it was through this struggle with form that he became the master, the culture hero, whom we have come to know and admire.

It was suggested that it might be of interest if I discussed here this evening some of my notions of the writer's experience in the United States, hence I have evoked the name of Hemingway, not by way of inviting far-fetched comparisons but in order to establish a perspective, a set of assumptions

From Ralph Ellison, *Shadow and Act* (New York: Random House, 1966), pp. 148-168.

from which I may speak, and in an attempt to avoid boring you by emphasizing those details of racial hardship which for some forty years now have been evoked whenever writers of my own cultural background have essayed their experience in public.

I do this *not* by way of denying totally the validity of these by now stylized recitals, for I have shared and still share many of their detailed injustices—what Negro can escape them?—but by way of suggesting that they are, at least in a discussion of a writer's experience, as *writer*, as artist, somewhat beside the point.

For we select neither our parents, our race nor our nation; these occur to us out of the love, the hate, the circumstances, the fate, of others. But we *do* become writers out of an act of will, out of an act of choice; a dim, confused and ofttimes regrettable choice, perhaps, but choice nevertheless. And what happens thereafter causes all those experiences which occurred before we began to function as writers to take on a special quality of uniqueness. If this does not happen then as far as writing goes, the experiences have been misused. If we do not make of them a value, if we do not transform them into forms and images of meaning which they did not possess before, then we have failed as artists.

Thus for a writer to insist that his personal suffering is of special interest in itself, or simply because he belongs to a particular racial or religious group, is to advance a claim for special privileges which members of his group who are not writers would be ashamed to demand. The kindest judgment one can make of this point of view is that it reveals a sad misunderstanding of the relationship between suffering and art. Thomas Mann and André Gide have told us much of this and there are critics, like Edmund Wilson, who have told of the connection between the wound and the bow.

As I see it, it is through the process of making artistic forms—plays, poems, novels—out of one's experience that one becomes a writer, and it is through this process, this struggle, that the writer helps give meaning to the experience of the group. And it is the process of mastering the discipline, the techniques, the fortitude, the culture, through which this is made possible that constitutes the writer's real experience as *writer,* as artist. If this sounds like an argument for the artist's withdrawal from social struggles, I would recall to you W. H. Auden's comment to the effect that:

> In our age, the mere making of a work of art is itself a political act. So long as artists exist, making what they please, and think they ought to make, even if it is not terribly good, even if it appeals to only a handful of people, they remind the Management of something managers need to be reminded of, namely, that the managed are people with faces, not anonymous members, that *Homo Laborans* is also *Homo Ludens*. . . .

Without doubt, even the most *engagé* writer—and I refer to true artists, not to artists *manqués*—begin their careers in play and puzzlement, in dreaming over the details of the world in which they become conscious of themselves.

Let Tar Baby, that enigmatic figure from Negro folklore, stand for the world. He leans, black and gleaming, against the wall of life utterly noncommittal under our scrutiny, our questioning, starkly unmoving before our naïve attempts at intimidation. Then we touch him playfully and before we can say *Sonny Liston!* we find ourselves stuck. Our playful investigations become a labor, a fearful struggle, an *agon*. Slowly we perceive that our task is to learn the proper way of freeing ourselves to develop, in other words, technique.

Sensing this, we give him our sharpest attention, we question him carefully, we struggle with more subtlety; while he, in his silent way, holds on, demanding that we perceive the necessity of calling him by his true name as the price of our freedom. It is unfortunate that he has so many, many "true names"—all spelling chaos; and in order to discover even one of these we must first come into the possession of our own names. For it is through our names that we first place ourselves in the world. Our names, being the gift of others, must be made our own.

Once while listening to the play of a two-year-old girl who did not know she was under observation, I heard her saying over and over again, at first with questioning and then with sounds of growing satisfaction, "I am Mimi Livisay? . . . *I am* Mimi Livisay. I *am* Mimi Livisay . . . I am *Mimi* Li-vi-say! I am Mimi . . ."

And in deed and in fact she was—or became so soon thereafter, by working playfully to establish the unit between herself and her name.

For many of us this is far from easy. We must learn to wear our names within all the noise and confusion of the environment in which we find ourselves; make them the center of all of our associations with the world, with man and with nature. We must charge them with all our emotions, our hopes, hates, loves, aspirations. They must become our masks and our shields and the containers of all those values and traditions which we learn and/or imagine as being the meaning of our familial past.

And when we are reminded so constantly that we bear, as Negroes, names originally possessed by those who owned our enslaved grandparents, we are apt, especially if we are potential writers, to be more than ordinarily concerned with the veiled and mysterious events, the fusions of blood, the furtive couplings, the business transactions, the violations of faith and loyalty, the assaults; yes, and the unrecognized and unrecognizable loves through which our names were handed down unto us.

So charged with emotion does this concern become for some of us, that we have, earlier, the example of the followers of Father Divine and, now, the Black Muslins, discarding their original names in rejection of the bloodstained, the brutal, the sinful images of the past. Thus they would declare new identities, would clarify a new program of intention and destroy the verbal evidence of a willed and ritualized discontinuity of blood and human intercourse.

Not all of us, actually only a few, seek to deal with our names in this manner. We take what we have and make of them what we can. And there are even those who know where the old broken connections lie, who recognize their relatives across the chasm of historical denial and the artificial barriers of society, and who see themselves as bearers of many of the qualities which were admirable in the original sources of their common line (Faulkner has made much of this); and I speak here not of mere forgiveness, nor of obsequious insensitivity to the outrages symbolized by the denial and the division, but of the conscious acceptance of the harsh realities of the human condition, of the ambiguities and hypocrisies of human history as they have played themselves out in the United States.

Perhaps, taken in aggregate, these European names which (sometimes with irony, sometimes with pride, but always with personal investment) represent a certain triumph of the spirit, speaking to us of those who rallied, reassembled and transformed themselves and who under dismembering pressures refused to die. "Brothers and sisters," I once heard a Negro preacher exhort, "let us make up our faces before the world, and our names shall sound throughout the land with honor! For we ourselves are our *true* names, not their epithets! So let us, I say, Make Up Our Faces and Our Minds!"

Perhaps my preacher had read T. S. Eliot, although I doubt it. And in actuality, it was unnecessary that he do so, for a concern with names and naming was very much part of that special area of American culture from which I come, and it is precisely for this reason that this example should come to mind in a discussion of my own experience as a writer.

Undoubtedly, writers begin their *conditioning* as manipulators of words long before they become aware of literature—certain Freudians would say at the breast. Perhaps. But if so, that is far too early to be of use at this moment. Of this, though, I am certain: that despite the misconceptions of those educators who trace the reading difficulties experienced by large numbers of Negro children in Northern schools to their Southern background, these children are, in *their* familiar South, facile manipulators of words. I know, too, that the Negro community is deadly in its ability to create nicknames and to spot all that is ludicrous in an unlikely name or that which is incongruous in conduct. Names are not qualities; nor are words, in this particular sense, actions. To assume that they are could cost one his life many times a day. Language skills depend to a large extent upon a knowledge of the details, the manners, the objects, the folkways, the psychological patterns, of a given environment. Humor and wit depend upon much the same awareness, and so does the suggestive power of names.

"A small brown bowlegged Negro with the name 'Franklin D. Roosevelt Jones' might sound like a clown to someone who looks at him from the outside," said my friend Albert Murray, "but on the other hand he just might turn out to be a hell of a fireside operator. He might just lie back in all of that comic juxtaposition of names and manipulate you deaf, dumb and blind

—and you not even suspecting it, because you're thrown out of stance by his name! There you are, so dazzled by the F.D.R. image—which you *know* you can't see—and so delighted with your own superior position that you don't realize that it's *Jones* who must be confronted."

Well, as you must suspect, all of this speculation on the matter of names has a purpose, and now, because it is tied up so ironically with my own experience as a writer, I must turn to my own name.

For in the dim beginnings, before I ever thought consciously of writing, there was my own name, and there was, doubtless, a certain magic in it. From the start I was uncomfortable with it, and in my earliest years it caused me much puzzlement. Neither could I understand what a poet was, nor why, exactly, my father had chosen to name me after one. Perhaps I could have understood it perfectly well had he named me after his own father, but that name had been given to an older brother who died and thus was out of the question. But why hadn't he named me after a hero, such as Jack Johnson, or a soldier like Colonel Charles Young, or a great seaman like Admiral Dewey, or an educator like Booker T. Washington, or a great orator and abolitionist like Frederick Douglass? Or again, why hadn't he named me (as many Negro parents had done) after President Teddy Roosevelt?

Instead, he named me after someone called Ralph Waldo Emerson, and then, when I was three, he died. It was too early for me to have understood his choice, although I'm sure he must have explained it many times, and it was also too soon for me to have made the connection between my name and my father's love for reading. Much later, after I began to write and work with words, I came to suspect that he was aware of the suggestive powers of names and of the magic involved in naming.

I recall an odd conversation with my mother during my early teens in which she mentioned their interests in, of all things, prenatal culture! But for a long time I actually knew only that my father read a lot, and that he admired this remote Mr. Emerson, who was something called a "poet and philosopher"—so much that he named his second son after him.

I knew, also, that whatever his motives, the combination of names he'd given me caused me no end of trouble from the moment when I could talk well enough to respond to the ritualized question which grownups put to very young children. Emerson's name was quite familiar to Negroes in Oklahoma during those days when World War I was brewing, and adults, eager to show off their knowledge of literary figures, and obviously amused by the joke implicit in such a small brown nubbin of a boy carrying around such a heavy moniker, would invariably repeat my first two names and then to my great annoyance, they'd add "Emerson."

And I, in my confusion, would reply, "No, *no, I'm* not Emerson, he's the little boy who lives next door." Which only made them laugh all the louder. "Oh, no," they'd say, "*you're* Ralph Waldo Emerson," while I had fantasies of blue murder.

For a while the presence next door of my little friend, Emerson, made it unnecessary for me to puzzle too often over this peculiar adult confusion. And since there were other Negro boys named Ralph in the city, I came to suspect that there was something about the combination of names which produced their laughter. Even today I know of only one other Ralph who had as much comedy made out of his name, a campus politician and deep-voiced orator whom I knew at Tuskegee, who was called in friendly ribbing, *Ralph Waldo Emerson Edgar Allan Poe,* spelled Powe. This must have been quite a trial for him, but I had been initiated much earlier.

During my early school years the name continued to puzzle me, for it constantly evoked in the faces of others some secret. It was as though I possessed some treasure or some defect, which was invisible to my own eyes and ears; something which I had but did not *possess,* like a piece of property in South Carolina, which was mine but which I could not have until some future time. I recall finding, about this time, while seeking adventure in back alleys—which possess for boys a superiority over playgrounds like that which kitchen utensils possess over toys designed for infants—a large photographic lens. I remember nothing of its optical qualities, of its speed or color correction, but it gleamed with crystal mystery and it was beautiful.

Mounted handsomely in a tube of shiny brass, it spoke to me of distant worlds of possibility. I played with it, looking through it with squinted eyes, holding it in shafts of sunlight, and tried to use it for a magic lantern. But most of this was as unrewarding as my attempts to make the music come from a phonograph record by holding the needle in my fingers.

I could burn holes through newspapers with it, or I could pretend that it was a telescope, the barrel of a cannon, or the third eye of a monster—*I* being the monster—but I could do nothing at all about its proper function of making images, nothing to make it yield its secret. But I could not discard it.

Older boys sought to get it away from me by offering knives or tops, agate marbles or whole zoos of grass snakes and horned toads in trade, but I held on to it. No one, not even the white boys I knew, had such a lens, and it was my own good luck to have found it. Thus I would hold on to it until such time as I could acquire the parts needed to make it function. Finally I put it aside and it remained buried in my box of treasures, dusty and dull, to be lost and forgotten as I grew older and became interested in music.

I had reached by now the grades where it was necessary to learn something about Mr. Emerson and what he had written, such as the "Concord Hymn" and the essay "Self-Reliance," and in following his advice, I reduced the "Waldo" to a simple and, I hope, mysterious "W," and in my own reading I avoided his works like the plague. I could no more deal with my name—I shall never really master it—than I could find a creative use for my lens. Fortunately there were other problems to occupy my mind. Not that I forgot my fascination with names, but more about that later.

Negro Oklahoma City was starkly lacking in writers. In fact, there was only

Roscoe Dungee, the editor of the local Negro newspaper and a very fine editorialist in that valuable tradition of personal journalism which is now rapidly disappearing; a writer who in his emphasis upon the possibilities for justice offered by the Constitution anticipated the anti-segregation struggle by decades. There were also a few reporters who drifted in and out, but these were about all. On the level of *conscious* culture the Negro community was biased in the direction of music.

These were the middle and late twenties, remember, and the state was still a new frontier state. The capital city was one of the great centers for southwestern jazz, along with Dallas and Kansas City. Orchestras which were to become famous within a few years were constantly coming and going. As were the blues singers—Ma Rainey and Ida Cox, and the old bands like that of King Oliver. But best of all, thanks to Mrs. Zelia N. Breaux, there was an active and enthusiastic school music program through which any child who had the interest and the talent could learn to play an instrument and take part in the band, the orchestra, the brass quartet. And there was a yearly operetta and a chorus and a glee club. Harmony was taught for four years and the music appreciation program was imperative. European folk dances were taught throughout the Negro school system, and we were also taught complicated patterns of military drill.

I tell you this to point out that although there were no incentives to write, there was ample opportunity to receive an artistic discipline. Indeed, once one picked up an instrument it was difficult to escape. If you chafed at the many rehearsals of the school band or orchestra and were drawn to the many small jazz groups, you were likely to discover that the jazzmen were apt to rehearse far more than the school band, it was only that they seemed to enjoy themselves better and to possess a freedom of imagination which we were denied at school. And one soon learned that the wild, transcendent moments which occurred at dances or "battles of music," moments in which memorable improvisions were ignited, depended upon a dedication to a discipline which was observed even when rehearsals had to take place in the crowded quarters of Halley Richardson's shoeshine parlor. It was not the place which counted, although a large hall with good acoustics was preferred, but what one did to perfect one's performance.

If this talk of musical discipline gives the impression that there were no forces working to nourish one who would one day blunder, after many a twist and turn, into writing, I am misleading you. And here I might give you a longish lecture on the Ironics and Uses of Segregation. When I was a small child there was no library for Negroes in our city, and not until a Negro minister invaded the main library did we get one. For it was discovered that there was no law, only custom, which held that we could not use these public facilities. The results were the quick renting of two large rooms in a Negro office building (the recent site of a pool hall), the hiring of a young Negro librarian, the installation of shelves and a hurried stocking of the walls with any and every book possible. It was, in those first days, something of a literary chaos.

But how fortunate for a boy who loved to read! I started with the fairy tales and quickly went through the junior fiction; then through the Westerns and the detective novels, and very soon I was reading the classics—only I didn't know it. There were also the Haldeman Julius Blue Books, which seem to have floated on the air down from Girard, Kansas; the syndicated columns of O. O. McIntyre, and the copies of *Vanity Fair* and the *Literary Digest* which my mother brought home from work—how could I ever join uncritically in the heavy-handed attacks on the so-called Big Media which have become so common today?

There were also the pulp magazines and, more important, that other library which I visited when I went to help my adopted grandfather, J. D. Randolph (my parents had been living in his rooming house when I was born), at his work as custodian of the law library of the Oklahoma State Capitol. Mr. Randolph had been one of the first teachers in what became Oklahoma City, and he'd also been one of the leaders of a group who walked from Gallatin, Tennessee, to the Oklahoma Territory. He was a tall man, as brown as smoked leather, who looked like the Indians with whom he'd herded horses in the early days.

And while his status was merely the custodian of the law library, I was to see the white legislators come down on many occasions to question him on points of law, and often I was to hear him answer without recourse to the uniform rows of books on the shelves. This was a thing to marvel at in itself, and the white lawmakers did so, but even more marvelous, ironic, intriguing, haunting—call it what you will—is the fact that the Negro who knew the answers was named after Jefferson Davis. What Tennessee lost, Oklahoma was to gain, and after gaining it (a gift of courage, intelligence, fortitude and grace), used it only in concealment and, one hopes, with embarrassment.

So, let us, I say, make up our faces and our minds!

In the loosely structured community of the time, knowledge, news of other ways of living, ancient wisdom, the latest literary fads, hate literature—for years I kept a card warning Negroes away from the polls, which had been dropped by the thousands from a plane which circled over the Negro community—information of all kinds, found its level, catch-as-catch can, in the minds of those who were receptive to it. Not that there was no conscious structuring— I read my first Shaw and Maupassant, my first Harvard Classics in the home of a friend whose parents were products of that stream of New England education which had been brought to Negroes by the young and enthusiastic white teachers who staffed the schools set up for the freedmen after the Civil War. These parents were both teachers and there were others like them in our town.

But the places where a rich oral literature was truly functional were the churches, the schoolyards, the barbershops, the cotton-picking camps; places where forklore and gossip thrived. The drug store where I worked was such a place, where on days of bad weather the older men would sit with their pipes and tell tall tales, hunting yarns and homely versions of the classics. It was here that I heard stories of searching for buried treasure and of headless horsemen, which I was told were my own father's versions told long before. There were even recitals of popular verse, "The Shooting of Dan McGrew," and, along with these, stories of Jesse James, of Negro outlaws and black United States marshals, of slaves who became the chiefs of Indian tribes and of the exploits of Negro cowboys. There was both truth and fantasy in this, intermingled in the mysterious fashion of literature.

Writers, in their formative period, absorb into their consciousness much that has no special value until much later, and often much which is of no special value even then—perhaps, beyond the fact that it throbs with affect and mystery and in it "time and pain and royalty in the blood" are suspended in imagery. So, long before I thought of writing, I was claimed by weather, by speech rhythms, by Negro voices and their different idioms, by husky male voices and by the shrill singing voices of certain Negro women, by music, by tight spaces and by wide space in which the eyes could wander, by death, by newly born babies, by manners of various kinds, company manners and street manners, the manners of white society and those of our own high society, and by interracial manners; by street fights, circuses and minstrel shows, by vaudeville and moving pictures, by prize fights and foot races, baseball games and football matches. By spring floods and blizzards, catalpa worms and jack rabbits, honeysuckle and snapdragons (which smelled like old cigar butts); by sunflowers and hollyhocks, raw sugar cane and baked yams; pigs' feet, chili and blue haw ice cream. By parades, public dances and jam sessions, Easter sunrise ceremonies and large funerals. By contests between fire-and-brimstone preachers and by presiding elders who got "laughing-happy" when moved by the spirit of God.

I was impressed by expert players of the "dozens" and certain notorious bootleggers of corn whiskey. By jazz musicians and fortunetellers and by men who did anything well; by strange sicknesses and by interesting brick or razor scars; by expert cursing vocabularies as well as by exalted praying and terrifying shouting, and by transcendent playing or singing of the blues. I was fascinated by old ladies, those who had seen slavery and those who were defiant of white folk and black alike; by the enticing walks of prostitutes and by the limping walks affected by Negro hustlers, especially those who wore Stetson hats, expensive shoes with well-starched overalls, usually with a diamond stickpin (when not in hock) in their tieless collars as their gambling uniforms.

And there were the blind men who preached on corners, and the blind men who sang the blues to the accompaniment of washboard and guitar; and the white junkmen who sang mountain music and the famous hucksters of fruit and vegetables.

And there was the Indian-Negro confusion. There were Negroes who were part Indian and who lived on reservations, and Indians who had children who lived in towns as Negroes, and Negroes who were Indians and traveled back and forth between the groups with no trouble. And Indians who were wild as wild Negroes and others who were as solid and steady as bankers. There were the teachers, too, inspiring teachers and villainous teachers who chased after the girl students, and certain female teachers who one wished would chase after young male students. And a handsome old principal of military bearing who had been blemished by his classmates at West Point when they discovered on the eve of the graduation that he was a Negro. There were certain Jews, Mexicans, Chinese cooks, a German orchestra conductor and an English grocer who owned a Franklin touring car. And certain Negro mechanics—"Cadillac Slim," "Sticks" Walker, Buddy Bunn and Oscar Pitman—who had so assimilated the automobile that they seemed to be behind a steering wheel even as they walked the streets or danced with girls. And there were the whites who despised us and the others who shared our hardships and joys.

There is much more, but this is sufficient to indicate some of what was present even in a segregated community to form the background of my work, my sense of life.

And now comes the next step. I went to Tuskegee to study music, hoping to become a composer of symphonies and there, during my second year, I read *The Waste Land* and that, although I was then unaware of it, was the real transition to writing.

Mrs. L. C. McFarland had taught us much of Negro history in grade school and from her I'd learned of the New Negro Movement of the twenties, of Langston Hughes, Countee Cullen, Claude McKay, James Weldon Johnson and the others. They had inspired pride and had given me a closer identification with poetry (by now, oddly enough, I seldom thought of my hidden name), but with music so much on my mind it never occurred to me to try to imitate them. Still I read their work and was excited by the glamour of the Harlem which emerged from their poems and it was good to know that there were Negro writers.—Then came *The Waste Land*.

I was much more under the spell of literature than I realized at the time. *Wuthering Heights* had caused me an agony of unexpressible emotion and the same was true of *Jude the Obscure,* but *The Waste Land* seized my mind. I was intrigued by its power to move me while eluding my understanding. Somehow its rhythms were often closer to those of jazz than were those of the Negro poets, and even though I could not understand then, its range of allusion was as mixed and as varied as that of Louis Armstrong. Yet there were its discontinuities, its changes of pace and its hidden system of organization which escaped me.

There was nothing to do but look up the references in the footnotes to the poem, and thus began my conscious education in literature.

For this, the library at Tuskegee was quite adequate and I used it. Soon I was reading a whole range of subjects drawn upon by the poet, and this led, in turn, to criticism and to Pound and Ford Madox Ford, Sherwood Anderson and Gertrude Stein, Hemingway and Fitzgerald and "round about 'til I was come" back to Melville and Twain—the writers who are taught and doubtlessly overtaught today. Perhaps it was my good luck that they were not taught at Tuskegee, I wouldn't know. But at the time I was playing, having an intellectually interesting good time.

Having given so much attention to the techniques of music, the process of learning something of the craft and intention of modern poetry and fiction seemed quite familiar. Besides, it was absolutely painless because it involved no deadlines or credits. Even then, however, a process which I described earlier had begun to operate. The more I learned of literature in this conscious way, the more the details of my background became transformed. I heard undertones in remembered conversations which had escaped me before, local customs took on a more universal meaning, values which I hadn't understood were revealed; some of the people whom I had known were diminished while others were elevated in stature. More important, I began to see my own possibilities with more objective, and in some ways, more hopeful eyes.

The following summer I went to New York seeking work, which I did not find, and remained there, but the personal transformation continued. Reading had become a conscious process of growth and discovery, a method of reordering the world. And that world had widened considerably.

At Tuskegee I had handled manuscripts which Prokofiev had given to Hazel Harrison, a Negro concert pianist who taught there and who had known him in Europe, and through Miss Harrison I had become aware of Prokofiev's symphonies. I had also become aware of the radical movement in politics and art, and in New York had begun reading the work of André Malraux, not only the fiction but chapters published from his *Psychology of Art.* And in my search for an expression of modern sensibility in the works of Negro writers I discovered Richard Wright. Shortly thereafter I was to meet Wright, and it was at his suggestion that I wrote both my first book review and my first short story. These were fatal suggestions.

For although I had tried my hand at poetry while at Tuskegee, it hadn't occurred to me that I might write fiction, but once he suggested it, it seemed the most natural thing to try. Fortunately for me, Wright, then on the verge of his first success, was eager to talk with a beginner and I was able to save valuable time in searching out those works in which writing was discussed as a craft. He guided me to Henry James' prefaces, to Conrad, to Joseph Warren Beach and to the letters of Dostoievsky. There were other advisers and other books involved, of course, but what is important here is that I was consciously concerned with the art of fiction, that almost from the beginning I was grappling quite consciously with the art through which I wished to realize myself. And this was not done in isolation; the Spanish Civil War was now in progress and the Depression was still on. The world was being shaken up, and through one of those odd instances which occur to young provincials in

New York, I was to hear Malraux make an appeal for the Spanish Loyalists at the same party where I first heard the folk singer Leadbelly perform. Wright and I went there seeking money for the magazine which he had come to New York to edit.

Art and politics; a great French novelist and a Negro folk singer; a young writer who was soon to publish *Uncle Tom's Children;* and I who had barely begun to study his craft. It is such accidents, such fortuitous meetings, which count for so much in our lives. I had never dreamed that I would be in the presence of Malraux, of whose work I became aware on my second day in Harlem when Langston Hughes suggested that I read *Man's Fate* and *Days of Wrath* before returning them to a friend of his. And it is this fortuitous circumstance which led to my selecting Malraux as a literary "ancestor," whom, unlike a relative, the artist is permitted to choose. There was in progress at the time all the agitation over the Scottsboro boys and the Herndon Case, and I was aware of both. I had to be; I myself had been taken off a freight train at Decatur, Alabama, only three years before while on my way to Tuskegee. But while I joined in the agitation for their release, my main energies went into learning to write.

I began to publish enough, and not too slowly, to justify my hopes for success, and as I continued, I made a most perplexing discovery; namely, that for all his conscious concern with technique, a writer did not so much create the novel as he was created *by* the novel. That is, one did not make an arbitrary gesture when one sought to write. And when I say that the novelist is created by the novel, I mean to remind you that fictional techniques are not a mere set of objective tools, but something much more intimate: a way of feeling, of seeing and of expressing one's sense of life. And the process of *acquiring* technique is a process of modifying one's responses, of learning to see and feel, to hear and observe, to evoke and evaluate the images of memory and of summoning up and directing the imagination; of learning to conceive of human values in the ways which have been established by the great writers who have developed and extended the art. And perhaps the writer's greatest freedom, as artist, lies precisely in his possession of technique; for it is through technique that he comes to possess and express the meaning of his life.

Perhaps at this point it would be useful to recapitulate the route—perhaps as mazelike as those of *Finnegan's Wake*—which I have been trying to describe, that which leads from the writer's discovery of a sense of purpose, which is that of becoming a writer, and then the involvement in the passionate struggle required to master a bit of technique, and then, as this begins to take shape, the disconcerting discovery that it is *technique* which transforms the individual before he is able in turn to transform it. And in that personal transformation he discovers something else: he discovers that he had taken on certain obligations, that he must not embarrass his chosen form, and that in order to avoid this he must develop taste. He learns—and this is most discouraging—that he is involved with values which turn in their *own* way, and not in the ways of politics, upon the central issues affecting his nation and his time. He learns that the American novel, from its first consciousness of itself as a literary form, has grappled with the meaning of the American experience, that it has been aware and has sought to define the nature of that experience by addressing itself to the specific details, the moods, the landscapes, the cityscapes, the tempo of American change. And that it has borne, at its best, the full weight of that burden of conscience and consciousness which Americans inherit as one of the results of the revolutionary circumstances of our national beginnings.

We began as a nation not through the accidents of race or religion or geography (Robert Penn Warren has dwelled on these circumstances) but when a group of men, *some* of them political philosophers, put down, upon what we now recognize as being quite sacred papers, their conception of the nation which they intended to establish on these shores. They described, as we know, the obligations of the state to the citizen, of the citizen to the state; they committed themselves to certain ideas of justice, just as they committed us to a system which would guarantee all of its citizens equality of opportunity.

I need not describe the problems which have arisen from these beginnings. I need only remind you that the contradiction between these noble ideas and the actualities of our conduct generated a guilt, an unease of spirit, from the very beginning, and that the American novel at its best has always been concerned with this basic moral predicament. During Melville's time and Twain's, it was an implicit aspect of their major themes, by the twentieth century and after the discouraging and traumatic effect of the Civil War and the Reconstruction it had gone underground, had become *understated.* Nevertheless it did not disappear completely and it is to be found operating in the work of Henry James as well as in that of Hemingway and Fitzgerald. And then (and as one who believes in the impelling moral function of the novel and who believes in the moral seriousness of the form) it pleases me no end that it comes into explicit statement again in the works of Richard Wright and William Faulkner, writers who lived close to moral and political problems which would not stay put underground.

I go into these details not to recapitulate the history of the American novel but to indicate the trend of thought which was set into motion when I began to discover the nature of that process with which I was actually involved. Whatever the opinion and decisions of critics, a novelist must arrive at his own conclusions as to the meaning and function of the form with which he is engaged, and these are, in all modesty, some of mine.

In order to orient myself I also began to learn that the American novel had long concerned itself with the puzzle of the one-and-the-many; the mystery of how each of us, despite his origin in diverse regions, with our diverse racial, cultural, religious backgrounds, speaking his own diverse idiom of the American in his own accent, is, nevertheless, American. And with this concern with the implicit pluralism of the country and with the composite nature of the ideal character called "the American," there goes a concern with gauging the health of the American promise, with depicting the extent to which it was being achieved, being made manifest in our daily conduct.

And with all of this there still remains the specific concerns of literature. Among these is the need to keep literary standards high, the necessity of exploring new possibilities of language which would allow it to retain that flexibility and fidelity to the common speech which has been its glory since Mark Twain. For me this meant learning to add to it the wonderful resources of Negro American speech and idiom and to bring into range as fully and eloquently as possible the complex reality of the American experience as it shaped and was shaped by the lives of my own people.

Notice that I stress as "fully" as possible, because I would no more strive to write great novels by leaving out the complexity of circumstances which go to make up the Negro experience and which alone go to make the obvious injustice bearable, than I would think of preparing myself to become President of the United States simply by studying Negro American history or confining myself to studying those laws affecting civil rights.

For it seems to me that one of the obligations I took on when I committed myself to the art and form of the novel was that of striving for the broadest range, the discovery and articulation of the most exalted values. And I must squeeze these from the life which I know best. (A highly truncated impression of that life I attempted to convey to you earlier.)

If all this sounds a bit heady, remember that I did not destroy that troublesome middle name of mine, I only suppressed it. Sometimes it reminds me of my obligations to the man who named me.

It is our fate as human beings always to give up some good things for other good things, to throw off certain bad circumstances only to create others. Thus there is a value for the writer in trying to give as thorough a report of social reality as possible. Only by doing so may we grasp and convey the cost of change. Only by considering the broadest accumulation of data may we make choices that are based upon our own hard-earned sense of reality. Speaking from my own special area of American culture, I feel that to embrace uncritically values which are extended to us by others is to reject the validity, even the sacredness, of our own experience. It is also to forget that the small share of reality which each of our diverse groups is able to snatch from the whirling chaos of history belongs not to the group alone, but to all of us. It is a property and a witness which can be ignored only to the danger of the entire nation.

I could suppress the name of my namesake out of respect for the achievements of its original bearer but I cannot escape the obligation of attempting to achieve some of the things which he asked of the American writer. As Henry James suggested, being an American is an arduous task, and for most of us, I suspect, the difficulty begins with the name.

Address sponsored by the Gertrude Clarke Whittall Foundation, Library of Congress, January 6, 1964.

How "Bigger" Was Born

Richard Wright

I am not so pretentious as to imagine that it is possible for me to account completely for my own book, *Native Son*. But I am going to try to account for as much of it as I can, the sources of it, the material that went into it, and my own years' long changing attitude toward that material.

In a fundamental sense, an imaginative novel represents the merging of two extremes; it is an intensely intimate expression on the part of a consciousness couched in terms of the most objective and commonly known events. It is at once something private and public by its very nature and texture. Confounding the author who is trying to lay his cards on the table is the dogging knowledge that his imagination is a kind of community medium of exchange: what he has read, felt, thought, seen, and remembered is translated into extensions as impersonal as a worn dollar bill.

The more closely the author thinks of why he wrote, the more he comes to regard his imagination as a kind of self-generating cement which glued his facts together, and his emotions as a kind of dark and obscure designer of those facts. Always there is something that is just beyond the tip of the tongue that could explain it all. Usually, he ends up by discussing something far afield, an act which incites skepticism and suspicion in those anxious for a straight-out explanation.

Yet the author is eager to explain. But the moment he makes the attempt his words falter, for he is confronted and defied by the inexplicable array of his own emotions. Emotions are subjective and he can communicate them only when he clothes them in objective guise; and how can he ever be so arrogant as to know when he is dressing up the right emotion in the right Sunday suit? He is always left with the uneasy notion that maybe *any* objective drapery is as good as *any* other for any emotion.

And the moment he does dress up an emotion, his mind is confronted with the riddle of that "dressed up" emotion, and he is left peering with eager dismay back into the dim reaches of his own incommunicable life. Reluctantly, he comes to the conclusion that to account for his book is to account for his life, and he knows that that is impossible. Yet, some curious, wayward motive urges him to supply the answer, for there is the feeling that his dignity as a living being is challenged by something within him that is not understood.

So, at the outset, I say frankly that there are phases of *Native Son* which I shall make no attempt to account for. There are meanings in my book of

From Richard Wright, *Native Son* (New York: Random House, 1940), pp. vii-xxxiv.

which I was not aware until they literally spilled out upon the paper. I shall sketch the outline of how I *consciously* came into possession of the materials that went into *Native Son,* but there will be many things I shall omit, not because I want to, but simply because I don't know them.

The birth of Bigger Thomas goes back to my childhood, and there was not just one Bigger, but many of them, more than I could count and more than you suspect. But let me start with the first Bigger, whom I shall call Bigger No. 1.

When I was a bareheaded, barefoot kid in Jackson, Mississippi, there was a boy who terrorized me and all of the boys I played with. If we were playing games, he would saunter up and snatch from us our balls, bats, spinning tops, and marbles. We would stand around pouting, sniffing, trying to keep back our tears, begging for our playthings. But Bigger would refuse. We never demanded that he give them back; we were afraid, and Bigger was bad. We had seen him clout boys when he was angry and we did not want to run that risk. We never recovered our toys unless we flattered him and made him feel that he was superior to us. Then, perhaps, if he felt like it, he condescended, threw them at us and then gave each of us a swift kick in the bargain, just to make us feel his utter contempt.

That was the way Bigger No. 1 lived. His life was a continuous challenge to others. At all times he *took* his way, right or wrong, and those who contradicted him had him to fight. And never was he happier than when he had someone cornered and at his mercy; it seemed that the deepest meaning of his squalid life was in him at such times.

I don't know what the fate of Bigger No. 1 was. His swaggering personality is swallowed up somewhere in the amnesia of my childhood. But I suspect that his end was violent. Anyway, he left a marked impression upon me; maybe it was because I longed secretly to be like him and was afraid. I don't know.

If I had known only one Bigger I would not have written *Native Son.* Let me call the next one Bigger No. 2; he was about seventeen and tougher than the first Bigger. Since I, too, had grown older, I was a little less afraid of him. And the hardness of this Bigger No. 2 was not directed toward me or the other Negroes, but toward the whites who ruled the South. He bought clothes and food on credit and would not pay for them. He lived in the dingy shacks of the white landlords and refused to pay rent. Of course, he had no money, but neither did we. We did without the necessities of life and starved ourselves, but he never would. When we asked him why he acted as he did, he would tell us (as though we were little children in a kindergarten) that the white folks had everything and he had nothing. Further, he would tell us that we were fools not to get what we wanted while we were alive in this world. We would listen and silently agree. We longed to believe and act as he did, but we were afraid. We were Southern Negroes and we were hungry and we wanted to live, but we were more willing to tighten our belts than risk conflict. Bigger No. 2 wanted to live and he did; he was in prison the last time I heard from him.

There was Bigger No. 3, whom the white folks called a "bad nigger." He carried his life in his hands in a literal fashion. I once worked as a ticket-taker in a Negro movie house (all movie houses in Dixie are Jim Crow; there are movies for whites and movies for blacks), and many times Bigger No. 3 came to the door and gave my arm a hard pinch and walked into the theater. Resentfully and silently, I'd nurse my bruised arm. Presently, the proprietor would come over and ask how things were going. I'd point into the darkened theater and say: "Bigger's in there." "Did he pay?" the proprietor would ask. "No, sir," I'd answer. The proprietor would pull down the corners of his lips and speak through his teeth: "We'll kill that goddam nigger one of these days." And the episode would end right there. But later on Bigger No. 3 was killed during the days of Prohibition: while delivering liquor to a customer he was shot through the back by a white cop.

And then there was Bigger No. 4, whose only law was death. The Jim Crow laws of the South were not for him. But as he laughed and cursed and broke them, he knew that some day he'd have to pay for his freedom. His rebellious spirit made him violate all the taboos and consequently he always oscillated between moods of intense elation and depression. He was never happier than when he had outwitted some foolish custom, and he was never more melancholy than when brooding over the impossibility of his ever being free. He had no job, for he regarded digging ditches for fifty cents a day as slavery. "I can't live on that," he would say. Ofttimes I'd find him reading a book; he would stop and in a joking, wistful, and cynical manner ape the antics of the white folks. Generally, he'd end his mimicry in a depressed state and say: "The white folks won't let us do nothing." Bigger No. 4 was sent to the asylum for the insane.

Then there was Bigger No. 5, who always rode the Jim Crow streetcars without paying and sat wherever he pleased. I remember one morning his getting into a streetcar (all streetcars in Dixie are divided into two sections: one section is for whites and is labeled—FOR WHITES; the other section is for Negroes and is labeled—FOR COLORED) and sitting in the white section. The conductor went to him and said: "Come on, nigger. Move over where you belong. Can't you read?" Bigger answered: "Naw, I can't read." The conductor flared up: "Get out of that seat!" Bigger took out his knife, opened it, held it nonchalantly in his hand, and replied: "Make me." The conductor turned red, blinked, clenched his fists, and walked away, stammering: "The goddamn scum of the earth!" A small angry conference of white men took place in the front of the car and the Negroes sitting in the Jim Crow section overheard: "That's that Bigger Thomas nigger and you'd better leave 'im alone." The Negroes experienced an intense flash of pride and the streetcar moved on its journey without incident. I don't know what happened to Bigger No. 5. But I can guess.

The Bigger Thomases were the only Negroes I know of who consistently violated the Jim Crow laws of the South and got away with it, at least for a sweet brief spell. Eventually, the whites who restricted their lives made them pay a terrible price. They were shot, hanged, maimed, lynched, and generally hounded until they were either dead or their spirits broken.

There were many variations to this behavioristic pattern. Later on I encountered other Bigger Thomases who did not react to the locked-in Black Belts with this same extremity and violence. But before I use Bigger Thomas as a springboard for the examination of milder types, I'd better indicate more precisely the nature of the environment that produced these men, or the reader will be left with the impression that they were essentially and organically bad.

In Dixie there are two worlds, the white world and the black world, and they are physically separated. There are white schools and black schools, white churches and black churches, white businesses and black businesses, white graveyards and black graveyards, and, for all I know, a white God and a black God. . . .

This separation was accomplished after the Civil War by the terror of the Ku Klux Klan, which swept the newly freed Negro through arson, pillage, and death out of the United States Senate, the House of Representatives, the many state legislatures, and out of the public, social, and economic life of the South. The motive for this assault was simple and urgent. The imperialistic tug of history had torn the Negro from his African home and had placed him ironically upon the most fertile plantation areas of the South; and, when the Negro was freed, he outnumbered the whites in many of these fertile areas. Hence, a fierce and bitter struggle took place to keep the ballot from the Negro, for had he had a chance to vote, he would have automatically controlled the richest lands of the South and with them the social, political, and economic destiny of a third of the Republic. Though the South is politically a part of America, the problem that faced her was peculiar and the struggle between the whites and the blacks after the Civil War was in essence a struggle for power, ranging over thirteen states and involving the lives of tens of millions of people.

But keeping the ballot from the Negro was not enough to hold him in check; disfranchisement had to be supplemented by a whole panoply of rules, taboos, and penalties designed not only to insure peace (complete submission), but to guarantee that no real threat would ever arise. Had the Negro lived upon a common territory, separate from the bulk of the white population, this program of oppression might not have assumed such a brutal and violent form. But this war took place between people who were neighbors, whose homes adjoined, whose farms had common boundaries. Guns and disfranchisement, therefore, were not enough to make the black neighbor keep his distance. The white neighbor decided to limit the amount of education his black neighbor could receive; decided to keep him off the police force and out of the local national guards; to segregate him residentially; to Jim Crow him in public places; to restrict his participation in the professions and jobs; and to build up a vast, dense ideology of racial superiority that would justify any act of violence taken against him to defend white dominance; and further, to condition him to hope for little and to receive that little without rebelling.

But, because the blacks were so *close* to the very civilization which sought to keep them out, because they could not *help* but react in some way to its incentives and prizes, and because the very tissue of their consciousness received its tone and timbre from the strivings of that dominant civilization, oppression spawned among them a myriad variety of reactions, reaching from outright blind rebellion to a sweet, other-worldly submissiveness.

In the main, this delicately balanced state of affairs has not greatly altered since the Civil War, save in those parts of the South which have been industrialized or urbanized. So volatile and tense are these relations that if a Negro rebels against rule and taboo, he is lynched and the reason for the lynching is usually called "rape," that catchword which has garnered such vile connotations that it can raise a mob anywhere in the South pretty quickly, even today.

Now for the variations in the Bigger Thomas pattern. Some of the Negroes living under these conditions got religion, felt that Jesus would redeem the void of living, felt that the more bitter life was in the present the happier it would be in the hereafter. Others, clinging still to that brief glimpse of post-Civil War freedom, employed a thousand ruses and stratagems of struggle to win their rights. Still others projected their hurts and longings into more naïve and mundane forms—blues, jazz, swing—and, without intellectual guidance, tried to build up a compensatory nourishment for themselves. Many labored under the hot suns and then killed the restless ache with alcohol. Then there were those who strove for an education, and when they got it, enjoyed the financial fruits of it in the style of their bourgeois oppressors. Usually they went hand in hand with the powerful whites and helped to keep their groaning brothers in line, for that was the safest course of action. Those who did this called themselves "leaders." To give you an idea of how completely these "leaders" worked with those who oppressed, I can tell you that I lived the first seventeen years of my life in the South without so much as hearing of or seeing one act of rebellion from *any* Negro, save the Bigger Thomases.

But why did Bigger revolt? No explanation based upon a hard and fast rule of conduct can be given. But there were always two factors psychologically dominant in his personality. First, through some quirk of circumstances, he had become estranged from the religion and the folk culture of his race. Second, he was trying to react to and answer the call of the dominant civilization whose glitter came to him through the newspaper, magazines, radios, movies, and the mere imposing sight and sound of daily American life. In many respects his emergence as a distinct type was inevitable.

As I grew older, I became familiar with the Bigger Thomas conditioning and its numerous shadings no matter where I saw it in Negro life. It was not, as I have already said, as blatant or extreme as in the originals; but it was there, nevertheless, like an undeveloped negative.

Sometimes, in areas far removed from Mississippi, I'd hear a Negro say: "I wish I didn't have to live this way. I feel like I want to burst." Then the anger would pass; he would go back to his job and try to eke out a few pennies to support his wife and children.

Sometimes I'd hear a Negro say: "God, I wish I had a flag and a country of my own." But that mood would soon vanish and he would go his way placidly enough.

Sometimes I'd hear a Negro ex-soldier say: "What in hell did I fight in the war for? They segregated me even when I was offering my life for my country." But he, too, like the others, would soon forget, would become caught up in the tense grind of struggle for bread.

I've even heard Negroes, in moments of anger and bitterness, praise what Japan is doing in China, not because they believed in oppression (being objects of oppression themselves), but because they would suddenly sense how empty their lives were when looking at the dark faces of Japanese generals in the rotogravure supplements of the Sunday newspapers. They would dream of what it would be like to live in a country where they could forget their color and play a responsible role in the vital processes of the nation's life.

I've even heard Negroes say that maybe Hitler and Mussolini are all right; that maybe Stalin is all right. They did not say this out of any intellectual comprehension of the forces at work in the world, but because they felt that these men "did things," a phrase which is charged with more meaning than the mere words imply. There was in the back of their minds, when they said this, a wild and intense longing (wild and intense because it was suppressed!) to belong, to be identified, to feel that they were alive as other people were, to be caught up forgetfully and exultingly in the swing of events, to feel the clean, deep, organic satisfaction of doing a job in common with others.

It was not until I went to live in Chicago that I first thought seriously of writing of Bigger Thomas. Two items of my experience combined to make me aware of Bigger as a meaningful and prophetic symbol. First, being free of the daily pressure of the Dixie environment, I was able to come into possession of my own feelings. Second, my contact with the labor movement and its ideology made me see Bigger clearly and feel what he meant.

I made the discovery that Bigger Thomas was not black all the time; he was white, too, and there were literally millions of him, everywhere. The extension of my sense of the personality of Bigger was the pivot of my life; it altered the complexion of my existence. I became conscious, at first dimly, and then later on with increasing clarity and conviction, of a vast, muddied pool of human life in America. It was as though I had put on a pair of spectacles whose power was that of an x-ray enabling me to see deeper into the lives of men. Whenever I picked up a newspaper, I'd no longer feel that I was reading of the doing of whites alone (Negroes are rarely mentioned in the press unless they've committed some crime!), but of a complex struggle for life going on in my country, a struggle in which I was involved. I sensed, too, that the Southern scheme of oppression was but an appendage of a far vaster and in many respects more ruthless and impersonal commodity-profit machine.

Trade-union struggles and issues began to grow meaningful to me. The flow of goods across the seas, buoying and depressing the wages of men, held a fascination. The pronouncements of foreign governments, their policies, plans, and acts were calculated and weighted in relation to the lives of people about me. I was literally overwhelmed when, in reading the works of Russian revolutionists, I came across descriptions of the "holiday energies of the masses," "the locomotives of history," "the conditions prerequisite for revolution," and so forth. I approached all of these new revelations in the light of Bigger Thomas, his hopes, fears, and despairs; and I began to feel far-flung kinships, and sense, with fright and abashment, the possibilities of *alliances* between the American Negro and other people possessing a kindred consciousness.

As my mind extended in this general and abstract manner, it was fed with even more vivid and concrete examples of the lives of Bigger Thomas. The urban environment of Chicago, affording a more stimulating life, made the Negro Bigger Thomases react more violently than even in the South. More than ever I began to see and understand the environmental factors which made for this extreme conduct. It was not that Chicago segregated Negroes more than the South, but that Chicago had more to offer, that Chicago's physical aspect—noisy, crowded, filled with the sense of power and fulfillment—did so much more to dazzle the mind with a taunting sense of possible achievement that the segregation it did impose brought forth from Bigger a reaction more obstreperous than in the South.

So the concrete picture and the abstract linkages of relationships fed each other, each making the other more meaningful and affording my emotions an opportunity to react to them with success and understanding. The process was like a swinging pendulum, each to and fro motion throwing up its tiny bit of meaning and significance, each stroke helping to develop the dim negative which had been implanted in my mind in the South.

During this period the shadings and nuances which were filling in Bigger's picture came, not so much from Negro life, as from the lives of whites I met and grew to know. I began to sense that they had their own kind of Bigger Thomas behavioristic pattern which grew out of a more subtle and broader frustration. The waves of recurring crime, the silly fads and crazes, the quicksilver changes in public taste, the hysteria and fears—all of these had long been mysteries to me. But now I looked back of them and felt the pinch and pressure of the environment that gave them their pitch and peculiar kind of being. I began to feel with my mind the inner tensions of the people I met. I don't mean to say that I think that environment *makes* consciousness (I suppose God makes that, if there is a God), but I do say that I felt and still feel that the environment supplies the instrumentalities through which the organism expresses itself, and if that environment is warped or tranquil, the mode and manner of behavior will be affected toward deadlocking tensions or orderly fulfillment and satisfaction.

Let me give examples of how I began to develop the dim negative of Bigger. I met white writers who talked of their responses, who told me how whites reacted to this lurid American scene. And, as they talked, I'd translate what they said in terms of Bigger's life. But what was more important still, I read their novels. Here, for the first time, I found ways and techniques of gauging meaningfully the effects of American civilization upon the personalities of people. I took these techniques, these ways of seeing and feeling, and twisted them, bent them, adapted them, until they became *my* ways of apprehending the locked-in life of the Black Belt areas. This association with white writers was the life preserver of my hope to depict Negro life in fiction, for my race possessed no fictional works dealing with such problems, had no background in such sharp and critical testing of experience, no novels that went with a deep and fearless will down to the dark roots of life.

Here are examples of how I culled information relating to Bigger from my reading:

There is in me a memory of reading an interesting pamphlet telling of the friendship of Gorky and Lenin in exile. The booklet told of how Lenin and Gorky were walking down a London street. Lenin turned to Gorky and, pointing, said: "Here is *their* Big Ben." "There is *their* Westminster Abbey." "There is *their* library." And at once, while reading that passage, my mind stopped, teased, challenged with the effort to remember, to associate widely disparate but meaningful experiences in my life. For a moment nothing would come, but I remained convinced that I had heard the meaning of those words sometime, somewhere before. Then, with a sudden glow of satisfaction of having gained a little more knowledge about the world in which I lived, I'd end up by saying: "That's Bigger. That's the Bigger Thomas reaction."

In both instances the deep sense of exclusion was identical. The feeling of looking at things with a painful and unwarrantable nakedness was an experience, I learned, that transcended national and racial boundaries. It was this intolerable sense of feeling and understanding so much, and yet living on a plane of social reality where the look of a world which one did not make or own struck one with a blinding objectivity and tangibility, that made me grasp the revolutionary impulse in my life and the lives of those about me and far away.

I remember reading a passage in a book dealing with old Russia which said: "We must be ready to make endless sacrifices if we are to be able to overthrow the Czar." And again I'd say to myself: "I've heard that somewhere, sometime before." And again I'd hear Bigger Thomas, far away and long ago, telling some white man who was trying to impose upon him: "I'll kill you and go to hell and pay for it." While living in America I heard from far away Russia the bitter accents of tragic calculation of how much human life and suffering it would cost a man to live as a man in a world that denied him the right to live with dignity. Actions and feelings of men ten thousand miles from home helped me to understand the moods and impulses of those walking the streets of Chicago and Dixie.

I am not saying that I heard any talk of revolution in the South when I was a kid there. But I did hear the lispings, the whispers, the mutters which some day, under one stimulus or another, will surely grow into open revolt unless the conditions which produce Bigger Thomases are changed.

In 1932 another source of information was dramatically opened up to me and I saw data of a surprising nature that helped to clarify the personality of Bigger. From the moment that Hitler took power in Germany and began to oppress the Jews, I tried to keep track of what was happening. And on innumerable occasions I was startled to detect, either from the side of the Fascists or from the side of the oppressed, reactions, moods, phrases, attitudes that reminded me strongly of Bigger, that helped to bring out more clearly the shadowy outlines of the negative that lay in the back of my mind.

I read every account of the Fascist movement in Germany I could lay my hands on, and from page to page I encountered and recognized familiar emotional patterns. What struck me with particular force was the Nazi preoccupation with the construction of a society in which there would exist among all people (*German* people, of course!) *one* solidarity of ideals, *one* continuous circulation of fundamental beliefs, notions, and assumptions. I am not now speaking of the popular idea of regimenting people's thought; I'm speaking of the implicit, almost unconscious, or pre-conscious, assumptions and ideals upon which whole nations and races act and live. And while reading these Nazi pages I'd be reminded of the Negro preacher in the South telling of a life beyond this world, a life in which the color of men's skins would not matter, a life in which each man would know what was deep down in the hearts of his fellow man. And I could hear Bigger Thomas standing on a street corner in America expressing his agonizing doubts and chronic suspicions, thus: "I ain't going to trust nobody. Everything is a racket and everybody is out to get what he can for himself. Maybe if we had a true leader, we could do something." And I'd know that I was still on the track of learning about Bigger, still in the midst of the modern struggle for solidarity among men.

When the Nazis spoke of the necessity of a highly ritualized and symbolized life, I could hear Bigger Thomas on Chicago's South Side saying: "Man, what we need is a leader like Marcus Garvey. We need a nation, a flag, an army of our own. We colored folks ought to organize into groups and have generals, captains, lieutenants, and so forth. We ought to take Africa and have a national home." I'd know, while listening to these childish words, that a white man would smile derisively at them. But I could not smile, for I knew the truth of those simple words from the facts of my own life. The deep hunger in those childish ideas was like a flash of lightning illuminating the whole dark inner landscape of Bigger's mind. Those words told me that the civilization which had given birth to Bigger contained no spiritual sustenance, had created no culture which could hold and claim his allegiance and faith, had sensitized him and had left him stranded, a free agent to roam the streets of our cities, a hot and whirling vortex of undisciplined and unchannelized impulses. The results of these observation made me feel more than ever estranged from the civilization in which I lived, and more than ever resolved toward the task of creating with words a scheme of images and symbols whose direction could enlist the sympathies, loyalties, and yearnings of the millions of Bigger Thomases in every land and race. . . .

But more than anything else, as a writer, I was fascinated by the similarity of the emotional tensions of Bigger in America and Bigger in Nazi Germany and Bigger in old Russia. All Bigger Thomases, white and black, felt tense, afraid, nervous, hysterical, and restless. From far away Nazi Germany and old Russia had come to me items of knowledge that told me that certain modern experiences were creating types of personalities whose existence ignored racial and national lines of demarcation, that these personalities carried with them a more universal drama-element than anything I'd ever encountered before; that these personalities were mainly imposed upon men and women living in a world whose fundamental assumptions could no longer be taken for granted: a world ridden with national and class strife; a world whose metaphysical meanings had vanished; a world in which God no longer existed as a daily focal point of men's lives; a world in which men could no longer retain their faith in an ultimate hereafter. It was a highly geared world whose nature was conflict and action, a world whose limited area and vision imperiously urged men to satisfy their organisms, a world that existed on a plane of animal sensation alone.

It was a world in which millions of men lived and behaved like drunkards, taking a stiff drink of hard life to lift them up for a thrilling moment, to give them a quivering sense of wild exultation and fulfillment that soon faded and let them down. Eagerly they took another drink, wanting to avoid the dull, flat look of things, then still another, this time stronger, and then they felt that their lives had meaning. Speaking figuratively, they were soon chronic alcoholics, men who lived by violence, through extreme action and sensation, through drowning daily in a perpetual nervous agitation.

From these items I drew my first political conclusions about Bigger: I felt that Bigger, an American product, a native son of this land, carried within him the potentialities of either Communism or Fascism. I don't mean to say that the Negro boy I depicted in *Native Son* is either a Communist or a Fascist. He is not either. But he is product of a dislocated society; he is a dispossessed and disinherited man; he is all of this, and he lives amid the greatest possible plenty on earth and he is looking and feeling for a way out. Whether he'll follow some gaudy, hysterical leader who'll promise rashly to fill the void in him, or whether he'll come to an understanding with the millions of his kindred fellow workers under trade-union or revolutionary guidance depends upon the future drift of events in America. But, granting the emotional state, the tensity, the fear, the hate, the impatience, the sense of exclusion, the ache for violent action, the emotional and cultural hunger, Bigger Thomas, conditioned as his organism is, will not become an ardent, or even a lukewarm, supporter of the *status quo*.

The difference between Bigger's tensity and the German variety is that Bigger's, due to America's educational restrictions on the bulk of her Negro population, is in a nascent state, not yet articulate. And the difference between Bigger's longing for self-identification and the Russian principle of self-determination is that Bigger's, due to the effects of American oppression, which has not allowed for the forming of deep ideas of solidarity among Negroes, is still in a state of individual anger and hatred. Here, I felt, was *drama!* Who will be the first to touch off these Bigger Thomases in America, white and black?

For a long time I toyed with the idea of writing a novel in which a Negro Bigger Thomas would loom as a symbolic figure of American life, a figure who would hold within him the prophecy of our future. I felt strongly that he held within him, in a measure which perhaps no other contemporary type did, the outlines of action and feeling which we would encounter on a vast scale in the days to come. Just as one sees when one walks into a medical research laboratory jars of alcohol containing abnormally large or distorted portions of the human body, just so did I see and feel that the conditions of life under which Negroes are forced to live in America contain the embryonic emotional prefiguration of how a large part of the body politic would react under stress.

So, with this much knowledge of myself and the world gained and known, why should I not try to work out on paper the problem of what will happen to Bigger? Why should I not, like a scientist in a laboratory, use my imagination and invent test-tube situations, place Bigger in them, and, following the guidance of my own hopes and fears, what I had learned and remembered, work out in fictional form an emotional statement and resolution of this problem?

But several things militated against my starting to work. Like Bigger himself, I felt a mental censor—product of the fears which a Negro feels from living in America—standing over me, draped in white, warning me not to write. This censor's warnings were translated into my own thought processes thus: "What will white people think if I draw the picture of such a Negro boy? Will they not at once say: 'See, didn't we tell you all along that niggers are like that? Now, look, one of their own kind has come along and drawn the picture for us!' " I felt that if I drew the picture of Bigger truthfully, there would be many reactionary whites who would try to make of him something I did not intend. And yet, and this was what made it difficult, I knew that I could not write of Bigger convincingly if I did not depict him as he *was*: that is, resentful toward whites, sullen, angry, ignorant, emotionally unstable, depressed and unaccountably elated at times, and unable even, because of his own lack of inner organization which American oppression has fostered in him, to unite with the members of his own race. And would not whites misread

Bigger and, doubting his authenticity, say: "This man is preaching hate against the whole white race"?

The more I thought of it the more I became convinced that if I did not write of Bigger as I saw and felt him, if I did not try to make him a living personality and at the same time a symbol of all the larger things I felt and saw in him, I'd be reacting as Bigger himself reacted: that is, I'd be acting out of *fear* if I let what I thought whites would say constrict and paralyze me.

As I contemplated Bigger and what he meant, I said to myself: "I must write this novel, not only for others to read, but to free *myself* of this sense of shame and fear." In fact, the novel, as time passed, grew upon me to the extent that it became a necessity to write it; the writing of it turned into a way of living for me.

Another thought kept me from writing. What would my own white and black comrades in the Communist party say? This thought was the most bewildering of all. Politics is a hard and narrow game; its policies represent the aggregate desires and aspirations of millions of people. Its goals are rigid and simply drawn, and the minds of the majority of politicians are set, congealed in terms of daily tactical maneuvers. How could I create such complex and wide schemes of associational thought and feeling, such filigreed webs of dreams and politics, without being mistaken for a "smuggler of reaction," "an ideological confusionist," or "an individualistic and dangerous element"? Though my heart is with the collectivist and proletarian ideal, I solved this problem by assuring myself that honest politics and honest feeling in imaginative representation ought to be able to meet on common healthy ground without fear, suspicion, and quarreling. Further, and more importantly, I steeled myself by coming to the conclusion that whether politicians accepted or rejected Bigger did not really matter; my task, as I felt it, was to free myself of this burden of impressions and feelings, recast them into the image of Bigger and make him *true*. Lastly, I felt that a right more immediately deeper than that of politics or race was at stake; that is, a *human* right, the right of a man to think and feel honestly. And especially did this personal and human right bear hard upon me, for temperamentally I am inclined to satisfy the claims of my own ideals rather than the expectations of others. It was this obscure need that had pulled me into the labor movement in the beginning and by exercising it I was fulfilling what I felt to be the laws of my own growth.

There was another constricting thought that kept me from work. It deals with my own race. I asked myself: "What will Negro doctors, lawyers, dentists, bankers, school teachers, social workers and business men, think of me if I draw such a picture of Bigger?" I knew from long and painful experience that the Negro middle and professional classes were the people of my own race who were more than others ashamed of Bigger and what he meant. Having narrowly escaped the Bigger Thomas reaction pattern themselves—indeed, still retaining traces of it within the confines of their own timid personalities—they would not relish being publicly reminded of the low, shameful depths of life above which they enjoyed their bourgeois lives. Never did they want people, especially *white* people, to think that their lives were so much touched by anything so dark and brutal as Bigger.

Their attitude toward life and art can be summed up in a single paragraph: "But, Mr. Wright, there are so many of us who are *not* like Bigger. Why don't you portray in your fiction the *best* traits of our race, something that will show the white people what we have done in *spite* of oppression? Don't represent anger and bitterness. Smile when a white person comes to you. Never let him feel that you are so small that what he has done to crush you has made you hate him! Oh, above all, save your *pride*!"

But Bigger won over all these claims; he won because I felt that I was hunting on the trail of more exciting and thrilling game. What Bigger meant had claimed me because I felt with all of my being that he was more important than what any person, white or black, would say or try to make of him, more important than any political analysis designed to explain or deny him, more important, even, than my own sense of fear, shame, and diffidence.

But Bigger was still not down upon paper. For a long time I had been writing of him in my mind, but I had yet to put him into an image, a breathing symbol draped out in the guise of the only form of life my native land had allowed me to know intimately, that is, the ghetto life of the American Negro. But the basic reason for my hesitancy was that another and far more complex problem had risen to plague me. Bigger, as I saw and felt him, was a snarl of many realities; he had in him many levels of life.

First, there was his personal and private life, that intimate existence that is so difficult to snare and nail down in fiction, that elusive core of being, that individual data of consciousness which in every man and woman is like that in no other. I had to deal with Bigger's dreams, his fleeting, momentary sensations, his yearning, visions, his deep emotional responses.

Then I was confronted with that part of him that was dual in aspect, dim, wavering, that part of him which is so much a part of *all* Negroes and *all* whites that I realize that I could put it down upon paper only by feeling out its meaning first within the confines of my own life. Bigger was attracted and repelled by the American scene. He was an American, because he was a native son; but he was also a Negro nationalist in a vague sense because he was not allowed to live as an American. Such was his way of life and mine; neither Bigger nor I resided fully in either camp.

Of this dual aspect of Bigger's social consciousness, I placed the nationalistic side first, not because I agreed with Bigger's wild and intense hatred of white people, but because his hate had placed him, like a wild animal at bay, in a position where he was most symbolic and explainable. In other words, his nationalist complex was for me a concept through which I could grasp more of the total meaning of his life than I could in any other way. I tried to approach Bigger's *snarled* and *confused* nationalist feelings with *conscious* and *informed* ones of my own. Yet, Bigger was not nationalist enough to feel the need of religion or the folk culture of his own people. What made Bigger's social consciousness most complex was the fact that he was hovering unwanted between two worlds—between powerful America and his own stunted place in life—and I took upon myself the task of trying to make the reader feel this No Man's Land. The most that I could say of Bigger was that he felt the *need* for a whole life and *acted* out that need; that was all.

Above and beyond all this, there was that American part of Bigger which is the heritage of us all, that part of him which we get from our seeing and hearing, from school, from the hopes and dreams of our friends; that part of him which the common people of America never talk of but take for granted. Among millions of people the deepest convictions of life are never discussed openly; they are felt, implied, hinted at tacitly and obliquely in their hopes and fears. We live by an idealism that makes us believe that the Constitution is a good document of government, that the Bill of Rights is a good legal and humane principle to safeguard our civil liberties, that every man and woman should have the opportunity to realize himself, to seek out his own individual fate and goal, his own peculiar and untranslatable destiny. I don't say that Bigger knew this in the terms in which I'm speaking of it; I don't say that any such thought ever entered his head. His emotional and intellectual life was never that articulate. But he knew it emotionally, intuitively, for his emotions and his desires were developed, and he caught it, as most of us do, from the mental and emotional climate of our time. Bigger had all of this in him, dammed up, buried, implied, and I had to develop it in fictional form.

There was another level of Bigger's life that I felt bound to account for and render, a level as elusive to discuss as it was to grasp in writing. Here again, I had to fall back upon my own feelings as a guide, for Bigger did not offer in his life any articulate verbal explanations. There seems to hover somewhere in that dark part of all our lives, in some more than in others, an objectless, timeless, spaceless element of primal fear and dread, stemming, perhaps, from our birth (depending upon whether one's outlook upon personality is Freudian or non-Freudian!), a fear and dread which exercises an impelling influence upon our lives all out of proportion to its obscurity. And, accompanying this *first fear*, is, for the want of a better name, a reflex urge toward ecstasy, complete submission, and trust. The springs of religion are here, and also the origins of rebellion. And in a boy like Bigger, young, unschooled, whose subjective life was clothed in the tattered rags of American "culture," this primitive fear and ecstasy were naked, exposed, unprotected by religion or a framework of government or a scheme of society whose final faiths would gain his love and trust; unprotected by trade or profession, faith or belief; opened to every trivial blast of daily or hourly circumstance.

There was yet another level of reality in Bigger's life: the impliedly political. I've already mentioned that Bigger had in him impulses which I had felt were present in the vast upheavals of Russia and Germany. Well, somehow, I had to make these political impulses felt by the reader in terms of Bigger's daily actions, keeping in mind as I did so the probable danger of my being branded as a propagandist by those who would not like the subject matter.

Then there was Bigger's relationship with white America, both North and South, which I had to depict, which I had to make known once again, alas; a relationship whose effects are carried by every Negro, like scars, somewhere in his body and mind.

I had also to show what oppression had done to Bigger's relationships with his own people, how it had split him off from them, how it had baffled him; how oppression seems to hinder and stifle in the victim those very qualities of character which are so essential for an effective struggle against the oppressor.

Then there was the fabulous city in which Bigger lived, an indescribable city, huge, roaring, dirty, noisy, raw, stark, brutal; a city of extremes: torrid summers and sub-zero winters, white people and black people, the English language and strange tongues, foreign born and native born, scabby poverty and gaudy luxury, high idealism and hard cynicism! A city so young that, in thinking of its short history, one's mind, as it travels backward in time, is stopped abruptly by the barren stretches of wind-swept prairie! But a city old enough to have caught within the homes of its long, straight streets the symbols and images of man's age-old destiny, of truths as old as the mountains and seas, of dramas as abiding as the soul of man itself! A city which has become the pivot of the Eastern, Western, Northern, and Southern poles of the nation. But a city whose black smoke clouds shut out the sunshine for seven months of the year; a city in which, on a fine balmy May morning, one can sniff the stench of the stockyards; a city where people have grown so used to gangs and murders and graft that they have honestly forgotten that government can have a pretense of decency!

With all of this thought out, Bigger was still unwritten. Two events, however, came into my mind and accelerated the process, made me sit down and actually start work on the typewriter, and just stop the writing of Bigger in my mind as I walked the streets.

The first event was my getting a job in the South Side Boys' Club, an institution which tried to reclaim the thousands of Negro Bigger Thomases from the dives and the alleys of the Black Belt. Here, on a vast scale, I had an opportunity to observe Bigger in all of his moods, actions, haunts. Here I felt for the first time that the rich folk who were paying my wages did not really give a good goddam about Bigger, that their kindness was prompted at bottom by a selfish motive. They were paying me to distract Bigger with ping-pong, checkers, swimming, marbles, and baseball in order that he might not roam the streets and harm the valuable white property which adjoined the Black Belt. I am not condemning boys' clubs and ping-pong as such; but these little stopgaps were utterly inadequate to fill up the centuries-long chasm of emptiness which American civilization had created in these Biggers. I felt that I was doing a kind of dressed-up police work, and I hated it.

I would work hard with these Biggers, and when it would come time for me to go home I'd say to myself, under my breath so that no one could hear: "Go to it, boys! Prove to the bastards that gave you these games that life is stronger than ping-pong. . . . Show them that full-blooded life is harder and hotter than they suspect, even though that life is draped in a black skin which at heart they despise. . . ."

They did. The police blotters at Chicago are testimony to how *much* they did. That was the only way I could contain myself for doing a job I hated; for a moment I'd allow myself, vicariously, to feel as Bigger felt—not much, just a little, just a *little*—but, still, there it was.

The second event that spurred me to write of Bigger was more personal and subtle. I had written a book of short stories which was published under the title of *Uncle Tom's Children.* When the reviews of that book began to appear, I realized that I had made an awfully naïve mistake. I found that I had written a book which even bankers' daughters could read and weep over and feel good about. I swore to myself that if I ever wrote another book, no one would weep over it; that it would be so hard and deep that they would have to face it without the consolation of tears. It was this that made me get to work in deep earnest.

Now, until this moment I did not stop to think very much about the plot of *Native Son.* The reason I did not is because I was not for one moment ever worried about it. I had spent years learning about Bigger, what had made him, what he meant; so, when the time came for writing, *what had made him and what he meant* constituted my plot. But the far-flung items of his life had to be couched in imaginative terms, terms known and acceptable to a common body of readers, terms which would, in the course of the story, manipulate the deepest held notions and convictions of their lives. That came easy. The moment I began to write, the plot fell out, so to speak. I'm not trying to oversimplify or make the process seem oversubtle. At bottom, what happened is very easy to explain.

Any Negro who has lived in the North or the South knows that times without number he has heard of some Negro boy being picked up on the streets and carted off to jail and charged with "rape." This thing happens so often that to my mind it had become a representative symbol of the Negro's uncertain position in America. Never for a second was I in doubt as to what kind of social reality or dramatic situation I'd put Bigger in, what kind of test-tube life I'd set up to evoke his deepest reactions. Life had made the plot over and over again, to the extent that I knew it by heart. So frequently do these acts recur that when I was halfway through the first draft of *Native*

Son a case paralleling Bigger's flared forth in the newspapers of Chicago. (Many of the newspaper items and some of the incidents in *Native Son* are but fictionalized versions of the Robert Nixon case and rewrites of news stories from the *Chicago Tribune.*) Indeed, scarcely was *Native Son* off the press before Supreme Court Justice Hugo L. Black gave the nation a long and vivid account of the American police methods of handling Negro boys.

Let me describe this stereotyped situation: A crime wave is sweeping a city and citizens are clamoring for police action. Squad cars cruise the Black Belt and grab the first Negro boy who seems to be unattached and homeless. He is held for perhaps a week without charge or bail, without the privilege of communicating with anyone, including his own relatives. After a few days this boy "confesses" anything that he is asked to confess, any crime that handily happens to be unsolved and on the calendar. Why does he confess? After the boy had been grilled night and day, hanged up by his thumbs, dangled by his feet out of twenty-story windows, and beaten (in places that leave no scars—cops have found a way to do that), he signs the papers before him, papers which are usually accompanied by a verbal promise to the boy that he will not go to the electric chair. Of course, he ends up by being executed or sentenced for life. If you think I'm telling tall tales, get chummy with some white cop who works in a Black Belt district and ask him for the lowdown.

When a black boy is carted off to jail in such a fashion, it is almost impossible do anything for him. Even well-disposed Negro lawyers find it difficult to defend him, for the boy will plead guilty one day and then not guilty the next, according to the degree of pressure and persuasion that is brought to bear upon his frightened personality from one side or the other. Even the boy's own family is scared to death; sometimes fear of police intimidation makes them hesitate to acknowledge that the boy is a blood relation of theirs.

Such has been America's attitude toward these boys that if one is picked up and confronted in a police cell with ten white cops, he is intimidated almost to the point of confessing anything. So far removed are these practices from what the average American citizen encounters in his daily life that it takes a huge act of his imagination to believe that it is true; yet, this same average citizen, with his kindness, his American sportsmanship and good will, would probably act with the mob if a self-respecting Negro family moved into his apartment building to escape the Black Belt and its terrors and limitations. . . .

Now, after all of this, when I sat down to the typewriter, I could not work; I could not think of a good opening scene for the book. I had defintely in mind the kind of emotion I wanted to evoke in the reader in that first scene, but I could not think of the type of concrete event that would convey the motif of the entire scheme of the book, that would sound, in varied form, the note that was to be resounded throughout its length, that would introduce to the reader just what kind of organism Bigger's was and the environment that was bearing hourly upon it. Twenty or thirty times I tried and failed; then I argued that if I could not write the opening scene, I'd start with the scene that followed. I did. The actual writing of the book began with the scene in the pool room.

Now, for the writing. During the years in which I had met all of these Bigger Thomases, those varieties of Bigger Thomases, I had not consciously gathered material to write of them; I had not kept a notebook record of their sayings and doings. Their actions had simply made impressions upon my sensibilities as I lived from day to day, impressions which crystallized and coagulated into clusters and configurations of memory, attitudes, moods, ideas. And these subjective states, in turn, were automatically stored away somewhere in me. I was not even aware of the process. But excited over the book which I had set myself to write, under the stress of emotion, these things came surging up, tangled, fused, knotted, entertaining me by the sheer variety and potency of their meaning and suggestiveness.

With the whole theme in mind, in an attitude almost akin to prayer, I gave myself up to the story. In an effort to capture some phase of Bigger's life that would not come to me readily, I'd jot down as much of it as I could. Then I'd read it over and over, adding each time a word, a phrase, a sentence until I felt that I had caught all the shadings of reality I felt dimly were there. With each of these rereadings and rewritings it seemed that I'd gather in facts and facets that tried to run away. It was an act of concentration, of trying to hold within one's center of attention all of that bewildering array of facts which science, politics, experience, memory, and imagination were urging upon me. And then, while writing, a new and thrilling relationship would spring up under the drive of emotion, coalescing and telescoping alien facts into a known and felt truth. That was the deep fun of the job: to feel within my body that I was pushing out to new areas of feeling, strange landmarks of emotion, tramping upon foreign soil, compounding new relationships of perceptions, making new and—until that very split second of time!—unheard-of and unfelt effects with words. It had a buoying and tonic impact upon me; my senses would strain and seek for more and more of such relationships; my temperature would rise as I worked. That is writing as I feel it, a kind of significant living.

The first draft of the novel was written in four months, straight through, and ran to some 576 pages. Just as a man rises in the mornings to dig ditches for his bread, so I'd work daily. I'd think of some abstract principle of Bigger's conduct and at once my mind would turn it into some act I'd seen Bigger perform, some act which I hoped would be familiar enough to the American reader to gain his credence. But in the writing of scene after scene I was guided by but one criterion: to tell the truth as I saw it and felt it. That is, to objectify in words some insight derived from my living in the form of action, scene, and dialogue. If a scene seemed improbable to me, I'd not tear it up, but ask myself: "Does it reveal enough of what

I feel to stand in spite of its unreality?" If I felt it did, it stood. If I felt that it did not, I ripped it out. The degree of morality in my writing depended upon the degree of felt life and truth I could put down upon the printed page. For example, there is a scene in *Native Son* where Bigger stands in a cell with a Negro preacher, Jan, Max, the State's Attorney, Mr. Dalton, Mrs. Dalton, Bigger's mother, his brother, his sister, Al, Gus, and Jack. While writing that scene, I knew that it was unlikely that so many people would ever be allowed to come into a murderer's cell. But I wanted those people in that cell to elicit a certain important emotional response from Bigger. And so the scene stood. I felt that what I wanted that scene to say to the reader was *more important than its surface reality or plausibility*.

Always, as I wrote, I was both reader and writer, both the conceiver of the action and the appreciator of it. I tried to write so that, in the same instant in time, the objective and subjective aspects of Bigger's life would be caught in a focus of prose. And always I tried to *render, depict,* not merely to tell the story. If a thing was cold, I tried to make the reader *feel* cold, and not just tell about it. In writing in this fashion, sometimes I'd find it necessary to use a stream of consciousness technique, then rise to an interior monologue, descend to a direct rendering of a dream state, then to a matter-of-fact depiction of what Bigger was saying, doing, and feeling. Then I'd find it impossible to say what I wanted to say without stepping in and speaking outright on my own; but when doing this I always made an effort to retain the mood of the story, explaining everything only in terms of Bigger's life and, if possible, in the rhythms of Bigger's thought (even though the words would be mine). Again, at other times, in the guise of the lawyer's speech and the newspaper items, or in terms of what Bigger would overhear or see from afar, I'd give what others were saying and thinking of him. But always, from the start to the finish, it was Bigger's story, Bigger's fear, Bigger's fight, and Bigger's fate that I tried to depict. I wrote with the conviction in mind (I don't know if this is right or wrong; I only know that I'm temperamentally inclined to feel this way) that the main burden of all serious fiction consists almost wholly of character-destiny and the items, social, political, and personal, of that character-destiny.

As I wrote I followed, almost unconsciously, many principles of the novel which my reading of the novels of other writers had made me feel were necessary for building of a well-constructed book. For the most part the novel is rendered in the present; I wanted the reader to feel that Bigger's story was happening *now*, like a play upon the stage or a movie unfolding upon the screen. Action follows action, as in a prize fight. Wherever possible, I told of Bigger's life in close-up, slow-motion, giving the feel of the grain in the passing of time. I had long had the feeling that this was the best way to "enclose" the reader's mind in a new world, to blot out all reality except that which I was giving him.

Then again, as much as I could, I restricted the novel to what Bigger saw and felt, to the limits of his feeling and thoughts, even when I was conveying *more* than that to the reader. I had the notion that such a manner of rendering made for a sharper effect, a more pointed sense of the character, his peculiar type of being and consciousness. Throughout there is but one point of view: Bigger's. This, too, I felt, made for a richer illusion of reality.

I kept out of the story as much as possible, for I wanted the reader to feel that there was nothing between him and Bigger; that the story was a special *première* given in his own private theater.

I kept the scenes long, made as much happen within a short space of time as possible; all of which, I felt, made for greater density and richness of effect.

In a like manner I tried to keep a unified sense of background throughout the story; the background would change, of course, but I tried to keep before the eyes of the reader at all times the forces and elements against which Bigger was striving.

And, because I had limited myself to rendering only what Bigger saw and felt, I gave no reality to the other characters than that which Bigger himself saw.

This, honestly, is all I can account for in the book. If I attempted to account for scenes and characters, to tell why certain scenes were written in certain ways, I'd be stretching facts in order to be pleasantly intelligible. All else in the book comes from my feelings reacting upon the material, and any honest reader knows as much about the rest of what is in the book as I do; that is, if, as he reads, he is willing to let his emotions and imagination become as influenced by the materials as I did. As I wrote, for some reason or other, one image, symbol, character, scene, mood, feeling evoked its opposite, its parallel, its complementary, and its ironic counterpart. Why? I don't know. My emotions and imagination just like to work that way. One can account for just so much of life, and then no more. At least, not yet.

With the first draft down, I found that I could not end the book satisfactorily. In the first draft I had Bigger going smack to the electric chair; but I felt that two murders were enough for one novel. I cut the final scene and went back to worry about the beginning. I had no luck. The book was one-half finished, with the opening and closing scenes unwritten. Then, one night, in desperation—I hope that I'm not disclosing the hidden secrets of my craft! —I sneaked out and got a bottle. With the help of it, I began to remember many things which I could not remember before. One of them was that Chicago was overrun with rats. I recalled that I'd seen many rats on the streets, that I'd heard and read of Negro children being bitten by rats in their beds. At first I rejected the idea of Bigger battling a rat in his room; I was afraid that the rat would "hog" the scene. But the rat would not leave me; he presented himself in many attractive guises. So, cautioning myself to allow the rat scene to disclose *only* Bigger, his family, their little room, and their relationships, I let the rat walk in, and he did his stuff.

Many of the scenes were torn out as I reworked the book. The mere rereading of what I'd written made me think of the possibility of developing themes which had been only hinted at in the first draft. For example, the entire guilt theme that runs through *Native Son* was woven in *after* the first draft was written.

At last I found out how to end the book; I ended it just as I had begun it, showing Bigger living dangerously, taking his life into his hands, accepting what life had made him. The lawyer, Max, was placed in Bigger's cell at the end of the novel to register the moral—or what *I* felt was the moral—horror of Negro life in the United States.

The writing of *Native Son* was to me an exciting, enthralling, and even a romantic experience. With what I've learned in the writing of this book, with all of its blemishes, imperfections, with all of its unrealized potentialities, I am launching out upon another novel, this time about the status of women in modern American society. This book, too, goes back to my childhood just as Bigger went, for, while I was storing away impressions of Bigger, I was storing away impressions of many other things that made me think and wonder. Some experience will ignite somewhere deep down in me the smoldering embers of new fires and I'll be off again to write yet another novel. It is good to live when one feels that such as that will happen to one. Life becomes sufficient unto life; the rewards of living are found in living.

I don't know if *Native Son* is a good book or a bad book. And I don't know if the book I'm working on now will be a good book or a bad book. And I really don't care. The mere writing of it will be more fun and a deeper satisfaction than any praise or blame from anybody.

I feel that I'm lucky to be alive to write novels today, when the whole world is caught in the pangs of war and change. Early American writers, Henry James and Nathaniel Hawthorne, complained bitterly about the bleakness and flatness of the American scene. But I think that if they were alive, they'd feel at home in modern America. True, we have no great church in America; our national traditions are still of such a sort that we are not wont to brag of them; and we have no army that's above the level of mercenary fighters; we have no group acceptable to the whole of our country upholding certain humane values; we have no rich symbols, no colorful rituals. We have only a money-grubbing, industrial civilization. But we do have in the Negro the embodiment of a past tragic enough to appease the spiritual hunger of even a James; and we have in the oppression of the Negro a shadow athwart our national life dense and heavy enough to satisfy even the gloomy broodings of a Hawthorne. And if Poe were alive, he would not have to invent horror; horror would invent him.

New York, March 7, 1940.

Many Thousands Gone

James Baldwin

It is only in his music, which Americans are able to admire because a protective sentimentality limits their understanding of it, that the Negro in America has been able to tell his story. It is a story which otherwise has yet to be told and which no American is prepared to hear. As is the inevitable result of things unsaid, we find ourselves until today oppressed with a dangerous and reverberating silence; and the story is told, compulsively, in symbols and signs, in hieroglyphics; it is revealed in Negro speech and in that of the white majority and in their different frames of reference. The ways in which the Negro has affected the American psychology are betrayed in our popular culture and in our morality; in our estrangement from him is the depth of our estrangement from ourselves. We cannot ask: what do we *really* feel about him—such a question merely opens the gates on chaos. What we really feel about him is involved with all that we feel about everything, about everyone, about ourselves.

The story of the Negro in America is the story of America—or, more precisely, it is the story of Americans. It is not a very pretty story: the story of a people is never very pretty. The Negro in America, gloomily referred to as that shadow which lies athwart our national life, is far more than that. He is a series of shadows, self-created, intertwining, which now we helplessly battle. One may say that the Negro in America does not really exist except in the darkness of our minds.

This is why his history and his progress, his relationship to all other Americans, has been kept in the social arena. He is a social and not a personal or a human problem; to think of him is to think of statistics, slums, rapes, injustices, remote violence; it is to be confronted with an endless cataloguing of losses, gains, skirmishes; it is to feel virtuous, outraged, helpless, as though his continuing status among us were somehow analogous to disease—cancer, perhaps, or tuberculosis—which must be checked, even though it cannot be cured. In this arena the black man acquires quite another aspect from that which he has in life. We do not know what to do with him in life; if he breaks our sociological and sentimental image of him we are panic-stricken and we feel ourselves betrayed. When he violates this image, therefore, he stands in the greatest danger (sensing which, we uneasily suspect that he is very often playing a part for our benefit); and, what is not

From James Baldwin, *Notes of a Native Son* (Boston: Beacon Press, 1955), pp. 24-45.

always so apparent but is equally true, we are then in some danger ourselves —hence our retreat or our blind and immediate retaliation.

Our dehumanization of the Negro then is indivisible from our dehumanization of ourselves: the loss of our own identity is the price we pay for our annulment of his. Time and our own force act as our allies, creating an impossible, a fruitless tension between the traditional master and slave. Impossible and fruitless because, literal and visible as this tension has become, it has nothing to do with reality.

Time has made some changes in the Negro face. Nothing has succeeded in making it exactly like our own, though the general desire seems to be to make it blank if one cannot make it white. When it has become blank, the past as thoroughly washed from the black face as it has been from ours, our guilt will be finished—at least it will have ceased to be visible, which we imagine to be much the same thing. But, paradoxically, it is we who prevent this from happening; since it is we, who, every hour that we live, reinvest the black face with our guilt; and we do this—by a further paradox, no less ferocious—helplessly, passionately, out of an unrealized need to suffer absolution.

Today, to be sure, we know that the Negro is not biologically or mentally inferior; there is no truth in those rumors of his body odor or his incorrigible sexuality; or no more truth than can be easily explained or even defended by the social sciences. Yet, in our most recent war, his blood was segregated as was, for the most part, his person. Up to today we are set at a division, so that he may not marry our daughters or our sisters, nor may he—for the most part—eat at our tables or live in our houses. Moreover, those who do, do so at the grave expense of a double alienation: from their own people, whose fabled attributes they must either deny or, worse, cheapen and bring to market; from us, for we require of them, when we accept them, that they at once cease to be Negroes and yet not fail to remember what being a Negro means—to remember, that is, what it means to us. The threshold of insult is higher or lower, according to the people involved, from the bootblack in Atlanta to the celebrity in New York. One must travel very far, among saints with nothing to gain or outcasts with nothing to lose, to find a place where it does not matter—and perhaps a word or a gesture or simply a silence will testify that it matters even there.

For it means something to be a Negro, after all, as it means something to have been born in Ireland or in China, to live where one sees space and sky or to live where one sees nothing but rubble or nothing but high buildings. We cannot escape our origins, however hard we try, those origins which contain the key—could we but find it—to all that we later become. What it means to be a Negro is a good deal more than this essay can discover; what it means to be a Negro in America can perhaps be suggested by an examination of the myths we perpetuate about him.

Aunt Jemima and Uncle Tom are dead, their places taken by a group of amazingly well-adjusted young men and women, almost as dark, but ferociously literate, well-dressed and scrubbed, who are never laughed at, who are not likely ever to set foot in a cotton or tobacco field or in any but the most modern of kitchens. There are others who remain, in our odd idiom, "underprivileged"; some are bitter and these come to grief; some are unhappy, but, continually presented with the evidence of a better day soon to come, are speedily becoming less so. Most of them care nothing whatever about race. They want only their proper place in the sun and the right to be left alone, like any other citizen of the republic. We may all breathe more easily. Before, however, our joy at the demise of Aunt Jemima and Uncle Tom approaches the indecent, we had better ask whence they sprang, how they lived? Into what limbo have they vanished?

However inaccurate our portraits of them were, these portraits do suggest, not only the conditions, but the quality of their lives and the impact of this spectacle on our consciences. There was no one more forebearing than Aunt Jemima, no one stronger or more pious or more loyal or more wise; there was, at the same time, no one weaker or more faithless or more vicious and certainly no one more immoral. Uncle Tom, trustworthy and sexless, needed only to drop the title "Uncle" to become violent, crafty, and sullen, a menace to any white woman who passed by. They prepared our feast tables and our burial clothes; and, if we could boast that we understood them, it was far more to the point and far more true that they understood us. They were, moreover, the only people in the world who did, and not only did they know us better than we know ourselves, but they knew us better than we knew them. This was the piquant flavoring to the national joke, it lay behind our uneasiness as it lay behind our benevolence: Aunt Jemima and Uncle Tom, our creations, at the last evaded us; they had a life—their own, perhaps a better life than ours—and they would never tell us what it was. At the point where we were driven most privately and painfully to conjecture what depths of contempt, what heights of indifference, what prodigies of resilience, what untamable superiority allowed them so vividly to endure, neither perishing nor rising up in a body to wipe us from the earth, the image perpetually shattered and the word failed. The black man in our midst carried murder in his heart, he wanted vengeance. We carried murder too, we wanted peace.

In our image of the Negro breathes the past we deny, not dead but living yet and powerful, the beast in our jungle of statistics. It is this which defeats us, which continues to defeat us, which lends to interracial cocktail parties their rattling, genteel, nervously smiling air: in any drawing room at such a gathering the beast may spring, filling the air with flying things and an unenlightened wailing. Wherever the problem touches there is confusion, there is danger. Wherever the Negro face appears a tension is created, the tension of a silence filled with things unutterable. It is a sentimental error, therefore, to believe that the past is dead; it means nothing to say that it is all forgotten, that the Negro himself has forgotten it. It is not a question of memory. Oedipus did not remember the thongs that bound his feet; nevertheless the marks they left testified to that doom toward which his feet were leading him. The man does not remember the hand that struck him, the darkness that frightened him, as a child; nevertheless, the hand and the darkness remain with him, indivisible from himself forever, part of the passion that drives him wherever he thinks to take flight.

The making of an American begins at that point where he himself rejects all other ties, any other history, and himself adopts the vesture of his adopted land. This problem has been faced by all Americans throughout our history—in a way it *is* our history—and it baffles the immigrant and sets on edge the second generation until today. In the case of the Negro the past was taken from him whether he would or no; yet to forswear it was meaningless and availed him nothing, since his shameful history was carried, quite literally, on his brow. Shameful; for he was heathen as well as black and would never have discovered the healing blood of Christ had not we braved the jungles to bring him these glad tidings. Shameful; for, since our role as missionary had not been wholly disinterested, it was necessary to recall the shame from which we had delivered him in order more easily to escape our own. As he accepted the alabaster Christ and the bloody cross —in the bearing of which he would find his redemption, as, indeed, to our outraged astonishment, he sometimes did—he must, henceforth, accept that image we then gave him of himself: having no other and standing, moreover, in danger of death should he fail to accept the dazzling light thus brought into such darkness. It is this quite simple dilemma that must be borne in mind if we wish to comprehend his psychology.

However we shift the light which beats so fiercely on his head, or *prove*, by victorious social analysis, how his lot has changed, how we have both improved, our uneasiness refuses to be exorcized. And nowhere is this more apparent than in our literature on the subject—"problem" literature when written by whites, "protest" literature when written by Negroes—and nothing is more striking than the tremendous disparity of tone between the two creations. *Kingsblood Royal* bears, for example, almost no kinship to *If He Hollers Let Him Go,* though the same reviewers praised them both for what were, at bottom, very much the same reasons. These reasons may be suggested, far too briefly but not at all unjustly, by observing that the presupposition is in both novels exactly the same: black is a terrible color with which to be born into the world.

Now the most powerful and celebrated statement we have yet had of what it means to be a Negro in America is unquestionably Richard Wright's *Native Son.* The feeling which prevailed at the time of its publication was that such a novel, bitter, uncompromising, shocking, gave proof, by its very existence, of what strides might be taken in a free democracy; and its indisputable success, proof that Americans were now able to look full in the face without flinching the dreadful facts. Americans, unhappily, have the most remarkable ability to alchemize all bitter truths into an innocuous but piquant confection and to transform their moral contradictions, or public discussion of such contradictions, into a proud decoration, such as are given for heroism on the field of battle. Such a book, we felt with pride, could never have been written before—which was true. Nor could it be written today. It bears already the aspect of a landmark; for Bigger and his brothers have undergone yet another metamorphosis; they have been accepted in baseball leagues and by colleges hitherto exclusive; and they have made a most favorable appearance on the national screen. We have yet to encounter, nevertheless, a report so indisputably authentic, or one that can begin to challenge this most significant novel.

It is, in a certain American tradition, the story of an unremarkable youth in battle with the force of circumstance; that force of circumstance which plays and which has played so important a part in the national fables of success or failure. In this case the force of circumstances is not poverty merely but color, a circumstance which cannot be overcome, against which the protagonist battles for his life and loses. It is, on the surface, remarkable that this book should have enjoyed among Americans the favor it did enjoy; no more remarkable, however, than that it should have been compared, exuberantly, to Dostoevsky, though placed a shade below Dos Passos, Dreiser, and Steinbeck; and when the book is examined, its impact does not seem remarkable at all, but becomes, on the contrary, perfectly logical and inevitable.

We cannot, to begin with, divorce this book from the specific social climate of that time: it was one of the last of those angry productions, encountered in the late twenties and all through the thirties, dealing with the inequities of the social structure of America. It was published one year before our entry into the last world war—which is to say, very few years after the dissolution of the WPA and the end of the New Deal and at a time when bread lines and soup kitchens and bloody industrial battles were bright in everyone's memory. The rigors of that unexpected time filled us not only with a genuinely bewildered and despairing idealism—so that, because there at least was *something* to fight for, young men went off to die in Spain—but also with a genuinely bewildered self-consciousness. The Negro, who had been during the magnificent twenties a passionate and delightful primitive, now became, as one of the things we were most self-conscious about, our most oppressed minority. In the thirties, swallowing Marx whole, we discovered the Worker and realized—I should think with some relief—that the aims of the Worker and the aims of the Negro were one. This theorem—to which we shall return—seems now to leave rather too much out of account; it became, nevertheless, one of the slogans of the "class struggle" and the gospel of the New Negro.

As for this New Negro, it was Wright who became his most eloquent spokesman; and his work, from its beginning, is most clearly committed to the social struggle. Leaving aside the considerable question of what relationship precisely the artist bears to the revolutionary, the reality of man as a social being is not his only reality and the artist is strangled who is forced to deal with human beings solely in social terms; and who has, moreover, as Wright had, the necessity thrust on him of being the representative of some thirteen million people. It is a false responsibility (since writers are not congressmen) and impossible, by its nature, of fulfillment. The unlucky shepherd soon finds that, so far from being able to feed the hungry sheep, he has lost the wherewithal for his own nourishment: having not been allowed—so fearful was his burden, so present his audience!—to recreate his own experience. Further, the militant men and women of the thirties were not, upon examination, significantly emancipated from their antecedents, however bitterly they might consider themselves estranged or however gallantly they struggled to build a better world. However they might extol Russia, their concept of a better world was quite helplessly American and betrayed a certain thinness of imagination, a suspect reliance on suspect and badly digested formulae, and a positively fretful romantic haste. Finally, the relationship of the Negro to the Worker cannot be summed up, nor even greatly illuminated, by saying that their aims are one. It is true only insofar as they both desire better working conditions and useful only insofar as they unite their strength as workers to achieve these ends. Further than this we cannot in honesty go.

In this climate Wright's voice first was heard and the struggle which promised for a time to shape his work and give it purpose also fixed it in an ever more unrewarding rage. Recording his days of anger he has also nevertheless recorded, as no Negro before him had ever done, that fantasy Americans hold in their minds when they speak of the Negro: that fantastic and fearful image which we have lived with since the first slave fell beneath the lash. This is the significance of *Native Son* and also, unhappily, its overwhelming limitation.

Native Son begins with the *Brring!* of an alarm clock in the squalid Chicago tenement where Bigger and his family live. Rats live there too, feeding off the garbage, and we first encounter Bigger in the act of killing one. One may consider that the entire book, from that harsh *Brring!* to Bigger's weak "Good-by" as the lawyer, Max, leaves him in the death cell, is an extension, with the roles inverted, of this chilling metaphor. Bigger's situation and Bigger himself exert on the mind the same sort of fascination. The premise of the book is, as I take it, clearly conveyed in these first pages: we are confronting a monster created by the American republic and we are, through being made to share his experience, to receive illumination as regards the manner of his life and to feel both pity and horror at his awful and inevitable doom. This is an arresting and potentially rich idea and we would be discussing a very different novel if Wright's execution had been more perceptive and if he had not attempted to redeem a symbolical monster in social terms.

One may object that it was precisely Wright's intention to create in Bigger a social symbol, revelatory of social disease and prophetic of disaster. I think, however, that it is this assumption which we ought to examine more carefully. Bigger has no discernible relationship to himself, to his own life, to his own people, nor to any other people—in this respect perhaps he is most American—and his force comes, not from his significance as a social (or anti-social) unit, but from his significance as the incarnation of a myth. It is remarkable that, though we follow him step by step from the tenement room to the death cell, we know as little about him when this journey is ended as we did when it began; and, what is even more remarkable, we know almost as little about the social dynamic which we are to believe created him. Despite the details of slum life which we are given, I doubt that anyone who has thought about it, disengaging himself from sentimentality, can accept this most essential premise of the novel for a moment. Those Negroes who surround him, on the other hand, his hard-working mother, his ambitious sister, his poolroom cronies, Bessie, might be considered as far richer and far more subtle and accurate illustrations of the ways in which Negroes are controlled in our society and the complex techniques they have evolved for their survival. We are limited however, to Bigger's view of them, part of a deliberate plan which might not have been disastrous if we were not also limited to Bigger's perceptions. What this means for the novel is that a necessary dimension has been cut away; this dimension being the relationship that Negroes bear to one another, that depth of involvement and unspoken recognition of shared experience which creates a way of life. What the novel reflects—and at no point interprets—is the isolation of the Negro within his own group and the resulting fury of impatient scorn. It is this which creates its climate of anarchy and unmotivated and unapprehended disaster; and it is this climate, common to most Negro protest novels, which has led us all to believe that in Negro life there exists no tradition, no field of manners, no possibility of ritual or intercourse, such as may, for example, sustain the Jew even after he has left his father's house. But the fact is not that the Negro has no tradition but that there has as yet arrived no sensibility sufficiently profound and tough to make this tradition articulate. For a tradition expresses, after all, nothing more than the long and painful experience of a people; it comes out of the battle waged to maintain their integrity or, to put it more simply, out of their struggle to survive. When we speak of the Jewish tradition we are speaking of centuries of exile and persecution, of the strength which endured and the sensibility which discovered in it the high possibility of the moral victory.

This sense of how Negroes live and how they have so long endured is hidden from us in part by the very speed of the Negro's public progress, a progress so heavy with complexity, so bewildering and kaleidoscopic, that he dare not pause to conjecture on the darkness which lies behind him; and by the nature of the American psychology which, in order to apprehend or be made able to accept it, must undergo a metamorphosis so profound as to be literally unthinkable and which there is no doubt we will resist until we are compelled to achieve our own identity by the rigors of a time that has yet to come. Bigger, in the meanwhile, and all his furious kin, serve only to whet the notorious national taste for the sensational and to reinforce all that we now find it necessary to believe. It is not Bigger whom we fear, since his appearance among us makes our victory certain. It is the others, who smile, who go to church, who give no cause for complaint, whom we sometimes consider with amusement, with pity, even with affection—and in whose faces we sometimes surprise the merest arrogant hint of hatred, the faintest, withdrawn, speculative shadow of contempt—who make us uneasy; who we cajole, threaten, flatter, fear; who to us remain unknown, though we are not (we feel with both relief and hostility and with bottomless confusion) unknown to them. It is out of our reaction to these hewers of wood and drawers of water that our image of Bigger was created.

It is this image, living yet, which we perpetually seek to evade with good works; and this image which makes of all our good works an intolerable mockery. The "nigger," black, benighted, brutal, consumed with hatred as we are consumed with guilt, cannot be thus blotted out. He stands at our shoulders when we give our maid her wages, it is his hand which we fear we are taking when struggling to communicate with the current "intelligent" Negro, his stench, as it were, which fills our mouths with salt as the monument is unveiled in honor of the latest Negro leader. Each generation has shouted behind him, *Nigger!* as he walked our streets; it is he whom we would rather our sisters did not marry; he is banished into the vast and wailing outer darkness whenever we speak of the "purity" of our women, of the "sanctity" of our homes, of "American" ideals. What is more, he knows it. He is indeed the "native son": he is the "nigger." Let us refrain from inquiring at the moment whether or not he actually exists; for we *believe* that he exists. Whenever we encounter him amongst us in the flesh, our faith is made perfect and his necessary and bloody end is executed with a mystical ferocity of joy.

But there is a complementary faith among the damned which involves their gathering of the stones with which those who walk in the light shall stone them; or there exists among the intolerably degraded the perverse and powerful desire to force into the arena of the actual those fantastic crimes of which they have been accused, achieving their vengeance and their own destruction through making the nightmare real. The American image of the

Negro lives also in the Negro's heart; and when he has surrendered to this image life has no other possible reality. Then he, like the white enemy with whom he will be locked one day in mortal struggle, has no means save this of asserting his identity. This is why Bigger's murder of Mary can be referred to as an "act of creation" and why, once this murder has been committed, he can feel for the first time that he is living fully and deeply as a man was meant to live. And there is I should think, no Negro living in America who has not felt, briefly or for long periods, with anguish sharp or dull, in varying degrees and to varying effect, simple, naked and unanswerable hatred; who has not wanted to smash any white face he may encounter in a day, to violate, out of motives of the cruelest vengeance, their women, to break the bodies of all white people and bring them low, as low as the dust into which he himself has been and is being trampled; no Negro, finally, who has not had to make his own precarious adjustment to the "nigger" who surrounds him and to the "nigger" in himself.

Yet the adjustment must be made—rather, it must be attempted, the tension perpetually sustained—for without this he has surrendered his birthright as a man no less than his birthright as a black man. The entire universe is then peopled only with his enemies, who are not only white men armed with rope and rifle, but his own far-flung and contemptible kinsmen. Their blackness is his degradation and it is their stupid and passive endurance which makes his end inevitable.

Bigger dreams of some black man who will weld all blacks together into a mighty fist, and feels, in relation to his family, that perhaps they had to live as they did precisely because none of them had ever done anything, right or wrong, which mattered very much. It is only he who, by an act of murder, has burst the dungeon cell. He has made it manifest that *he* lives and that his despised blood nourishes the passions of a man. He has forced his oppressors to see the fruit of that oppression: and he feels, when his family and his friends come to visit him in the death cell, that they should not be weeping or frightened, that they should be happy, *proud* that he has dared, through murder and now through his own imminent destruction, to redeem their anger and humiliation, that he has hurled into the spiritless obscurity of their lives the lamp of his passionate life and death. Henceforth, they may remember Bigger—who has died, as we may conclude, for them. But they do not feel this; they only know that he has murdered two women and precipitated a reign of terror; and that now he is to die in the electric chair. They therefore weep and are honestly frightened—for which Bigger despises them and wishes to "blot" them out. What is missing in his situation and in the representation of his psychology—which makes his situation false and his psychology incapable of development—is any revelatory apprehension of Bigger as one of the Negro's realities or as one of the Negro's roles. This failure is part of the previously noted failure to convey any sense of Negro life as a continuing and complex group reality. Bigger, who cannot function therefore as a reflection of the social illness, having, as it were, no society to reflect, likewise refuses to function on the loftier level of the Christ-symbol. His kinsmen are quite right to weep and be frightened, even to be appalled: for it is not his love for them or for himself which causes him to die, but his hatred and his self-hatred; he does not redeem the pains of a despised people, but reveals, on the contrary, nothing more than his own fierce bitterness at having been born one of them. In this also he is the "native son," his progress determinable by the speed with which the distance increases between himself and the auction-block and all that the auction-block implies. To have penetrated this phenomenon, this inward contention of love and hatred, blackness and whiteness, would have given him a stature more nearly human and an end more nearly tragic; and would have given us a document more profoundly and genuinely bitter and less harsh with an anger which is, on the one hand, exhibited and, on the other hand, denied.

Native Son finds itself at length so trapped by the American image of Negro life and by the American necessity to find the ray of hope that it cannot pursue its own implications. This is why Bigger must be at the last redeemed, to be received, if only by rhetoric, into that community of phantoms which is our tenaciously held ideal of the happy social life. It is the socially conscious whites who receive him—the Negroes being capable of no such objectivity—and we have, by way of illustration, that lamentable scene in which Jan, Mary's lover, forgives him for her murder; and, carrying the explicit burden of the novel, Max's long speech to the jury. This speech, which really ends the book, is one of the most desperate performances in American fiction. It is the question of Bigger's humanity which is at stake, the relationship in which he stands to all other Americans—and, by implication, to all people—and it is precisely this question which it cannot clarify, with which it cannot, in fact, come to any coherent terms. He is the monster created by the American republic, the present awful sum of generations of oppression; but to say that he is a monster is to fall into the trap of making him subhuman and he must, therefore, be made representative of a way of life which is real and human in precise ratio to the degree to which it seems to us monstrous and strange. It seems to me that this idea carries, implicitly, a most remarkable confession: that is, that Negro life is in fact as debased and impoverished as our theology claims; and, further, that the use to which Wright puts this idea can only proceed from the assumption—not entirely unsound—that Americans, who evade, so far as possible, all genuine experience, have therefore no way of assessing the experience of others and no way of establishing themselves in relation to any way of life which is not their own. The privacy or obscurity of Negro life makes that life capable, in our imaginations, of producing anything at all; and thus the idea of Bigger's monstrosity can be presented without fear of contradiction, since no American has the knowledge or authority to contest it and no Negro has the voice. It is an idea, which, in the framework of the novel, is dignified by the possibility it promptly affords of presenting Bigger as the herald of disaster, the danger signal of a more bitter time to come when not Bigger alone but all his kindred will rise, in the name of the many thousands who have perished in fire and flood and by rope and torture, to demand their rightful vengeance.

But it is not quite fair, it seems to me, to exploit the national innocence in this way. The idea of Bigger as a warning boomerangs not only because it is quite beyond the limit of probability that Negroes in America will ever achieve the means of wreaking vengeance upon the state but also because it cannot be said that they have any desire to do so. *Native Son* does not convey the altogether savage paradox of the American Negro's situation, of which the social reality which we prefer with such hopeful superficiality to study is but, as it were, the shadow. It is not simply the relationship of oppressed to oppressor, of master to slave, nor is it motivated merely by hatred; it is also literally and morally, a *blood* relationship, perhaps the most profound reality of the American experience, and we cannot begin to unlock it until we accept how very much it contains of the force and anguish and terror of love.

Negroes are Americans and their destiny is the country's destiny. They have no other experience besides their experience on this continent and it is an experience which cannot be rejected, which yet remains to be embraced. If, as I believe, no American Negro exists who does not have his private Bigger Thomas living in the skull, then what most significantly fails to be illuminated here is the paradoxical adjustment which is perpetually made, the Negro being compelled to accept the fact that this dark and dangerous and unloved stranger is part of himself forever. Only this recognition sets him in any wise free and it is this, this necessary ability to contain and even, in the most honorable sense of the word, to *exploit* the "nigger," which lends to Negro life its high element of the ironic and which causes the most-well-meaning of their American critics to make such exhilarating errors when attempting to understand them. To present Bigger as a warning is simply to reinforce the American guilt and fear concerning him, it is most forcefully to limit him to that previously mentioned social arena in which he has no human validity, it is simply to condemn him to death. For he has always been a warning, he represents the evil, the sin and suffering which we are compelled to reject. It is useless to say to the courtroom in which this heathen sits on trial that he is their responsibility, their creation, and his crimes are theirs; and that they ought, therefore, to allow him to live, to make articulate to himself behind the walls of prison the meaning of his existence. The meaning of his existence has already been most adequately expressed, nor does anyone wish, particularly not in the name of democracy, to think of it any more; as for the possibility of articulation, it is this possibility which above all others we most dread. Moreover, the courtroom, judge, jury, witnesses and spectators, recognize immediately that Bigger is their creation and they recognize this not only with hatred and fear and guilt and the resulting fury of self-righteousness but also with that morbid fullness of pride mixed with horror with which one regards the extent and power of one's wickedness. They know that death is his portion, that he runs to death; coming from darkness and dwelling in darkness, he must be, as often as he rises, banished, lest the entire planet be engulfed. And they know, finally, that they do not wish to forgive him and that he does not wish to be forgiven; that he dies, hating them, scorning that appeal which they cannot make to that irrecoverable humanity of his which cannot hear it; and that he *wants* to die because he glories in his hatred and prefers, like Lucifer, rather to rule in hell than serve in heaven.

For, bearing in mind the premise on which the life of such a man is based, i.e., that black is the color of damnation, this is his only possible end. It is the only death which will allow him a kind of dignity or even, however horribly, a kind of beauty. To tell this story, no more than a single aspect of the story of the "nigger," is inevitably and richly to become involved with the force of life and legend, how each perpetually assumes the guise of the other, creating that dense, many-sided and shifting reality which is the world we live in and the world we make. To tell his story is to begin to liberate us from his image and it is, for the first time, to clothe this phantom with flesh and blood, to deepen, by our understanding of him and his relationship to us, our understanding of ourselves and of all men.

But this is not the story which *Native Son* tells, for we find here merely, repeated in anger, the story which we have told in pride. Nor, since the implications of this anger are evaded, are we ever confronted with the actual or potential significance of our pride; which is why we fall, with such a positive glow of recognition, upon Max's long and bitter summing up. It is addressed to those among us of good will and it seems to say that, though there are whites and blacks among us who hate each other, we will not; there are those who are betrayed by greed, by guilt, by blood lust, but not we; we will set our faces against them and join hands and walk together into that dazzling future when there will be no white or black. This is the dream of all liberal men, a dream not at all dishonorable, but, nevertheless, a dream. For, let us join hands on this mountain as we may, the battle is elsewhere. It proceeds far from us in the heat and horror and pain of life itself where all men are betrayed by greed and guilt and blood-lust and where no one's hands are clean. Our good will, from which we yet expect such power to transform us, is thin, passionless, strident: its roots, examined, lead us back to our forebears, whose assumption it was that the black man, to become truly human and acceptable, must first become like us. This assumption once accepted, the Negro in America can only acquiesce in the obliteration of his own personality, the distortion and debasement of his own experience, surrendering to those forces which reduce the person to anonymity and which make themselves manifest daily all over the darkening world.

Notes on a Native Son

Eldridge Cleaver

After reading a couple of James Baldwin's books, I began experiencing that continuous delight one feels upon discovering a fascinating, brilliant talent on the scene, a talent capable of penetrating so profoundly into one's own little world that one knows oneself to have been unalterably changed and *liberated,* liberated from the frustrating grasp of whatever devils happen to possess one. Being a Negro, I have found this to be a rare and infrequent experience, for few of my black brothers and sisters here in America have achieved the power, which James Baldwin calls his revenge, which outlasts kingdoms: the power of doing whatever cats like Baldwin do when combining the alphabet with the volatile elements of his soul. (And, like it or not, a black man, unless he has become irretrievably "white-minded," responds with an additional dimension of his being to the articulated experience of another black—in spite of the universality of human experience.)

I, as I imagine many others did and still do, lusted for anything that Baldwin had written. It would have been a gas for me to sit on a pillow beneath the womb of Baldwin's typewriter and catch each newborn page as it entered this world of ours. I was delighted that Baldwin, with those great big eyes of his, which one thought to be fixedly focused on the macrocosm, could also pierce the microcosm. And although he was so full of sound, he was not a noisy writer like Ralph Ellison. He placed so much of my own experience, which I thought I had understood, into new perspective.

Gradually, however, I began to feel uncomfortable about something in Baldwin. I was disturbed upon becoming aware of an aversion in my heart to part of the song he sang. Why this was so, I was unable at first to say. Then I read *Another Country,* and I knew why my love for Baldwin's vision had become ambivalent.

Long before, I had become a student of Norman Mailer's *The White Negro,* which seemed to me to be prophetic and penetrating in its understanding of the psychology involved in the accelerating confrontation of black and white in America. I was therefore personally insulted by Baldwin's flippant, schoolmarmish dismissal of *The White Negro*. Baldwin committed a literary crime by his arrogant repudiation of one of the few gravely important expressions of our time. *The White Negro* may contain an excess of esoteric verbal husk, but one can forgive Mailer for that because of the solid kernel of truth he gave us. After all, it is the baby we want and not the blood of afterbirth. Mailer

---

From Eldridge Cleaver, *Soul On Ice* (New York: McGraw-Hill, 1968), pp. 97-111.

described, in that incisive essay, the first important chinks in the "mountain of white supremacy"—important because it shows the depth of ferment, on a personal level, in the white world. People are feverishly, and at great psychic and social expense, seeking *fundamental and irrevocable liberation*—and, what is more important, *are succeeding in escaping*—from the big white lies that compose the monolithic myth of White Supremacy/Black Inferiority, in a desperate attempt on the part of a new generation of white Americans to enter into the cosmopolitan egalitarian spirit of the twentieth century. But let us examine the reasoning that lies behind Baldwin's attack on Mailer.

There is in James Baldwin's work the most grueling, agonizing, total hatred of the blacks, particularly of himself, and the most shameful, fanatical, fawning, sycophantic love of the whites that one can find in the writings of any black American writer of note in our time. This is an appalling contradiction and the implications of it are vast.

A rereading of *Nobody Knows My Name* cannot help but convince the most avid of Baldwin's admirers of the hatred for blacks permeating his writings. In the essay "Princes and Powers," Baldwin's antipathy toward the black race is shockingly clear. The essay is Baldwin's interpretation of the Conference of Black Writers and Artists which met in Paris in September 1956. The portrait of Baldwin that comes through his words is that of a mind in unrelenting opposition to the efforts of solemn, dedicated black men who have undertaken the enormous task of rejuvenating and reclaiming the shattered psyches and culture of the black people, a people scattered over the continents of the world and the islands of the seas, where they exist in the mud of the floor of the foul dungeon into which the world has been transformed by the whites.

In his report of the conference, Baldwin, the reluctant black, dragging his feet at every step, could only ridicule the vision and efforts of these great men and heap scorn upon them, reserving his compliments—all of them left-handed—for the speakers at the conference who were themselves rejected and booed by the other conferees because of their reactionary, sychophantic views. Baldwin felt called upon to pop his cap pistol in a duel with Aimé Césaire, the big gun from Martinique. Indirectly, Baldwin was defending his first love—the white man. But the revulsion which Baldwin felt for the blacks at this conference, who were glorying in their blackness, seeking and showing their pride in Negritude and the African Personality, drives him to self-revealing sortie after sortie, so obvious in "Princes and Powers." Each successive sortie, however, become more expensive than the last one, because to score each time he has to go a little farther out on the limb, and it takes him a little longer each time to hustle back to the cover and camouflage of the perfumed smoke screen of his prose. Now and then we catch a glimpse of his little jive ass—his big eyes peering back over his shoulder in the mischievous retreat of a child sneak-thief from a cookie jar.

In the autobiographical notes of *Notes of a Native Son* Baldwin is frank to confess that, in growing into his version of manhood in Harlem, he discovered that, since his African heritage had been wiped out and was not accessible to him, he would appropriate the white man's heritage and make it his own. This terrible reality, central to the psychic stance of all American Negroes, revealed to Baldwin that he hated and feared white people. Then he says: "This did not mean that I loved black people; on the contrary, I despised them, possibly because they failed to produce Rembrandt." The psychic distance between love and hate could be the mechanical difference between a smile and a sneer or it could be the journey of a nervous impulse from the depths of one's brain to the tip of one's toe. But this impulse in its path through North American nerves may, if it is honest, find the passage disputed: may find the leap from the fiber of hate to that of love too taxing on its meager store of energy—and so the long trip back may never be completed, may end in a reconnaissance, a compromise, and then a lie.

Self-hatred takes many forms; sometimes it can be detected by no one, not by the keenest observer, not by the self-hater himself, not by his most intimate friends. Ethnic self-hate is even more difficult to detect. But in American Negroes, this ethnic self-hatred often takes the bizarre form of a racial death-wish, with many and elusive manifestations. Ironically, it provides much of the impetus behind the motivations of integration. And the attempt to suppress or deny such drives in one's psyche leads many American Negroes to become ostentatious separationists, Black Muslims, and back-to-Africa advocates. It is no wonder that Elijah Muhammad could conceive of the process of controlling evolution whereby the white race was brought into being. According to Elijah, about 6300 years ago all the people of the earth were Original Blacks. Secluded on the island of Patmos, a mad black scientist by the name of Yacub set up the machinery for grafting whites out of blacks through the operation of a birth-control system. The population on this island of Patmos was 59,999 and whenever a couple on this island wanted to get married they were only allowed to do so if there was a difference in their color, so that by mating black with those in the population of a brownish color and brown with brown—but never black with black—all traces of the black were eventually eliminated; the process was repeated until all the brown was eliminated, leaving only men of the red race; the red was bleached out, leaving only yellow; then the yellow was bleached out, and only white was left. Thus Yacub, who was long since dead, because this whole process took hundreds of years, had finally succeeded in creating the white devil with the blue eyes of death.

This myth of the creation of the white race, called "Yacub's History," is an inversion of the racial death-wish of American Negroes. Yacub's plan is still being followed by many Negroes today. Quite simply, many Negroes believe, as the principle of assimilation into white America implies, that the race problem in America cannot be settled until all traces of the black race are eliminated. Toward this end, many Negroes loathe the very idea of two very dark Negroes mating. The children, they say, will come out ugly. What they mean is that the children are sure to be black and this is not desirable. From the widespread use of cosmetics to bleach the black out of one's skin and other concoctions to take Africa out of one's hair, to the extreme resorted to by more Negroes than one might wish to believe, of undergoing nose-thinning and lip-clipping operations, the racial death-wish of American Negroes—Yacub's goal—takes its terrible toll. What has been happening for the past four hundred years it that the white man, through his access to black women, has been pumping his blood and genes into the blacks, has been diluting the blood and genes of the blacks—i.e., has been fulfilling Yacub's plan and accelerating the Negroes' racial death-wish.

The case of James Baldwin aside for a moment, it seems that many Negro homosexuals, acquiescing in this racial death-wish, are outraged and frustrated because in their sickness they are unable to have a baby by a white man. The cross they have to bear is that, already bending over and touching their toes for the white man, the fruit of their miscegenation is not the little half-white offspring of their dreams but an increase in the unwinding of their nerves although they redouble their efforts and intake of the white man's sperm.

In this land of dichotomies and disunited opposites, those truly concerned with the resurrection of black Americans have had eternally to deal with black intellectuals who have become their own opposites, taking on all of the behavior patterns of their enemy, vices and virtues, in an effort to aspire to alien standards in all respects. The gulf between an audacious, bootlicking Uncle Tom and an intellectual buckdancer is filled only with sophistication and style. On second thought, Uncle Tom comes off much cleaner here because usually he is just trying to survive, choosing to pretend to be something other than his true self in order to please the white man and thus receive favors. Whereas the intellectual sycophant does not pretend to be other than he actually is, but hates what he is and seeks to redefine himself in the image of his white idols. He becomes a white man in a black body. A self-willed, automated slave, he becomes the white man's most valuable tool in oppressing other blacks.

The black homosexual, when his twist has a racial nexus, is an extreme embodiment of this contradiction. The white man has deprived him of his masculinity, castrated him in the center of his burning skull, and when he submits to this change and takes the white man for his lover as well as Big Daddy, he focuses on "whiteness" all the love in his pent up soul and turns the razor edge of hatred against "blackness"—upon himself, what he is, and all those who look like him, remind him of himself. He may even hate the darkness of night.

The racial death-wish is manifested as the driving force in James Baldwin. His hatred for blacks, even as he pleads what he conceives as their cause, makes him the apotheosis of the dilemma in the ethos of the black bourgeoisie who have completely rejected their African heritage, consider the loss irrevocable, and refuse to look again in that direction. This is the root of Baldwin's violent repudiation of Mailer's *The White Negro*.

To understand what is at stake here, and to understand it in terms of the life of this nation, is to know the central fact that the relationship between black and white in America is a power equation, a power struggle, and that power struggle is not only manifested in the aggregate (civil rights, black nationalism, etc.) but also in the interpersonal relationships, actions, and reactions between blacks and whites where taken into account. When those "two lean cats," Baldwin and Mailer, met in a French living room, it was precisely this power equation that was at work.

It is fascinating to read (in *Nobody Knows My Name*) in what terms this power equation was manifested in Baldwin's immediate reaction to that meeting: "And here we were, suddenly, circling around each other. We liked each other at once, but each was frightened that the other would pull rank. He could have pulled rank on me because he was more famous and *had more money* and also *because he was white*; but I could have pulled rank on him precisely because I was black and I knew more about that periphery he so helplessly maligns in *The White Negro* than he could ever hope to know." [Italics added.]

Pulling rank, it would seem, is a very dangerous business, especially when the troops have mutinied and the basis of one's authority, or rank, is devoid of that interdictive power and has become suspect. One would think that for Baldwin, of all people, these hues of black and white were no longer armed with the power to intimidate—and if one thought this, one would be exceedingly wrong: for behind the structure of the thought of Baldwin's quoted above, there lurks the imp of Baldwin's unwinding, of his tension between love and hate—love of the white and hate of the black. And when we dig into this tension we will find that when those "two lean cats" crossed tracks in that French living room, one was a Pussy Cat, the other a Tiger. Baldwin's purr was transmitted magnificently in *The Fire Next Time*. But his work is the fruit of a tree with a poison root. Such succulent fruit, such a painful tree, what a malignant root!

It is ironic, but fascinating for what it reveals about the ferment in the North American soul in our time, that Norman Mailer, the white boy, and James Baldwin, the black boy, encountered each other in the eye of a social storm, traveling in opposite directions; the white boy, with knowledge of white Negroes, was traveling toward a confrontation with the black, with Africa; while the black boy, with a white mind, was on his way to Europe. Baldwin's nose, like the North-seeking needle on a compass, is forever pointed toward his adopted fatherland. Europe, his by intellectual osmosis and in Africa's stead. What he says of Aimé Césaire, one of the greatest black writers of the twentieth century, and intending it as an ironic rebuke, that "he had penetrated into the heart of the great wilderness which was Europe and stolen the sacred fire . . . which . . . was . . . the assurance of his power," seems only too clearly to speak more about Peter than it does about Paul. What Baldwin seems to forget is that Césaire explains that fire, whether sacred or profane, burns. In Baldwin's case, though the fire could not burn the black off his face, it certainly did burn it out of his heart.

I am not interested in denying anything to Baldwin. I, like the entire nation, owe a great debt to him. But throughout the range of his work, from *Go Tell It on the Mountain*, through *Notes of a Native Son*, *Nobody Knows My Name*, *Another Country*, to *The Fire Next Time*, all of which I treasure, there is a decisive quirk in Baldwin's vision which corresponds to his relationship to black people and to masculinity. It was this same quirk, in my opinion, that compelled Baldwin to slander Rufus Scott in *Another Country*, venerate Andrè Gide, repudiate *The White Negro*, and drive the blade of Brutus into the corpse of Richard Wright. As Baldwin has said in *Nobody Knows My Name*, "I think that I know something about the American masculinity which most men of my generation do not know because they have not been menaced by it in the way I have been." O.K., Sugar, but isn't it true that Rufus Scott, the weak, craven-hearted ghost of *Another Country*, bears the same relation to Bigger Thomas of *Native Son*, the black rebel of the ghetto and a man, as you yourself bore to the fallen giant, Richard Wright, a rebel and a man?

Somewhere in one of his books, Richard Wright describes an encounter between a ghost and several young Negroes. The young Negroes rejected the homosexual, and this was Wright alluding to a classic, if cruel, example of a ubiquitous phenomenon in the black ghettos of America: the practice by Negro youths of going "punk-hunting." This practice of seeking out homosexuals on the prowl, rolling them, beating them up, seemingly just to satisfy some savage impulse to inflict pain on the specific target selected, the "social outcast," seems to me to be not unrelated, in terms of the psychological mechanisms involved, to the ritualistic lynchings and castrations inflicted on Southern blacks by Southern whites. This was, as I recall, one of Wright's few comments on the subject of homosexuality.

I think it can safely be said that the men in Wright's books, albeit shackled with a form of impotence, were strongly heterosexual. Their heterosexuality was implied rather than laboriously stated or emphasized; it was taken for granted, as we all take men until something occurs to make us know otherwise. And Bigger Thomas, Wright's greatest creation, was a man in violent, though inept, rebellion against the stifling, murderous, totalitarian white world. There was no trace in Bigger of a Martin Luther King-type self-effacing love for his oppressors. For example, Bigger would have been completely baffled, as most Negroes are today, at Baldwin's advice to his nephew (*The Fire Next Time*), concerning white people: "You must accept them *and accept them with love.* For these innocent people have no other hope." [Italics added.]

Rufus Scott, a pathetic wretch who indulged in the white man's pastime of committing suicide, who let a white bisexual homosexual fuck him in his ass, and who took a Southern Jezebel for his woman, with all that these tortured relationships imply, was the epitome of a black eunuch who has completely submitted to the white man. Yes, Rufus was a psychological freedom rider, turning the ultimate cheek, murmuring like a ghost, *"You took the best so why not take the rest,"* which has absolutely nothing to do with the way Negroes have managed to survive here in the hells of North America! This all becomes very clear from what we learn of Erich, the arch-ghost of *Another Country,* of the depths of his alienation from his body and the source of his need: "And it had taken him almost until this very moment, on the eve of his departure, to begin to recognize that part of Rufus' great power over him had to do with the past which Erich had buried in some deep, dark place; was connected with himself, in Alabama, *when I wasn't nothing but a child*; with the cold white people and the warm black people, warm at least for him. . . ."

So, too, who cannot wonder at the source of such audacious madness as moved Baldwin to make this startling remark about Richard Wright, in his ignoble essay "Alas, Poor Richard": "In my relations with him, I was always exasperated by his notions of society, politics, and history, for they seemed to me utterly fanciful. I never believed that he had any real sense of how a society is put together."

Richard Wright is dead and Baldwin is alive and with us. Baldwin says that Richard Wright held notions that were utterly fanciful, and Baldwin is an honorable man.

> "O judgment; thou art fled to
> brutish beasts,
> And men have lost their reason!"

Wright has no need, as Caesar did, of an outraged Antony to plead his cause: his life and his work are his shield against the mellow thrust of Brutus' blade. The good that he did, unlike Caesar's, will not be interred with his bones. It is, on the contrary, only the living who can be harmed by Brutus.

Baldwin says that in Wright's writings violence sits enthroned where sex should be. If this is so, then it is only because in the North American reality hate holds sway in love's true province. And it is only through a rank perversion that the artist, whose duty is to tell us the truth, can turn the two-dollar trick of wedding violence to love and sex to hate—if, to achieve this end, one has basely to transmute rebellion into lamblike submission—*"You took the best,"* sniveled Rufus, *"so why not take the rest?"* Richard Wright was not ghost enough to achieve this cruel distortion. With him, sex, being not a spectator sport or a panacea but the sacred vehicle of life and love, is itself sacred. And the America which Wright knew and which *is*, is not the Garden of Eden but its opposite. Baldwin, embodying in his art the self-flagellating policy of Martin Luther King, and giving out falsely the news that the Day of the Ghost has arrived, pulled it off in *Another Country*.

Of all black American novelists, and indeed of all American novelists of any hue, Richard Wright reigns supreme for his profound political, economic, and social reference. Wright had the ability, like Dreiser, of harnessing the gigantic, overwhelming environmental forces and focusing them, with pin-point sharpness, on individuals and their acts as they are caught up in the whirlwind of the savage, anarchistic sweep of life, love, death, and hate, pain, hope, pleasure, and despair across the face of a nation and the world. But, ah! "O masters," it is Baldwin's work which is so void of a political, economic, or even a social reference. His characters all seem to be fucking and sucking in a vacuum. Baldwin has a superb touch when he speaks of human beings, when he is inside of them—especially his homosexuals—but he flounders when he looks beyond the skin; whereas Wright's forte, it seems to me, was in reflecting the intricate mechanisms of a social organization, its functioning as a unit.

Baldwin's essay on Richard Wright reveals that he despised—not Richard Wright, but his masculinity. He cannot confront the stud in others—except that he must either submit to it or destroy it. And he was not about to bow to a *black* man. Wright understood and lived the truth of what Norman Mailer meant when he said ". . . for being a man is the continuing battle of one's life, and one loses a bit of manhood with every stale compromise to the authority of any power in which one does not believe." Baldwin, compromised beyond getting back by the white man's *power,* which is real and has nothing to do with *authority*, but to which Baldwin has ultimately succumbed psychologically, is totally unable to extricate himself from that horrible pain. It is the scourge of his art, because the only way out for him is psychologically to embrace Africa, the land of his fathers, which he utterly refuses to do. He has instead resorted to a despicable underground guerrilla war, waged on paper, against black masculinity, playing out the racial death-wish of Yacub, reaching, I think, a point where Mailer hits the spot: "Driven into defiance it is natural if regrettable, that many homosexuals go to the direction of assuming that there is something intrinsically superior in homosexuality, and carried far enough it is a viewpoint which is as stultifying, as ridiculous, and as anti-human as the heterosexual's prejudice."

I, for one, do not think homosexuality is the latest advance over heterosexuality on the scale of human evolution. Homosexuality is a sickness, just as are baby-rape or wanting to become the head of General Motors.

A grave danger faces this nation, of which we are as yet unaware. And it is precisely this danger which Baldwin's work conceals; indeed, leads us away from. We are engaged in the deepest, the most fundamental revolution and reconstruction which men have ever been called upon to make in their lives, and which they absolutely cannot escape or avoid except at the peril of the very continued existence of human life on this planet. The time of the sham is over, and the cheek of the suffering saint must no longer be turned twice to the brute. The titillation of the guilt complexes of bored white liberals leads to doom. The grotesque hideousness of what is happening to us is reflected in this remark by Murray Kempton, quoted in *The Realist*: "When I was a boy Stepin Fetchit was the only Negro actor who worked regularly in the movies. . . . The fashion changes, but I sometimes think that Malcolm X and, to a degree even James Baldwin, are *our* Stepin Fetchits."

Yes, the fashion does change. "Will the machinegunners please step forward," said LeRoi Jones in a poem. "The machine gun on the corner," wrote Richard Wright, "is the symbol of the twentieth century." The embryonic spirit of kamikaze, real and alive, grows each day in the black man's heart and there are dreams of Nat Turner's legacy. The ghost of John Brown is creeping through suburbia. And I wonder if James Chaney said, as Andrew Goodman and Michael Schwerner stood helplessly watching, as the grizzly dogs crushed his bones with savage blows of chains—did poor James say, after Rufus Scott—"*You took the best, so why not take the rest?*" Or did he turn to his white brothers, seeing their plight, and say, after Baldwin, "That's your problem, baby!"

I say after Mailer, "There's a shit-storm coming."

Gwendolyn Brooks: Poet of the Unheroic

Arthur P. Davis

Most of the twentieth century poets have found it necessary to write about the spiritual sterility, the loss of direction and meaning, and the general lack of "bigness" which characterize our times. From T. S. Eliot's *Wasteland* down to the most recent work by the most recent "beat" poet or angry young man, the chorus of condemnation has been loud and full. And the voice of Gwendolyn Brooks, though not as strident as that of others, has helped to swell the chorus. Unlike many of the other poets, however, she has tended to *appraise* rather than *to condemn*. For her the modern world may be described in one word—*unheroic*. We twentieth century men, she seems to be saying, lack bigness; we are little creatures contented with little things and little moments. But she understands and sympathizes with our littleness.

Miss Brooks has published three major poetical works: *A Street in Bronzeville* (1945); *Annie Allen* (1949), which won her the Pulitzer Prize in Poetry; and *The Bean Eaters* (1960). In this study, I shall use only the poems in these three volumes. Moreover, I shall not attempt any consideration of her diction, imagery, and versification—subjects which warrant much more space than I can give here. My present concern will be limited to what I believe is the prevailing mood in Miss Brooks's works—the unheroic—and the ways in which she uses this mood to delineate, not only the Bronzeville world of her poems, but also symbolically the larger world of modern living.

Bronzeville, the scene on which Miss Brooks's characters act out their drab and shabby lives, is not only Chicago's Southside, but also Harlem, South Philadelphia, and every other black ghetto in the North. It is a place of rundown tenements, of beauty and funeral parlors, of old roomers growing old without graciousness, of "cool" young hoodlums headed for trouble, and of young girls having abortions. It is a community of stenches—urine, cabbage, *heavy* diapers, and chitterlings. It is an old section—not picturesquely and majestically old—but just plain and generally old, with old wood, old marble, old tile, and old dirt. Unlike the South, it is not an area of racial violence, but in other respects it is worse than the South. A dingy, drab, impersonalized "corner" of a metropolitan center, it is the place into which the Negro, rootless and alone, has been pushed, a place in which are found

From *CLA Journal,* VII (December, 1963), 114-25.

men estranged
From music and from wonder and from joy
But far familiar with the guiding awe
Of foodlessness.[1]

The men and women who walk the streets of Bronzeville are Negroes, but as Miss Brooks writes about their small lives we tend to forget their race and think only about their human qualities.

Gwendolyn Brooks is first of all the chronicler of the commonplace, of little men, of little actions. There are few, if any, truly heroic moments delineated in her poems. In fact, she seems to find a certain consolation in the little, the unheroic moment:

Exhaust the little moment. Soon it dies.
And be it gash or gold it will not come
Again in this identical disguise.[2]

Here is a new kind of low pressure *carpe diem* attitude. Take the present small moment, she seems to be saying, because it is very much like all other moments. There will be very few if any really great moments.

Moreover, she implies in several other pieces that modern men do not want to face big moments or big decisions. We like the "dear thick shelter / Of the familiar." In a poem entitled "The Explorer," the persona seeking a "still spot in the noise," seeking a "satin peace" can find only the "scream of nervous affairs, / . . . And choices. / He feared most of all the choices that cried to be taken."[3] When Miss Brooks has considered our reluctance to face big decisions, she has used on two occasions the second-coming-of-Christ theme. In one of these poems, "In Emmanuel's Nightmare," Christ came down "to clear the earth of the dirtiness of War," but returned with his mission unfulfilled. Finding that men liked friction, discord, and war, he was too considerate to disturb their littleness. War was their "chief sweet delectation." The decision to give it up would be too big for them to handle.

Twentieth century men, Miss Brooks suggests again and again, are not only small creatures but are no longer even ashamed of their smallness. On the contrary, they are inclined to be smug about it. In a poem, entitled "Strong Men Riding Horses," the speaker looking at a Western, complacently contrasts *his* life with that depicted on the TV screen: "I am not like that," he says. "I pay rent . . . / . . . run if robbers call . . . / I am not brave at all."[4] The self satisfaction of these little men may be great enough to arouse in them actual pity for those of a more heroic mold, and Miss Brooks understands their attitude. Using as a title, Edward Young's line: "pygmies are pygmies still, though percht on Alps," the poet adds

But can see better there, and laughing there
Pity the giants wallowing on the plain.[5]

[1] *A Street in Bronzeville*, p. 27.
[2] *Annie Allen*, p. 51.
[3] *The Bean Eaters*, p. 13.
[4] *Ibid.*, p. 15.
[5] *Annie Allen*, p. 14.

On occasion, however, there are stirrings of a minor rebellion among the complacent moderns. Perhaps rebellion is too strong a word, but a few, aware of the emptiness of their lives, begin to question the meaning of things. One of the best poems in this vein is "A Man of the Middle Class." It shows a successful citizen taking stock of himself:

> I've antique firearms. Blackamoore. Chinese
> Rugs. Ivories.
> Bronzes. Everything I Wanted.
> But have I answers? Oh methinks
> I've answers such as have
> The Executives I copied long ago,
> The ones who, forfeiting Vicks salve,
> Prayer book and Mother, shot themselves last Sunday.[6]

In this search for an answer, several of Miss Brooks's characters contemplate suicide, another indication of the spiritual bankruptcy of our times. In "A Sunset of the City,"[7] an aging woman, "no longer looked at with lechery or love," wonders "Whether to dry / In humming pallor or to leap and die." Thinking of her life, she asks if: "Somebody muffed it? Somebody wanted to joke." The same kind of despair is found in "The Contemplation of Suicide: The Temptation of Timothy" in which we are told: "One poises, poses at track, or range, or river, / Saying, What is the fact of my life, to what do I tend?"[8] One notes in passing, however, that the speakers in these poems do not *commit* suicide. They merely contemplate it, held back, as Miss Brooks suggests, by "Some little thing, remarkless and daily," some "common cliche."

The meaningless of modern living indicated by these suicide poems stems in part from our loss of faith, and Miss Brooks's comment on this is a plea for guidance:

> One wants a Teller in a time like this . . .
> . . . .
> One wonders if one has a home . . .
> One is not certain if or why or how.
> One wants a Teller now:—[9]

Although men may need a Teller, they are more than skeptical about his very existence. In a poem ironically titled, "God works in a mysterious way," the speaker asks God to come

> Out from Thy shadows, from Thy pleasant meadows,
> Quickly, in undiluted light . . .
> If Thou be more than hate or atmosphere
> Step forth in splendor, mortify our wolves.
> Or we assume a sovereignty ourselves.[10]

[6] *The Bean Eaters*, p. 42.
[7] *Ibid.*, p. 39.
[8] *Ibid.*, p. 57.
[9] *Annie Allen*, p. 52.
[10] *A Street in Bronzeville*, p. 54.

The threat to assume sovereignty need not be taken too seriously. Unfortunately, most of the inhabitants of Bronzeville do not have enough faith in themselves or in their fellow men to assume sovereignty. In "when I die," a young woman cynically tells us that one little short man will follow her body to the grave, place some "buck-a-dozen" roses there, and

Then off he'll take his mournin' black,
And wipe his tears away.
And the girls, they will be waitin'.
There's nothin' more to say.[11]

Among the few characters in these three works who do assume a kind of sovereignty are those like Cousin Vit, characters who unashamedly seize the present small moment and live it up to the fullest. Even in death, Cousin Vit is impressive:

Carried her unprotesting out the door.
Kicked back the casket stand. But it can't hold her,
That stuff and satin aiming to enfold her, . . .
Even now she does the snake hips with a hiss,
Slops the bad wine across her shantung, talks . . .[12]

Cousin Vit dead is more alive than these would-be-suicides and other shoddy and cynical Bronzeville inhabitants. Whatever her shortcomings, Cousin Vit has asserted her pagan self without asking questions or whining. It may be that she, Sadie,[13] and others like them, girls "who scraped life / With a fine-tooth comb," girls who seize their love in hallways and alleys and other unconventional places—it may be that these carefree souls have a deeper understanding of the modern scene than any of their sedate sisters and friends. Perhaps they are the only ones who do understand. In any case, Miss Brooks, their creator, obviously admires them and enjoys writing about them.[14]

But they are the exceptions. Gwendolyn Brooks's main concern is with the little people who do the usual and expected, who find joy in the familiar. In her assessment of modern man, it is the constant surprise of the ordinary that intrigues her; that is her ever-recurring theme. As she tells us:

Wonders do not confuse. We call them that
And close the matter there. But common things
Surprise us.[15]

Although the poems discussed above presumably concern Bronzeville citizens, there is almost nothing about them to suggest that the characters portrayed are Negroes. In these poems she has succeeded, as did James Joyce,

[11] *Ibid.*, p. 36.
[12] *Annie Allen*, p. 45.
[13] *A Street in Bronzeville*, p. 14.
[14] *Annie Allen*, p. 31.
[15] *The Bean Eaters*, p. 67.

in writing about the members of a group or nationality in such "human" terms, all special, national, or group considerations are forgotten. This is really not a world-shaking achievement. Successful writing in all ages for all peoples has this kind of universality. And yet, because everything about the Negro is so often considered "different" or "special," one feels its necessary to mention this aspect of her work.

But Miss Brooks also has many poems dealing specifically and directly with racial matters, including racial protest. In any treatment of these pieces, we must realize that she writes in a peculiar period, the integration period—a period between the era of blanket segregation on the one hand, and on the other, the promise of *full* citizenship in the future. In the meanwhile she is living between two worlds, and her racial poems will show the ambivalent quality of the age in which she writes. They will also show the emphasis on the unheroic which is present in much of her work, an attitude which stems in part from the very nature of the dilemma in which all Negroes now find themselves.

One of Miss Brooks's most subtly conceived racial characters is the title-figure in "The Sundays of Satin-Legs Smith." A superb creation—with his wonder suits in "yellow and in wine," all drapes, his scented lotion, his feather flower, and his hysterical ties—Satin-Legs could easily have become another Sporting Beasley, humorously and heroically rising above the sordid Bronzeville environment through sheer sartorial splendor. But Miss Brooks does not yield to that temptation. She has placed Satin-Legs on a board and dissected him as she would a laboratory specimen; and she has found that

> The pasts of his ancestors lean against
> Him. Crowd him. Fog out his identity.
> Hundreds of hungers mingle with his own,
> Hundreds of voices advise so dexterously
> He quite considers his reactions his,
> Judges he walks most powerfully alone,
> That everything is—simply what it is.[16]

In short, Satin-Legs for all his fine dress and self-assurance is not heroic. He is an acceptor of things as they are, a creature of dry hours and emptiness. A twofold symbol, he is another twentieth century man, and just as much the victim of his age as of his Bronzeville background.

When many of us think of protest poetry we tend to recall the fiery lines of "If We Must Die," written by McKay during those exciting days of the New Negro Movement. Moreover, we have somehow come to expect the same kind of bitterness and defiance in all poetry of this kind. But Miss Brooks's protest poems, written in an integration age, are usually quite different in spirit and approach from those of the New Negro generation. She has subtle irony, a quiet humor, and oftentimes a sense of pity, not only

[16] *A Street in Bronzeville,* p. 28.

for the black victims of prejudice but also for the whites who are guilty. But her works as a rule are not fiery or defiant, and they are seldom bitter.

Note for example the gentleness and restraint of a group of Negroes driving through "Beverly Hills, Chicago" and comparing the houses there with those in which they live:

> Nobody is furious. Nobody hates these people.
> At least, nobody driving by in this car.
> It is only natural, however, that it should occur to us
> How much more fortunate they are than we are.[17]

Although the statement is calm, as they drive away, the persona is forced to add the following remark: "When we speak to each other our voices are a little gruff," a subtle acknowledgement of the source of much Negro ugliness, unfairness from the outside.

In another poem which comes at the end of *Annie Allen*, Miss Brooks expresses in typical low key protest the desire of the Negro to be accepted:

> Open my rooms, let in the light and air.
> Reserve my service at the human feast.
> And let the joy continue. Do not hoard silence
> For the moment when I enter, tardily,
> To enjoy my height among you.[18]

And in the rest of this restrained poem, she ridicules the polite denial of brotherhood based on traditional wisdom. There is no lynching here to protest, no mob violence which requires heroic defense. And there is no "heroic" undisguised hatred on the part of the whites. It is just the silence —the damning silence—that comes when a Negro enters a gathering; it is the nice-nasty logic of little "reasonable" people who "can sugar up our prejudice with politeness." Cruelty now "flaunts diplomas, is elite, / Delicate, has polish, knows how to be discreet: . . ."

Miss Brooks can also express in a few telling lines the ambivalence which all Negroes have when they experience the tension that comes when patriotism is brought face to face with second-class status. The characters in the following poem are World War II soldiers. Note how deftly she suggests our hesitancies:

> And still we wear our uniforms, follow
> The cracked cry of the bugles, comb and brush
> Our pride and prejudice, doctor the sallow
> Initial ardor, wish to keep it fresh . . .
>
> . . . .
>
> But inward grows a soberness, an awe,
> A fear, a deepening hollow through the cold.[19]

[17] *Annie Allen*, p. 49. [18] *Ibid.*, p. 59.

[19] *A Street in Bronzeville*, p. 57. The same distrust of American democracy also occurs in "Negro Hero," *Ibid.*, p. 30.

One of Miss Brooks's most effective protest poems, it seems to me, is one that has no word of protest in it. It simply tells "of DeWitt Williams on his way to Lincoln Cemetery." It is a brief saga of a young man who was

Born in Alabama.
Bred in Illinois.
He was nothing but a
Plain black boy.
Swing low swing low sweet sweet chariot.
Nothing but a plain black boy.[20]

There is a world of suggestion in that repeated last line. Although no charges are made, the words somehow seem to be an indictment.

Miss Brooks is often ironic in her treatment of well-meaning but obtuse whites. In "The Lovers of the Poor" she describes the confusion of the ladies from the Betterment League when confronted with actual conditions among the Bronzeville poor:

Keeping their scented bodies in the center
Of the hall as they walk down the hysterical hall,
They allow their lovely skirts to graze no wall,
Are off at what they manage of a canter, . . .[21]

She is equally as amused by the slumming white folks who come to a Bronzeville night spot and who are hurt, who "feel overwhelmed by subtle treasons" because "The colored people will not *clown*."[22]

Although she may laugh at the naivete of whites or resent their injustice, Miss Brooks is always willing to look beyond color at the essential "humanness" of all people. In one of her longer poems—a poem with the involved title, "A Bronzeville Mother Loiters in Mississippi. / Meanwhile, a Mississippi Mother Burns Bacon"[23]—she tells the Emmett Till tragedy from the viewpoint of the white woman involved. It is an excellent study in pity and understanding. There is no hatred here but a deep human sympathy for the white mother who dreamed romantically of herself as "the milk-white maid" of the ballads and of her husband as the noble and heroic defender who rescued her from the "Dark Villain." But when the white mother comes to her senses and fully understands the horror of the lynching; when she realizes that her brutish husband is no hero but a murderer, her hatred for him becomes unbearable. Emmett's mother suffers, but so does the white mother; and of the two crosses the white is the harder to bear.

The same understanding attitude is taken in the poem, "The Chicago Defender Sends a Man to Little Rock."[24] The Negro reporter discovers that he cannot write a story he was sent to write because it isn't there. He also finds out that the story that *was* there would not be accepted by his editor

20 *Ibid.*, p. 21.
21 *The Bean Eaters,* p. 38.
22 *Annie Allen,* p. 46.
23 *The Bean Eaters,* p. 19.
24 *Ibid.*, p. 32.

because the biggest news in Little Rock was that "they are like people everywhere." Oh, yes, there was hatred and mob-violence in Little Rock, but the world is but a series of Little Rocks. People are human and therefore small and weak and to be pitied rather than condemned and hated. "The loveliest lynchee was our Lord."

But Gwendolyn Brooks is not *always* restrained and detached when she writes about race. On occasion, she seems to step into the picture and to express through her characters an intense personal feeling. Miss Brooks evidently believes that the ballad form should have the "beat inevitable," should have "blood," should have "A wildness cut up, and tied in little bunches,"[25] and when she uses this form for racial protest, she can become almost strident. For example, in "The Ballad of Rudolph Reed," a poem presumably based on the Chicago housing riots, the passion is evident:

> He ran like a mad thing into the night.
> And the words in his mouth were stinking.
> By the time he had hurt his first white man
> He was no longer thinking.
>
> By the time he had hurt his fourth white man
> Rudolph Reed was dead.
> His neighbors gathered and kicked his corpse.
> "Nigger—" his neighbors said.[26]

Rudolph Reed is perhaps the one heroic figure, or the nearest approach to it, in these three volumes; and yet he is just a plain man goaded to violence by an attack on his home. Evidently for the Bronzeville inhabitant a decent place to live is far more important than many other so-called ideals for which men fight and die. For Rudolph Reed, a house takes on mystical qualities:

> "Oh my house may have its east or west
> Or north or south behind it.
> All I know is I shall know it,
> And fight for it when I find it."[27]

Miss Brooks touches on the housing theme in at least three other poems—"Lovers of the Poor," "Kitchenette Building," and "Beverly Hills, Chicago." Her concern with the subject is natural. It is typical of her emphasis on the importance of the commonplace. But the intensity of feeling expressed in the ballad is unusual for her.

There is another subject on which Miss Brooks seems to feel strongly—the plight of the dark Negro girl in our color-conscious society.[28] There are poems on this theme in each of her three volumes. Outstanding among these works are "the ballad of chocolate Mabbie," "Ballad of Pearl May Lee,"

[25] *Ibid.*, p. 19. [26] *Ibid.*, p. 64. [27] *Ibid.*, p. 63.

[28] See Arthus P. Davis, "The Black-and-Tan Motif in the Poetry of Gwendolyn Brooks," *CLA Journal* (December, 1962), pp. 90-97.

and "Jessie Mitchell's Mother." Perhaps the most forthright expression of the theme is found in the following poem in *Annie Allen*:

> Stand off, daughter of the dusk,
> And do not wince when the bronzy lads
> Hurry to cream-yellow shining.
> It is plausible. The sun is a lode.
>
> True, there is silver under
> The veils of the darkness.
> But few care to dig in the night
> For the possible treasure of stars.

Even though she seems to have strong feelings on this particular aspect of the color problem, she does not make heroines or martyrs or tragic African Queens of these Daughters of the Dusk. They are just plain girls. As I have stated elsewhere: "In the New Negro Renaissance of 1925, many of the poets glorified black beauty. The following lines of Countee Cullen are typical:

> My love is dark as yours is fair,
> Yet lovelier I hold her,
> Than listless maids with pallid hair
> And blood that's thin and colder.

But there is none of this black-but-beautiful attitude, there is no glorification of blackness in the poems of Miss Brooks. Her suffering dark girls are too realistic and disillusioned to find solace in self deception. They *know* that it is tough to be "cut from chocolate" and to have "boisterous hair" in a land where "white is right." To be black is to be rejected; this is the never-changing burden of their complaint."[29]

When one compares Miss Brooks's racial problems with those of an earlier generation of Negro writers, he finds this significant difference. In most of the earlier poems, regardless of the bitterness expressed, there is an implied faith in a better day which will come either through the fulfillment of the American Dream or through the workings of a Just God. In these earlier works, there was also on occasion the kind of self-abasement one finds in Corrother's lines: "To be a Negro in a day like this— / Alas! Lord God, what evil have we done?" There is no self-pity in Gwendolyn Brooks's racial poems and precious little optimism. She doesn't seem to have much faith in either the American Dream or a Just God. Expressing neither hope nor fear, she is content to describe conditions as they are in Bronzeville. She seems to be saying: these things are so, and they are bad; but modern men, white or black, are not heroic. One can't expect too much.

In summary then, Gwendolyn Brooks is a modern poet who finds our present age far from impressive. She tells us that we are addicted to little

[29] *Ibid.*, p. 97.

things, little visions, little actions; she describes us, using appropriately commonplace symbols, images, and situations. But there is no contempt in her delineation; on the contrary, she has a deep understanding of and an even deeper sympathy for our weaknesses. Her characters are the citizens of Bronzeville, but she handles *race* with ease and naturalness. She neither exploits "Negro-ness" unduly, nor does she shy away from it. Race for her has no mystical overtones. As a result, her characters above all else are convincing and three-dimensional.

Gwendolyn Brooks is not a simple poet. As a rule she writes with disarming clearness, but she can also be thoroughly "modern" and difficult, as she is in *The Anniad*. But whether using the idiom of colloquial speech or the involved and oftentimes obscure diction of a certain type of contemporary verse, she is generally rewarding. In her verse experiments, in her diction, and in her imagery she is frequently daring and unique. In these characteristics and in her deeper-than-surface understanding of the modern mind, Miss Brooks proves herself an original, sensitive, and significant American poet.

The Negro Novel in America: In Rebuttal

Darwin T. Turner

Hearing no protests and seeing no pickets, Yale University Press has published a paperback, "revised" edition of Robert A. Bone's *The Negro Novel in America.* Now, too late to prevent publication but perhaps in time to caution readers avidly seeking to learn about the artistic contributions of Negroes, it is necessary to point out the shortcomings, the fallacies, and the biases which vitiate Mr. Bone's commendable effort to evaluate Negro writers' novels according to literary criteria. Although I must become caustic, I write with regret, for such a book is needed, and Mr. Bone frequently demonstrates both the requisite critical acuteness and literary talent to write perceptively and engagingly. Unfortunately, not content to confine himself to the role of critic and historian of individual writers, he has presumed to serve as psychiatrist, philosopher, and teacher not only for all Negro writers but for all Negroes. Forgetting his own admonition that "extraordinary" experience with another race is required of a writer who wishes to write perceptively of that race (p. 252), he has set forth a creed for the Negro writer and intellectual, and he has defended that creed by errors of fact and inference, inconsistencies and contradictions, supercilious lectures, and flippant remarks often in bad taste.

The characteristic weaknesses appear in the first two paragraphs of the introduction:

> The advocates of naive brotherhood will object in advance to the notion of a "Negro" novel. They will deny, usually without having read them, that novels written by American Negroes differ significantly from novels written by other Americans. . . .
>
> To this line of argument the classic rebuttal has been advanced by J. Saunders Redding. "Season it as you will," he writes, "the thought that the Negro American is different from other Americans is still unpalatable to most Negroes." Nevertheless, he continues, "the Negro is different. An iron ring of historical circumstances has made him so." As if to restore the balance, he adds, "But the difference is of little depth." With this balanced view I agree. It is a serious mistake to gloss over or ignore strong cultural differences, in order to speed the process of integration. (pp. 1-2).

Bone covers an amazing amount of ground. He intends to persuade "the advocates of naive brotherhood" that a "Negro" novel exists. First, therefore, his audience becomes indefinite. I know what is meant by the phrase "naive

From *CLA Journal,* X (December, 1966), 122-134.

advocates of brotherhood," but I do not know what is meant by "naive brotherhood." Second, Bone seems determined to tilt with Don Quixote's giants. Few, if any, people question the fact that "Negro" novels have been written. The more critical issue is whether *all* "novels written by American Negroes differ significantly from novels written by other Americans" in such a way that a reader can determine the difference. The impossibility of ever proving this statement is easily evidenced by the mistakes which have been made in identifying the racial origins of non-Negroes who have written about Negroes or of Negroes who have written about white people. Readers ignorant of the race of Henrietta Buckmaster or Frank Yerby do not instinctively recognize the truth.

But Bone wanted to prove that there is a significant difference, and in the age of Madison Avenue advertising, he chose to prove it by testimony from one who should know—a Negro writer. Bone's misuse of Saunders Redding's words should provide teachers of Freshman Composition with at least one lecture on propaganda devices. Redding says that most Negroes do not like to think that they are different from other Americans, but because of historical circumstances, they have a difference which "is of little depth." To Bone this proves "strong cultural differences" which produce a readily identifiable "Negro" novel. Even this triumph is not enough for Bone, who jumps from a literary question not solved to a social question not asked, as he advises the reader not to ignore the strong differences, "in order to speed the process of integration." The literary critic has become the social teacher.

These two paragraphs are a microcosm of the work. The remainder of the introduction is similarly marred. The dominant thesis is that as a minority group stripped ("denuded" is Bone's word) of its native culture, the Negro in America has been sundered in a psychic tug-of-war between Assimilationism and Negro Nationalism. Wishing to be White, he has repulsed lower-class members of his race while he has aped the mannerisms of middle-class white people. Cognizant that he is restricted within the dominant culture, he has militantly marshaled his hatred against the white majority while he has aggrandized the minor successes of his own race.

> Assimilationism and Negro nationalism, concepts indispensable to understanding the cultural history of the American Negro, are employed throughout the . . . work not only in interpreting the consciousness of individual authors, but in gauging the temper of whole periods. . . . They provide . . . a fixed point of reference from which to view the changing attitudes of the Negro novelist—attitudes which are often fundamental to the content of his art. (p. 7).

This framework, he says, will provide analytical tools for studying the cultural history of the ethnic minority, the American Negro.

Historians like Benjamin Quarles would argue that Mr. Bone's one-sentence stripping of African culture from the American Negro is a dubious oversimplification. By failing to adopt a similar framework for analyzing the work of writers of the Irish Renaissance or Jewish writers in America, literary historians seem to distrust Bone's approach. The major objection, however, is Bone's continuing to quote such respected writers as Redding, Wright, and Ellison to verify conclusions which would be accepted without argument (by a Negro at least) while he postulates as incontrovertible other theories which he has established by dexterous implication, fallacious inference, and wit.

For instance, I would not dispute that, if one wishes to simplify, one may study the history of any minority group—from the Hebrews in an Egyptian society to the present—in terms of the attempt of that group to become part of or to rebel against the dominant culture. But that fact does not justify the implication that a Negro is hypocritical or assimilationistic if he likes Beethoven's music, attends a "staid Episcopalian" rather than a "shouting Baptist" church, and develops a patriarchal family structure. (p. 5). The implication itself reveals the essential weakness in Mr. Bone's thought: having a preconceived image of the Negro and of the lives of Negroes, he defends those writers who support his image and attacks those who create contrary images. Although he admonishes scholars who attempt to base literary judgments on social bases (p. 7), too soon he lies in the pit against which he warned.

It is tempting but impossible in a paper of this length to refute Mr. Bone point by point, to call attention to all the errors of fact (for many of which I would excuse him, knowing the difficulty of dredging out some of the information), to cite the many fallacious and inexcusable inferences, and to note the instances in which the zest for turning a phrase has created a breach of good taste. For the sake of illustration, however, I must discuss some of the more glaring.

The work is structured in six parts: Part I, "The Novel of The Rising Middle Class: 1890–1920"; Part II, "The Discovery of the Folk: 1920–1930"; Part III, "The Search for a Tradition, 1930–1940"; Part IV, "The Revolt Against Protest"; a Postscript, an essay on James Baldwin which constitutes the only new material in the "revised" edition; and an Epilogue, advice to Negro writers. Parts III and IV and the Postscript have value, as has the bibliography. The book would be better if the other sections had not been written.

The poorest of the histori-literary sections is Part I. Aggrieved by what he believes to be deplorable assimilationism by the Negro middle-class and contemptuous of the popular literary traditions before 1920, Bone devotes considerable verbiage to an attack on both, but principally the middle-class.

He begins his attack with a spurious history of the rise of the middle-class: "The historical origins of the Negro middle-class, can be traced back to the nocturnal escapades of countless male aristocrats who tried valiantly to wash a face whiter than snow." (p. 12). Less offensive than the tasteless facetiousness is the amusing fact, that, despite his contempt for the Negro writers who echoed the plantation tradition, Bone himself accepted one of the cardinal myths by implying that the South was populated only by aristocrats. Ignoring such dark-skinned house servants as Paul Laurence Dunbar's mother, he continues his myth by asserting that the house servants were mulatto children of the master who, after the Civil War, naturally turned for assistance to the Southern democrats who were their kin. Therefore, they wrote novels addressed to "their" white folks. Reluctant to abandon the benefits of paternalism, they still hoped to solve the problem of the color line *within the family* (both branches). (p. 20).[1] Since Bone is vague about the identity of the "early novelists," it is difficult to refute him specifically. One mentioned in the chapter, however, is Charles W. Chesnutt, who certainly did not believe that he was addressing his novels to his white kinfolk.

The middle-class next appears, Bone states, under the guise of the Talented Tenth, a term which "is used synonymously with 'Negro middle-class.' " (p. 13). Bone's ambiguous phrasing makes it impossible to determine whether he is explaining that he wilfully uses it as a synonym or whether he mistakenly assumed that W. E. B. DuBois considered it a synonym. Needless to say, DuBois had too keen a sense of figures to have any difficulty distinguishing between the upper intellectual tenth of any group and the middle socio-economic section of that same group. For Bone, however, "Talented Tenth" equals middle-class equals Assimilationist.

Bone reprimands this Talented Tenth group of early novelists (one must assume that he includes all novelists before 1920) for adopting the Horatio Alger success formula and for attempting to inculcate middle-class morality into their readers. He concludes his reprimand with the dramatically irrelevant allegation that "the early Negro novelist had the soul of a shopkeeper" (p. 15), a note reminiscent of some diatribes about the "Butcher Boy of Stratford."

This is not Bone's only grievance against the early novelists. Assuming that "we are inclined to assume that this early protest literature . . . was based on a catholic concern for the brotherhood of man" (p. 17)—an assumption never made by a Negro literary historian, he hastens to point out that the early novelists were prejudiced against Jews, immigrants, and non-whites (p. 17). Even worse, they sometimes betrayed their own race, as when Chesnutt's protagonist protested his unwillingness to sit beside a group of Negro farm hands. Here Bone repeats the moral judgment uttered by "Liberals" and by Negroes themselves: the Negro should not be a snob. Any member of another group may despise the less talented, less strong, less intelligent, less wealthy, less healthy members of his group, but the Negro must love his fellowman.

[1] The italics are Bone's.

Worst of all, Bone continues, the desire to assimilate caused the Talented Tenth to imitate outworn literary traditions of Romanticism and melodrama rather than to recognize that American literature of the future would be that emulating the realism and naturalism and the styles of Twain, Garland, Howells, Dreiser, Norris, and James. This is certainly the only instance in which a literary historian has found in social aspirations an explanation of the literary style of not one but an entire group of writers. Harassed by Bone's allegations and inconsistencies the early Negro novelist has no chance for respectability. If, like Chesnutt, he realistically expressed the attitudes of Negroes, he is chastized for lacking a brotherly spirit. If he wrote a Horatio Alger story, he is derided as an assimilationist. The obvious implication is that success stories should have been written only by white authors for white readers, for the Negro should never have expected such success. But that is exactly the attitude stated in "One Man's Fortune" by Paul Laurence Dunbar, whom Bone denounces as an arch-Assimilationist. If the early novelist wrote in the melodramatic tradition of his time, he is castigated for lacking the perceptivity missing equally from hundreds of non-Negro novelists who were writing the same kind of melodrama.

In the second chapter Bone finally identifies the "Talented Tenth" novelists. And a motley group they are. Whereas Bone distinguished the writing of Twain from that of Howells and Henry James, he gathers into a single group the following diverse personalities: Paul Laurence Dunbar, a provincial, highschool educated, Ohio-born and reared, dark-skinned youth, who distrusted mulattoes and considered prose inferior to poetry; Charles Waddell Chesnutt, a talented short-story writer born in Ohio but reared in North Carolina, sensitive to the problems of light-colored Negroes, outspoken and determined to carve his fortune; W. E. B. DuBois of Massachusetts, aristocratically proud of his ancestry, educated as a scholar, arrogant and militant, a talented essayist who sometimes collected his essays as history and sometimes as novels; and James Weldon Johnson, cosmopolite from Florida, trained in education and in law, attuned to the theatrical world of New York and to the diplomatic world of Washington. Never has there been such a bundling under a single blanket since the bees flew in with Aunt Matilda.

To enforce the nonexistent unity, Bone digs out surprising similarities. Chesnutt and Dunbar both wrote their first stories in the plantation tradition. In the case of Chesnutt, this refers to the fact that his first published collection of tales focused on Uncle Julius, a shrewd Southern Negro who, to advance his own ends, tells his Negro employer tales based on the folk superstitions of Negroes in North Carolina. Unlike the typical stories of the "plantation tradition," they do not glorify the ante-bellum South. As Bone knew, or should have known, Chesnutt once protested that he would not write about Negroes contented with peonage under their ex-masters even though he knew such Negroes existed. To identify Chesnutt with the plantation tradition is, therefore, akin to describing Guy de Maupassant as a pastoral writer because he wrote about rural people.

Furthermore, Bone asserts, Chesnutt and Dunbar had white literary patrons—Walter Hines Page and William Dean Howells, respectively. The term "patron" insults all four men, for it implies support far beyond that given or received. Page, it is true, was the first editor to accept Chesnutt's stories, but the decision to publish the first collection of Chesnutt's stories and his novels required authority which Page lacked. The relationship of Howells to Dunbar is even more tenuous. Howells introduced the poetry of Dunbar to national attention by writing a favorable review of *Majors and Minors* and by writing an introduction to *Lyrics of a Lowly Life*. If these acts define a patron, then Baudelaire was a patron of Edgar Allan Poe. Actually, Dunbar, unlike Chesnutt, did have white patrons but they were far less eminent than Howells.

Injudicious appraisals mar the attention which Bone gives to these writers as individuals. Although he magnanimously contends that extenuating circumstances motivated Dunbar's "Uncle Tom" behavior he writes,

> Whenever Dunbar had something to say which transcended the boundaries of the plantation tradition, he resorted to the subterfuge of employing white characters, rather than attempting a serious literary portrait of the Negro. (p. 39).

Obviously, Mr. Bone failed to read *The Strength of Gideon and Other Stories*.

Bone sees in the relationship of Bles and Zora, in *The Silver Fleece* (1911), DuBois's unconscious allegory of his attempt to embrace the Negro masses, an action which he can undertake only if Zora redeems herself. It is scarcely necessary to point out that in American novels of 1910, one rarely finds heroes being wed to unredeemed or even to slightly stained heroines. Were all these writers revealing their unconscious antipathy for the masses, or is such biographical symbolism to be exercised only in reading novels written by Negroes?

Bone describes DuBois's diction as a schizophrenic clash of "20th-century intellectual veneer" against "19th-century idiom." (p. 45). DuBois's new meanings strain against the old idiom, "but it will not yield." When Mark Twain observed that James Fenimore Cooper wrote dialogue badly, he explained that Cooper wrote it badly because he did not listen to the way that people talk or did not have occasion to talk with characters of the type about whom he wrote. But Twain considered himself a judge of literature not a psychiatrist.

Bone's comments on James Weldon Johnson reveal his inconsistency, and—if I may be forgiven for adopting his critical approach—reveal the subliminal tension between his aesthetic judgments and his social biases. Pleased with the artistic merits of *The Autobiography of an Ex-Coloured Man* and with Johnson's defense of ragtime and the cakewalk, Bone treats lightly the fact that Johnson's protagonist has higher aspirations: "the low-life milieu of the Harlem School is hardly his [Johnson's] natural habitat." (p. 48). A less competent novelist would have been condemned as Assimilationist for implying that there are higher aspirations.

Part II—the discussion of the Renaissance—is markedly superior to the first but weakens eventually from Bone's stubborn effort to fit all the writings into the framework of Assimilationism versus Negro Nationalism. To indicate his approval of the talented rebels of the Renaissance, Bone describes them as "the intellegensia," a term unfortunately more restrictive and less appropriate than "Talented Tenth," which he continues to use as a cudgel against the middle-class. Before he ends his introduction, however, Bone dumps the intelligensia into the camp of Harlem Nationalists at war with the Talented Tenth-middle-class advocates of the Genteel Tradition.

Even in his discussion of the Harlem School, Mr. Bone's biases govern his aesthetic judgments. He condemns the "early novelists" because they revealed their contempt for the masses by introducing in their works characters resembling those of the minstrel shows. He praises the Harlem writers for daring to create characters who "run dangerously close to the stereotype." (p. 66). And he continues to reveal unconsciously the limitations in his knowledge of Negro life, limitations which affect both his social theories and his interpretations of the works. For instance, he writes,

> In the early Negro novel a 'professor' was a school teacher (inflated achievement); in the Harlem School novel a 'professor' is strictly the third party to a rickety piano and a precarious glass of beer. (p. 66).

But one familiar with idiom of the South knows that well into the Forties "Fessuh" was the generic title for all male teachers. A novelist failing to use the term would have violated the idiom which Bone wishes to protect.

It is difficult not to suspect that Bone praises the Harlem writers not merely because they are competent craftsmen but because, despite occasional extravagances, they more honestly reveal the Negro as Bone believes him to be. Bone, for instance, examines Claude McKay's characters as "symbols" whereas he derides the characters of the early novelists as "counterstereotypes" or "minstrels." His chief criticism of *Home to Harlem* and *Banjo* is that Ray, McKay's spokesman, is too intellectual to permit McKay to renounce Anglo-Saxon civilization as emphatically as Bone expects. He extols McKay's achievement in *Banana Bottom,* in which Bita, the protagonist, marrying Jubban, embraces the beauty of peasant life.

Similarly, although Bone mentions the structural defects of Langston Hughes' *Not Without Laughter,* his principal criticism is that by sending the protagonist back to school, Hughes contradicts his major theme—that Negroes cultivate the spirit of joy because "achievement" is largely illusory for them. Since Bone finds no ambivalence or inconsistency in Hughes' attitudes toward racial matters in other works, one wonders whether Hughes did not say exactly what he desired—that the Negro must embrace joy and seek success. Perhaps it is merely Bone who believes that one cannot exist in company with the other.

Bone's eloquent praise of Jean Toomer compensates for the fact that almost all of the biographical information is inexact. Toomer's parents were not "cultivated Negroes of Creole stock." At least Toomer never assumed that his Georgia-born father was. The household tradition of tales of slavery exists factually only in Bone's imagination. In fact, Toomer was eighteen before he became fully aware of the dramatic role which his grandfather, P. B. S. Pinchback, had played in the Reconstruction. Toomer did not study law. He did not turn to literature as quickly as Bone implies. But he did undertake "a brief literary apprenticeship in cosmopolitan New York." It is ironic that Toomer, whom he praises for having "never underestimated the importance of his Negro identity" (p. 82), should have been the very one to proclaim loudest the statement which Bone ridicules as the self-deluding myth of the Assimilationist: "I am not a Negro; I am an American." On this issue, of which he must have been aware, Bone is silent.

Although Bone cannot be blamed for wanting to discuss Toomer, *Cane* is not a novel. Neither Toomer nor the Liveright publishers considered it such. Bone's other errors in interpreting *Cane* result merely from his excusable ignorance of the man and his other writings; the errors, however, illustrate the danger of building a man, a philosophy, and a myth upon the subjective reading of one literary work.

In the final chapter of Part II, the hapless middle-class become "spokesman of Negro Philistia," principally because of their attacks on the Harlem artists. In this chapter, more perhaps than in any other, Bone suffers a colorblindness which prevents his recognizing that DuBois's objections to subject matter of novels and Benjamin Brawley's objections to jazz do not reflect racial posture but artistic standards. It is difficult to draw a significant racial distinction between W. D. Howell's attack upon Russian naturalistic novels and DuBois's disgust with what he believed to be the filth of *Home to Harlem*. Similarly, English-teacher Brawley's criticism of the "grammar" of the lyrics of jazz is echoed today by many non-Negro critics of rock and roll. But subconsciously believing that all worthy Negroes should possess identical artistic standards, Bone flails them with arguments sometimes supported by misused quotations:

> James Weldon Johnson, whose instinct was always sound in such matters, vigorously defended the lower-class Negro as "higher" literary material. "It takes nothing less than supreme genius," he once remarked, "to make middle-class society, black or white, interesting—to say nothing of making it dramatic." (p. 96).

Johnson says nothing here about "higher" literary material, whatever that may be. He says that it is hard to write dramatically about middle-class people. If he implies that it is, therefore, easier to write about lower-class people, he implies equally that it is easier to write about upperclass people.

Such a blatant misuse of a source is as reprehensible as is the laudatory statement on the back cover of *The Negro Novel in America,* which implies endorsement by the *CLA Journal* when, in fact, the quotation was taken from an article in the *Journal,* not even from a review.

Suffering most in the chapter is Jessie Fauset, who "was never able to transcend the narrow limits" of her sheltered background. (p. 102). Granted that Miss Fauset's novels do not please, surely the cause must be more than the kind of family background which Edith Wharton used advantageously. Miss Fauset's literary sin is not her failure to rebel against the kind of family which Bone implies a Negro ought not have; her sins are a diction which was outmoded by 1890 and an inability to structure a plot effectively. But Bone ignores these artistic weaknesses to concern himself only with her family and her literary intentions even though he averred in the beginning that he would always "establish the work of art in its own right before viewing it as part of the cultural process." (p. 7).

In Part III Bone insists less on the struggle between Assimilationism and Nationalism. It is just as well, for some of the novelists he must discuss demonstrate a basic weakness of Bone's thesis—it fails to consider that the writer, by the very fact of his publishing, is becoming a part of the dominant culture regardless of the thesis he expresses in his work. In his private life, Arna Bontemps surely must represent the middle-class Negroes or the Talented Tenth who have adopted, or have inherited, the values identified with white, middle-class Americans of the Protestant ethnic group and who, by Bone's definition, are Assimilationist. Yet Bontemps' novel which Bone praises most highly is *Black Thunder*, which Bone believes is marred primarily by excessive race pride, i.e., Negro Nationalism.

Commendably, Bone calls attention to George Henderson and William Attaway, whose novels should be better known. While discussing these and Richard Wright, he demonstrates that he has competence when he restricts himself to literary judgments.

Zora Neale Hurston benefits from Bone's appraisal which points to the virtues of her work and minimizes her exploitation of the exotic in the speech and habits of Negroes, her caricaturing of Negroes whose philosophies differed from hers, her acceptance of the caste philosophy characteristic of the plantation tradition, and her focus upon the atypical culture of Eatonville, Florida. As might be expected, he judges harshly *Seraph on the Suwanee,* which lacks the exotic charm of her earlier novels about Negroes. Curiously, he ignores *Moses, Man of the Mountain,* which is perhaps Miss Hurston's most delightful work.

Part IV challenged Bone because, for the first time, he was forced to discuss a number of novelists who wrote non-Negro novels. He met the challenge by dismissing Frank Yerby as "the prince of pulpsters," an allegation irrelevant to his thesis that novels by Negroes must be significantly different, and by defining as Assimilationist such writers as Richard Wright, Chester Himes,

Zora Neale Hurston, and Ann Petry when they wrote about white protagonists.

In Parts IV and V, he reveals his best work. Judging Ellison and Baldwin, who lend themselves to mythic or symbolic interpretation, he can propound explications which are provocative even if they do not always reflect the artists' intentions.

Near the conclusion of his book, Bone states the truth which should have disuaded him from the thesis upon which he based literary as well as social judgments: "Little remains to be said of these novelists as a group, for like all real artists, their work is highly individualistic." (p. 171). Having reached this understanding, he can merely vacillate in the advice he offers Negro novelists in a postscript. The Negro novelist should not sacrifice his art to the non-literary attempt to correct social injustices:

> Let the Negro novelist as citizen, as political man, vent his fury and indignation through the appropriate protest organizations, but as novelist, as artist, let him pursue his vision, his power of seeing and revealing which is mankind's rarest gift. (p. 246).

Absorbed with the beauty of his phrases, Bone fails to observe that if man's rare gift makes him see injustice, then artistic integrity requires him to reveal it. This will be called protest—if it is ineptly written.

Furthermore, Bone continues, the Negro writer should not seek to evade writing about the ghetto because, if he does, then it will lack an interpreter (p. 248). As soon as one judges art by adding the historical dimension, Bone states, one realizes that the novelist is not "free to deal with Negro life" when he does not write about the ghetto (p. 248). Thus Bone finally unmasks to reveal himself as one of those whom he cited Richard Gibson as castigating—the "Professional Liberal," who reminds the Negro writer "that he cannot possibly know anything else but Jim Crow, sharecropping, slum ghettoes, Georgia crackers . . . " (p. 247).

Bone concludes his advice with the reminder that although the Negro novelist can write about anything he knows, his early novel should be about Negroes because "most Negro novelists will produce only one or two novels" (p. 253). He knows this to be a fact because most Negro novelists have produced only one or two novels.

In the beginning was Mr. Bone's assertion of the need for a book which evaluated Negro writers' novels according to artistic standards. If Mr. Bone had limited himself to that task, he would have succeeded despite his predilection for works lending themselves to mythic interpretation. As a cultural historian or as a psychiatrist of the mentalities of millions of Negroes, however, he is less than adequate.

The Failure of William Styron

Ernest Kaiser

The problem of creating Negro characters in historical fiction (within the veil and in slavery) is very difficult even for Negro writers. Margaret Walker's novel *Jubilee* (1967) written after talking with people who knew the early characters and steeping herself in the family history and Arna Bontemps's novel *Black Thunder* (1935, 1964) about Gabriel's Virginia slave insurrection of 1800 are just two examples of this. Du Bois in parts of *The Souls of Black Folk* and James Weldon Johnson's poem "O Black and Unknown Bards" succeed in evoking the slaves' emotional reaction to slavery. Historical fiction about Negroes that has real characters and is true to history is almost impossible even for the most understanding white writers in the racist, separatist United States.

There have been, nevertheless, a few novels dealing with Negro slave uprisings and unrest: Harriet Beecher Stowe's *Dred* (1856), G. P. R. James's *The Old Dominion* (1858), Mary Johnston's *Prisoners of Hope* (1899), Pauline C. Bouve's *The Shadows Before* (1899), A. Bontemps's *Black Thunder* (1935, 1964), Frances Gaither's *The Red Cock Crows* (1944) and Daniel Panger's *Ol' Prophet Nat* (1967). There are also the plays *Nat Turner* by Paul Peters (published in Edwin Seaver's *Cross Section,* 1944) and *Harpers Ferry: A Play about John Brown* (1967) by Barrie Stavis that have been produced in our time. In addition to these works, there were Herbert Aptheker's *American Negro Slave Revolts* (1943) and his 1937 master's thesis at Columbia University (published as *Nat Turner's Slave Rebellion* in 1966) plus a long bibliography in each book. Lately we have had F. Roy Johnson's *The Nat Turner Slave Insurrection* (1966) and John Lofton's *Insurrection in South Carolina: The Turbulent World of Denmark Vesey* (1964). So this was the considerable body of writing available to William Styron when he, in the late 1940's, began to look for material on Nat Turner. Now Finkelstein, in his book *Existentialism and Alienation in American Literature* (1965), calls Styron a disciple of Faulkner and an existentialist whose fiction is technically good but more subjective and narrower in focus than Faulkner's and thus of less significance. Mike Newberry's review of Styron's third novel *Set This House on Fire* (1960) (the other two are *Lie Down in Darkness* [1951] and *The Long March* [1952]) in *Mainstream* (Sept. 1960) calls him a writer of overwhelming ability who is extremely

From *William Styron's* Nat Turner: *Ten Black Writers Respond,* edited by John H. Clarke (Boston: Beacon Press, 1968), pp. 50-65.

pessimistic and without a moral point of view in this novel. John Howard Lawson, in an essay "Styron: Darkness and Fire in the Modern Novel" (*Mainstream,* Oct. 1960), disagrees somewhat with Newberry. He calls Styron a brilliant and sensitive writer who has moved from the Freudian, psychoanalytic frame of reference of his first novel to the existentialism of the third. Comparing his compassion to Chekhov's in the first novel and his social understanding to that of Thomas Wolfe's last novel *You Can't Go Home Again* in the third, Lawson says that Styron is angry at the evil of the social environment which destroys people but also feels that the trouble is mystical and hidden in the soul. This conflict, he says, creates faults in his writing. Styron, Lawson continues, must face the fact that he is abetting in his writing the corruption of life and art which he passionately opposes and is thus another promising American talent deteriorating like Mailer, James Jones, and others. I would add that *Set This House on Fire* is obviously a very heavily autobiographical novel like the novels of Thomas Wolfe. Lawson comments that this third book has anti-Italian, anti-Semitic, and anti-Negro stereotypes. Cass (Styron), the central character in the novel, speaks of his nightmares being tied up with Negroes. His guilt, says Lawson, is specifically related to his feeling as a white southerner that he has participated in shameful treatment of Negroes.

But when Styron comes to write his fourth novel *The Confessions of Nat Turner* (1967) which has haunted him since 1948, his talent really deteriorates and goes downhill as Lawson had noted earlier. His social view, instead of developing, has remained where it was in his third novel or even gone backward. He has read all of the works on Nat Turner and slave rebellions and rejected them. Herbert Aptheker points out in a footnote to his article-review of Styron's *The Confessions* ("Styron-Turner and Nat Turner: Myth and Truth," *Political Affairs,* Oct. 1967) that Styron borrowed a few years ago the manuscript of his master's thesis written in 1936 and published as *Nat Turner's Slave Rebellion* in 1966. It was kept several months and then returned. In a review of Aptheker's *American Negro Slave Revolts* and Stanley M. Elkins's *Slavery,* Styron attacks Aptheker's book, retitles and reduces it to *Signs of Slave Unrest* and the U.S. slaves' organized rebellion to very little. But he praises highly the Elkins book describing the dehumanized, Sambo slave (*New York Review of Books,* Sept. 26, 1963).

In his article "This Quiet Dust" (*Harper's* Apr. 1965) which was reprinted in the book *Best Magazine Articles 1966,* Styron says that he distrusts any easy generalizations about the South by white sociologists, Negro playwrights, southern politicians, and northern editors since his own "knowledge" of Negroes as a southern youth was gained at a distance through folklore and hearsay. (Why Negro playwrights, who are on the other side of the racial fence, should be thrown in is beyond me.) Then he proceeds to project his own generalization that although Ralph Ellison is right about the constant preoccupation of southern whites with Negroes, perpetual sexual tension between Negroes and whites in the South is greatly exaggerated, so effective have been the segregation laws from the 1890's to the present. And this assertion is based solely on his own experiences. But the sociologists, playwrights, and editors (never mind the southern politicians) have better information than mere personal experience on which to base their generalizations. The corollary of Styron's idea of little interracial sex in the South is the mythology that white women are put on pedestals by white men in the South. Harry Golden, a northern liberal now living in the South, believes this along with Styron. He restates the myth in his book *Mr. Kennedy and the Negroes* (1964). Styron admits that there was enormous interracial sex during slavery. (The southerner Ross Lockridge Jr.'s mammoth historical novel *Raintree County* [1948] has the white wife become insane when the white slaver moves his Negro woman into the same house with her.) The article "The Plight of Southern White Women" (*Ebony,* Nov. 1957) says that southern women told that they were nice ladies by the men, were kept home off juries, away from high-paying jobs and voting booths—out of competition. Also that white women were enslaved along with the Negroes in the South and that the freedom of these two groups has always run closely parallel; that white women were used as a shield behind which white men committed cowardly acts of violence against Negroes, and that southern white women hate playing the roles of Scarlett O'Haras.

Styron's writing of *The Confessions,* he says further in "This Quiet Dust," is an attempt to *know* the Negro. And yet, he rejects here, as he has elsewhere, Aptheker's documented books on American Negro slave revolts when he states baldly that in 250 years of slavery, there were no uprisings, plots or rebellions except those led by Gabriel Prosser in Virginia in 1800, Denmark Vesey in South Carolina in 1882 and Nat Turner in Virginia in 1831. He again accepts wholeheartedly the fraudulent and untenable thesis of Frank Tannenbaum and Stanley M. Elkins (see my refutation in an essay in *Freedomways,* Fall 1967) that American slavery was so oppressive, despotic and emasculating psychologically that revolt was impossible and Negroes could only be Sambos.

The problems of Negro-white relations in the South that come up in Styron's essay reveal the level of his understanding of the Negro problem: he doubts that there are sexual relations to any degree between the races in the segregated South; he explains the question of Nat Turner's intelligence, precocity, and apprehension; he states boldly that Americans believe that the slave system, though morally wrong, was conducted with such charity and restraint that insurrection and murder were unthinkable; he has a constant preoccupation with "knowing" Negroes; and he seems to relish the horrible details of the whites' bestiality toward Negroes. Examples of bestial descriptions in his article are his unnecessary, gruesome explanation that the doctors skinned Nat Turner's dead body, after he was hanged along with 17 other Negroes, and made grease of his flesh; and the lurid details in his novel of the killings of whites by Negroes.

Styron, after having read Aptheker's master's thesis on Nat Turner, put all the ideas that Aptheker refuted in his essay. Styron says that the greedy cultivation of tobacco caused the economic depression in Tidewater Virginia before 1831; Aptheker says that the fall in the price of cotton caused the disaster. Styron largely accepts W. S. Drewry's book *The Southampton Insurrection* (1900); Aptheker rejects it as untruthful; Styron says that stringent codes for policing slaves followed the revolt; Aptheker says that many of these stringent codes preceded Nat's revolt. Styron says that Virginia was edging close to emancipation; Aptheker's book says that there never was in the South a flourishing emancipation movement. Nat Turner's rebellion in which many whites were killed, says Styron further in this essay, was an act of futility. It caused about 200 Negroes to be tortured and killed and obviously should never have taken place at all. Aptheker shows that Nat Turner's revolt was the culminating blow of a period of rising slave unrest which began about 1827 and played itself out in 1832; it brought historic social forces to a head. The revolt blew off the lid which the slavocracy had clamped down upon the press and the rostrums of debate and lecture. From then on until the Civil War, continues Aptheker, there was a confrontation of Abolitionists and slavocrats, of North and South. Styron also says that today in southeast Virginia Negroes are living amiably with white paternalism which includes restricting Negroes from owning new-model Buicks or their children from going to school with whites. This is a total lie. I am a native of that part of Virginia and have scores of relatives there who not only carry on large-scale, mechanized farming and own and drive big automobiles if they are able to; they also are activists in the NAACP chapters there, and there have been court suits all over the area in the past several years which have resulted in some desegregation of the public schools in that area. Styron should look at the quarterly *Race Relations Law Reporter* (published at Vanderbilt University School of Law, Nashville, Tenn.) for the last eight years and see the scores of Virginia desegregation cases there.

It is clear from this essay's whole approach to and attitude toward Negroes that Styron has no equipment either factually or psychologically to write a novel about Nat Turner or any other Negro for that matter. His essay is a 20- or 30-year throwback to the racism and paternalism of the 1930's and 1940's. In the author's note in *The Confessions,* Styron says Nat Turner's rebellion was the only effective, sustained revolt in the annals of American Negro slavery. That makes Aptheker's 409-page doctoral dissertation at Columbia University, published as the book *American Negro Slave Revolts* in 1943 and twice since, just a pack of lies! Styron says further in his review of Aptheker's *American Negro Slave Revolts* mentioned above that the view of the slave as in revolt against slavery is a part of the white man's fantasy. On the contrary, his view of the slaves as Sambos is but a common variety of southern racist fantasy based on ignorance and buttressed by Tannenbaum and Elkins's false thesis while the revolt thesis is based on solid historical research by Aptheker and many others, Negro and white.

He also says further in his note that his novel is not so much an historical novel as it is a meditation on history. It is a meditation all right and that of an unreconstructed southern racist.

He says in his essay that the novel has a psychoanalytical emphasis upon Nat's so-called tormented relationship with his father following psychoanalyst Erik Erikson's book *Young Man Luther*. Aptheker's article-review of *The Confessions* shows that while Styron quotes from Turner's *Confessions,* he also twists certain facts to suit his Freudian thesis in the novel. In many other cases, says Aptheker, he falsifies the known facts of Nat Turner's history, and Styron admits in the author's note that he has allowed himself the utmost freedom of imagination in reconstructing Turner's early life and the motivations for the revolt. The unspeakable arrogance of this young southern writer daring to set down his own personal view of Nat's life as from inside Nat Turner in slavery! Instead of trying to get the true feeling of the Negroes of the period as Howard Fast did in *Freedom Road* (to say nothing of Margaret Walker's and Arna Bontemps's hard historical work in *Jubilee* and *Black Thunder* respectively), Styron, who doesn't really know the Negroes living in Virginia today, deigns to speak personally for the slaves.

As Lawson has pointed out, Styron's early novels had only anti-Negro stereotypes. But *The Confessions* is infinitely worse. All of the Negro stereotypes are here: the filthy, racist language of American whites: nigger, nigger, nigger on almost every page, black toadeater, darky, pickininny, ginger-colored Negro with thick lips. He puts in over and over the Negro's black color: the white woman's fingers upon the Negro's black arm. Aptheker's article-review also gives many other examples of Styron's despicable, racist descriptions of Negroes. The language of *The Confessions* equals in its vile racist filth that found in J. C. Furna's *Goodbye to Uncle Tom* (1956) which I pilloried in *Freedomways,* Spring 1961. Other stereotypes in the novel are the servile, cringing slave, the slave who loves his slave-master, the slave craving a white woman and the main stereotype which the whole book points up: the slave who confesses the details of the plot or revolt against slavery for freedom to a white man when caught like a child who has done something wrong against his parents. The ignorant Styron even has the temerity to attempt to explain how much hatred Negroes have for the white man and why. His ignorance and arrogance know no bounds. Like every white southerner, Styron has to know the Negro, as he says in "This Quiet Dust," although he really knows nothing and wants to find out nothing of Negro life and history.

This novel is a witches' brew of Freudian psychology, Elkins's "Sambo" thesis on slavery and Styron's vile racist imagination that makes especially Will and Nat Turner animals or monsters. Styron has to rationalize the oppression of Negroes in one way or another. Elkins says that the American slave system was so oppressive that Negroes had to be Sambos and Freud says that there were dark, ineradicable, primitive drives or instincts in Turner that made him a beast. Aptheker says in his article-review that the fictional image of the Dunning school of history was *The Clansman, Gone with the Wind* of the U. B. Phillips school, and William Styron's *The Confessions of Nat Turner* of the Elkins school. Having rejected the Negro people's history, Styron cannot see Turner as the hero he was and as the Negro people see him; as a slave who led a heroic rebellion against the dehumanization of chattel slavery. This novel makes Styron look like a Rip Van Winkle who has slept through the Negro people's twelve-year freedom struggle of the 1950's and 1960's.

But just as Michael Harrington, Jason Epstein, Norman Podhoretz and other reviewers seized upon Elkin's *Slavery* as a rationale of the Negro slave as a "Sambo" personality thus relieving themselves of the great guilt of American Negro chattel slavery, so, as Aptheker has pointed out in his article-review, reviewers of Styron's *The Confessions* have seized upon this book as pointing up the current Negro ghetto uprising as led by mad Negroes, as futile, stupid rebellions which should be put down ruthlessly. Critics Elizabeth Hardwick and Norman Podhortz have written about the decline of book reviewing in the U.S. into advertising blurbs. Historian Christopher Lasch, in *The New Radicalism in America* (1965), says that journalism has degenerated into public relations, advertising and propaganda. An outstanding literary critic, Stanley Edgar Hyman, in *Standards: A Chronicle of Books for Our Time* (1966), talks about truth as unfashionable in literary journalism. Harry Golden, in an essay in the "What I Have Learned" series (*Saturday Review,* June 17, 1967) states that "journalists are writers who have no education and disdain looking up words in dictionaries or subjects in encyclopedias, relying on their memories." Certainly the decline of book reviewing and the ignorance of journalists are sharply pointed up by the near unanimity of high brow, middle brow, low brow, liberal and conservative reviewers in praising Styron's novel. But they all, with no research behind the novel or historical knowledge of the South in the 1820's and 1830's, seem to be basically approving of the novel's thesis rather than really reviewing the historical novel which they were not equipped to do. As Thomas Lask says in a review of Kenneth Tynan's *Tynan Right and Left* (*New York Times,* Dec. 12, 1967), under the cover of esthetics these reviewers are condemning what they hate in politics or approving what they like.

Newsweek (Oct. 16, 1967) in a cover story called *The Confessions* an act of revelation to a whole society. Wilfred Sheed, the book review editor of *Commonweal,* in a front page review in *The New York Times Book Review* (Oct. 8, 1967), called the novel artificial but knowing no history he could only accept Styron's view of history; Eliot Fremont-Smith, in a two-part review in the *New York Times* (Oct. 3–4, 1967), also knowing nothing of Negro history, goes all out. He calls the book a triumph, a rare book that shows us our American past, our present, ourselves, compelling, convincing, a rich and powerful novel. The *New Republic's* reviewer was C. Vann Woodward, a historian who has already swallowed Elkins's thesis whole and uncritically in "The Anti-Slavery Myth" (*American Scholar,* Spring 1962). In the Oct. 7, 1967, issue, Woodward repeats the lie that Nat's rebellion was the only slave rebellion of consequence in the largest slave society in the nineteenth century world as well as the Elkins thesis that Negro slaves were servile Sambos. Accepting and repeating all of Styron's slave stereotypes, he says that the novel shows a respect for history and has a sure feeling for Nat's period. Woodward calls the novel the most profound fictional treatment of slavery in our literature embracing all the subtleties and ambivalences of race in the South.

In *The Nation* (Oct. 16, 1967), the reviewer Shaun O'Connell, a young English teacher at the University of Massachusetts, is completely overwhelmed by Styron's novel. Obviously knowing nothing of Negro history, O'Connell accepts all of Styron's false psychological twistings and all of his invented "facts" about Turner's life as valid and sensible. He thinks that Styron, a twentieth century southerner, has really gotten inside a nineteenth century Negro slave and portrayed him accurately. He says that Styron has improved his craft and modulated his style; that *The Confessions* is the best of his novels. He also calls Styron's "The Quiet Dust" an important essay. And all of this is called fiction criticism by *The Nation* editor's note. *The Nation* does carry in the same Oct. 16th issue "A Note on the History" by Herbert Aptheker which says more briefly what Aptheker spells out in his *Political Affairs* (Oct. 1967) article-review on the novel. And that is plenty as we have seen above. We will only say here that Aptheker again nails the lie repeated by the historian Woodward and Styron that the Nat Turner revolt was the only sustained U.S. Negro slave revolt, armed attack or uprising. He says that there were slave uprisings from 1691 in Virginia to 1864 in Mississippi. He also points out that Styron lyingly makes a monster of Will who in reality was not like that at all.

Other reviewers, with no knowledge, just accepted the novel as accurate. *The National Observer* (Oct. 9, 1967) headed the review "Fiction Vivifies the Facts of a Tidewater Tale." Poppy Cannon White, in a review of the book in her column in the Negro newspaper *New York Amsterdam News* (Nov. 25, 1967) says that *The Confessions* seems persuasive, historically accurate, and is a remarkable document. She says that the hero of the novel looks, sounds, and feels like truth, but she finds Turner protrayed as a madman hard to take. The book wallows in violence, she says, but she thinks of the violence as she thinks of Truman Capote's nonfiction, violent novel about multiple murder *In Cold Blood* (1965): these are books, she says, about tortured minds and dark recesses of the spirit. Mrs. White disagrees about Nat Turner's revolt being the only one; she says that there were hundreds of revolts. In a later column (Dec. 9, 1967) devoted to *The Confessions,* she says that she received a lot of mail about her previous column reviewing the novel; that some letters agreed and some disagreed with her statement that Nat's revolt wasn't the only sustained revolt in American slavery. Mrs. White then contrasts *The Confessions* and other slave novels with another new novel, Harold Courlander's *The African,* a book, she says, concerned with a man, with real people who have a past and a culture. *Time* magazine called the book a new peak in the literature of the South. *Harper's* called it a masterpiece of storytelling. The historian Arthur Schlesinger, Jr., called the book in *Vogue* the finest American novel published in many years. Philip Rahv, in *New York Review of Books,* called it a first-rate novel . . . the best by an American writer that has appeared in some years. Edmund Fuller in the *Wall Street Journal* said that Styron without doubt is the foremost writer of his generation in American fiction. *Commentary* magazine said it is a superb novel with immense understanding. The *Los Angeles Times* called it one of the great novels by an American author in this century.

One of the mostly southern liberals working for the Southern Regional Council reviewed the novel in *New South* (Fall 1967), the Council's magazine. He found the novel richly deserving of its critical acclaim since it is an important work of fiction dealing successfully with race and the whole historical setting of slavery, one of the more important themes in American life. The reviewer defends the novel against the two critical reviews of the novel that he had seen: (1) the mild criticism of Wilfred Sheed in *The New York Times Book Review* who doubts the ability of a twentieth century white southerner like Styron to speak from the consciousness of a nineteenth century black slave and also finds technical faults in the novel; (2) H. Aptheker's charges in *The Nation* that the novel has all the rationalizations of slavery plus the slave stereotypes. The *New South* reviewer again drags out the Elkins thesis and compares the Negro slaves to the Jews in the Nazi concentration camps. But this has been refuted. (See my essay in *Freedomways* Fall 1967.) He also sidesteps Aptheker's charge of historical inaccuracy; says the novel's main achievement is its showing of the horror and cruelty of slavery. He agrees with other reviewers when they seized upon this novel and used it as an argument against today's riots. They also say that Nat's revolt prevented Virginia from solving its slavery problem. He thinks that the real moral issue today as in history is not the violence but the cause for violence.

Even James Baldwin, Styron's friend, chimes in by saying that Styron has begun the common history—ours. And the veteran biographical and historical novelist Irving Stone, deploring the decline of what he calls the "great school of historical novelists" (*New York Times,* Jan 19, 1968), says that *The Confessions* is the one recent historical novel that impressed him. Robert Coles, a Harvard psychiatrist, the author of the book *Children of Crisis* (1967) and the latest self-styled white "authority" on Negroes, finds Styron's psychological and historical explanations of Nat Turner completely satisfying and valid in his long, six-page review in *Partisan Review* (Winter 1968).

Another high-brow magazine *Dissent* (Jan.–Feb. 1968), in its review by James MacPherson, is also favorable and uncritical in its approach to Styron's novel. The historian Martin Duberman, in a very long, uncritical, glowing review in the *Village Voice* (December 14, 1967), swallows Styron's novel hook, line and sinker. Agreeing with Styron that the Elkins "Sambo" thesis is the most valid explanation of American slavery, Duberman thinks that the novel is very accurate history as well.

There were some dissenting reviews. Herbert Aptheker, an authority on Negro history and especially slave revolts, in addition to the short piece in *The Nation,* wrote a devastatingly critical article-review in *Political Affairs* (Oct. 1967) which we have mentioned several times. Richard Greenleaf's review of the novel in *The Worker* (Oct. 8, 1967) called it anti-Negro and a libel on Nat Turner. Another *New York Amsterdam News* columnist Gertrude Wilson wrote on Oct. 21, 1967, that Styron had done a good job in *The Confessions* and that she hoped that her column readers would read the novel; also that the novel showed that white people could understand what it is like to be black. Later she had second thoughts. In her Dec. 30, 1967, column titled "Styron's Folly," she asked: why is the book such a success among whites? She concludes that the book is so popular with whites because it proves that if Negroes retaliate against injustice by violence, they will be quelled by violence. The book also gives, she says, the blessing of history for continued violence against Negroes. Mrs. Wilson also found in Howard H. Meyer's recent biography of Thomas W. Higginson that Nat had a slave wife (with a different master from his) whom he couldn't protect at all in slavery. (There is a brief account of Nat's wife in Samuel Warner's *The Authentic and Impartial Narrative of the Tragical Scene of the Twenty Second of August, 1831* [1831] as well as an article on Nat Turner's family and descendants in the *Negro* History Bulletin [Mar. 1955].) She concludes that Styron's stereotyped picture of Nat as a celibate, as one of repressed lusts who is violently aroused by a sweet young white girl is a lie. This book is history twisted, she says, to fit the sexual fantasies of her own times.

As anyone who has read the Negro critic Albert Murray's essay "Something Different, Something More" (in Herbert Hill's *Anger and Beyond,* 1966) knows, he denounces social fiction by Negro writers which attacks our system and society and takes refuge in the art-as-mostly-technique approach to creative writing. So Murray, familiar with Styron's considerable technique in his first three novels, hoped that Styron, a so-called reconstructed southerner, would bring his fourth novel off even though he had picked a difficult subject for a white American novelist. But Murray is compelled to put *The Confessions* down and he does this in a brilliant essay-review (*The New Leader*, Dec. 4, 1961). He says that Styron failed to identify intimately with Nat Turner; that his Turner is one whom many white people will accept at a safe distance but not the hero with whom Negroes identify. Accusing Styron of building a weak Turner character according to the Elkins Sambo thesis and Freudian castration (he also calls this pro-slavery image Marxist which it isn't), he says that Styron has added a neo-Reichean hypothesis about the correlation between sex repression and revolutionary leadership; between Negro freedom from slavery and sexual desire for a white woman. Styron, he says, never realized that the Negro conception of Nat Turner as an epic hero, a special, dedicated breed of man who had given his last full measure of devotion to liberation and dignity was already geared to the dynamics of rituals and myth and hence to literature. Criticizing Styron for ignoring the many slave revolts, Murray accuses Elkins of making slavery overwhelming for Negroes but letting such a monstrous system have little effect on the whites who operated it. Murray uses Kenneth Stampp's *The Peculiar Institution* (1956) to document the great impact of the Nat Turner and other slave revolts on the slavocracy. When Styron has Nat Turner say that Negroes were bragging in brass when they said that they would kill whites, Murray replies that Negroes fought in the Revolutionary War, the War of 1812 and very bravely a little later against their Confederate slave masters in the Civil War. Describing the characters Nat Turner in *The Confessions* and the female Peyton in *Lie Down in Darkness* as having a lot of Styron's own personality in them, Murray says that if white writers want to think Negro and create Negro characters, they must be able to sing the spirituals and/or swing the blues, or, in other words, know the rugged facts and the psychological subtleties and nuances of Negro life.

Loyle Hairston did a fine critical essay-review of the novel for *Freedomways* (Winter 1968). Cecil M. Brown, a perceptive Negro critic, also did a brilliant, analytical job on Styron in his long review in *Negro Digest* (February 1968). And there are two long critical reviews of *The Confessions* by the late black psychologist Lloyd T. Delany and the sociologist Gerald M. Platt in the new magazine *Psychology Today* (January 1968). Platt accepts some of the false "facts" in Styron's novel and Delany calls the book a valiant and honest attempt to view the horrible institution of slavery. But Delany also calls the book Styron's confessions which are historically inaccurate, stereotyped and racist. Both Delany and Platt say that the novel presents the revolt in a vacuum with no historical context; but most important, they both show clearly and in great detail that the novel is psychologically false through and through in terms of human motivation and psychological theory and is morally wrong as well.

This novel is a good example of the absurdity of the separation of art and politics, art and sociology. This separation is nourished and encouraged by all liberal magazines such as *The New Republic, The Nation, Commentary, New York Review of Books, Dissent, Commonweal, The New Leader, The Progressive, The Reporter* and others—magazines that fight for progressive social policies and measures but take a stand-pat, art-for-art's-sake approach to fiction, plays, cinema, music and painting. Styron has lived through twelve years of the Negro social revolution and struggle in the U.S., but this upheaval has not touched him as a novelist. He wrote *The Confessions* just as he would have written it in 1948. His writing is impervious to Negro social change and struggle and to the facts of Negro history. His book is a throwback to the racist writing of the 1930's and 1940's. The decline in the writing of Styron, Ellison and many other American novelists is directly traceable to this tragic American separation of art and politics, art and sociology—as John Howard Lawson pointed out in his essay on Styron (*Mainstream,* Oct. 1960).

Sidney Finkelstein calls truthful fiction (in his book *Existentialism and Alienation* and in a review of two of Philip Stevenson's novels [*Political Affairs,* Oct. 1962]) those novels and short stories that take up the central problem of American life: that is, the conflict between the democratic principles on which the nation was founded and the forces of violence against the working people—a conflict which has been continuous throughout American history. Novelists like Stevenson, Albert Maltz, and Phillip Bonosky are attempting to help humanize U.S. human relations and extend democracy to the dispossessed even if this interferes with property and profits. This struggle, says Finkelstein further, for a more rational, realistic and truthful view of life, which includes the fight for Negro equality and rights, is a struggle for humanization of nature and social relations against alienation. The artists who depict this many-sided struggle of alienated human beings moving toward more humanization are a force in the humanization of reality. But, as Finkelstein points out, when the writers themselves are alienated and psychologically sick, as in Styron's case, their view of society and of other human beings is colored by their subjective, Freudian views of their own problems and the effect of their art is further alienation rather than humanization.

III

CHRONOLOGY OF BLACKAMERICAN HISTORY AND LITERAURE

Significant Events, 1501-1968

1501 Spain removes ban on transport of Blacks to the New World: Spaniards migrating may take as many as 12 slaves. The African slave trade begins.

1562 John Hawkins, British "sea dog," brings 300 Blacks from Africa to Haiti, trading them for ginger and sugar. Additional expeditions bring him knighthood in 1565.

1591 Using firearms, Spanish and Portuguese mercenaries hired by Morocco defeat the Black kingdom of Songhai; the entire culture is destroyed.

1595 First foothold of Dutch on Guinea Coast of Africa.

1600 Charter of East India Company, English trading company authorized to explore, trade with, and occupy lands in Far East, Africa, and the Americas.

1606 English companies are chartered to colonize the coast of North America.

1608 John Smith, *A True Relations of Such Occurrences and Accidents of Noate as Hath Hapned in Virginia Since the First Planting of that Collony,* a promotion tract.

1617 Plague decimates Indians along New England coast.

1619 100 children from London slums transported to Virginia as apprentices; a shipload of marriageable girls sent by Virginia Company for sale to planters at 120 pounds of tobacco each.
First Blacks brought to Virginia and sold as servants.

1620 Pilgrims join *Mayflower* voyage; Mayflower Compact signed in Provincetown Harbor. By 1630 there are 300 settlers.

1624 Dutch West India Company sends settlers to Manhattan Island.

1628 Puritans establish Massachusetts Bay Colony; by 1640 there are 16,000 settlers.

1630 John Winthrop begins his *Journal.* (Printed in part in 1790; the whole printed in 1825 as *The History of New England from 1630-1649.*)
William Bradford begins *History of Plimouth Plantation.*

1631 Massachusetts Bay Colony decrees only freemen may vote, and only members of approved Church shall be declared freemen.

1635 Roger Williams is banished from Massachusetts Bay Colony.

1636 Harvard College founded to educate ministers.

1637 Thomas Morton, *New English Canaan,* satire on the Pilgrims.

1639 First printing press established at Cambridge, Mass.; *Bay Psalm Book* printed 1640.

1642 Massachusetts law enables authorities to require that all children be taught to read.

1643 Ironworks at Lynn, Mass.; woolen and fulling mills at Rowley, Mass. Skilled workers imported from England.

1644 John Cotton, *The Keyes of the Kingdom of Heaven.*

1645 Sugar plantations in Caribbean Islands flourish and the importation of Black slaves accelerates. The introduction of stringent slave codes and their enforcement becomes necessary. The problem of runaways besets the planters; ex-slaves known as Maroons organize rebellions; conspiracies, uprisings, bloodshed are common all during 17th century.

1650 Anne Bradstreet, *The Tenth Muse, Lately Sprung Up in America*—the first volume of original verse written in America.

1652 First law against slavery in North America enacted in Rhode Island.

1656 Connecticut passes law against Quakers.

1662 Children declared slave or free according to status of mother.
Michael Wigglesworth, *The Day of Doom*—exceedingly popular poem depicting Judgment Day.
England authorizes judges to send rogues, vagabonds, and sturdy beggars to the American colonies.

1663 In Carolina every settler (in his first year) allowed 20 acres for each male slave, 10 acres for each female slave. Slavery legalized in Maryland with strict enforcement.

1667 Slaves allowed baptism with understanding it does not alter their status.

1670 Connecticut restricts movement of Blacks; Massachusetts enacts law that children of slaves may be sold.
Suffrage in Virginia and Maryland limited to property owners.

1675 Penn receives West Jersey for settlement of Quakers.

1676 Indian Wars throughout New England frontier, extending to frontiers of Virginia and Maryland, continuing until 1678.

1680 Massachusetts restricts movement of Blacks.

1682 Edward Taylor, *Preparatory Meditations*—theological poems.

1684 Slavery legalized in New York.
Increase Mather, *An Essay for the Recording of Illustrious Providences.*

1685 Massachusetts revokes requirement of church membership for right to vote.

1687 A rebellion by slaves in Northern Neck, Virginia thwarted.

1688 *Germantown Friends'* (Quaker) *Protest against Slavery*—first anti-slavery document in America.

1692 Salem witchcraft mania.

1693 Cotton Mather, *Wonders of the Invisible World*—justifies the execution of witches.

1694 Virginia slave code in force providing clear description of punishments for specific crimes: slaves may not be party to lawsuit; testify, unless against another Black man; be party to any legal contract; have legal marriage; consider children legitimate; strike a White person; rape a female slave; travel without permit; possess arms; hire out; possess drums or blow horns; visit at the houses of whites or free Blacks; assemble without the presence of a white; or learn to read, write, or cipher. Violations punished by fine, imprisonment, whipping, branding, or death. Capital crimes are arson, rape, conspiracy.

1698 English parliament extends slave-trade privileges to private merchants. Beginning of New England domination of slave traffic between Africa and Caribbean Islands.

1703 Indians resist spread of White settlers; Massachusets leads in organizing for defense of colonists.

1705 New York provides that runaway slaves found 40 miles north of Albany may be executed; slave revolt in 1712 ends with execution of 21 Blackamericans.

1707 Philadelphia mechanics protest the hiring of Black slaves from their owners as unfair competition.

1713 England secures the exclusive right to transport slaves to the Spanish colonies in America.

John Wise, *Churches Quarrel Espoused*; 1717, *Vindication of Government of the New England Churches*—the first explicit argument for more democratic government.

1721 Inoculation against smallpox accepted by Puritans indicating a shift in interpretation of events as God's providences.

1724 Black Code in New Orleans.

1727 Cadwallader Colden, *History of the Five Indian Nations.*

1732 Benjamin Franklin, *Poor Richard's Almanack,* issued annually to 1757.

1734 John Peter Zenger arrested for libel; his acquittal a victory for free press in America.

1740 "The Great Awakening"; George Whitefield's tour through the colonies, preaching Methodist doctrine, stimulates religious revival with dramatic repentences and conversions taking place outside organized church structure, causing great excitement.

1750 Georgia repeals law against the keeping of slaves.

1751 Franklin, *Experiments and Observations in Electricity Made at Philadelphia in America.*

John Bartram, *Observations on American Plants.*

1754 John Woolman, *Some Considerations on the Keeping of Negroes Recommended to the Professors of Christianity of every Denomination*; Woolman was one of the first to engage in active protest against slavery.

American phase of the conflict between France and England begins, the "French and Indian War."

1760 Briton Hammon, *Narrative of the Uncommon Sufferings and Surprizing Deliverance of Briton Hammon*—a slave narrative, usually considered to be the first dictated by a Blackamerican.

1767 Thomas Godfrey, *The Prince of Parthia*—first American drama, performed in Philadelphia.

1769 Daniel Boone begins to explore Kentucky.

1770 The Boston Massacre: Crispus Attucks is fatally wounded when he knocks down a British soldier firing into a crowd of unruly colonists.

1773 First Blackamerican Baptist Church formed, in Silver Bluff, Georgia.
Ezra Stiles, president of Yale, advocates colonization of free Blacks in West Africa.
Phillis Wheatley, *Poems on Various Subjects, Religious and Moral*—published in London, first volume by a Blackamerican slave of Boston.

1774 Address to the Massachusetts General Court by Blackamericans insisting they too have a natural right to their freedom.

1775 George Washington appointed commander-in-chief of Continental Army; battle of Bunker Hill. Washington reverses his earlier policy of rejecting the services of slaves and freedmen in the army; 5000 Blackamericans serve during the Revolutionary War; two predominantly Black units in Massachusetts, one in Connecticut, one in Rhode Island.
First Abolition Society meeting in Philadelphia; Franklin presides.

1776 Thomas Paine, *Common Sense;* first number of *American Crisis* appears.
American colonies declare themselves independent of England. That portion containing indictment of slave trade stricken out of draft of Declaration of Independence.

1777 New Jersey opens school for Black children; Vermont abolishes slavery.
Massachusetts legislature considers a law against slavery.
Jupiter Hammon, "A Dialogue, Intitled, The Kind Master and the Dutiful Servant"—poem written by a Long Island Black slave, published in America.

1780 Pennsylvania manumits all children of slaves upon their reaching 28 years; gradual emancipation follows in Connecticut, Rhode Island, New York, and New Jersey.
Founding of American Academy of Art and Sciences in Boston.

1784 United States begins trade with China. First bale of cotton shipped to England.

1785 Cartwright's mechanical loom stimulates demand for cotton.
John Marrant, *A Narrative of the Lord's Wonderful Dealings with J. Marrant, A Black.*

1786 Philip Freneau, *Poems*—uses American issues and subject matter.

1787 Philadelphia opens school for Blackamerican children; New York follows. Constitutional Convention agrees to allow representation based on slaves counted as people, but with stipulation that each slave be counted as three-fifths of a man; agrees to prohibit slave trade after 1808; agrees that no state may protect a fugitive slave.
Free African Society organized by Absalom Jones and Richard Allen.

Jefferson's *Notes on Virginia;* Hamilton, Madison, and Jay, *The Federalist.*

British acquire Sierra Leone from the natives; in 1791 it will become the place for settlement of freed slaves.

1789 *The Interesting Narrative of the Life of Olaudah Equiano, or Gustavus Vassa, the African,* a Black narrator who eventually purchases his freedom and goes to England to work for abolition of slavery.

1792 Denmark is the first country to prohibit the slave trade.

1793 Eli Whitney's cotton gin begins the "cotton economy" of the South based upon slavery.

First fugitive slave act.

1794 Mulattoes and Blacks of Haiti (a French Colony), acting under the impetus of the French Revolution, assert their equality and independence. They defeat an army sent by Napoleon and eject the White inhabitants.

Bethel Church organized in Philadelphia; eventually known as Bethel African Methodist Episcopal Church; branches of AME Church in Baltimore, Wilmington, spreading to Pennsylvania and New Jersey towns.

1796 The African Methodist Episcopal Zion Church in New York.

1803 Louisiana Territory annexed to United States; slavery allowed.

1808 African slave trade ends; slaves may no longer be imported into America.

1811 400 slaves revolt in Louisiana; 75 slaves die.

1816 Slavery of Christians in Morocco ended.

1819 Washington Irving, "Rip Van Winkle."

1820 Steamboat line between New York and New Orleans.

Missouri Compromise provides for balanced entry of slave and non-slave states into the Union.

1821 Mexico declares itself independent of Spain.

Liberia, an African nation, founded by freed Blackamericans.

1822 Denmark Vesey (free since 1800) lays careful plans for revolt in Charleston; results in stricter enforcement of Black codes throughout the South.

United States recognizes independence of Mexico.

Brazil independent of Portugal; Greece begins to free herself from Turkey.

1823 Monroe Doctrine: no continents of America may be colonized by Europe; United States will not interfere with European colonization elsewhere.

1823 James Fenimore Cooper, *The Pioneers.*

1825 Erie Canal completed, providing impetus for the first great expansion West.

1827 *Freedom's Journal* begins publication, edited by Cornish and Russwurm.

1829 First steam locomotive, on line from Carbondale to Honesdale, Pa. David Walker, *Walker's Appeal, in Four Articles*—a fiery pamphlet by a free Black exhorting Blackamericans to take the fight for their freedom into their own hands.

1830 Choctaw Indians cede their lands east of the Mississippi. This pattern is followed by the Seminoles, the Creeks, the Sauk and Fox, the Sioux, until in 1871 all treaties are nullified by the U.S. government and Indians become national wards.
Joseph Smith, *Book of Mormon.*

1831 Garrison begins publication of *Liberator*—leading organ of abolitionist activity.
Nat Turner's revolt in Southampton County, Virginia.
First convention of "People of Color" held in Philadelphia.

1833 Oberlin, first coeducational college, founded; admits Black students. American Anti-slavery Society founded at Philadelphia; in New York, 1834, antislavery meeting generates rioting because of presence of Blackamericans in the audience.

1834 Britain begins emancipation of slaves in colonies, part of widespread social reform.

1835 Noyes Academy in New Canaan, New Hampshire closed by violence for accepting Black students.
In Charleston antislavery mails seized and burned.

1837 Hosea Easton, *A Treatise on the Intellectual Character and Civil and Political Condition of the Coloured People of the U.S., and the Prejudice Exercised Towards Them*—a radical analysis of the brutalizing effects of the American institution of slavery.
Emerson, *The American Scholar*—calling for reliance on native abilities rather than pallid, decadent European culture.
Narrative of the Adventures and Escapes of Moses Roper from American Slavery—typical of hundreds of slave narratives to appear with greater frequency until the outbreak of the Civil War.
Proslavery mob kills Abolitionist Elijah P. Lovejoy in Alton, Illinois.
American Peace Society passes resolution against all wars.

1838 Only Whites may vote in Pennsylvania. Mob in Pennsylvania destroys Lundy's "Pennsylvania Hall" because of antislavery meetings held there.
Underground Railroad organized.

1839 The *Amistad* sails from Havana with 53 Blacks. Led by Joseph Cinque they revolt. The ship is captured by Americans and the slaves transported to New London, Conn. John Quincy Adams argues the case for the Blacks before the Supreme Court; in 1841 they are freed and sail for home.

David and Lydia Maria Child edit *National Anti-Slavery Standard.*

1841 The *Creole* sails from Richmond with 130 slaves who revolt and force the ship to Nassau where they are liberated by British authorities.

1842 Supreme Court rules that the owner of a fugitive slave may recover him under the Fugitive Slave Act of 1793.

1843 Henry Highland Garnet delivers "An Address to the Slaves of the United States of America" calling for active resistance.

1844 Baptist Church splits over slavery; in 1845 Methodist Episcopal Church splits into a Northern and Southern conference.

W. H. Smith, *The Drunkard, or The Fallen Saved*—a temperance drama, plays to vast audiences everywhere.

Joseph Smith, head of Mormon Church, killed by mob at Nauvoo, Ill.; Brigham Young becomes leader; Mormon exodus to the west begins in 1846.

1845 Frederick Douglass publishes first edition of his *Narrative;* expanded to *My Bondage and My Freedom* in 1855.

1847 Frederick Douglass begins publication of *The North Star,* a fiery Black abolitionist paper; 1851 changed to *Frederick Douglass' Paper.*

1849 California gold rush; first population push to the far west, incentive for building the transcontinental railroad.

Henry David Thoreau, *Civil Disobedience.*

1850 William Nell, *Services of Colored Americans in the Wars of 1776 and 1812; 1855 The Colored Patriots in the American Revolution*—these are compilations of biographies and excerpts from the writings of Black patriots.

Herman Melville, *Moby Dick.*

1852 *The Pro-Slavery Argument* published—contains explicit defense of the institution by Southerners.

Harriet Beecher Stowe, *Uncle Tom's Cabin.*

1853 W. W. Brown, *Clotel, or the President's Daughter,* first novel by a Blackamerican.

1854 "Bleeding Kansas" conflict begins between free soil and proslavery factions.

Henry David Thoreau, *Walden.*

1855 Great wave of immigration into the United States reaches peak.

Walt Whitman, *Leaves of Grass*; Samuel Ringgold Ward, *The Autobiography of a Fugitive Negro: His Anti-Slavery Labours in the United States, Canada, and England.*

1856 Governor of South Carolina asks for repeal of 1807 law outlawing slave trade.

1857 Dred Scott decision: Supreme Court rules a Blackamerican cannot bring suit in federal court.

Hinton Rowan Helper, *The Impending Crisis of the South.*

1858 Campaign for U. S. Senate seat in Illinois waged between Lincoln and Douglas.

1859 John Brown's raid at Harper's Ferry. Georgia legislature acts to allow sale of free Blackamericans picked up as vagrants.

1861 South Carolina secedes; Civil War begins.
Freedman's Relief Association formed in Boston, New York, Philadelphia.

1862 General David Hunter (Union Army) issues certificates of emancipation to slaves employed by Confederacy, later to all slaves in his Department of the South; Lincoln countermands the order.
"First Regiment of South Carolina Volunteers" organized under T. W. Higginson, first slave company.

1863 Enlistment of Blackamericans authorized by War Department, limit put at 5,000.
First all-Black regiment from the North, the 54th Massachusetts under Robert Gould Shaw, attacks Fort Wagner in Charleston Harbor.
Emancipation Proclamation abolishes slavery in states at war.

1864 Fugitive Slave Law repealed. General Sherman begins his march from Atlanta to the sea.

1865 Surrender of General Lee at Appomattox ending Civil War. Assassination of Lincoln. Ratification of 13th amendment—the Black man is free. Eventually, ratification of 14th amendment—the Black man is a citizen. And 15th amendment—the Black man shall vote.
Mississippi legislation against vagrancy reintroduces the Black Codes.

1866 Civil Rights Act passed, conferring citizenship to Blacks.
Fisk University founded.
Ku Klux Klan formed at Pulaski, Tenn.
Race riots in New Orleans and Memphis against Blackamerican suffrage. Higginson publishes first article on Spirituals in *Atlantic Monthly;* W. F. Allen edits *Slave Songs of the U. S.*
Howard University for Blackamericans chartered in Washington D. C.
Congress takes over Reconstruction; imposes military rule on South, disfranchises all former Confederates.
Horatio Alger's first story, *Ragged Dick,* a phenomenally successful series teaching that virtue is always rewarded with success and money.

1868 Impeachment of President Johnson fails; amnesty proclaimed for all concerned in Rebellion.

1869 Union Pacific (transcontinental railroad) completed. San Francisco street riots against Chinese laborers. In 1871, 15 Chinese laborers lynched in Los Angeles.

1871 The Paris Workers' Commune crushed by the government.
The African Gold Coast annexed by England.

1872 Act of Congress ends Freedmen's Bureau, established to help liberated slaves.

1874 Race riots in Vicksburg, Mississippi; 75 Blackamericans killed.

1875 Civil Rights Act, guaranteeing equal public accommodations to Blackamericans, passed by Congress; Supreme Court ruling, 1883 invalidates it. White League of New Orleans revolts against the State Government. Federal troops called in.

1876 Queen Victoria proclaimed Empress of India.

1877 Federal troops withdrawn from the South.
Transvaal (South Africa) annexed by England.

1880 Joel Chandler Harris, *Uncle Remus: His Songs and Sayings*—begins the restoration of the plantation myth of the lovable, happy darky.

1881 Booker T. Washington opens Tuskegee Institute.
Henry James, *Portrait of a Lady.*
American Federation of Labor organized.

1883 Supreme Court upholds Tennessee Jim Crow laws which sanction separate public facilities for Blacks and Whites.
George Washington Williams, *History of the Negro Race,* in 2 vols.

1884 Somaliland annexed to England; Southwest Africa, Togo, the Cameroons to Germany.

1885 Italians raid Abyssinian coast; annex all of Abyssinia (Ethiopia) in 1895.

1886 The Haymarket Riot, Chicago—major clash between strikers and police, commemorated in many foreign countries as "May Day."
Rich gold mines discovered in southern Transvaal.

1887 Charles Chesnutt publishes "The Goophered Grapevine," a story in dialect using Uncle Remus-like character; William J. Simmons, *Men of Mark,* a 1200 page biographical dictionary of Blackamerican leaders; Thomas Nelson Page, *In Ole Virginia,* a novel depicting the charm of the old South.

1890 The first edition of a small collection of poems by Emily Dickinson achieves critical approval.

1893 First publication of poems by Paul Laurence Dunbar, *Oak and Ivy*; later, his dialect poems make his reputation.

1894 Congress repeals Civils Rights Act of 1866.

1895 Stephen Crane, *The Red Badge of Courage;* Bob Cole, *A Trip to Coontown,* first musical produced by Blackamerican; Booker T. Washington's *Atlanta Exposition Address.*

1896 Case of Plessy *v.* Ferguson argued before Supreme Court; that Southern segregation (Jim Crow) conflicts with the 13th and 14th amendments is denied by the Court, which defends its decision by articulating the "separate but equal" doctrine.

1897 Alexander Crummell founds the American Negro Academy in Washington.

1898 Spanish American War; United States gains the Hawaiian Islands, Puerto Rico, and the Phillippine Islands.
Louisiana introduces the "Grandfather Clause" into its constitution:

only males whose fathers or grandfathers were qualified to vote Jan. 1, 1867 are automatically registered; others must comply with educational or property requirements.

1899 United Fruit Co. organized, extending United States influence throughout Latin America.
Thorstein Veblen, *Theory of the Leisure Class.*

1900 National Negro Business League founded to promote Negro business.
Theodore Dreiser, *Sister Carrie.*

1901 J. P. Morgan's iron and steel trust founded; first billion-dollar corporation.
Great wave of strikes begins; by 1905, 14,000 strikes recorded.
President Theodore Roosevelt dines at White House with Booker T. Washington, generating bitter Southern reaction.
Roosevelt recommends regulating trusts and corporations.

1902 *McClure's* publishes Ida M. Tarbell's "History of the Standard Oil Company," beginning era of muckraking journalism.
Chinese Exclusion Act broadened to prevent Chinese from entering U. S. from island territories; in 1907 Roosevelt orders exclusion of all Japanese laborers coming from Mexico, Canada, or Hawaii.
Thomas Dixon, *The Leopards' Spots,* generally conceded to be the most extreme of racist novels.
Ford Motor Company formed; 1911 established the assembly line means of production.
W. E. Burghardt DuBois, *Souls of Black Folk.*

1905 In a Pacific war, Russia is defeated by Japan. United States mediates peace treaty giving certain ports to Japan, making Korea a Japanese protectorate, and freeing Chinese Manchuria of both Russian and Japanese occupation.
Einstein's theory of relativity revolutionizes concepts of space and time held since Newton.

1906 Race riots break out in Springfield, Ohio; Atlanta, Georgia; Brownsville, Texas. More rioting in Springfield, Illinois in 1908; East St. Louis in 1917; Chicago and Washington in 1919; and Tulsa in 1921.

1907 Great waves of immigrants from southern and eastern Europe reach peak with 1,285,349 arrivals.
NAACP formed; 1911 campaign to arouse public opinion against lynching is begun.
The Transvaal government (white South African) restricts immigration of Indians from Asia. Opposition led by Mohandas Gandhi; in 1914 Gandhi returns to India and eventually begins the movement against the British.

1909 Admiral Peary and Mat Henson plant U.S. flag at North Pole.

1910 Gustavus Myers, *History of Great American Fortunes.*
Hollywood becomes know as a film town; the first sound film, "The Jazz Singer" in 1927.

1912 Chinese Emperor abdicates; Sun Yat Sen first president of a parliamentary government. Thirty-five years of instability follows.

1914 World War I breaks out.
Mamie Smith makes first Blues recording.
Robert Frost, *North of Boston.*

1915 Edgar Lee Masters, *Spoon River Anthology.*

1916 Great migration of Southern Blacks to Northern industrial centers begins; peaks in 1919.
Carl Sandburg, *Chicago Poems.*

1917 U. S. enters World War I. Blackamericans inducted into military service encounter discrimination; allowed to serve as menials in Navy; rejected by Air Force; overseas segregation.
The Bolshevik Revolution in Russia ends the rule of the Czars.
Closing of Red Light district in New Orleans increases the migration to Northern cities of blues singers and jazz musicians; the new music becomes popular all over the U.S. and parts of Europe.

1919 Father Divine (George Baker) organizes his "heavens."
Sherwood Anderson, *Winesburg, Ohio.*
Ku Klux Klan reactivated; over 200 appearances in 27 states. Seventy Blackamericans lynched, among them returning soldiers still in uniform. Twenty-five race riots in North and South.
First large all-Black musicians band plays Broadway.

1920 Women are granted the right to vote. Constitutional amendment prohibits the sale of alcoholic beverages in U.S. (repealed in 1933). Eugene O'Neill, *The Emperor Jones.*

1921 Sacco and Vanzetti, anarchists, accused of murder. Despite world-wide protest, they are executed in 1927 as part of a national wave of anti-communist sentiment.
Harlem Renaissance begins as a response to renewed interest in Afro-American culture by Whites. Broadway musicals such as *Shuffle Along* are great successes. James Weldon Johnson publishes *The Book of American Negro Poetry;* Benjamin Brawley, *A Social History of the American Negro.*
Immigration restrictions begin with introduction of quotas. Japanese are totally excluded.

1922 T. S. Eliot, *The Waste Land.*
Marcus Garvey's "Universal Negro Improvement Association," urging Negroes to return to Africa. Garvey imprisoned in 1925 for fraud.

1923 *Opportunity: Journal of Negro Life* begins publication, supplying a place where Blackamerican writers may publish.
Jean Toomer, *Cane*; e. e. cummings, *Tulips and Chimneys.*

1925 Carl Van Vechten, *Nigger Heaven*—the most popular novel depicting Harlem life by a white man; generated many imitations and refutations. 40,000 Ku Klux Klan members parade in Washington.

1926 Langston Hughes, *The Weary Blues;* Hemingway, *The Sun Also Rises.* 1,000,000 acres in Liberia leased to Firestone Rubber Company.

1929 U. S. stock market crash, part of worldwide financial crisis; worst depression begins.

1930 Wali Farad founds Black Muslim movement in Detroit; in 1934 Elijah Muhammad takes leadership, establishing headquarters in Chicago.

1931 Japan marches into Manchuria; in 1932 attacks Shanghai; in 1933 resigns from League of Nations. Spanish Revolution ends monarchy; 1936-1939 civil war in Spain.

1933 Franklin Delano Roosevelt inaugurated President of U.S. Major reforms of American society undertaken.
Adolf Hitler becomes Chancellor of Germany.

1935 Harlem race riots.
Gershwin's *Porgy and Bess*—a musical depicting Blackamerican life in Catfish Row by a white musician and lyricist, taken from a play by white writers. The production has traveled all over the world meeting with acclaim everywhere; never accepted by Black community as authentic.

1939 World War II.

1940 U.S. does not enter World War II but Roosevelt begins projects for national defense; Executive Order 8802 in 1941 bans discrimination in defense industries and government. Racial violence develops in Detroit, New York, Los Angeles, Chicago, and in the South.
Richard Wright, *Native Son.*

1941 Japanese attack Pearl Harbor. U.S. entry into World War.

1945 Termination of War in Europe. United States drops bomb on Hiroshima and Nagasaki. Surrender of Japanese.
United Nations established.

1946 Postwar growth of Black population in Northern cities—4 million in 1940; 9 million in 1960.
Harry S. Truman's Executive Order 9808 creates President's Committee on Civil Rights to study minority rights and degree of protection under Federal law. *To Secure These Rights,* 1947, makes recommendations for improvement in administration of laws of the country.

1947 India becomes independent of Britain after agreeing to the formation of Pakistan out of disputed territory.

1948 Dr. Ralph J. Bunche, grandson of slave, sent to Palestine to mediate Israeli-Arab dispute as member of United Nations Commission.
Truman appoints committee to report on integration in the armed services. During Korean War (1950-1951) 30 percent of forces in Korea are integrated.
Jewish settlers in Palestine proclaim independent state of Israel as voted by United Nations. Arabs resist.

1949 Victory of Communists in China under Mao Tse-Tung decisively alters nation and ends direct Western influence.

1950 Korean War. United Nations forces confront Chinese Communists. Program to aid Navajo and Hopi Indians authorized by Congress.

1952 Egyptian monarchy overthrown by army coup under Colonel Nasser. Ralph Ellison, *Invisible Man.*

1953 James Baldwin, *Go Tell It on the Mountain.*

1954 French defeated in Indo-China (Vietnam), which is divided into North and South when the French leave. Cambodia and Laos also independent of France.

Supreme Court decision to outlaw segregation in all public schools in the U. S. nullifying the doctrine of "separate but equal" as an inherent contradiction.

1956 Blackamericans in Montgomery, Alabama boycott the bus lines; start of wide effort to secure equal rights by means of direct nonviolent action.

1957 Congress passes Civil Rights Act; creates Civil Rights Commission authorizing Department of Justice to institute injunction proceedings against persons conspiring to deprive citizens of their rights; enlarged in 1960. President Eisenhower sends Federal troops to protect Blackamerican students seeking to enter school in Little Rock, Arkansas. The Gold Coast in British West Africa becomes the independent state of Ghana as part of the rapid break-up of the British African Empire.

1959 Fidel Castro's revolutionary movement takes power in Cuba.

1960 Belgian Congo becomes Independent Congo Republic with Joseph Kasavubu as president and Patrice Lumumba as premier. Stormy political and military events follow; Lumumba executed.

1961 Pope John XXIII issues encyclical *Mater et Magistra* stressing need for improved social justice; in 1962, 21st Ecumenical Council opens to discuss Church reforms; in 1963 encyclical *Pacem in Terris* issued asking for a world community of nations to ensure the peace.

1962 Leaders of twenty African nations meeting in Nigeria establish the Organization of African States. Another group of African leaders, meeting in Casablanca, North Africa, agrees to set up an African common market and an African development bank. At Addis Ababa in 1963, leaders of thirty African nations sign a charter for the Organization of African Unity.

Constitutional amendment forbids the poll tax in U.S. federal elections. President Kennedy signs order prohibiting discrimination in federally assisted housing.

1963 Black and White liberals organize the March on Washington demanding jobs and equality for Blacks.

President Kennedy assassinated. His Civil Rights Act passes Congress after Johnson becomes President (1964).

U. S. commits itself to defend South Vietnam with whatever military aid is necessary in war against North Vietnam.

1964 The long hot summer: rioting in Philadelphia, New York, Chicago, New Jersey; murder of 3 civil-rights workers in Mississippi; murder in Georgia of a Black educator returning from reserve officer training. Martin Luther King, Jr. receives Nobel peace prize.

1965 Malcolm X assassinated. In 1963 he broke with Elijah Muhammed and founded the "Organization of Afro-American Unity." A militant and nonintegrationist leader, he urged links between Blacks and the rest of the world.

1968 Martin Luther King, Jr. assassinated. Through his organization, the Southern Christian Leadership Council, he led a nationwide campaign to achieve equality through nonviolent action.

Robert Kennedy assassinated. Brother of the former president and a leading liberal in American politics.

Massive American military intervention in South Vietnam fails to end North Vietnamese efforts to unify the nation under its aegis.